Tappin' at the Apollo

Tappin' at the Apollo

*The African American
Female Tap Dance Duo
Salt and Pepper*

CHERYL M. WILLIS

McFarland & Company, Inc., Publishers
Jefferson, North Carolina

LIBRARY OF CONGRESS CATALOGUING-IN-PUBLICATION DATA

Names: Willis, Cheryl M., author.
Title: Tappin' at the Apollo : the African American female tap dance duo Salt and Pepper / Cheryl M. Willis.
Other titles: Tapping at the Apollo
Description: Jefferson, North Carolina : McFarland & Company, Inc., Publishers. | Includes bibliographical references and index.
Identifiers: LCCN 2016002247 | ISBN 9781476662701 (softcover : acid free paper) ∞
Subjects: LCSH: Salt and Pepper (Dance company) | Tap dancers—United States—Biography. | Women tap dancers—United States—Biography. | African American women tap dancers—Biography. | Evelyn, Edwina, 1922–2011. | Welch, Jewel.
Classification: LCC GV1786.S323 W55 2016 | DDC 792.780922 [B]—dc23
LC record available at https://lccn.loc.gov/2016002247

BRITISH LIBRARY CATALOGUING DATA ARE AVAILABLE

**ISBN (print) 978-1-4766-6270-1
ISBN (ebook) 978-1-4766-2315-3**

© 2016 I Got an Idea, LLC. All rights reserved

No part of this book may be reproduced or transmitted in any form or by any means, electronic or mechanical, including photocopying or recording, or by any information storage and retrieval system, without permission in writing from the publisher.

On the cover: Edwina "Salt" Evelyn and Jewel "Pepper" Welch (from the memorabilia of Jewel Welch)

Printed in the United States of America

*McFarland & Company, Inc., Publishers
Box 611, Jefferson, North Carolina 28640
www.mcfarlandpub.com*

To Edwina "Salt" Evelyn
who shared her life experiences with me
and offered continuous encouragement
and support in all my undertakings.

Acknowledgments

Tappin' at the Apollo has been nourished by many people and experiences. Numerous encounters seemed disconnected at first, but, when added to the gumbo of information, I realized that each contributed an essential ingredient.

I am indebted to Edwina "Salt" Evelyn, Jewel "Pepper" Welch, and Mildred "Candi" Thorpe, who built friendships with me through numerous interviews, telephone conversations and visitations. Not only did these women share their knowledge of tap dance and entertainment, but they also touched my life by giving me a unique purpose and direction. My ambition is to preserve their legacies as African American women tap dancers and as respected entertainment headliners of the 1940s.

I extend my deepest appreciation to Vernita McNeil, the niece of Edythe Robinson and Edwina "Salt" Evelyn. Mrs. McNeil invited me to her home and embraced me as part of her family. For the writing and production of this book, she generously shared family stories and pictures, advertisements, and articles from Edwina Evelyn's scrapbook.

There are not enough thank-yous for my dear friend Dr. Nancy Barron, who spent an enormous amount of time editing my work. Her tireless efforts and encouragement are greatly appreciated and valued. A special thanks to my friend David Greenberg, who also read my work, assisted me in publishing negotiations, and encouraged me to continue going forward. Sharon Emmons, Maria Fama, Sharon Friedler, Candace Kane, Greg Tyson and Dr. Melayne Dixon White critiqued parts of my work and assisted me throughout the writing process. Their time and contributions are deeply appreciated.

I was fortunate to receive assistance from the professional contact of Professor Emeritus Thomas G. Field, Jr., Rusty Frank, Jim Lowe, and Judy Pritchett. Many others offered specific data to guide me in my research, particularly O. P. Van Auken, Bill Henle, Geri Kennedy, Mark Koenigsberg, Addam Stell and Sharon Spencer.

I am beholden to those who many years ago contributed information through personal interviews and/or telephone conversations about their Swing Era experiences: Mary Blow, Charles "Honi" Coles, Marion Coles, Chris Colombo, Isabelle "Eleanor Byrd" Fambro, Lillian Fitzgerald, Edith Evelyn Gettings, Edith "Baby Edwards" Hunt, Ludie Jones, Edythe Robinson, and LaVaughn Robinson.

My relatives and friends offered continuous support and listened to my long arduous writing procedure, while remaining my friends through it all. I am most thankful to them: Lisa Bates, Susan Berg, Carol Daigle, Lois Ann and Wayne Davisson,

Dr. Eva Gold, Carol Goodson, Lee-Ann Henle, Kathy Johnson, Candance Kagan, Bonnie Olson, Susan Starkey, Dr. Sara Wu, and the Marianites of Holy Cross at Our Lady of Prompt Succor Nursing Home.

Secondary research was explored in the following institutions, where the staffs were extremely helpful and knowledgeable:

In the New Orleans area: Amistad Research Center, kindly assisted by Andrew Salinas, reference archivist, Tulane University, New Orleans; Howard-Tilton Memorial Library, kindly assisted by Sean Benjamin, Public Services of Louisiana Research Collection, Tulane University, New Orleans; William Ransom Hogan Jazz Archive, kindly assisted by Lynn Abbott, Special Collections of Howard-Tilton Memorial Library, Tulane University, New Orleans; Jefferson Parish Library, East Bank Regional, Metairie, Louisiana; New Orleans Public Library, kindly assisted by Yvonne Losille, New Orleans.

On the East Coast: Atlantic City Free Public Library and Atlantic City Historical Museum, kindly assisted by Heather Perez, curator and archivist, Atlantic City, New Jersey; Beinecke Rare Book and Manuscript Library, assisted through email by Matthew Daniel Mason, Ph.D. archivist, Yale University, New Haven, Connecticut; Free Library of Philadelphia, kindly assisted by Wayne B. Saunders, Central Library, Philadelphia; National Museum of African American History & Culture, kindly assisted through email by Paul Gardullo, museum curator, Smithsonian Institution, Washington, D.C.; Smithsonian Institution Scholarly Press, kindly assisted through email by Stephanie Summerhays, production specialist, and Mary Markey, Smithsonian Institution Archives, Washington, D.C.

In the Northwest: Fort Vancouver Regional Library District, kindly assisted by Supisa Oliver, Vancouver, Washington; Multnomah County Central Library, Portland, Oregon; Portland State Univeristy, Portland, Oregon; and Suzzallo Library of the University of Washington, Seattle, Washington.

Table of Contents

Acknowledgments vii
Preface 1
Introduction 3

1. A Look at the Years That Roared 7
2. Dancing on the Corner 11
3. Steppin' on Stage 17
4. Candi and Pepper 35
5. Salt and Pepper 52
6. The Apollo Theater 64
7. The Best Year of My Life 78
8. All Aboard for the East Coast 91
9. Crossing the Line 106
10. Down in Dixie 121
11. Chicago 133
12. On Midwestern Soil 151
13. "The Girls" 165
14. Canadian Jazz 174
15. A Sweet Moment Slips Away 181

Epilogue: What Do We Do Now? 187
Appendix I: Schedule of Performances 195
Appendix II: In Memory of a Generation Who Performed 207
Chapter Notes 217
Bibliography 230
Index 237

Preface

The riveting sounds produced by the beat, the rhythm, and the improv of tap dancers connect one not only to each unique performer but also to a tap dance rhapsody. This biography of "Salt and Pepper" invites the audience into a world of their rhythmic sound—one in which these tap dancers experienced the groove of Swingin' harmony contrasted with the cacophony of injustice.

"Salt and Pepper," an African American tap dance duo, exuberantly performed a man's style of tap dance in male attire and received the male stamp of approval: "That girl could dance her ass off." In the 1920s and 1930s, "Salt" and "Pepper" learned to tap dance on the street corners of New York and Philadelphia. By the 1940s, they found themselves featured at New York's legendary Apollo Theatre with jazz giants Count Basie, "Fats" Waller, and Earl "Fatha" Hines.

Edwina "Salt" Evelyn and Jewel "Pepper" Welch danced into my life in 1989 during my research on African American women tap dancers. My twenty-year friendship with Salt is the driving force behind this book. It is designed to acknowledge them as two independent women who enjoyed their entertainment work and made a financially sound living. While most African American women were domestics, Salt and Pepper were headliners in Black show business.

An abundance of performing opportunities came their way in part through the country's need for entertainment during World War II, which left Salt and Pepper free to travel to the hundreds of established nightclubs and theaters. Along their journey, they performed with numerous African American dancers, singers, comedians, and novelty acts. Through its story and one hundred photographs, this book preserves the legacy of Salt and Pepper and many of those who performed during this time period. My primary sources of information were Salt and Pepper's memorabilia and the show business stories they shared with me. This information is supported by research into newspapers, magazines, books and electronic documents from the era.

The stage is set through the relevant history of the cities, clubs, and theaters where Salt and Pepper performed. The success of theaters and nightclubs featuring the best in Swing, Bop, and Bebop music rested on the peoples of the Great Migration (generally between 1915 and 1960) coupled with a nation that wanted to Swing but not necessarily integrate.

Salt and Pepper beat the odds against racism, sexism, and homophobia. Traveling by rail in designated Black cars, they journeyed throughout the East Coast, the Midwest, and the South. They performed in magnificent theaters where they could not enter through the front door due to restrictive laws or straightforward prejudice. Jazz clubs, both black- and white-owned, featured black performers for predominately white audiences. Mob-owned jazz slave masters demanded anywhere from three to seven high-energy shows a day, but a simple housing clause was never included in the contract. Gambling and alcohol were presumed parts of the scene, but Salt and Pepper largely avoided them. They sang and danced a male-style tap dance, but they didn't receive a salary equal to that earned by Black male dancers, much less white performers.

Within the nonjudgmental atmosphere of show business, gay and lesbian lifestyles were accepted as normal. Outside show business, however, many presented themselves as heterosexual and even married. It deterred the public from questioning their lifestyle. Salt and Pepper found freedom to be who they were in entertainment's safe environment. Outside entertainment, homosexuality was looked upon with disdain. For African Americans moreover, it was considered a stigma that debauched efforts for liberty in a prejudiced America.

Salt and Pepper traveled within the African American community, where competition was "sweet" and community solidarity was the outcome. Celebration of community was imperative. The stardom of one was a splendid achievement enjoyed by all, which stood in contrast to the competitive rivalry of white American society.

Tappin' at the Apollo captures a period of history that continues to be relevant today. Tap has been passed down as an expressive dance form; many African American women continue to struggle for equality; racial conflicts are part of the daily news; and the need for African American solidarity is absolutely essential.

Take the journey with Salt and Pepper to preserve their legacy and learn the history that helped pave the way for the success of today's African Americans in the entertainment industry.

Introduction

In March 1989, the "Silver Belles" (under the management of Geri Kennedy) performed at the Uptown Theatre in Philadelphia. The Silver Belles, former Cotton Club and Apollo Theatre chorus girls (1920s–1950s), graced the stage with Charles "Honi" Coles as the master of ceremonies.

I had known Honi for several years, and he was aware that I was writing my dissertation on African American women tap dancers from the Swing Era. After the show, I went onstage to congratulate him.

A rather large African American woman dressed in black slacks with a loose-fitting black-and-white figured shirt came dancing on the stage. With a huge grin, she called out, "Hey, Mr. Coles, do you remember me?" They both laughed and hugged each other. Honi turned to me and said, "This person was one of the greatest women tap dancers." He went on to tell me that she could "dance her ass off" and that her team was called "Candi and Pepper." The woman lengthened her body and swayed her head from side to side in an extremely proud manner at the compliment. She introduced herself as Jewel "Pepper" Welch. After a brief chat about her life's accomplishments, Pepper agreed to be interviewed for my dissertation research. And on that note, I entered a world that deeply touched my life.

The racial tensions in Philadelphia at that time made it difficult for me to cross boundaries. Interviewing many of the African American women dancers from the 1930s and 1940s was a slow process of introduction, suspicion, scrutiny, and, in most cases, acceptance. It was not a pop in, interview, and leave process. My role as a researcher depended on establishing relationships, building trust, and developing lifelong friendships.

I was enthusiastic about meeting Pepper because she was willing to share her memories about show business and participate in the interview process. Pepper, however, had a preconceived dream that my work would get her on the *Oprah Winfrey Show* (1986–2011).

Despite our disparate expectations, Pepper made it possible for me to meet her former dance partners: Mildred "Candi" Thorpe and Edwina "Salt" Evelyn. Candi had performed for about nine years and benefited from the great success of dancing as part of "Candi and Pepper." When the team disbanded, Candi did not continue in show business. Yet she was gracious and welcoming to me and the interview process.

In April 1990, I headed to Greenwich Village to interview Edwina "Salt" Evelyn. She met me at the subway station with a cheerful hug. We walked quickly as she gave me a tour of the neighborhood: the Blue Note Jazz Club, the Village Underground, and Comedy Cellar. She also offered a little history about the stars who got their big breaks in the clubs.

As we opened the door to her apartment, her little poodle, Bandit, greeted us. The living room décor was French provincial, with a burgundy couch and two high-back chairs, period paintings, cut-glass lamps, and a chandelier over the dining room table. A wall of windows connected Edwina's life to the sounds of buses, ambulances, motorcycles, and police sirens. She remarked that the noises were music to her ears.

On the dining room table was a gargantuan scrapbook of Edwina's performing life during the Swing Era. She was eager to get started with the interview. As she opened the scrapbook, my heart fluttered with amazement. The book contained clippings of programs, contracts, menus, advertisements, and newspaper reviews from the 1940s and 1950s. The pages were embellished with pictures of Swing bands, dancers, singers, chorus girls, and comedians.

A few minutes into the interview, the door opened, and Edythe Robinson entered. Edwina and Edythe had been life partners for over forty years. During the next two years, as many interviews followed, Edwina shared stories of her life and her years in show business. Edythe added to the stories and shared our laughing, chatting and reminiscing about the Swing Era.

On the dining room table in this small Greenwich Village apartment was a historical scrapbook of a bygone era, and standing beside me was Edwina, the historian, who was to become my lifelong friend. It was a dream come true for any researcher.

Over the years, Edwina and I looked at her scrapbook many times as she reminisced. Often, when I telephoned her, she said she was reading my dissertation about African American women tap dancers. Edwina felt that it was a work long overdue and worthy of publication. It seemed as if I was always "getting ready" to publish it, but I never took the time to focus on the process. However, in 2010, when Edwina told me she had cancer, I was jolted into reality. Here was my friend of twenty years ready to leave, and I hadn't fulfilled her request of publication. During her last days, I promised Edwina that I would write her story and publish her scrapbook. She seemed pleased. Regrettably, the promise was late in coming, since she would never be able to enjoy it.

Tappin' at the Apollo is a biographical portrait of Edwina "Salt" Evelyn, and it also highlights the lives of Jewel "Pepper" Welch and Mildred "Candi" Thorpe.

I definitely had my own ideas of how I was going to write the book and what was important. But throughout the writing process, I could feel Edwina guiding me as to where I should go next. Although it was a personal struggle, I abandoned my outline and followed Edwina's impulses.

I began by organizing the items from the scrapbook by cities, clubs and theaters. This information was coordinated with the interviews and video-taped stories that Edwina had shared with me. The final steps were to assemble the story and verify it through both historical research and personal interviews with other dancers from the period.

Edwina's itinerary was used as the focal point. It illuminated the evolution of the jazz scene in clubs and theaters while also casting light on the transformation of the

Broadway stage with the music and dances that swept America. It also revealed the influencing cultures of Alcohol Prohibition and organized crime with their effects on entertainment, African American migration and the intensification of racism, and the demand for entertainment stimulated by World War II.

The direct quotes of Edwina, Pepper and Candi found throughout this book were taken from formal interviews between 1989 and 1991 and from personal communications in the years that followed. Many of these quotes are not footnoted.

Edwina underlined her name or the team's name on all the items found in the scrapbook. Unfortunately, many of the supporting newspaper articles found in the scrapbook were not dated, nor were the newspapers identified. Weeks, months and years of searching microfilm produced some of the evidence that was lacking. When articles were quoted and the date or title of the newspaper was not established, the text states that the information was taken from an article found in the scrapbook. Additional supporting research of the era, the clubs and theaters, and other stars was cited and included in the endnotes and bibliography.

The Swing Era burst out of the Harlem Renaissance, and over the next twenty-five years the sound was altered to express the times with Bop and Bebop music. The period came alive through several generations actively engaged in the art of jazz. The African American stars on the playbills found in Edwina's scrapbook contributed to the evolution and expansion of the jazz scene, which included music, dance, comedy, song and novelty acts. *Tappin' at the Apollo* is intended to shine a light on many of those who performed and thus preserve their legacies. Regrettably, the entire scrapbook could not be printed due to copyright laws and the quality of the original items.

Jewel "Pepper" Welch and Mildred "Candi" Thorpe are referred to by their stage names of "Pepper" and "Candi" throughout the book, since these were the names that they used throughout their lives. Edwina "Salt" Evelyn is referred to as Edwina in the first part of the book, which details when she danced with early partners and as a solo act. She is also referred to as Edwina in sections of the book that focus on her time after her show business years. However, when dancing in the team "Salt and Pepper," she is referred to as "Salt."

There was a considerable amount of research and discussion regarding the racial vocabulary used in this book. Paralleling American history, and with respect to each time period, the words *Negro, Colored, Black, Afro-American*, and *African American* were used. The word *Black* with a capital "B" denotes the race and encompasses ethnic culture. The word *black* with a small "b" is used as an adjective (e.g., black and white audiences). Trying to decide if the term *black* referred to culture, race, or color turned out to be a complicated task. Hopefully, readers will not be offended by my choices and efforts. The term *white* refers to and describes Caucasians of all ethnic diversities.

The railroad was the primary form of transportation between cities for many African Americans from the turn of the twentieth century. Each train was identified by a name such as the Ambassador, the Bluegrass, and the Indianapolis Express. The names of the trains that were probably used by Salt and Pepper are identified at the beginning of each chapter.

In the text, many performers are acknowledged without extensive biographies or comments about their role in history. Rather than placing that information in the notes, I decided that it deserved its own section. Appendix II contains biographical information and/or comments about significant performers mentioned in the text. The information in the appendix was passed along to me through interviews with the principals and other performers from the era, and also through secondary sources.

Hopefully, the shared memories, the stars of the period, and the history written in *Tappin' at the Apollo* will shed light on the lives of these women who were tap dance pioneers, as well as further developing an understanding of the history that shaped their lives.

1

A Look at the Years That Roared

The Roaring Twenties charged on to the American scene with freeing jazz rhythms and improvisational impact. Dixieland jazz had migrated from New Orleans to Chicago on the Illinois Central Railroad as early as 1910 with musicians Jelly Roll Morton and Tony Jackson.[1] Over the following decade, jazz absorbed cultural styles and influences from many Southern areas as well as from European-based music. By the 1920s, jazz found another home in New York's Harlem. African American clubs or clubs that featured African American talent opened in Chicago and Harlem. The jazz sound and its dance became all the rage.

The country had emerged from World War I in 1918 with the goal of making the world safe for democracy. On the home front, democracy was an accepted privilege for most Americans, but not for African Americans. The number of race riots and lynchings of African Americans grew as the years went by. Hundreds of people both black and white were killed and thousands injured. Although the Fourteenth Amendment of the Constitution (1868) gave all citizens the right to "life, liberty or property ... and equal protection of the laws," restrictions for African Americans were imposed. Jim Crow laws, resulting from the "separate but equal" mandate,[2] sprang up throughout the country. These laws prohibited African Americans from using all public facilities.

Organizations dedicated to white supremacy, such as the Ku Klux Klan, grew in size, sponsoring terrorist activities. In response, the National Association for the Advancement of Colored People (NAACP) was organized to pursue equality under the Constitution.

Despite racism, the decade of the 1920s was a period of liberation, creativity, and political independence for African Americans—a cultural restoration known as the Harlem Renaissance. Intellectual, artistic, and political African American leaders took center stage, not only in the Harlem district of New York but also in a cultural movement that reached throughout the United States.

Tap Was in the Air

On May 22, 1921, Black theater returned to the Broadway stage in a landmark production of *Shuffle Along*.[3] The success of its music and choreography legitimized ragtime jazz music and tap/vernacular dance for the white world.[4] *Shuffle Along* was humorous and featured the first sophisticated African American love story. It presented African Americans in the glory of their talents, freed from the blackfaced stereotype of minstrelsy.[5]

The comedy team of Flournoy Miller and Aubrey Lyles wrote and starred in the play, while Noble Sissle and Eubie Blake created and performed ragtime songs such as "Shuffle Along" and "I'm Just Wild About Harry" (which became Harry Truman's campaign anthem in 1948).[6] *Shuffle Along* also featured innovative chorus girls like Florence Mills and Josephine Baker. The improvisational style of the chorus girls introduced dances never before performed on Broadway.[7]

The success of *Shuffle Along* paved the way for other African American musical plays featuring tap and vernacular dances. Some of these plays were *Running Wild* (1923), Lew Leslie's *Blackbirds of 1928*, and Leonard Reed's *Connie's Hot Chocolates* (1929).[8] These shows provided performing opportunities and stardom for many entertainers, such as singers Adelaide Hall and Ethel Waters, actor/singer/lawyer Paul Robeson, singer/dancer/comedian Johnny Hudgins, and tap dancer Bill Robinson.

These musicals and the hope of being on stage awakened dreams in the public. Children and teenagers in many large cities were encouraged to tap. They learned on the street corner and from the tap masters.

In Harlem, many got their inspiration from the Hoofers Club, which was started in the 1920s. The Hoofers Club was housed in the back basement of the Comedy Club, a gambling hall on 133rd Street between Lenox and 7th Avenue. It was the headquarters for predominantly African American tap dance competitions and was largely by invitation only. The Hoofers Club served as a place of camaraderie and competition primarily for great male tap dancers such as Bill "Bojangles" Robinson, John Sublett of "Buck and Bubbles," Baby Laurence, Teddy Hale, Charles "Honi" Coles and Charles "Cholly" Atkins, Bunny Briggs, Pete Peaches & Duke (Pete Nugent, Irving "Peaches" Beaman, and Duke Miller[9]), and Chuck Green.

The unwritten law of the Hoofers Club was "Thou Shalt Not Copy Another's Steps Exactly." You could imitate anybody inside the club, which was taken as a compliment. But a dancer was forbidden to use another's step in public or for pay.[10] This protocol fostered the creation of new steps.

Competition led to emphasis on technique as well as complex rhythms. In 1922, John "Bubbles" Sublett was given credit for a new style of dance known as Rhythm Tap, which emphasized counterpoint rhythms and exhibited the dancer as a musician. He led the way in tap dance for almost a century. Nevertheless, it appears that William Henry Lane (a.k.a. "Master Juba") performed a similar style of counterpoint as early as the 1840s.

Rhythm Tap paralleled the rhythms of Big Band Swing music. During the Bop and Bebop Era of the late 1940s and 1950s, Rhythm Tap transitioned to Jazz Tap. Yet, from the 1920s onward, musicians were often influenced by tap dancers, and, in turn, tap dancers were inspired by the music and rhythms of Louis Armstrong, Art Tatum, Charlie Parker, and Dizzy Gillespie.[11]

Harlem Puts on a New Face

The 1920s was a time of change. A brief overview of the period will illuminate several of the events that changed Harlem and affected the world of entertainment.

Harlem was a beautiful community—safe and well lit with paved streets and beautiful homes. The area was linked to downtown Manhattan by major avenues and public transportation.

Originally named Haarlem by early Dutch settlers, it was a white neighborhood of European immigrants who tried to hold on to their Old World roots and traditions. After World War I, the demographics shifted as African Americans moved to Harlem and established businesses. By the late 1920s, 70 percent of Harlem's real estate belonged to African Americans in small businesses. In this new community, a cultural elite came together to express themselves in poetry, fiction, visual arts, music, history, sociology, and other areas in which creativity flourished. The period was known as the Harlem Renaissance.[12]

On January 16, 1919, the Eighteenth Amendment of the U.S. Constitution was ratified, forbidding the manufacture, sale, barter, transport, import, export, delivery or furnishing of any intoxicating liquor (although it did not actually prohibit the *use* of alcohol). The Volstead Act clarified the terminology of the amendment, stating that intoxicating liquors were those containing 0.5 percent alcohol. The Volstead Act superseded all existing prohibition laws in effect in states with such legislation.[13] Prohibition remained the law in the United States for thirteen years.

Prohibition reduced the amount of consumed alcohol. However, it stimulated the spread of organized criminal activity in bootlegging and other gang-related crimes of power and control. Saloons, originally for men, were banned, and private establishments known as speakeasies flourished. Women were welcomed into speakeasies, and it became fashionable for women to drink. In New York City alone, over 100,000 speakeasies sprang up.[14]

Simultaneously, *Shuffle Along* (1921) began the process of marketing the Harlem Renaissance to white America. This renaissance lasted until the crash of the stock market in 1929. It lured the curious wealthy white community to Harlem (a phenomenon known as slumming) to enjoy and experience African American entertainment, with its mystic sound, free dance movement, and good times.[15]

Theaters were established with stage shows and plays that provided all-Black entertainment. Some theaters in New York City were the Lafayette Theatre, the Lincoln Theatre, and Harlem Opera House.[16] Plush nightclubs, including Connie's Inn, Ed Small's Paradise, and the Cotton Club, opened their doors to white patrons. The Cotton Club opened in 1923 and provided an elegant environment that catered to a "whites only" elite clientele. In this environment, whites could observe African Americans without mixing with them.

In reminiscing about the elaborate shows at the Cotton Club, bandleader Cab Calloway said:

> The bandstand was a replica of a southern mansion, with large white columns and a backdrop painted with weeping willows and slave quarters. The band played on the

veranda of the mansion, and in front of the veranda, down a few steps, was the dance floor, which was also used for the shows. The waiters were dressed in red tuxedos, like butlers in a southern mansion, and the tables were covered with red-and-white-checked gingham tablecloths. There were huge cut-crystal chandeliers, and the whole set was like the sleepy-time-down-South during slavery. Even the name, Cotton Club, was supposed to convey the southern feeling. I supposed the idea was to make whites, who came to the club, feel like they were being catered to and entertained by black slaves.[17]

Spectators in the Cotton Club's audience represented the elite of the elite in contemporary society.[18] And on the stage was the best in African American entertainment, with such stars as tap dancers Bill "Bojangles" Robinson and the Nicholas Brothers, singers Lena Horne and Ethel Waters, comedian Dusty Fletcher, and the big bands of Duke Ellington, Cab Calloway, and Jimmie Lunceford.

Tap dance made a spectacular appearance in the Cotton Club. It was performed by male dancers exhibiting Rhythm Tap and Flash. Chorus girls and boys also performed Rhythm Tap, Soft Shoe, and other vernacular dance styles such as Truckin',[19] the Suzy-Q,[20] and Shorty George.[21]

With Prohibition in force, these clubs were controlled by members of organized crime, who provided their clientele with bootleg liquor, the lure of exotic entertainment, and the adventure of the gangster world.[22]

In addition to the elite who visited Harlem, the 1920s brought an influx of African Americans predominantly from the South. They sought industrial jobs, an escape from the hardship of sharecropping, and liberty. Although many had aspirations of financial stability, they experienced a considerable deficit in wages compared to whites. Large apartments were subdivided into several small units, with African American rent double that of white city dwellers. Many of the tenants took in lodgers or rented to other tenants who worked different shifts in order to meet the financial burden. In Harlem, 5,000 people resided in a single block, with 250,000 people crammed into an area fifty blocks long and eight blocks wide.[23] By the time of the Great Depression, beginning in late 1929, overcrowded conditions, low salaries, and a harsh economy began to turn Harlem into a slum.

Cab Calloway reflected on the economic condition of Harlem during his years at the Cotton Club:

> By 1929 investors had lost $40 billion and more than 32,000 businesses were bankrupt. There were breadlines everywhere and near-riots in New York. Everybody was angry with poor old Herbert Hoover. Everybody except people in the entertainment world.... It's a funny thing, when things get really bad, when the bottom falls out of the economy, that's when people really need entertainment... Jazz was swinging, the theaters on Broadway were cleaning up, and in Harlem the nightclubs, speakeasies, and Jazz spots were packed every night.... I suppose that people figure, what the hell, let's go out and have a ball. It's one way to get away from the gloom.[24]

2

Dancing on the Corner

We danced on the stoop. We danced on the street corner. We learned to dance in Harlem with the neighborhood children. It was a form of recreation. We created steps and dance routines. Then, we challenged each other for the best step. We used to dance around the street ... we used to dance for fun, really.[1]

Saturday afternoons were supposedly reserved for Alice Garrett's Dancing School in Harlem.[2] Edwina "Salt" Evelyn's mother, Christina Hall Evelyn, paid 25 cents for dance lessons for Edwina and her sister Edith. In a mischievous manner, Edwina and Edith put their tap shoes in a bag, took the money, and left the house. But they rarely went to dancing school. Instead, they'd go to Nedick's[3] to buy a hot dog and a root beer for a nickel. When it was almost time for the dance recital, Edwina and Edith finally attended classes. Edwina explained that the children in the class told them what to do: "'OK we're going to do the time step.' We did the time step. The kids said, 'Now do the half break.' We'd do the half break. 'Now we're going to do falling off the log.'"[4] The dance progressed with the other kids calling out the names of the steps. Edwina and Edith said they learned the routines quickly, because they had mastered the steps on the street corner.

Most professional tap dancers of that time period didn't learn to dance in a school. As Edwina said, "The dancing school was right out there on the street. Doing the dance and challenging each other, that was the main thing."

"We'd move rather than paint"

Throughout the years, Edwina spent a lot of time laughing over the phrase,

Tap dancer Edwina Grace Evelyn.

"We'd move rather than paint." It appeared that moving was very much part of her young life.

Her father, John Edward Evelyn (1888–1957), was a sea captain from Roseau, Dominica, in the French West Indies. He settled in New Bedford, Massachusetts, and married Edwina's mother, Christina Coblins (1894–1963), whose family was from the Dutch West Indies. The Evelyns moved to New London, Connecticut, when Edwina (born September 19, 1922) was two years old. They were a middle-class African American family with middle-class values. Edwina stated that in the early 1900s, "there was no such thing as a two-income family." Her father was the sole provider, and the family lived on his earnings. Her mother, an accomplished piano player, was a homemaker who raised six children: Prescott Leroy Evelyn (1913–1952), a boat captain who drowned in an accident while carrying parts for the Lotas Elevator; Donald Norman Evelyn (1915–2010); Ivy Evelyn Golden (1917–2002); Edith Yvonne Evelyn Gettings (ca. 1920–2009); Edwina Grace Evelyn (1922–2011); and Edward Evelyn (1925–2005).

Like most families of seamen, the Evelyns were always concerned for the safety of their father. Many of the men were at sea for two or three months at a time. This was before cell phones or computers, and communication with those at sea was limited. The Evelyns lived in a neighborhood where all of the houses had a widow's walk. When the ships were scheduled to come in, the wives went out on the widow's walk, trying to spot their husband's boats. Unfortunately, some of these men were lost at sea and didn't come back—thus, a widow's walk.

The Great Depression of 1929 brought the Evelyns to the New York area. As the first African American barge captain on the East Coast, John Evelyn's job was to carry coal on the river. In the summer, the family lived in Long Island, where they joined John on the boat. During the winter, they moved to Harlem to go to school.

From a child's perspective, living in Harlem had a humorous side because the family moved so much. As Edwina put it, "We'd move rather than paint."

> We lived all over Harlem.... There was never a housing shortage and all kinds of incentives to move. Two months rent free, one month rent free. So we'd never paint, we'd move. [laughter] Everybody did that. Now, you can't find places to live. Every apartment building had vacancy signs with all kinds of incentives. We don't paint, we move. I moved all over, all over.

Building a Church

Around 1933, with tap dance flourishing, Edwina and her sister Edith launched their dancing/singing careers as the "Evelyn Sisters." During one interview, Edwina's sister Edith arrived in time to tell/act out her side of the story.

Edith was short, with large bones and a rounded shape, which, coupled with her powerful, assertive presence, made her appear much larger than she actually was. Her beautiful smile was framed by a shoulder-length black pageboy hairdo. Edith was into "looking good" with beautiful clothes and jewelry.

Edith stated that the first ambition for the "Evelyn Sisters" was to earn enough money to build a church. The young sisters were good performers; yet it appeared that they had lofty goals.

At the time, the girls lived on Long Island, where there was no Catholic church. The priest, Father McCabe, celebrated Mass in a makeshift basement. His dream was to have a church, and he had many fundraisers to support his ambition.

This is where the "Evelyn Sisters" made their entrance. McCabe took the girls to New York City to perform at the homes of wealthy Catholics who contributed sizable donations for the new church. These young girls felt that dancing was a God-given talent, and they wanted to put their talents to good use. They believed that they were doing a good thing, so they didn't take any money for themselves. Edwina said that McCabe treated them like his own children, and on the evenings that they performed he let them sleep in a private room in the rectory. In the morning, McCabe put the girls on the trolley for a lengthy ride back to Long Island. At that time, there was no 8th Street subway. The trolley ended at 159th Street, and the girls walked the rest of the long distance to their home in Jamaica, Queens.

The high point of this experience came when Father McCabe took them to see the Warner Brothers movie *42nd Street*, which was nominated for the Academy Award's Best Picture prize in 1934. During the interview, as Edith shared this part of the story, she and Edwina burst into the songs from *42nd Street*, complete with some quick tap dance steps of their own. Their energy pulsed, and the room was filled with joy and laughter.

After many dance performances in New York, Father McCabe, with the help of the Evelyn Sisters, was able to buy a pool hall, which he turned into St. Benedict the Moor Catholic Church. From the memory of their childhood, the "Evelyn Sisters" prided themselves on the fact that they had "built a Catholic Church."

Let's Lindy

The "Evelyn Sisters" danced and sang together throughout their elementary school years. But during their teens, Edith began to focus her talent on Swing dance at the exquisite Savoy Ballroom.

The Savoy, opened in 1926, was a hotbed for the development of jazz and vernacular dance. It was in the center of Harlem on Lenox Avenue between 140th and 141st Streets. The ballroom was owned by the Jewish Moe Gale and managed by African American Charles Buchanan. The Savoy was one of the first culturally and racially integrated establishments in the United States.

The Savoy Ballroom set a precedent for jazz music and Swing dance. It was all the rage with teenagers. Two bands alternated sets every twenty minutes. The Savoy house bands were the best Swing bands of the time, such as the Chick Webb Orchestra, Al Cooper's Savoy Sultans, and Chris Columbo and His Gentleman of Swinging Jazz.

Columbo later recalled that the Savoy, the "Home of Feet," opened at six o'clock in the evening and closed at two o'clock in the morning, seven days a week. Attendance reached quotas of 4,000 to 5,000 people per night. The dance area, which was one block square, was on the second floor, where wine and food were sold. Columbo stated that the floor rested on ball bearings to support the weight of the people who bounced to the popular dance of the Lindy Hop.[5]

The Savoy was known for its fierce competitions, ranging from the Battle of the Big Bands to the Lindy Hop. Cab Calloway said that during the the Battle of the Big Bands, "each band would play a couple of sets, trying to blow the other band away, and the audience would clap and cheer to decide which had won."[6] It was a similar routine for the dancers who competed with the Lindy Hop: they danced each other "under the table."

Herbert "Whitey" White, a former boxer and the bouncer at the Savoy, watched the dancers and chose the best for exhibitions, competitions, and performance gigs. At one time, Whitey employed more than 70 Swing dancers. The group, known as Whitey's Lindy Hoppers, performed at the Cotton Club, in films, for the Queen of England and throughout the world. Choreographer Frankie Manning and the youngest dancer, Norma Miller (14 years old, born 1919), were the stars of the Lindy Hoppers, and their work influenced the social dances of the 1930s–1950s.[7] Norma Miller, known as the "Queen of Swing," was still dancing and teaching into 2015.

As her face brightened and her arms flailed, Edith said that she gave up her tap dance aspirations, found a male partner, and began to do the Lindy. Moving her feet in the basic Lindy Hop steps, she said was chosen as one of the Lindy Hoppers when she was around 17 years old. The group rehearsed for hours every week, and soon Edith competed and performed at the Savoy and other dance venues. Edwina promoted her sister's efforts, stating that Edith was a wonderful Lindy Hopper and performed with the group for several years.

A Budding Career

Edwina learned her tap dance craft from the streets and perfected her style. She took risks by putting herself on the performance stage. Dancing in a skirt, shirt and Mary Jane tap shoes with huge bows, Edwina was the main attraction for a Woman's Club at the YMCA in Harlem near 125th Street. Viewing a photograph taken at that time, she laughed at the audience's reaction to her. It appeared that the men enjoyed her dancing, while the women seemed to have mixed responses. Nevertheless, Edwina thought the audience was amazed by her work, and she proudly boasted, "They can't believe it!"

With her positive outlook, Edwina declared that while this gig was not a benefit financially speaking (bringing maybe $7–$10), it was one that was intended to benefit her career. Her goal was to get her name out there and keep it in front of the public.

Whenever the issue of money arose, Edwina stressed that she gave her earnings to her mother in appreciation for all she had done. She often stated that her parents had raised her to contribute to the family. Fortunately, Edwina's mother established a savings account for her, providing a nest egg for Edwina's future and implanting a value of responsibility.

Her family survived the Great Depression and was able to provide Edwina with

Top: **Edwina takes on the YMCA.** *Bottom:* **In her high school play, Judge Edwina proclaims, "Justice shall be done."**

an education in the New York public schools: PS 103 (Elementary), PS 81 Junior High School and Wadleigh High School. Edwina was a very good student; she loved learning and delighted in her academic accomplishments. On her graduation day, she proudly received a certificate for never being tardy or absent during her high school years. Her desire to perform was also deeply rooted, and in 1940 Edwina had the lead as a judge in her high school senior play.

Edwina enjoyed performing tap dance, but her deepest ambition was to become a teacher. She believed that teaching was a wonderful career and a profession to which she could dedicate herself. After high school, she pursued her life's ambition to attend college.

One evening, Edwina's mother came into the room with an envelope. Inside was the money she had saved for Edwina's college education. Edwina opened it to find $30, which would pay for her admission to Brooklyn College and for her college books. Edwina enrolled in night classes because these were less expensive than taking classes during the day. Her dream was on its way to being fulfilled.

After one semester, however, the needs of the family outweighed the available funds for college. There were no grants or college loans during that period, so Edwina's dream of going to college was crushed. Nevertheless, her family supported her through her disappointment and encouraged her to pursue a career in show business.

3

Steppin' on Stage

In Edwina's first interview, she revealed that she had won the Apollo Theatre Amateur Night and performed there many times over the years. She then shared her experience of breaking into show business.

As the country struggled through the Great Depression, talent contests lured people with the promise of fame and fortune. In 1933, "The Harlem Amateur Hour," with live radio broadcasts on WMCA, was kicked off by African American host Ralph Cooper. The contests were held at New York's Lafayette Theatre, owned by Frank Schiffman. The following year, these radio contests moved to 253 West 125th Street and Lenox Avenue at the Apollo Theatre, then owned by Sidney Cohen and Morris Sussman. They were then picked up and transmitted on a national network of twenty-one stations.[1]

In 1935, Frank Schiffman and Leo Brecher bought the Apollo. The goal of the theater was to produce the best shows featuring African American stars and entertainment. "The Harlem Amateur Night" continued to be broadcast on Wednesday nights at the Apollo Theatre hosted by Ralph Cooper; later Joe O'Brian, a white man, became the announcer.[2]

The search for talent at the Apollo Theatre and other theaters in the United States added to the momentum of tap dance. Everyone wanted to be on stage, display their talents, and make it to the top. The Amateur Night launched the careers of famed singers Ella Fitzgerald and Pearl Bailey in the 1930s, and it continued to produce superstars, including James Brown and the Jackson 5, in the 1960s and 1970s.

The Apollo Theatre began a new chapter in African American live entertainment. For the first time in American history, the Apollo established an institution in which African American entertainers could perform with pride and dignity.[3] The advertisement for the Apollo proclaimed, "World's Greatest Colored Shows," and the theater billed itself as a place "where stars are born and legends are made."

In the 1930s, the Apollo featured tap dancers like the Nicholas Brothers, the Berry Brothers, Bill "Bojangles" Robinson, and "Buck and Bubbles." Comedians Jackie "Moms" Mabley, Dewey "Pigmeat" Markham, and Clinton "Dusty" Fletcher made regular appearances. The Apollo also debuted Billie Holiday, Ella Fitzgerald, and the Count Basie Orchestra, and it featured numerous chorus girls.

Partnerships

Edwina and Anna Ree Gilliam were dance partners in high school. Their parents made them simple costumes of black satin pants, white blouses with Peter Pan collars, and black velvet cummerbunds. Edwina's biggest concern was her Mary Jane tap shoes that continually fell apart. Yet these two young girls felt like they were on their way to success and the big time.

Edwina and Anna (Anna Ree Gilliam), 1939.

They were offered small gigs and performed in many amateur contests. Finally, a change came with a dollar-prize win in an amateur contest at the RKO (Radio-Keith-Orpheum) Regent Theatre on 168th Street and 7th Avenue in Harlem. It was a thrilling experience that helped them gain access to other performing opportunities in New York. They won many local amateur contests after that.

During their senior year of high school, Anna announced that she was going be married. It came as quite a surprise for Edwina and brought an end to their tap dance partnership. Ann Ree Gilliam Shelton stayed in New York for a time, but eventually she moved to Cleveland with her husband and daughter. Edwina related proudly that Annie Ree became the first female trolley car driver in Cleveland during World War II.

The Performing Circuit

In late 1920s and early 1930s, interest in the vaudeville format declined, and a new format with the sound of the "big band" (meaning a jazz group of ten or more musicians) became all the rage. By the late 1930s, most theaters produced theme-styled shows followed by a movie segment. Within the themed show or full show, there were generally acts by show girls and boys, chorus girls and boys, a solo act, a dance team, an exotic (shake) dancer, a singer, a comedian, a novelty act and a full orchestra or Swing band.

Show girls and boys were used as framers for the act. For example, if the piano was featured center stage, the show girls and boys came out in beautiful costumes, moved about elegantly, and posed around the piano. Chorus girls and boys were the exceptional dancers. Chorus boys were featured at the Cotton Club and during the early years of the Apollo. Later, the focus was on the chorus girls, who drew crowds with their sexy bodies and their ability to dance. Chorus boys and girls are now featured in most stage shows and musical videos.

By the late 1930s, African American performers had their own agents and were booked in paramount theaters and clubs throughout the United States. These first-rate theaters presented shows with African American entertainers to predominantly African American audiences. One of the circuits thus created was called "Round the World" or "Going Around the World," consisting of the Apollo Theatre (Harlem, New York); the Royal Theatre (Baltimore, Maryland); the Howard Theatre (Washington, D.C.); the Paradise Theatre (Detroit, Michigan); and the Regal Theater (Chicago, Illinois). When performers were booked on this circuit, they usually played all five theaters within the year, but not always in the same order.

Edwina knew that in order to be noticed in the world of show business, it was extremely important to play the circuit. In addition to the theater circuits, thousands of nightclubs in cities throughout the country were established. Some of the ones Edwina mentioned were New York's Onyx Club, Kelly's Stables, the Hickory House, and Elk's Rendezvous; Chicago's Club DeLisa, Charlie Glenn's Rhumboogie Café, and the Plantation; Detroit's Club El Sino and Club B&C; Atlantic City's Paradise Club, Club Harlem, and the Blue Mirror; Asbury Park's Hall's Savoy Nite Club; Washington, D.C.'s Stardust; and St. Louis' Plantation Café.

Edwina and Ana

Edwina soon found a second partner: Ann Baxter. They were known as "Evelyn and Anne" or "Edwina and Anna." (It often happened that the newspapers or venues would change or misspell performers' names.)

Edwina and Ana were a fiercely competitive team determined to go to the top. Audiences cheered the girl dance team, which would compete on stage against the boys. Their costume was full-dress, which meant tuxedos. This was intended to prove

Edwina and Ann (Ann Baxter), 1940–1943.

their power, quickness, and finesse. Edwina boasted that they could tie their ties better than the men; in the same breath, she humbly admitted that they were the "best dressed team and the best dance team!"

Edwina and Ana entered the Apollo Amateur Night and won first place. This win gave them the endorsement of the Apollo and opened doors to the show biz world.

During one interview, Edwina unassumingly stated that on March 6, 1942, she and Ann were featured at the Apollo with Thomas Wright "Fats" Waller, composer

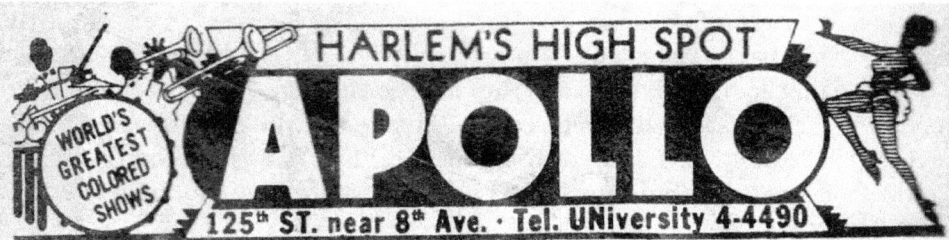

On the bill with "Fats" Waller, 1942.

of the song "Ain't Misbehavin.'" Waller was also known for his musical score from Broadway's *Hot Chocolates* (1929). Waller, with his enthusiastic personality and stride piano style,[4] was the main attraction of the Apollo show. During this performance, Waller introduced the "Jitterbug Waltz." Upon recounting this occasion, Edwina let out a big laugh and burst into song: "The night is getting on, the band is getting slow...."

During the "Fats" Waller week at the Apollo, the playbill included tap duo "Evelyn and Ann"; the dance team Burnham, Harris and Scott (Joe Scott); singers Three Shades of Rhythm; Blues singer Myra Johnson; and Leonard Harper's Dancing Girls and Boys as a chorus line. The movie feature was *Public Enemies*, a story of the law fighting crime that ran rampant.

On March 20, 1942, Edwina and Ann performed at the Royal Theatre in Baltimore with the International Sweethearts of Rhythm. The Sweethearts were a female orchestra billed as the "18 Queens of Swing." Jean Sparks was the band's director. Edwina commented, "It was an all-girl revue; the whole show was all girls. It was great. No recognition for them now."

A few weeks later, on April 3, 1942, Edwina and Ann probably hopped on the *Red Arrow* for their train ride to Detroit, Michigan. There they performed at the Paradise Theatre. A write-up from that time reads, "Big Show At the Paradise.... Ann and Edwina, a two-girl novelty dancing team and other acts will round out a fast entertainment." On the bill were some of the era's greatest performers, including the Berry Brothers, Sister Rosetta Tharpe, and Lucky Millinder's band. Edwina performed many times with Lucky Millinder at the Apollo and at Kelly's Stables.

Lucky Millinder was born August 8, 1900, in Anniston, Alabama. Lucius "Lucky" Millinder began his career as an errand boy for the producer Percy Venable at the Grand Terrace in Chicago. In addition to being taught to dance, Millinder had the job of memorizing all the steps and dances that Venable taught the chorus line. Soon, he was able to rehearse the dances in the show and became acquainted with the music.[5] Although he never studied music or played an instrument, Millinder began leading bands around 1930. By the mid–1940s, he fronted big bands with such well-known musicians as Dizzy Gillespie, John Kirby, Charlie Shaver and Theolonius Monk.[6]

Band leader Lucky Millinder.

"Lucky" appeared to be quite a character. Earl Hines later stated, "Lucky would fire anybody in the world. He fired himself one time. 'Yeah,' he said, 'You're fired, Lucky!' He would fire you to assert his authority, and then give you more money before the two weeks' notice was up."[7]

3. Steppin' on Stage

In Edwina's opinion, the Berry Brothers were one of the greatest acts in show business. They were three brothers: Ananias (Nyas), James, and Warren Berry. Nyas and James were born in New Orleans, while Warren was born in Denver.[8] Edwina thought Nyas was the handsome one. She described their act as

> all kinds of fantastic things you wouldn't think a human being could do. They were really wonderful. You just have to look in amazement. You couldn't believe it." They twirled and threw their canes to one another while dancing, spinning, and never missing a beat. They tap danced on a huge drum and performed splits, caught each other in jumps, and performed other acrobatic stunts never seen on the stage until that time.

In 1951, the act dissolved as Warren had suffered with his hips and Nyas died of a heart attack. The experts touted the Berry Brothers as one of the top dance acts in

Dancers par excellence, the Berry Brothers.

the business, along with the Four Step Brothers, the Nicholas Brothers and Tip Tap and Toe.⁹

On the bill with Edwina and Ana was Sister Rosetta Tharpe (1915–1973), who began her singing career at two years old. She accompanied her mother Katie Bell Nubin, who was a dynamic evangelist and mandolin player. They traveled throughout the South representing the Church of God in Christ (COGIC). Music was essential for converting sinners, saving souls, and healing the afflicted. Later Rosetta Tharpe, vocalist and guitar player, brought her brand of gospel blues to the very clubs and theaters sanctified churchgoers were forbidden to visit.¹⁰

Gospel Blues singer Sister Rosetta Tharpe.

Tharpe provided Millinder with a number of substantial hits: "Rock Me," "That's All," and "Shout, Sister, Shout." Her powerful mezzo-soprano voice was coupled with a signature biting attack and swinging rhythmic drive. Although Tharpe found great success on the Swing Era stage, she felt her true calling was religious singing. She left Millinder's band in 1942 but "sustained an outstanding career as a gospel-folk singer (and guitarist) well into the 1960s."¹¹

Among other clubs and theaters, Edwina and Ann performed at Harlem's Hollywood Cabaret, at 105 West 116th Street in Harlem. Advertised as the Becky Harding Shows, these performances were designed by Harding and produced by her husband Buster.

Edwina and Ann successfully danced and performed the circuit for about a year. Yet, during their time together, Ann experienced fatigue, coughing and sneezing. As the symptoms worsened, she checked into the hospital, only to be diagnosed with tuberculosis. Sady, there were no treatments or antibiotics for this disease until the 1950s. Ann Baxter ultimately died due to complications from tuberculosis.

An article that ran on October 24, 1929, in the *New York Times* (titled "Congestion Causes High Mortality"), stated that the crowded neighborhoods of Harlem had a 40 percent higher death rate than the rest of the city. This was caused by tuberculosis.¹² The illness was extremely contagious, as it was passed through the air from coughing and sneezing. Therefore, a stigma was attached to the disease and anyone associated with it.

Edwina was fortunate to have avoided tuberculosis and only whispered that it was the cause of Ann's death.

Harlem's Lure Dies

The Roaring Twenties petered out as the Great Depression plummeted in. Throughout the 1930s, many Americans were deprived of jobs and any chance of a decent living. Those working in mines, farms, the car industry, textiles, and steel plants formed industrial unions to protect their income and jobs. African Americans and immigrants were blamed for the lack of jobs for white workers. There were protests, strikes, and riots across the country.

On April 8, 1933, the Prohibition era ended. Harlem began to feel the effects of a decade of crime. An area that was once prosperous with clubs, entertainment, arts, and jobs was infiltrated by gangsters, alcohol, guns, the numbers game, prostitution, drugs, and an atmosphere of corruption.

On December 8, 1941, the country became immersed in World War II. During the war, about 12 million American troops were engaged in battle. One-twelfth were African Americans who fought in segregated troops. These men sacrificed their lives in the war for freedom, while their own freedom was denied in the United States.

Tensions and riots grew throughout Harlem. In mid–July 1943, fights started in front of the Braddock Hotel, around the corner from the Apollo Theatre. This prompted uniformed and plain-clothes policemen to be stationed at the hotel and on street corners throughout Harlem. On August 1, 1943, a policeman prohibited an interracial couple from entering the hotel. Later that evening, an African American woman, Marjorie Polite, was arrested for arguing with a hotel employee. As she was literally being dragged away, an African American soldier Robert Bandy came to Polite's aid. He and the police officer argued, a fight broke out, and Brandy was shot in the shoulder. When the news of the shooting reached the people, a riot erupted. A force of 6,600 city police, military police, and civil patrolmen charged into Harlem to restore order. An additional 8,000 State Guardsmen and 1,500 civilian volunteers were posted throughout the area. By August 3, 6 people lay dead, 400 people were injured, 550 arrested, and 1,485 stores were damaged or burned to the ground.[13]

Although Prohibition had been revoked ten years prior, crime continued and the riots of the 1940s brought the glory of Harlem to an end. Many of the nightclubs moved downtown to Manhattan as the memory of an era went up in smoke. By 1943, West 52nd Street became the new center for jazz, known as Swing Street.

On Her Own

When Ann Baxter became ill, Edwina ventured out into the professional world as a solo performer. She apparently never feared dangerous situations or let any political/social situation deter her ambitions. Edwina was always aware of troublesome conditions, but she was able to move through them (or else avoid them entirely). She had a drive and determination to achieve her goal of being an outstanding performer.

As a single act, the critics of African American newspapers quickly gave her the title "Little Lady of Taps." As Edwina emerged on New York City's Swing Street, she found herself in the entertainment center, performing at one jazz club after another, such as the Onyx Club, the Hickory House, the Down Beat, the Famous Door, and the Minton. However, the crowds on 52nd Street did not cater to the sophisticated clientele of Harlem's club scene. These clubs were boisterous places, popular with a heavy drinking crowd.[14]

As part of the "big time," Edwina performed at Kelly's Stables, 137 West 52nd Street, between 6th and 7th Avenue. (Kelly's eventually burned down in 1947.) This venue sought to create a "bucolic atmosphere," with sawdust on the floor and carriage lamps next to the stage.[15] The George Ward Orchestra often played at Kelly's with featured top-notch performers such as jazz singer Billie Holiday and saxophonist Coleman Hawkins.

Edwina debuted dressed in a white tuxedo coat and pants, a black boutonniere, black tie, black handkerchief, and white tap shoes. Her tap dance style concentrated on rhythms similar to those of John "Bubbles" Sublett—close-to-the-floor foot work filled with rhythms complemented by her expressive personality. Earning great reviews, she was featured nightly at Kelly's Stables.

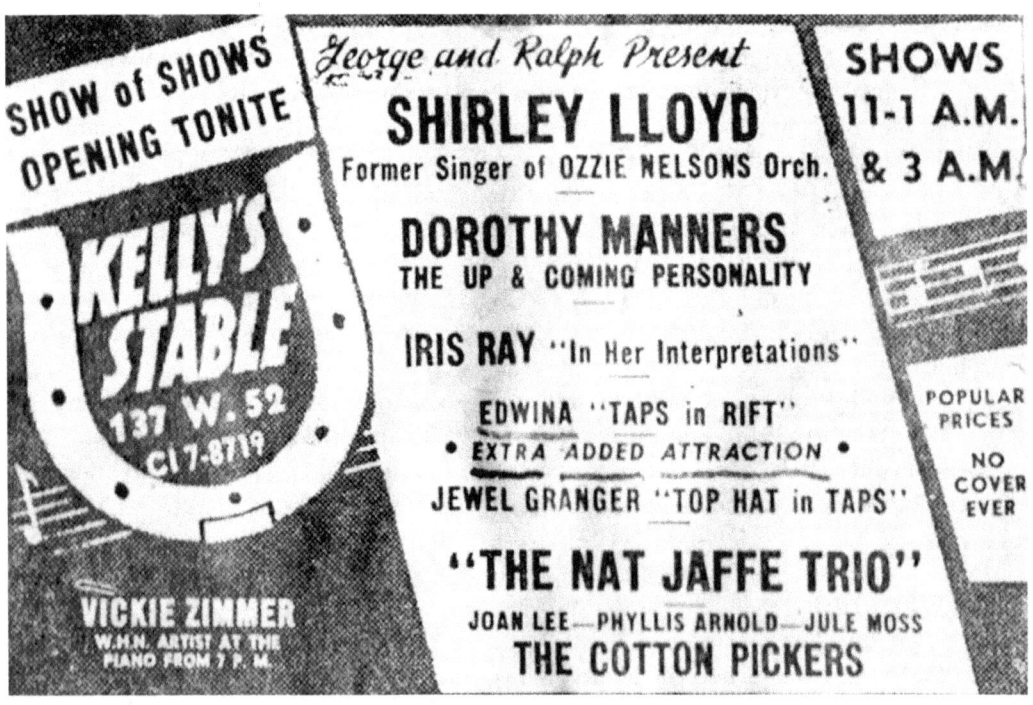

Kelly's Stable on New York's Swing Street.

3. Steppin' on Stage

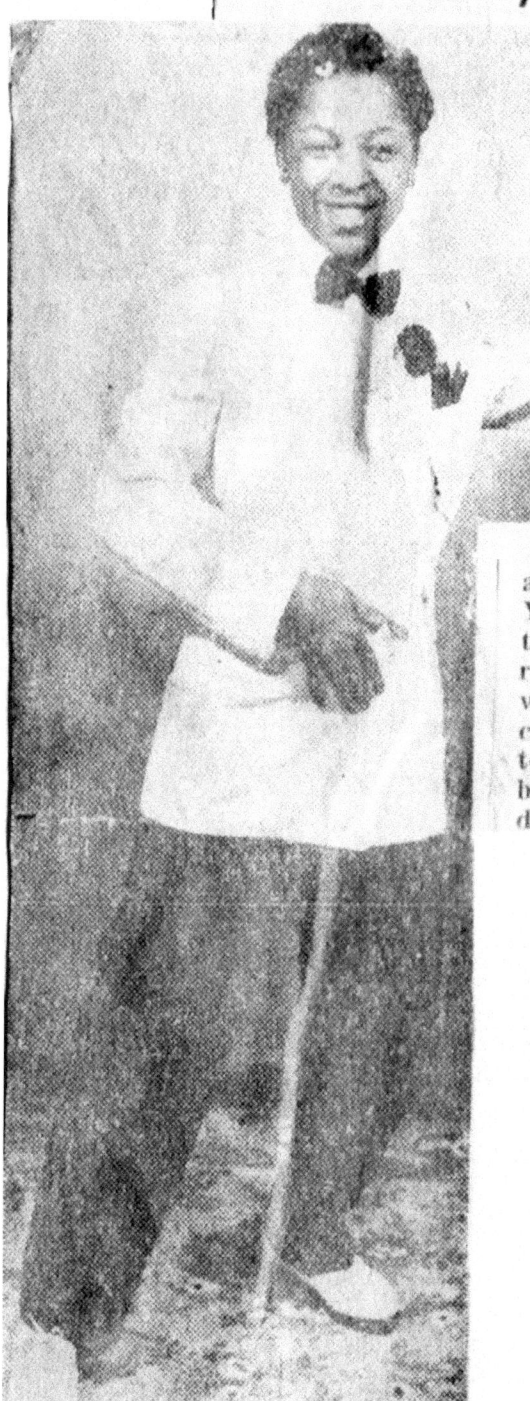

Hit At Kelly's Stables

Miss Edwina Evelyn, known around Kelly's Stable, in New York's 52nd Street, as the "Little Lady of Taps," is doing all right in the Gotham nitery, where her act has been well received. She went to Kelly's after having worked some of the best spots in Harlem and in downtown New York.

"Little Lady of Taps" scores a hit.

George Ward and his Orchestra.

Asbury Park's Savoy Nite Club

New Jersey provided several resort areas for entertainment. Asbury Park was a summer seashore resort area that served as a vacation spot for many residents from New York City and northern New Jersey. It was known for its luxury hotels, casinos, restaurants, theaters, entertainment clubs, beaches and boardwalk.[16]

Edwina, as the "Little Lady of Taps," jumped on the *Nellie Bly* for a ride to a performing niche at the Hall's Savoy Nite Club in Asbury Park. With great enthusiasm, Edwina eagerly reviewed the line-up for the show: Lacy Wharton and his Swing Band from Boston, the comedian and master of ceremonies (MC) Sam "Spo-De-O-De" Theard, exotic dancer Myrtle Hawkins, torch singer Ruth Warner, and singer Baby Hines (the first wife of Earl "Fatha" Hines).

Edwina said that Sam Theard "was a great stand-up comedian of the 1940s. In his unique style, he spelled his name Spo-dee-O-dee and wrote the song 'I'll Be Glad When You're Dead.'" She burst into song: "Now I'll be glad when you're dead, you rascal you, uh-huh." She added that he wrote that song sitting down at a table and gave it to a man for 25 bucks. It became a big hit.

Samual Allen Theard was born in New Orleans in 1904. He was an actor, comedian and song writer. In his style of dirty Blues and novelty Swing records, he composed songs such as "I Wonder Who's Boogiein' My Woogie Now," "She Skuffles That Ruff," and "Rubbin' on That Darned Old Thing." He was most famous for "I'll Be Glad When You're Dead (You Rascal You)" and "Let the Good Times Roll." Theard recorded under the alias "Lovin' Sam" or "Sam Tarpley," and he was a comedian with a 1940s style of sexual humor as "Spo-De-O-De."

Edwina explained that Myrtle "LaZonda" Hawkins was a tastefully alluring exotic dancer. At the time, an exotic dancer was also called a shake dancer. They were provocative, but not as risqué as contemporary strippers are. Hawkins' started out as a dancer with Grace Hall's Chorus Girls at the Howard Theatre and as one of Charlie Davis's Chorines at the Apollo. It appears that while Hawkins was dancing in Long Island, the contracted shake dancer did not show up for her performance. Hawkins took her place and later stated, "I've been shaking ever since."[17] Edwina performed with Hawkins in many theaters and clubs throughout the circuit. During the 1990s, Myrtle Hawkins continued to perform with the Swinging Seniors in New York.

Edwina was very clear that singer Babe Hines had once been married to Earl Hines. Hines himself stated that he and Laura Badge were friends in the 1920s. The band leader Lois Deppe asked Hines and Badge to stand up for his wedding, which they did. And after a few drinks, Hines and Badge got married, too. Shortly afterward, Badge, who was a singer,

Top: **Comedian/singer/composer Samuel Allen Theard ("Spo-De-O-De").** *Bottom:* **Exotic dancer Myrtle "LaZonda" Hawkins.**

assumed the name of Babe Hines. But when Hines realized that Badge was riding on his fame and money, and not true to him, the marriage ended.[18]

Singer Laura "Babe Hines" Badge.

Washington, D.C.'s Stardust Inn

Continuing her journey on the *Nellie Bly*, the "Little Lady of Taps" found herself at Frank Moore's Stardust Inn at 4th and Virginia Avenue SW, Washington, D.C. It was a club where Bebop musicians from the Dizzy Gillespie era became famous. Edwina was doing a single act. On the bill with her were singer and comedian MC Johnny Bragg, Broadway singer Gertrude Saunders, singer Cora Green, versatile singer Kay Hedgeman, and passion dancers (Billy) Cheers and Jerrie.

Edwina stated that Gertrude Saunders was a singer. Yet it appears that Saunders played the role of Ruth Little in Sissle and Blake's production of *Shuffle Along* (1921). She was also a singer in Maceo Pinkard's musical *Liza* (1922), *Sepia Cinderella* (1947) and *Blackberries of 1932*. In Saunders' personal life, she found herself involved in a love triangle with Bessie Smith and Smith's husband Jack Gee. Smith and Gee had a violent relationship torn apart by Bessie's bisexuality. It appears that Gee took Bessie's money to produce a show for the younger and lighter-skinned beauty Gertrude Saunders, and tempers erupted.[19]

Cora Green was famed as a vaudeville and Broadway performer. As a contralto singer, she teamed up with Florence Mills and Ada "Bricktop" Smith, performing as the Panama Trio. The legendary pianist Tony Jackson was part of their act. Green also partnered with "Hamtree" Harrington as "Harrington & Green," touring the Keith-Albee circuit for white audiences.

During this solo period, Edwina was featured at the Stardust Inn and many other clubs, getting her name before the public. She didn't talk much about it, other than mentioning the advertisements and pictures of the stars who were on the playbill with her. But later in her career, she spent a lot of time at the Stardust Inn.

"Little Lady of Taps" at the Stardust in Washington, D.C.

Singer Cora Green, vaudeville and Broadway star.

The Amphitheatre's Gala

There were often shows in D.C.'s public venues where nightclubs collaboratively showcased the top talent. Such collaboration functioned as advertising for the clubs and lured in patrons. In one such instance, Special Service Office Group II produced the "Gala All-Star Club Afternoon Matinee." It was held at the Amphitheatre on Sun-

Tap dancers: the Smith Sisters and Geri.

day, July 4, 1943, at 4:00 p.m., with representatives from each participating nightclub.

Representing Club Stardust were tap dancer Edwina Evelyn, Blues singer Kay Hedgeman and "Fats" Pinier (a 5'5", 250-pound man with a wonderful voice belting out the hottest numbers).[20] The Clores Cocktail Lounge starred Doris Knighton and MC Geo. Kraft. Republic Gardens featured TOTO Ellington, "Streamline" Sue, Smitty and Dotty, and tap dancer Jimmie Mordecai.[21] Off Beat presented three singers: Marshall Haley lyric tenor, Marie Ricardo "Blues Lady," and Ester Gardiner. Crystal Caverns showcased the Two Queens of Swing: Bea Morton and Betty Logan.

Club Bali presented the dance team of the Smith Sisters and "Call the Police

Girl" Monette Moore. The Smith Sisters were tap dancers Katherine and Verne Smith and Geraldine Ball. According to Edwina, they were a terrific trio, just like the Miller Brothers and Lois. With disappointment, she added, "The trio got recognition, but the females just never got too much recognition.... These girls were wonderful." The group dispersed when Geri died in 1944.

4

Candi and Pepper

"There was once upon a time that I was promoted as a star. Once upon a time, I was a star."—Jewel "Pepper" Welch

Everyone has secrets that they never want divulged. Jewel "Pepper" Welch's deepest secret was her age. She reported that she was born on May 23 around 1922 or 1923, but her dance partners revealed that the year of her birth was in fact closer to 1916. This six-to-seven-year difference made it difficult to correlate her activities with the time period. Nevertheless, the core of her life is intact.

It appears that Pepper's mother, whose maiden name was Walker, was a teacher in Richmond, Virginia. Her father was unknown. When Pepper was very young, her mother sent her to Camden, New Jersey, to live with her Aunt Tullie and her uncle, who was Mexican. When they took a trip to Canada, Tullie's husband, who didn't have a U.S. passport, wasn't allowed back into the country. Tullie felt that she was unable to care for Pepper and, when Pepper was about two years old, brought her to Philadelphia to live with her Aunt Annabelle Walker Welch and Annabelle's husband Thomas Welch. Annabelle "Mother" Welch was born in Emporia, Virginia. Pepper always considered Annabelle her mother.

Jewel "Pepper" Welch.

Thomas Welch, whose ancestors were from Barbados, moved to Philadelphia from North Carolina. Thomas, an alcoholic, and Annabelle divorced early in Pepper's life. Mother Welch then married Arthur Jamison, a steel worker. Together they raised Pepper in North Philadelphia. Unfortunately, Pepper did not know the story about her birth mother until very late in her life.

Pepper Learns to Dance

Mother Welch instilled within Pepper a love for entertainment. When Pepper was a young child, she and Mother Welch would go to the Standard Theatre in Philadelphia to see wonderful shows. They enjoyed listening to the Victrola, dancing the Charleston and singing. Pepper always said, "I got dancing in my bones."[1]

Pepper loved to dance. She spent a lot of time on the street corner learning to tap dance and challenging the boys, uncommon for most girls at that time.

When Pepper was about ten years old, her friends dared her to go into a tavern and perform a tap dance. In her bold style, Pepper walked into the bar, headed for the three-piece band on stage, and started dancing. The audience was amazed and threw money on the floor for her. This became the incentive to continue performing.

Between the 1920s and 1940s, Philadelphia theaters[2] presented large vaudeville shows that evolved into Swing Band revues featuring tap dance. As in most large cities during the Great Depression, the craze was to achieve stardom by participating in Kiddie Hour and amateur contests. These shows, held in theaters, were also aired on radio. The intention was to offer the community hope for the future and to promote attendance at theaters, nightclubs, and movies. There were all sorts of incentives to gain participants—for example, one could win $25 and a week's billing at the theater. Another prize was a dance lesson with Bill "Bojangles" Robinson; it was offered to the child who wrote the best letter explaining which Bill Robinson and Shirley Temple movie they liked and why.[3]

During one interview, Pepper, with a huge smile, described her first competition when she was about 12 or 13 years old. She was scared to death as she walked onstage. For her performance, she sang and danced to "Pennies from Heaven." Pepper acted out the story:

> I sang the chorus: "Every time it rains, it rains / pennies from heaven...." Then I executed a step where I jumped up on my toes. Instead of landing on the tips of my shoes, I slipped and fell forward almost into the orchestra pit. I landed on my chin and busted it open. When I got up, I kept dancing and didn't miss a beat. The audience went wild applauding me.

Pepper said that the hole in her chin was so big that it looked like she had two mouths! After the show, the female piano player took her to the hospital to get stitched up.

In speaking of her competitive experiences, Pepper said, "I won a couple and I lost a couple." These experiences, however, presented opportunities and opened the door to the world of entertainment.

Letter to Ella Fitzgerald

In 1937, Pepper made an attempt to receive guidance into the world of show business. She wrote a letter to Ella Fitzgerald, whom she admired. She was thrilled to received a personal response to her letter.

Although Pepper had wonderful memorabilia, she refused to let anything be copied because she feared that the copier would eat it up or that she wouldn't get it back. The following is a letter from Ella Fitzgerald that Pepper read aloud. Ella wrote:

> Dear Jewel,
>
> I'm afraid there isn't much that I can say concerning stage life. You see, I'm just getting into the swing of it myself. This much I know I enjoy ... that much what I haven't taken part in, and I'm going to keep on expressing my opinion.
>
> There are hundreds of dancers and singers. Don't get discouraged by that ... and profit by some of their mistakes and stick to their original material ... I'm going to keep on trying.
>
> Write to me at the Apollo Theatre 125th Street in New York in care of Chick Webb's Band. Will be there next week. I'd love to hear from one admirer who rates me so highly. I hope the picture is satisfactory until I can do better.
>
> I remain yours sincerely,
> Ella Fitzgerald

Jazz singer Ella Fitzgerald, 1937.

Pepper wrote a second time to express her show business expectations. Ella responded as follows: "Again, to you Pepper keep up the good work. You're really swell. Sincerely, Love to you." Pepper was quite impressed that the second letter was addressed to Pepper and not Jewel.

When Pepper got into show business, she met Ella and showed her the letters. It appears that Ella and Pepper were on a first-name basis, and Pepper implied that they remained friends from then on.

Early Dance Partners

Louis Garcia, assistant manager of the Nixon Grand, was an agent for Slatko's Theatrical Ventures.[4] Garcia discovered and arranged acts for children and teenagers, finding opportunities for them to perform. According to Pepper, in 1934 Garcia organized a tap dance team with Pepper and two sisters; they were called the "Rhythmettes." The girls performed together for a short time. Yet in the October 22, 1939, *Philadelphia Independent*, there was an advertisement that implied Pepper was dancing in a trio with Mabe Burley and Lula Mae. The group performed at the Hi-Hat Club in Lawnside, New Jersey.[5] It is uncertain if these women were the Rhythmettes or if Pepper was uncertain of the exact dates.

For many years, Mother Welch chaperoned Pepper to her dance performances. Pepper wasn't sure if a formalized contract existed or if she earned a salary during her time with Lou Garcia. She was doing the work for the enjoyment and relished the applause.

A major concern for African American performers was receiving payment for their work. During the 1940s, but continuing from the early nineteenth century, being cheated was common, and receiving payment equal to that of white performers was almost always out of the question. By the 1950s, many African American entertainers demanded half of their fee before going on stage, expecting the other half as they exited the stage. With this standard, they were at least assured of half payment.

As a child, Pepper was impressed that the audience threw money on the floor during her performances. The money was shoveled up after the show, and all the children received a portion. It appeared that any small amount of money was acceptable to her.

In the nightclub scene, there were several restrictions for children and young adults: They were not allowed to be in the area where liquor was sold, and they had to wait in the kitchen until it was time to perform. If their parents were not present, a guardian was appointed to supervise the children. Pepper said the reason for this rule was "to see that you don't get in trouble or get out there with the wild crowd."

Pepper was later partnered with Lulu Styles of Philadelphia, who could have been Lula Mae from the old trio (the Rhythmettes). They were known as "Pep and Pepper." She proudly accepted the name "Pepper" as her professional and personal name. The team performed in local nightclubs, and their parents made their costumes. Lulu "Pep" wore a short dainty dress, while Pepper wore slacks. She felt that she was a more masculine dancer, and, because of that, she believed she was "lucky enough to wear slacks."

As a teenager, Pepper became aware of and accepted her sexuality. In discussions about women, Pepper's face would brighten and her eyes sparkled. She spoke of how she was attracted to sexy females, saying that one of the joys of show business was that people didn't need to hide their sexuality.

As teenagers "Pep and Pepper" decided to run away to Annapolis, Maryland, and get a job in a nightclub. Annapolis was the home of the U.S. Naval Academy, and Pepper thought that there would be many sailors with money to attend clubs. Both girls were quite excited about the situation. When they arrived, the manager of the club was interested in their talents and decided to hire them. But he was a little suspicious about their situation, so he called their parents. That night during the show, Mother Welch walked into the club, watched Pepper perform, and then took her home.

"Pep and Pepper" performed together for about a year in Philadelphia; Bridgeton, New Jersey; and Wilmington, Delaware. During her interviews, Pepper seemed unsure of why the team broke up, but she thought it was because Lulu married. Yet, according to the *Philadelphia Independent*, Lula Styles was documented as dancing solo at Irene's Café on June 16, 1940.[6]

Pepper attended William Penn High School in Philadelphia. However, she found it hard to concentrate. Later she admitted that her only interests were tap dancing and having a good time. Show business permitted her to have both and make a good salary as well. Pepper dropped out of school in the eleventh grade and worked as a solo act in the Philadelphia area.

Waiting in the Wings

In South Philadelphia, another woman with a dance background similar to Pepper's was ready for the "big time." She was Mildred "Candi" Thorpe.

Candi was born in Philadelphia on Friday, March 21, 1919. As she sweetly cited, "Friday's child is loving and giving."[7] Her parents were Laura Decker Thorpe and William Thomas Thorpe. Their heritage was German, Cherokee and African American. William worked as a supervisor at the Campbell Soup Company while Laura raised William Thorpe (b. 1914), Sydney (b. 1917), Thelma Thorpe Taylor (b. 1918), and Mildred, better known as "Candi" (b. 1919).

Candi left school when she was in ninth grade because she wanted to dance, but she bragged that her sister Thelma completed high school. Candi chuckled as she recounted, "All I did was hang out at the Lincoln Theatre. It's a wonder I know how to read and write. When I tell people that, my sister says, 'Don't tell people that because they'll think you can't read.' I hooked school so many times. Every time I'd come home, [my sister would] be telling Pop I hooked school."

Dancer extraordinaire: Charles "Honi" Coles.

Candi learned to dance on the street corners of Philadelphia, challenging the boys. She hung out in the alley of the Lincoln Theatre, learning steps from the tap dancers who performed there, such as the great Bill Bailey, Derby Wilson and Honi Coles. She'd aggressively approach the dancers as they came out of the theater, asking, "Would you show me that step that you two did, on the stage…. It's the second step after you first come out." The dancer would do the step, and Candi would go through the motions with a little "old trickery" here and there. After she performed her version of one of Honi Coles' steps, he responded, "I liked the way you did it, better [than the way I did it]." Candi said, "He was jiving me." She took pride in herself, saying, "I was gifted. I had it. I had rhythm all the time."

Tallie's Minstrel

Around 1935, when Candi was about 16 years old, she joined a troupe of dancers called Tallie's Minstrels, a small Black minstrel show. The group traveled by car and joined with larger carnivals along the tour. They performed for a week in each locale.[8] The carnivals were made up of a circus, an African American band that played ragtime or jazz music, and tent shows like Tallie's Minstrels.

By the turn of the twentieth century, performing opportunities that showcased tap dancers were found in gillies and medicine shows.[9] These shows were usually one-nighters. African American minstrels, as Tallie's Minstrels, were often tent shows connected with larger carnivals.

With racial prejudice escalating, the Ku Klux Klan (KKK), Knights of the White Camellia, and the White Caps intimidated, tortured, killed, and lynched thousands of African Americans. When acts were successful and performers became able to buy cars and quality clothing, they were often suspected, stopped, and harassed by police. For personal safety, many joined larger Black performing groups. Some of the most influential touring groups were Black Patti's Troubadours (1896–1916), the Whitman Sisters (1900–1943), and Ma Rainey (1904–1924), appearing in such shows as Rabbit Foot Minstrels, Ma Rainey and Her Blues & Minstrel Show, Rainey and Rainey, and Assassinators of the Blues. As these shows faded, the performers joined vaudeville circuits or tried to get hired for an African American Broadway show.

Candi reported that Tallie's Minstrels performed in a tent with an hour of singing and dancing entertainment. There was one man who wore blackface, using charcoal or makeup paint to blacken his face for the show. Tallie's Minstrels had eight people in the show: Tallie, his three daughters, Candi, and three others.

The tradition of blackface started in the 1820s. The American minstrels were negative stereotypical caricatures of African Americans brought to the entertainment stage by white performers. The blackfaced whites performed dances, songs and skits that supposedly idealized the image of slave life. African Americans were portrayed as "naïve buffoons who sang and danced the days away, gobbling 'chitlins,' stealing the occasional watermelon, and expressing their inexplicable love for 'ol' massuh.'"[10] As time progress and African Americans searched for performing opportunities, they, too, had to resort to wearing blackface to be on stage.

Nevertheless, Candi believed that Tallie's Minstrels were not part of the old minstrelsy style, nor did they perpetuate a negative stereotype. It was simply an opportunity through which she could get some show business experience.

While Tallie's Minstrels were in Hopkinsville, Kentucky, Candi's minstrel days came to an end. As she walked down the street, she saw a dog resting in the grass. After she had passed him, he came up behind her and sank his teeth into her calf.

Although she was yelling and fighting to get him off, no one came to help. After hitting the dog on the head, he let go, and she was able to hobble away. She got back to the tent bleeding and in great pain. She received no sympathy from the others and was told that it was time for the show. She could hardly walk, but she was still expected to dance.

After the show, the performers retired for the night. When they woke up in the morning, the carnival had left town, taking all the proceeds. Tallie didn't get paid, and they were stranded. With no money and suffering from the dog attack, Candi had to get home. She wired her father for money. However, Candi's father knew that she would spend any money she had, and he wanted to be sure she could get home. So instead of sending money, her dad sent her a train ticket to return to Philadelphia.

A New Team Is Formed

In 1937, a columnist for the *Philadelphia Independent* newspaper wrote that he had observed two single performers in the Philadelphia area with contrasting dance styles. One was Jewel "Pepper" Welch, and the other was Mildred "Candi" Thorpe. Candi was an improvisational dancer who emphasized rhythms. Pepper's strength lay in Flash: acrobatic tricks such as jumping up and touching her toes, sliding into splits, and spinning. The columnist suggested that the two girls should join forces. In the July 16, 1937, *Philadelphia Independent*, there was a write-up in the "Stroller" section stating,"'Peppie' and 'Candy' Good 'Hoofers': The smart boys are whispering that 'Peppie' Welch and 'Candy' Tallie are envious of each other.... Both of these gals are good."[11] This statement may have thrust the two dancers together. But it also implies that Candi had continued working under the name of her previous employer, Tallie's Minstrels.

Pepper was working at a cabaret called Irene's Café, at 2200 Ridge Avenue in Philadelphia. It appears that Candi was performing a block away at the Congo Café, Old Bank Building, 2300 Ridge Avenue (advertised as Philadelphia's "Leading Nite Life Spot"). Although they had never formally met, they acted upon the columnist's information and found each other. They then became the outstanding tap dance team "Candi and Pepper."

The Team Reaches Stardom

Candi and Pepper's first engagement as a dance team was at Simm's Paradise Café in South Philadelphia. From Simm's, they performed with tap dancer Derby Wilson at O.V. Catto's Elks Lodge,[12] 16th and Fitzwater Streets, diagonally across from Simm's.

In an article advertising Erskine Hawkins at O.V. Catto's on April 28, 1940, a section read:

Jewel "Pepper" Welch and Mildred "Candi" Thorpe, 1940.

4. Candi and Pepper

Candi and Pepper tear up the floor.

Candy and Pepper Head O. V. Revue

One of the greatest comedy song and dance teams ever produced in Philadelphia, Candy and Pepper, is headlining the current show at the O. V. Catto Downstairs Grill, 16th and Fitzwater Streets. They came to the O. V. Catto direct from a successful engagement at the Apollo Theatre in Harlem.

These two performers, products of local amateur programs, have developed into headline attractions and are on their way up the theatrical ladder.[13]

During a later performance at Simm's, Candi and Pepper worked with producer Larry Steele. His shows were outstanding and, according to Candi, "any star that was [a star] worked Simm's," such as Moms Mabley and several incredible tap dancers, including Baby Laurence, Blackie, and Stump and Stumpy.

Candi and Pepper performed in the Philadelphia area for a while. Their big break came when their manager, Reiss DuPree, owner of the Strand Ballroom in Philadelphia, booked them at New York's Apollo Theatre on January 3, 1941. They probably boarded the *Liberty Bell* and began their adventures. Candi described the experience as follows:

> On opening day, I was so frightened. We'd never worked a theater, Pepper and I. We had come just out of Philadelphia. Philadelphia, New York, it's like day and night. New York is like fast pace. You have to be on top of everything. The first show ... we were the opening act ... we looked out [from behind the curtain]. Here's all these performers. They got from the first to the middle of the theater. [They were in] every row casing the new acts.
>
> We were scared to death when we hit that stage. And the introduction was, "Ladies and Gentleman, we got two girls who are going to dance for you out of Philadelphia; Candi is sweet, Pepper is hot; come on girls, show me what you got." It sounds corny now but it's the way he introduced us. "Candi is sweet, Pepper is hot; come on girls, show me what you got." And we tore 'em up. We tore 'em up.
>
> OK, we go on, we ran out of routines because the public liked [us] so well that they kept calling us back for an encore ... at the time, there was a theater manager ... his name was Frank Shiffman. And he called backstage on the PA System and told the stage hands ... that the opening act which was Candi and Pepper would now close the show. The stars of the show, Stump and Stumpy, were now opening the show.

Their basic act was a little singing to "Sunny Side of the Street." Candi improvised tap rhythms, never doing the same thing twice. She added wings, slides, and trenches to her rhythms when needed.[14] The music she liked was "I Got Rhythm," because it allowed her to do her rhythm breaks where she needed them.

Pepper likewise did her part of the routine. Candi said, "She was great, she was great, she was great! Tall, beautiful smile, flashy. She'd do a turn and her whole jacket would turn around [using her hands to show the flair of the jacket], she was good. She jumped up in the air and touched her toes." The act closed to "One O'Clock Jump" with over the tops and squatting leg thrusts. Candi raved that they brought the house down.

A May 5, 1940, *Philadelphia Independent* article with a picture of Candi and Pepper stated, "Make Hit: Pepper and Candy, local dance-comedy team, who are definitely on their way up the theatrical ladder. The girls recently completed successful engagements at the Apollo Theatre in Harlem, Howard in Washington and the O.V. Catto Club here in Philly."[15]

The Apollo Theatre performance was followed by a few years of jumping on and off trains—the *Black Diamond* to Buffalo, the *Red Arrow* to Detroit, and the *Michigan* to Chicago. It began with a roadshow with the New Jersey "Cotton Club Revue," which featured Louis Armstrong and his orchestra, Midge Williams, Sonny Woods, Luis Russell, Candi and Pepper, Big Time Crip, and Stump and Stumpy.

Candi and Pepper performed frequently at Bill Robinson's Mimo Club and Small's Paradise in New York. In addition, they were featured in Detroit's Club Congo with

Candi and Pepper with Louis Armstrong in Buffalo, 1940.

Twentieth-Century Theatre, Cotton Club Revue, Buffalo, New York.

Comedians Stump and Stumpy.

singer Una Mae Carlisle, interpretive dancers Tonalayo and Lopez, the Singing Weavers, singer Margaret Watkins and the Club Congo Orchestra. They also worked many gigs in Buffalo and Chicago.

Candi was proud of the team because, as women, they were appreciated for their talent. They only showed their hands and faces and didn't need to expose their bodies. Candi proudly said, "The audience heard and saw what was important."

Candi and Pepper were on the Apollo Theatre playbill several times, billed and documented as superlative tappers. The team performed at the Apollo with Count Basie on the week of January 3, 1941; Fats Waller the week of February 19, 1941; and the Sweethearts of Rhythm the week of January 19, 1942.

In the January 19, 1941, *Philadelphia Independent*, the

Big Time Crip, dancer.

"Brighter Lighter Banter" section by Earl Barnes cites the dancers: "Candy and Pepper, whirlwind dancing and singing duo, helped Count Basie wow capacity throngs at the Apollo in Harlem two weeks ago. These lassies are two more Phillyites who have made good in a big way."[16]

Off Stage

Candi and Pepper were both excited about being part of what they called the fast life. They enjoyed life, show business and the money they made. Unfortunately,

WEEK Beginning FRIDAY, JANUARY 3rd

AMERICA'S GREATEST SWING BAND
AND CLARENCE ROBINSON'S BIG REVUE CAST

COUNT BASIE
and his BAND

with JIMMIE RUSHING and HELEN HUMES

Happy, Pal and Pete
Two Men and a Mule

TWO LUCKY BUCKS
FIRST APPEARANCE A DANCE NOVELTY

CANDY & PEPPER
PRIDES OF PHILADELPHIA

Henry Wessels - John Mason
JIMMIE BASKETTE - SANDY BURNS
Beautiful Apollo Chorus

Candi and Pepper with Count Basie, 1941.

in between shows they gambled, played pool and cards, and spent most of what they earned.

Reflecting on her life in show business, Candi revealed that it was a great life, but at times a lonely one. The applause was great to hear because it made her feel like she was doing something right. But when the last show was over, she'd go home to four walls and nothing else.

Another difficult part was the expense of being a headline act. She and Pepper felt like they had to put up a front. Candi said, "So naturally, you'd say 'hey, give 'em a drink, give 'em a drink' because you're a name act. Between your music and your uniforms and the upkeep of your personal self, your living expense, your clothing and all this [it was expensive] ... it's a tough life, I'll tell you, it's a tough life. Beautiful, but tough."

Top: Jazz pianist, composer, and bandleader Count Basie. *Bottom:* Candi and Pepper with "Fats" Waller, 1941.

Candi made friends easily. She was never interested in men, other than competing with them in tap dance. During the interviews, she was open about her sexuality, but she didn't really talk about it with her family.[17]

Candi prided herself on having a personal relationship with Ella Fitzgerald. The innuendoes implied a sexual affair, and, of course, neither Ella nor Candi would have advertised a relationship that was taboo in the 1930s and 1940s. Candi also had a crush on a performer named Tondelayo (possibly of Tonalayo and Lopez). Whenever she mentioned this person's name, she'd roll her eyes, chuckling, "Tondelayo with those juicy red lips." Candi was an honest woman who would shoot from the hip. She didn't have an ego of personal

Left: **Jazz pianist and composer Thomas Wright "Fats" Waller.** *Below:* **Candi and Pepper reach a high pitch.**

glory, nor did she exaggerate the truth. Her stories reflected her personal life, and that's what it was—personal.

Candi and Pepper danced together for about five or six years. According to Pepper, their breakup story was as follows: One night in Chicago, Pepper brought a girlfriend to the hotel room. The girls were laughing, talking and playing; then they jumped in bed together. Pepper was on the outside, the girlfriend in the middle, and Candi on the other side of the bed. They soon went to sleep. During the night, Pepper felt the bed "a-rockin' and a-rollin'." Lying on her side, Pepper reached behind and felt a hand. It was Candi's hand in places where Pepper wanted to put hers. Furious, Pepper jumped out of bed, "hollerin' and yelling." She grabbed the mattress and flung it across the room, tossing the two women on the floor. And that was the end of the team, as well the end of their friendship.

After Pepper broke up the partnership, Candi ended her tap dance career. She stayed in Chicago doing odd jobs, but finally returned to the Philadelphia area in 1950. With great disappointment, she said, "We were on our way, but we split. We did, we had chemistry."

Pepper and Tillie

Pepper signed with professional manager Tillie Jenkins and worked as a solo performer on both coasts. Pepper shared many stories about her relationship with Tillie. In her dramatic manner, she told the story of how she and Tillie traveled to California, where Tillie's family lived. During their travels, they feared that Pepper would not be allowed in hotels for whites. Their gimmick was that Tillie would register at the hotel for herself and her maid. Pepper would walk behind her, carrying her bags and saying, "Yes, Ma'am." Then they walked up the stairs to the room and laughed aloud about the way they had fooled the management.

Pepper said that during her time in California, she and Tillie went to parties and visited Tillie's family. (It was important for Pepper to always relate to Tillie as Jewish.) Pepper implied that she and Tillie were "hot and heavy" in love, but she never gave details.

In time, Pepper wanted to go back to Philadelphia. She said that Mother Welch had told her to always keep enough money for a train ticket home, which she did. (However, the part about saving money did not feature very significantly in the information Pepper shared during her interviews.)

The story "Invades the Coast," which appeared in the *Chicago Defender* on April 3, 1943, included a picture of Pepper and the following information: "'PEPPER' The sensational 'IT' girl formerly of the team of 'Candy and Pepper,' passed through Chicago Sunday en route to the Coast where she's working as a single. She's managed by Tillie Jenkins, who is accompanying the dancer on the cross country hop."[18]

5

Salt and Pepper

Elk's Rendezvous

A trip uptown to Harlem's Lenox Avenue district found many Swingin' clubs, such as Small's Paradise, Minton's Playhouse, Lenox Lounge, and Dickie Wells' Theatrical Grill. Edwina found a home at Elk's Rendezvous, advertised as "America's Most Intimate Nite Club presenting a fast stepping hilarious Floor Show."

Elk's Rendezvous was recognized by its Art Deco neon awnings and a neon elk's head at the top curve of the storefront's sign located at 464 Lenox Avenue and 133rd Street. The building stands today, but now it has a red brick facade and a nondescript storefront.

Edwina proclaimed, "And this here was a great, great, great master of ceremonies Ralph Cooper. He used to also play in Black movies. That's why we used to call him Mugzy, 'cause that was his name in the movies. He was a gangster in the movies, yeah. I remember the name of one of the movies which was called *Bullets or Ballads*." As a master of ceremonies (MC), Cooper told jokes and got the crowd laughing and in the mood for what was to come.[1]

In 1933, Ralph Cooper introduced and hosted the Harlem Amateur Night at New York's Lafayette Theatre, and he continued to broadcast the show from the Apollo Theatre in 1935. Cooper was known for producing shows, fronting a band, playing the straight man with various acts, and working as a disc jockey in New York City. He was also a noted actor in early African American motion pictures, such as *Poor Little Rich Girl* (1936), *Bargain with Bullets* (1937), *Gang War* (1940), and *Am I Guilty?* (1940).

In late 1943, with MC Ralph Cooper, Elk's Rendezvous featured the following acts: "Baby Don't You Cry" Warren Evans, Continental favorites Moore and Larry, Jimmy Smith A World Wonder, *New Faces 1943* Ann Robinson, comedienne Cousin Ida, Harlem's Glamour Boy Manhattan Paul, precision in tap Edwina Evelyn, and the Copper Tan Rendezvouettes: Louise Peterson, Virginia Wright, Betty Mays (married to Ralph Cooper), Thelma Prince, and Ollie Prince (and one unknown).

Edwina described Jimmy Smith as follows: "He used to tap dance on the xylophone. He was a tap dancer. But he tap danced, not on the floor, he tap danced on the xylophone, a regular xylophone. He used to tap dance, and he used to make a tune. It was wonderful."

Ann Robinson was a performer in the Broadway show *New Faces 1943*. Edwina

5. Salt and Pepper

Above: Elk's Rendezvous. *Below:* Movie star and master of ceremonies Ralph Cooper.

explained that each year there was a show that promoted the new faces seen on stage and screen.

Manhattan Paul was a master of ceremonies in New York City's Small's Paradise, Moraine's, Elk's Rendezvous and other nightclubs.

Pepper Arrives

Edwina performed as a solo act in many of the Harlem clubs and downtown on Swing Street. At the same time, Jewel "Pepper" Welch was performing in the New York and the Philadelphia areas. Edwina was on the bill at Elk's Rendezvous from September 18 to October 24, 1943. Following her performance, that dance spot was filled by Pepper for the weeks of October 30 through December 4. A *New York Age* advertisement revealed Pepper Welch on the playbill for Elk's Rendezvous in a show called "Harlem to Hollywood" with MC Ralph Cooper (December 4, 1943).

One night after Edwina's performance at Elk's Rendezvous, Tillie Jenkins, Pepper's agent, went backstage for a chat with Edwina. After a brief introduction, Jenkins asked if Edwina knew Pepper, who was also doing a single act. Edwina said she had heard that Pepper was a wonderful dancer and had seen her act, but didn't know her personally.

Excitedly, Jenkins said it appeared that Edwina and Pepper were following each other on the touring circuit. When Edwina was at Moraine's in Harlem, Pepper was at Elk's Rendezvous, and vice versa. Jenkins implied that it seemed more than a coincidence, planting the bait. Then she added that their dancing styles were similar and that people even said they looked like sisters. Jenkins suggested that the girls team up, because they would be a great dance act, and there was more money for teams than for a single act.

Edwina pondered the idea. Later, when she and Pepper had a few free weeks, they met and rehearsed. Edwina viewed Pepper's Flash style (acrobatic stunts) as a complement to her rhythmic footwork style.

The girls decided to team up, and Edwina chose the stage name "Salt" to validate the team as "Salt and Pepper." "It worked out beautifully," she cynically chuckled. Salt and Pepper were complements on the dance floor, but in life they were as different as salt and pepper.

(During the narrative detailing this period of her performance life, Edwina will be referred to as Salt.)

Salt (Edwina) was private and sophisticated. She enjoyed a simple style of fun and was very interested in learning. She often spoke about how she read during her free time and went to museums while touring. On the other hand, Pepper was energized and daring, taking risks on a whim. She sought out thrilling moments and enjoyed the nightlife connected with entertainment. Over the years, they developed a solid friendship as Salt watched out for Pepper and kept her on the straight and narrow.

The tap dance team "Salt and Pepper" had its first performance on Friday, January 7, 1944, at the Apollo Theatre in Harlem. They appeared on the playbill with Erskine Hawkins and his band. They were obviously incredible, as they were held over for another week to appear with Louis Jordan on January 14, 1944. (These shows will be discussed in the next chapter.)

With a sensational introduction at the Apollo, the team was contracted with Elk's Rendezvous. It appears that the show ran from January 28 through April 13, 1944. It starred MC Ralph Cooper with Herman Flintall's Orchestra. On the playbill were Salt and Pepper, singer Warren Evans, contortionist and juggler Dolly Pembrook, singer Baby Hines, exotic dancer Joi-La-Joy, Manhattan Paul, Betty Mays, and the Rendezvouettes.

Trumpeter/composer/bandleader Erskine Hawkins.

Booking Agent

Salt and Pepper discontinued management with Tillie Jenkins, choosing instead to sign up with Hazel Green. Salt and Pepper turned out to be a profitable match. Green had solid bookings for them and promoted them with newspaper advertise-

> **HAZEL GREEN**
> *Theatrical Enterprises*
> C. B. S. THEATRE BUILDING
> **1697 BROADWAY   NEW YORK**
> 53rd & Broadway
> Phone COlumbus 5-8678   Room 1203
>
> ★
> **ARTIST'S CONTRACT**
>
> AGREEMENT, made this 25 day of Feb. 1944 between Manager/Proprietor of Elks Rendezvous
> Address 132 Lenox Ave.
>
> AND Salt & Pepper the Artist.
>
> The Manager engages the Artists as a dance team for a Period of 6 weeks with option of 6 weeks Commencing Feb. 25 1944, in consideration of which the Manager agrees to pay $150.00 per week. Transportation to be paid by
> The Artist agrees to perform from usual policy
>
> It is understood and agreed by both parties hereto that Hazel Green is in no way responsible for any damage or claims that may arise to either from this ageement.
>
> The Manager or Proprietor of Elks Rendezvous agrees to pay to Hazel Green, a sum equal to 10 % weekly for services rendered by said Hazel Green, as long as the Artist remains in said Manager's or Proprietor's services or is engaged by said Manager or Proprietor or if re-engaged by said Manager or Proprietor and said Artist, by these presents, does authorize said Manager or Proprietor to deduct and to pay to Hazel Green the said sum of 10 % for this engagement or for any future re-engagement by said Manager or Proprietor of
>
> The Manager reserves the right to terminate this contract after the first performance.
>
> IN WITNESS WHEREOF, the parties hereto have hereunto set their hands and seals the day and year first above written.
> Manager _____ Artist _____
> HAZEL GREEN   Phone _____
> Agents for Manager
> _____ Address _____

Contract with Hazel Green Theatrical Enterprises.

ments and write-ups for each show. When they weren't performing, Green kept their names before the public. Occasionally, the Santley Agency (a freelance group) also booked them.

Green was responsible for booking all the theaters on the "Round the World" circuit that catered to the upper echelon of Northern Black theaters[2] As mentioned earlier, this circuit included the Apollo in New York, the Royal in Baltimore, the Regal in Chicago, the Paradise in Detroit, and the Howard in Washington, D.C. Green also booked Salt and Pepper for jobs in smaller theaters and nightclubs. The larger jobs (called revues) ran for one week to three months. A gig was usually for one night or for a weekend.

Although they had their own agent, Salt explained that at times a talent or theater-booking agent would see an act in a show and offer them a job. Occasionally, the bandleader would ask a performer to tour with him/her. At other times, a performer was recommended for a job by other performers. Salt explained that performance was one way to get a contract, and one job led to another. "Maybe you'd appear at the Bali now. [The producer from] the Crystal Caverns would come over and say, 'We'd like to book you in the future for their show.' ... Many a time, you got your own jobs. The agents didn't always get you jobs." For example, on Friday nights every talent and booking agency had a representative in the audience.[3] If a performer freelanced, the agency that signed him/her took a percentage. In her generous manner, Salt justified the agent's percentage of freelanced jobs: "It was fair. It saved them the trouble, because most of your jobs, they are the ones that got them for you.... They are entitled to that. That's how they exist."

Dapper Dans in the Suits

While the team was performing at Chicago's Rhumboogie, a newspaper clipping in *Pittsburgh Courier* read, "The two dapper dans in the suits are Salt & Pepper, rhythm dancers." This led to a discussion about costumes and ages.

During an interview with Salt, the researcher commented, "It looks like you are younger than Pepper in this picture. Pepper said that you were about three years older than she." With loud, hearty laughter, Salt declared, "Pepper is not younger than me. She's about six years older." This was the first indication of Pepper's birth year.

When the laughter settled down, Salt brought the conversation back to the costumes. "Your costume was half your act ... your appearance was very, very important," she stated. Originally, Salt and Pepper wore short jackets called Eton suits[4] or Eisenhower jackets. They had a bellboy look, which Salt believed looked very attractive, and they were also comfortable for movement. She added, "Our shirts were pure white ... our shoes were pure white. People used to say, 'Where are those girls with those white ice cream shoes?'" Their costumes also included zoot suits and full-jacketed suits.

The purchase of wardrobe and upkeep were huge expenses out of their pockets. Their shirts were starched, and suits were professionally laundered. If they were doing three shows a night, they had two costume changes for each show, which came to about six different changes in one night. Salt felt that this gave them a different look every time they came on stage.

Salt reminisced, "People used to say, 'AAAAHHHH. Oooh!' You know what I mean, because it was important ... your appearance was very important." She felt that the male attire, a suit or tuxedo, was a symbol of elegance and emphasized the dance.

Success in the entertainment field means to "be better than the competition." Fred Astaire, a white male who danced an elegant style of tap while wearing a top hat and tails, was one who set the standard for costumes. Salt and Pepper learned to dance on the street corner while competing against the boys. They knew not only the style of clothing but also the level of rhythms and dance styles necessary to succeed in the world of tap dance.

The Manhattan Debs was the name of another team of two women tap dancers. Salt said that they were marvelous dancers. Their shoes had taps on the tips of the toes, which were used for toe stands (in addition to protecting their shoes). She also commented on their sexy little costumes, which she didn't think were effective. Yet, in Salt's opinion, the idea of tap dance and success seemed to work when the Debs wore male-style suits.

Salt and Pepper didn't feel that being dainty and feminine would have worked for them. Moreover, the American culture of the early twentieth century favored formal attire for evening entertainment. A suit and tie for men and dresses for women were appropriate. For African Americans, looking smart and adorning the body was part of the cultural aesthetic. The performers also took pride in their appearance, as did the audiences. Performers dressed in formal attire to delight those who came out to see them. They also dressed to be accepted by white audiences. In the 1940s, no one on stage would have been dressed in jeans and a T-shirt, unless it reinforced a scene in a play.

Aware of all the reasons outlined above, Salt and Pepper carefully chose their costumes. The male-style suits may have been their winning ticket to compete with male dancers in tap dance.

Rehearsals

Rehearsal times varied from show to show and often depended on transportation. Salt and Pepper usually arrived at a club or theater a day or two before their performance. One or two rehearsals were scheduled for the entire show if it were a musical revue or a theme-styled performance.

The acts arrived from different cities, bringing their own props, costumes, and sheet music. The bandleader worked with the performers and the orchestra to set the entrance, the tempo, and other particulars of the music. Sometimes the act did a full-out performance with the band for the rehearsal, and other times they walked through setting the music with the bandleader. In the latter cases, the members of the band didn't see the act until the night of the show.

Many times, the band, traveling by car or bus, arrived late, or performers would miss the train. This meant there was no time for rehearsal. The bandleader then went

5. Salt and Pepper

Manhattan Debs: Dinky (Ann Henry) and Junior.

to the dressing room for a "talk rehearsal." He'd ask what the performer was going to do, and they would talk about the music and what they needed.

Salt described the typical talk rehearsal:

> I'm going to do two choruses of "How High the Moon." ... The dancers would set their tempo with the band. [Or] they went out and they'd tell [the bandleader], "I want it right here" [demonstrates tempo by tapping with her foot]. The band gets it and it goes on from there.... You can have a talk rehearsal, talk it over and go right out there and do it before a big audience.... When you're getting ready to end the routine you say, "OK, let's

go or [take me home]." And they give you an extra four bars [or eight bars] and take you off the stage ... that's when they bring up the music loud because it's the ending.

Some of them [dancers] have tricks [with] the band. They'll do a step like this [demonstrates] and slow them down a little bit or they do a step and pick them up a little bit. Tricks of the trade!

That's it and that's rehearsal. [laughter] But that's show business for you. Some people think you've been doing the same show for a year. And it's the first time you've ever done it. That's improvising. And it turns out great.

When the whole show gets together for the finale, when everybody comes out and takes their places on the stage, we do that basic B.S. Chorus[5] and the basic Shim Sham.[6] The last one tags[7] it. The tag [dancer] comes back a couple of times ... that's the show. People think you've been doing it for years. [laughter] Some shows ... we didn't have any rehearsals.

Salt and Pepper usually worked with wonderful big band musicians like Earl Hines, Fletcher Henderson, George Hudson, and Fats Waller. Some of the musicians had studied music, while others learned it on their own. But according to Salt, "They all were wonderful musicians. They could play with anybody."

Gigs were plentiful and challenging. While Salt and Pepper had music for a full orchestra, they often performed in clubs that only had a small combo. They needed to adapt quickly or resort to general music. It went something like this:

> Many a time, the agent would call and say, "I have a gig for you over in Jersey, can you make it?" "Gig?" We'd say, "sure," maybe $50 or $75. Maybe the call came through at 3 o'clock in the afternoon and you'd have to be there for 7 o'clock for rehearsal. First show goes on at 9 o'clock. So you get over there and you don't even have chance to set up a routine, so you talk out a routine: "Let's do the time step, an eight-bar introduction, a chorus of "Lady Be Good," that's a great dancing number. We'll do the time step, then we'll do the half break, the shuffle off to Buffalo, then we'll do Pepper's step, and then we'll do Salt's step, then we'll take it out with the finale." So you talk over the rehearsal and you never do it until you get out there on the stage. It goes over better than, maybe, if you had rehearsed for six weeks. Now, if you're doing a single, you never know what you're going to do ... it's all according to how the music hits you."

Improvisation

The beautiful thing about jazz music is its freedom. Jazz has form and structure, but it requires improvisation, which allows the performer to deviate according to their feelings, the rhythm and the sound. A musical phrase takes a musician/dancer down a different path and then returns to the basic structure.

When dancing as part of a team or group in a rhythm or jazz style, the movement is set. There may be parts when each dancer "does his/her thing." If a solo dancer were a great improvisational dancer, like Walter Green, Baby Laurence, and Teddy Hale, he/she improvised the dance on the spot. They didn't have a set routine. They had close-to-the-floor rhythms and sounded like drummers. If they had a good band behind them, they improvised with the band or challenged a member of the band spontaneously.

Those who used improvisation seemed to be in a transcendant state. They were totally engrossed in what they were doing, which was making music. Salt clarified:

But the single dancer, they never knew what they were going to do till they got out there.... They didn't dance by the books; they danced according to their feeling. That's why they never did the same thing twice. If the music was good, they could get out there and dance, and wouldn't want to come off the stage.... The music behind you could really make you or break you.... Some of those dancers out there, they used to have to stand in the wings and tell them to come on off, because they would keep going. That Teddy Hale ... and that Walter Green was a great dancer. He used to dance close to the floor. Buster Brown dances something like him, close to the ground, rhythm [dance] close to the floor, and not a lot of hopping. Bunny Briggs does it. All that rhythm and everything.... But that music, they have a good band behind them, they don't need to have any rhythm music. They just talk to the band leader. "Give me a four-bar introduction, and just give me three choruses of 'Shining Stockings' and then take me out with eight bars or something like that." They didn't know what you were going to do. And some of them would stay out there, the band would be ready to take them off and they'd still be out there. [laughter] In the wings, they had to tell them to come off.

In the early 1930s, hardwood flooring was used in the construction of most theater stages and clubs. They looked beautiful, and for tap dancers this flooring allowed for a variety of sounds made by metal taps against the wood. In addition, the "fast" floor used for tap dance was polished and slippery, which enhanced slides, scrapes, splits, and other stunts. The dancer Jimmy Slyde preferred a fast floor because his style of dancing was filled with slides across the floor and slides of his feet together and apart. If the floor was sticky, it could knock off the dancer's balance and control.[8] Dancers needed to be cautious with the floor, or they could find themselves in a customer's lap.

The Act

Salt thought that Pepper was a wonderful dancer, and the contrast of Flash and rhythm would be the selling feature of the team. Pepper was slim and had long legs. She kicked her leg very high and held it straight up for several beats of the music. One of her best moves was to slide down into a split and immediately rise up again.

As their act developed, Budd Johnson, a saxophonist and clarinetist who worked with Earl Hines, composed their music for a sixteen-piece orchestra. Salt explained that the music was written to embellish the movement. Salt and Pepper's main act with music and lyrics was called "Rhythm and Rhyme."

The act began with a song that included their names, Salt and Pepper. Salt explained that every step was choreographed and the music accentuated the most important parts of their dance. The drummer or the saxophone player intensified their movements. When Pepper went down in a split, the movement was accented with the drum. Likewise, the cymbal would crash as Pepper kicked her leg straight up to her head. A piano run enhanced a split or turn, and a drum roll heightened a series of Flash steps. "The drummer would go 'da& DA1 da& da2' and you'd do your step with him. It was just marvelous ... it was so emphatic." Salt described the music and the dance as personified. This tailor-made music brought incredible applause at just the right moments.

The act began with their song:

Get down with Salt and Pepper.

> Dig that Salt, she's right on time.
> Here comes Pepper, she's right behind.
> And there's nothing like rhythm and rhyme.
> Boy, nothing like rhythm and rhyme.

Salt and Pepper then danced together for two choruses, followed by a few jokes. After that, they moved to opposite sides of the stage, where they would each perform two choruses in solo. This section was considered the challenge or the improvisation. Pepper did a combination of rhythm and Flash, and Salt performed Rhythm Tap.

Afterward, they faced each other and slid across the stage, crossing paths. With a quick turn, they then faced each other and began the penguin walk. (Pepper described the penguin walk as a maneuver in which hands are placed on the neck and elbows are raised high, and the dancers waddle from foot to foot like penguins.) This was followed by a straddle jump as the dancers touched their toes. Pepper remembered that they moved upstage toward the band, then quickly turned around and danced toward the audience. She stated that during this section they would "get down" with some vernacular dances, such as Shorty George[9] or Struttin'.[10]

The team then executed a series of Flash steps, such as Over the Tops[11] and Through the Trenches.[12] Pepper performed quick spins, then jumped in the air and landed in a split. She often did two or three splits in succession where she slid to the floor and rose up as she drew her legs together. The team also did a version of Kazatsky[13] kicks, and the act concluded with several quick spins and a pose that was usually an expressive use of the hands. Most tap dancers exited with a character-style strut that was showy or humorous (and usually asymmetrical).

Pepper described her performance style as follows: "I played to the audience. I looked to make each person think I was dancing for them. While I was doing a step, I would point to them. Like this [demonstrates a direct point], special for them.... And they'd think, 'OH to Me,' and that was the trick of it."

Pepper said that she and Salt often opened the show. It was their job to rouse the audience. And in a loud enthusiastic voice, speaking so fast that she could barely get all the words out, Pepper explained:

> I'd run out, do the split. We'd come out to each other; do the penguin.... Then I'd jump back into a back bend. I'd do a break: da, da, da, da, da, ah (1& 2 &3 4). Salt and I would face each other, [sings] da ah da& ah da& ah Da (&1 &2 &3 4). I'd come up and turn a spin around. Salt would be coming to me doing a step like this here [demonstrates]. I'd run pass Salt and do a split. Boom! Bow! Ra, ta, ta, ta, ta ta (&1e&a2). Ta, Ta, Ta, ta Ta, ta Ta (1&2 &3&4). Bbbrrrrrrr, TAAAA and this guy said, "WWWOOOOO!!!" That's the way we went, wild fiery. [lots of laughter]
>
> Salt danced very nice. She danced better [than] me, I thought. She used to do all those acrobatic steps, like Over the Top. I learned how to do the splits later on.... I used to run out and do a spin and ... then, fall right into a split.... Salt and I both, she use to jump down and do that with me. Then we'd come almost off the stage and then I'd jump up and do the split and "Brs rats, ta, ta, ta, ta Bow" (&a1 e&a2 3).

Salt was a rhythm dancer. Her specialty was to tap close to the floor, emphasizing Swing rhythms. She was short and her kicks weren't as dynamic as Pepper's. But over the years of working with Pepper, Salt's style became exhilarating. "And that's what made the team great," Salt said, "because we were different stylists."

Salt and Pepper were prepared with music for two or three encores. Before the show, they would talk with the bandleader: "Say, we'll take two choruses of 'How High the Moon' or a chorus of 'Perdido.'" With different music, the steps and style were changed.

Pepper would go out first and improv. Then Salt went out and did a chorus of rhythms. They'd switch off with high-energy steps and Flash. Applause determined the length of the encore. They would finish together and then add one or two musical tags that left the audience clapping and begging for more.

6

The Apollo Theatre

> Harlem ... you realize you're no longer talking about a place but a point of view, not a space but a spirit: It's when you realize that, when the Man says "Uptown," he isn't describing a point on the compass but a different dimension entirely.
>
> Frank Schiffman with Leo Brecher founded the Apollo Theatre ... responsible for its distinguished place among the world's black institutions. In no other single phenomenon, entertainment or otherwise, has the saga of the black American been so completely encapsulated, his sociology and psychology so graphically manifested, his poetry so brightly illuminated, as in the history of show business in Harlem. And that is especially true of the Apollo.
>
> For it is at the Apollo that the tragic past, the turbulent present, and the uncertain destiny of the black man are microcosmically portrayed in song, dance, and humor. In the course of an evening there, one may learn at a stroke more about the black experience than can be derived from a whole library of black studies: the bottomless despair, the soaring pleasure, the lyrical myths, the crushing realities, the successes poisoned by futility, the failures ennobled by dignity.[1]

Playing at the Apollo Theatre was the stamp of approval from the tribunal on high. Volumes have been written about the Apollo, and every performer has a collection of stories about this theater. Edwina Evelyn and Ann Baxter, as "Evelyn and Ann," once took the Apollo stage with the famous musician Fats Waller, and Candi and Pepper played the Apollo with Fats Waller and with Count Basie. Salt and Pepper performed almost every year on the Apollo stage and were featured with the outstanding bandleaders and orchestras of Ernie Fields, Erskine Hawkins, Earl Hines, Johnny Hodges, and Louis Jordan. These women gloried in their Apollo accomplishments.

The Workings of the Theater...

Harlem's Apollo Theatre controlled the block of 125th Street between 7th and 8th Avenues. Its marquee flashed on and off, drawing attention to the stars of the week and beckoning the community into its shabby, dingy lobby. According to Jack Schiffman, son of Frank Schiffman (the owner of the Apollo), the smell of urine and the abundance of dirt was part of the theater's allure.[2]

An articulate, educated, straight-laced man, Frank Schiffman was a short Jew with a potbelly.[3] Salt proclaimed that Schiffman knew show business better than the performers, because he was the owner, manager, and director, not to mention a businessman. He knew how to work with people to build an outstanding show. Schiffman's goal was to produce the "World's Greatest Colored Shows."

The format of the show changed throughout the years to meet the demands and interests of the audience. Salt described the format of the 1940s: a full show with a singer, a comedian, usually an exotic dancer or an acrobatic, a dance team, and the headliner. The Apollo featured the greatest bandleaders of the era, such as Louis Armstrong, Fletcher Henderson, Duke Ellington, Earl Hines, Count Basie, Cab Calloway, and Chris Columbo.

The show always started with a few arrangements by the orchestra to excite the audience. In the early years of the 1930s, Schiffman hired outstanding choreographers,[4] most of whom had their own dancers who starred as Apollo chorus line dancers. Later, the Apollo featured its own chorus girls and boys. Similar to the Cotton Club, the chorus girls were tall and usually had light skin, which was referred to as "high yeller" (high yella). Most of these biracial women could "pass" for white. The focus was on the women; the chorus boys were seen only on rare occasions. The chorus girls opened the show, had a dance number in the middle, and closed with the finale.

Every Friday at 10:00 a.m., the doors to the Apollo opened and featured a new show. For just a few nickels, a person could get in the theater and see the show four or five times before it closed. Salt recounted:

> You'd go in the show at 11:00 in the morning and you didn't come out until 7:00 at night. Cuz if you liked the show you'd stay and see it over.... They don't do like they do now. Now they open the show just for that performance. But then, you'd stay in the show all day and all night.
>
> The kids, they used to play hooky. They would come in and they would see the show. The Apollo, the biggest thing at the Apollo, they'd change the show every Friday. So every Friday all the truants would be in there. So after the first show all the lights would come up. And the truant officer would be there to get the kids who were cutting school. Now the budget doesn't allow that, we don't even hear of that now. But we had regular truant officers. Everybody would beat it when the lights would come on, everybody of school age. They would try to get them, but they couldn't catch everybody.

The setup of the theater was very basic. There was lighting for the performance and a microphone, but no special effects. Salt stressed that in her day special technological effects did not camouflage the sound and visuals of the performer. A performer had to be talented to become a star.

Salt and Pepper's act started with a song as a prelude to their dance:

> I'd bring Pepper around and Pepper would bring me on.... We could still do that, I'm sure, and that's something I'll never forget. We avoided jokes unless they were spontaneous. After the song, we did the dance routine. Many times, we were slated to open the show, because we were acts as well known [as the others]. When the show started and we went over, that's what they call "going over," being successful; then he [Schiffman] would rearrange the show.

Salt and Pepper were often scheduled to appear toward the end of the show, close to the headliner. And there were times when they were the headliner! Placement in the show was of great importance, as it acknowledged one's celebrity. In addition to her tap duet, Frank Schiffman often gave Salt the job of announcer. She stood behind the curtain to announce the incoming show on the microphone. On occasion, a person who had a comedy role didn't show up, and she filled in. Salt remembered playing the "straight man" with one of the Checker's (a singer) in a commercial comedy sketch for milk.

Producing the Show

Salt was amazed by Schiffman's ability to organize a show. She described him as a man who knew the business well, hired the acts, and arranged the show. The first and second shows on Friday at the Apollo were trial runs—rehearsals. If you stayed to watch the second show on Friday, it could be entirely different from the first show. The acts were slated for the first show. As it ran, Schiffman stood in the wings and watched. He was the major critic. He knew everything—the music, the bands, the dance numbers.

Salt described Schiffman's responses. After the first show, Schiffman scratched different numbers. For some, he'd say, "We'll take a chance on the act." At other times, "Mr. Schiffman was sitting there with the money in his hand, telling them to come off stage. [laughter] They cut it [the act] and in the next show a different performer came on." He'd say, "Keep the first number in and the third number in, but cut the second number." He'd shorten certain things and lengthen others. "Many people lost their jobs after the first show."

Around the corner from the Apollo, musicians and entertainers hung out at the bar of the Braddock Hotel and Grill, 126th Street and 8th Avenue. They hoped that the first show at the Apollo would have trouble, so they could be hired. If an act didn't show or a band was late, Schiffman went to the hotel searching for a replacement. He hired on the spot and brought them back to the Apollo. There was a rack of musician-style jackets backstage ready for use. The new band would put on the jackets and spontaneously play the next show. But once the show was set, it remained the same for the rest of the week.

The Audience Was the Show

The African American audience at the Apollo participated intensely and personally with the performers. In music, it's the call and response, which is similar to the pattern of an African American church service, civil rights rally or performance. The preacher/leader/entertainer competed with the congregation/rally/audience. Each demanded more from the other to generate emotional explosions—of faith, of anger, of ecstasy.[5]

The audiences expected and demanded change, which required an artist to stay fresh with his dance steps, songs, and jokes. The audience's attitude was "we paid to be entertained, and we will be entertained even at the performer's expense." The performer would sing or dance, which got an immediate response from the audience during or after the act. A performer could challenge the response with another song or dance or joke. And the banter continued.[6]

According to Jack Schiffman, the 1,500-seat Apollo auditorium had orchestra seats on the first floor and two balconies. The kids in the orchestra section were the most active, jumping up and down, swaying, clapping, waving at the performers, and dancing in the aisles. Some even rushed to the front of the stage to touch a performer or throw a handkerchief that the performer was expected to toss back after mopping his/her brow with it.

The second balcony was called the "buzzard's roost" because it was so high that people had to be related to mountain goats to get to it. Billows of smoke from cigarettes or reefers clouded the view down to the stage.[7] Schiffman referred to the audience in the roost as "the usual horde of kids, winos, junkies, toughs and their sluts, degenerates, and other endearing specimens [who] are fond of staking out in the second balcony."[8] Those in the Buzzard's Roost screamed and shrieked, cried and moaned, bayed and booed, and they could pick a carcass clean.[9] They called out pleasure or disapprobation in terms shockingly saturated with sexual suggestions and at times would just yell out, "Leave!" or "Get off the stage!"[10] According to Sandman Sims, people in the balcony would throw chairs or beer bottles. Other times, people who were overcome by the music jumped from the second balcony; Lionel Hampton's "Flyin' Home" inspired them to fly.[11]

The greatest stars at the Apollo, such as Ella Fitzgerald and Pearl Bailey, nervously paced and grimaced before it was their turn to face the audience. They knew that these spectators had the power to make or break their careers. Although the audience created a fiercely competitive atmosphere for the performers, a spirit of family support developed backstage. Salt stated, "We had pride, we had love, and, the main thing, we had respect." Being part of the competition strengthened the bonds and minimized the rivalry between performers.

At the Apollo, the predominantly African American audience was the judge of talent and extremely vocal about their opinions. The wise performer played to the second balcony. Even though they were crude and cruel, they knew excellence.[12] The audience was "the most astute judge of talent and the most appreciative audience in the world. If they [entertainers] could please the people at the Apollo, they could please any crowd."[13]

The Apollo's Wednesday Amateur Night show promoted new talent. It was responsible for fostering the careers of hundreds of important stars.[14] The Apollo's gimmick for Amateur Night was the "executioner." The first executioner, Norman Miller (stage name Porto Rico), was a superb tap dancer. Jack Schiffman described Rico and his act as follows:

> It all started one night when an especially poor amateur was on stage in full sight of Rico, who worked the microphones on stage left. Some evil spirit began working on his innards and suddenly he could stand it no longer. With black eyes blazing, he ran out on stage brandishing a starter's pistol in his raised hand. He stopped, turned, and went into a

grotesque dance. Round and round his transfixed victim he spun, weaving a tight magic spell. It is even likely that some incantations escaped from between his curled lips. It is certain that he fired off his weapon. There can be no question that the magic had worked. The amateur was dispatched before an audience that was convulsed with laughter yet fully aware that a device had been hatched, a myth born.[15]

Over the years, others perpetuated Rico's executioner style after performers fell afoul of the audience. Although the performer may have been disappointed for losing the competition, to be executed with artistry and style was no disgrace.[16]

When tap dancers were on the bill, the audience was filled with dancers wearing their tap shoes. If they thought the dancer wasn't good, they would challenge him/her while performing on stage. This participant/observer atmosphere developed the best talent in the United States. It was here in Harlem that performers received the stamp of approval that in turn opened the doors to the world of entertainment.

Stars of the Amateur Night

Ella Fitzgerald, at 15 years old, entered the competition at the Apollo Amateur Night in 1934. Salt shared the story: Ella entered the contest as a dancer. But while she was waiting for her turn, the Edwards Sisters (Ruth and Louise), an incredible tap dance team, performed. "And when she saw what they were doing, she said, 'Oh Lord, I can't go out there and dance after that ... because they were so sensational.' So what she did was to change her act to singing." At first, the audience booed, but when she calmed down and sang Hoagy Carmichael's "Judy" (and, as an encore, "The Object of My Affection"), Ella won the contest as a singer.[17]

Ella had a very difficult childhood, but her success at the Apollo thrust her into public view. Chick Webb heard Ella and hired her to be the singer with his band. It was with Webb that she sang the song that made her very popular: "A Tisket, A Tasket." Salt sang, "'A Tisket, a tasket, I lost my yellow basket / Won't someone help me, help me, please' ... that was great. That's the one that made her."

Salt also told the story about the fabulous Pearl Bailey, who got her big start at the Apollo Amateur Night. Pearl Bailey, her brother Bill Bailey, his partner Derby Wilson, and Pearl's sister Eura Bailey were all tap dancers. Bill Bailey and Derby Wilson, disciples of Bill Robinson, were outstanding professional tap dancers.[18] Bill was the focus of the famous song, "Won't You Come Home, Bill Bailey." Eura Bailey could also sing and dance, but she never received fame. Salt continued,

> There were a lot of acts that never went to the west or those in the west that never came to the east. The same thing happened to Bill Bailey's sister in Philadelphia, Eura Bailey. She could sing and dance better than Pearl Bailey could sing and better than Bill Bailey could dance. Her problem was she wasn't able to leave Philadelphia. She worked all around Philadelphia but wasn't able to leave. She had more talent than the both of them, but she just never wanted to travel.

Salt resumed Pearl Bailey's story: At 15 years old, Pearl went to the Strand Theatre in Philadelphia to tell her brother Bill that it was time for dinner. (There's conflicting information regarding whether it was the Strand Theatre or the Pearl Theatre.) While at the theater, Pearl, who could dance as well as she could sing, entered her first amateur contest. She won $5 and a week-long singing engagement on that stage. But after a week of performing, Pearl was unable to receive her money because the theater had closed down.[19]

Pearl was later extremely successful at the Apollo Amateur Night. Salt said that after a series of nightclub acts, Pearl got her big break when Sister Rosetta Tharpe, who was singing with Cab Calloway's band, got a cold and couldn't sing. Pearl, who was available, replaced her. "Calloway signed her up for 20 weeks at the Zanzibar, and she became a sensational hit. She went right up the ladder. Pearl Bailey, yeah [smiles], of course, was in *Hello Dolly!*, and a couple of other Broadway shows which were sensational."

Salt and Pepper at the Apollo

A visit to the Apollo will illuminate the scene and the stars on the playbill who were part of Salt and Pepper's memories.

On Friday, January 8, 1944, Salt and Pepper made their performing debut at the Apollo Theatre:

Hawkins and His Band	Jimmie Mitchell[20]
Effie Smith	The Kinneys
2 Swing Maniacs	Salt and Pepper
Tim and Vivian	

Singer/comedienne Effie Smith appeared in the 1940s as a guest on broadcasts of the Armed Forces Service Radio. She also performed with artists such as saxophonist Coleman Hawkins, bandleader and composer Benny Carter, and conductor Andre Previn. Some of Smith's recordings included "Answer to R. M. Blues" and "It's Been So Long" in 1947. Effie and her husband John L. Criner founded several recording studios, such as the G&G and Gem labels, as well as Aries Publishing and Spot Records. Effie Smith recorded into the 1960s with songs such as "Dial That Telephone," "Champagne Mind with a Soda Water Income," "Water, Water" and "You Ought to Be Ashamed."[21]

Tim and Vivian, by contrast, were a comedy team. Vivian Gravens was a longtime performing partner with Tim Moore, and they were married in 1957. Tim Moore (born Harry Roscoe Moore, 1887–1958) was best known as George "Kingfish" Stevens in the CBS television series *Amos 'n' Andy* (1951). Beginning at eleven years old, Tim worked in a traveling vaudeville act called "Cora Miskel and Her Gold Dust Twins." The successful act traveled around Europe to British music halls and medicine shows. He also worked as a tour guide in Hawaii, a fly-shooer controlling pests in a barn, and a boxer. Moore later developed a one-man version of *Uncle Tom's Cabin*, which involved performing Simon Legree with half of his face with white chalk and Uncle Tom with the other half of his face with burnt cork. His performing teams included his vaudeville companion and wife Gertie Moore, Mantan Moreland, and later his fourth wife Vivian Gravens Moore. His career continued in vaudeville and a successful run on Broadway in *Take the Air* (1927), Lew Leslie's *Blackbirds of 1928*, *Shuffle Along* (1928), and *Fast and Furious* (1931). Some of his movies include *His Great Chance* (1923), *Darktown Revue* (1931), and *Boy! What a Girl!* (1947). Moore wrote his own material as well as skits for other performers such as W.C. Fields. His extensive achievements included radio, recording as a comedian, television and *Amos 'n' Andy*.[22]

Friday, January 14, 1944, Salt and Pepper were held over for a second week at the Apollo. They had the pleasure of performing with Louis Jordan and the Tiffany Five:

Louis Jordan and His Typany Five	"Hot Lips" Page and His Band
Gertrude Saunders	Salt & Pepper
And Other Headliners	

Louis Jordan (1908–1975) was a pioneer in American music, working as a songwriter and bandleader. His popularity escalated during the Swing Era. He was known as "The King of the Jukebox," as his music was enjoyed by both black and white audiences. Jordan was ranked by *Billboard* magazine as the fifth all-time most successful Black recording artist. Selling at least four million hits during his career, Jordan "topped the R&B 'race' charts, and was one of the first black recording artists to achieve a significant crossover in popularity into the mainstream (predominantly white) American audience, scoring simultaneous Top Ten hits on the white pop charts on several occasions. After Duke Ellington and Count Basie, Louis Jordan was probably the most popular and successful African-American bandleader of his day."[23]

Salt raved that Jordan played the trumpet wonderfully and that his musicians were sensational. Among his popular records were "Choo Choo Ch'Boogie," "Nobody Knows You When You're Down and Out," "You Go Fifty Cents More Than You're Going to Keep," "Caldonia," "Ain't That Just Like a Woman," "Ain't Nobody Here but Us Chickens," "If You So Smart, How Come You Ain't Rich?," "Barnyard Boogie," "Fat Sam from Birmingham," "Run Joe," "Hog Wash," and "Got My Mojo Working."

Oran Thaddeus Page, known as "Hot Lips" Page, was a trumpeter, singer and bandleader born in Dallas, Texas (1908–1954). He was known as a scorching trumpet soloist, powerful vocalist, and emcee (MC). In the 1920s, Page started his career playing with Ma Rainey's band. From 1928 to 1931, he worked with Walter Page's Blue Devils, and in the 1930s, he played with Bennie Moten, Count Basie, and Artie Shaw. Page later developed his own big band and played in many cities, including New York, Chicago, and Boston. "Hot Lips" Page and his band recorded "Skull Duggery" (1938) on the Bluebird label, as well as "Pagin' Mr. Page" (1944) and "St. James Infirmary" (1947).[24]

The week of Friday, January 5, 1945, Salt and Pepper arrived at the Apollo with the Earl Hines Orchestra and Revue. (This took place during a one-year tour with Hines, which will be discussed in the following chapter.)

Earl Hines Orchestra and Revue	Ford Harris & Jones
3 Maniacs of Rhythm	Salt and Pepper

Janie Moses	Arthur Walker
4 Mello-Tones	Lord Essex
Red Lyons	Palmer "Fats" Davies
Wardell Gray	Kermit Scott

The week of Friday, November 22, 1946, Ernie Fields escorted Salt and Pepper to the stage. The cast of the show included the following:

Ernie Fields and his Band	Wynoni Harris, King of the Blues
4 Step Brothers	"Pigmeat"
Sybil Lewis	John Bunn
Salt & Pepper	Mel Moorerhy
Dobson's Comedy Dog Act	

Ernie Fields (1905–1997) was born in Nacogdoches, Texas, and raised in Oklahoma. He graduated from Tuskegee Institute, focusing on the trombone. Fields didn't want to leave the area, so he created a band in Tulsa called the Royal Entertainers. Finding it difficult to make a living, he traveled with his band to the Southwest. John Hammond invited Fields to New York, where he gained recognition as one of the great bandleaders of the period. He recorded on Vocalion label and with Columbia Records, and he toured the East Coast and Midwestern states. The band's featured vocalist was Mel Moore.[25]

"Blues Shouter" Wynonie Harris was known as Mr. Blues. Harris' voice registered more in decibels than in tone where he made a musical impact on audiences. Jack Schiffman said that Harris' "tonsils were probably made of leather, his larynx of steel, and his vocal chords of cat gut."[26] Salt thought that Wynonie Harris was a wonderful singer and a good-looking guy. The girls swooned over his lovely ballads.

The Four Step Brothers, a great dancing quartet, starred in the show.

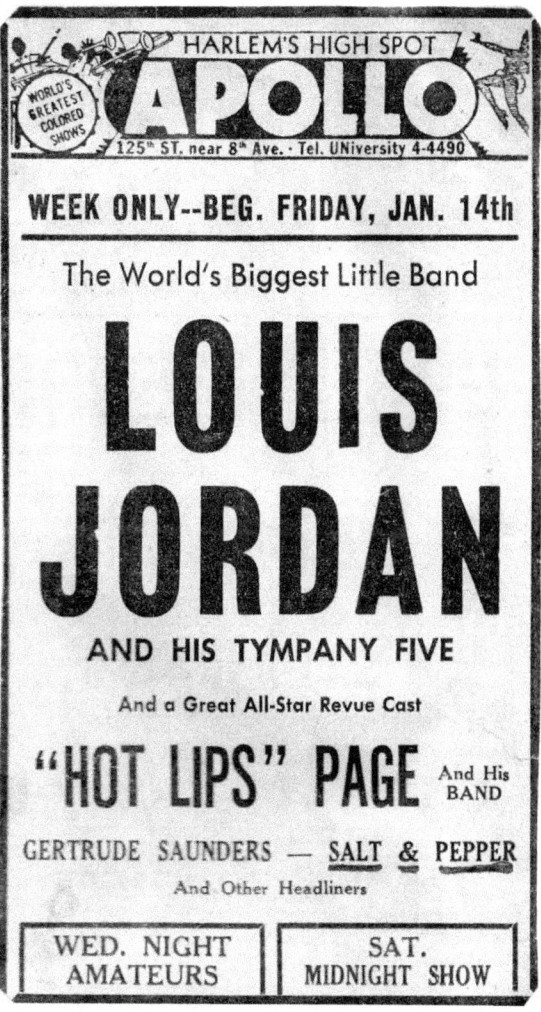

Louis Jordan, "Father of Rhythm & Blues" and "Grandfather of Rock 'n' Roll."

The team performed Rhythm Tap, comedy, and some Flash in their act. They progressed from the Cotton Club in the mid–1920s to the Hollywood Walk of Fame in 1988. The act started as a trio in 1925: Maceo Anderson, Al Williams, and Red Walker. Throughout their long career (1925–mid–1980s), they changed from a trio to a quartet. The Four Step Brothers included Al Williams, Maceo Anderson, "Flash" Rufus L. McDonald, and Red Walker. As the years progressed, several men took the role of the fourth Step Brother, but Prince C. Spencer danced the role in the final years. Prince and McDonald were so fantastic, they could challenge any tap dancer. This group was featured in movies, such as *Check and Double Check* (1930), *Shine On Harvest Moon* (1944), and *Road to Utopia* (1946).[27]

Blues shouter Wynonie Harris.

Dewey "Pigmeat" Markham, a regular at the Apollo Theatre, was an outstanding African American comedian, dancer and actor. Pigmeat was extremely funny. He played the Apollo more often than any other performer. Both Salt and Pepper raved about his sketch character of a judge, "Heah Come de Judge," where a variety of people came before Judge Pigmeat to hear their cases. Pigmeat passed sentences on their offenses that always ended with a unique and hilarious one-liner.[28]

Sybil Lewis was one of the most convincing actresses of Black cinema. She was in such films as *Mystery in Swing* (1940), *Broken Strings* (1940), *Am I Guilty?* (1940), *Midnight Menace* (1946), *Lucky Gamblers* (1946), *Boy! What a Girl!* (1947), and *Miracle in Harlem* (1948). She was

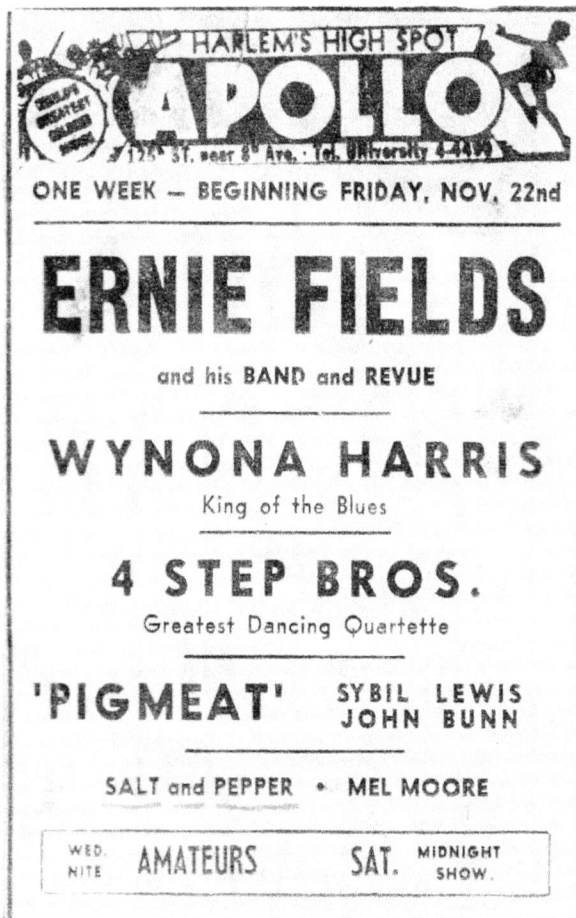

Ernie Fields and His Royal Entertainers.

viewed as an actress, not stereotyped as a black actress. Lewis was also seen in Hollywood movies such as *Revenge of the Zombies* (1943), *Going My Way* (1944), and *The Very Thought of You* (1944).[29]

Melvin Moore, born in Oklahoma, was a vocalist with a number of big bands, including groups led by Ernie Fields, Dizzy Gillespie and Fletcher Henderson. In 1952, Moore joined the world-famous Ink Spots as a singer and drummer, traveling with the group until 1963. He later promoted for Decca Records and Brunswick Records.[30]

The week of May 7, 1948, the Apollo stage was filled with the talent of Billy Eckstine:

Billy Eckstine
Strawberry Russel & Julia
Jesse James
Dick Merrill

George Paxton and his band
Wilkey & Dare
Salt and Pepper

Billy Eckstine (William Clarence "Billy" Eckstine) was selected by popularity polls as the "outstanding new singing star of the year" in 1948. MGM also stated that Eckstine was their "outstanding star," with record sales in the millions. Eckstine was backed by George Paxton, his band, and the band's vocalist Dick Merrill.

The *New York Amsterdam News* reported on May 15, 1948, that the Eckstine's show at the Apollo demonstrated "democracy in action": "The show has a famous colored headliner and a well known white band—a popular colored dancing team, and a popular white knock about comedy act. It also has two additional colored novelty and comedy acts." The article went on to say that Eckstine opened the show and gave a seven-song encore.

George Paxton and his band, who had appeared several times on Broadway, gave the audience a repertoire of old and new hits. Headliners on the bill were the tap dancing act Salt and Pepper, singing and talking comedians Strawberry Russell and Julia, comedy acrobats Wilkey and Dare, and handicapped acrobatic dancer Jesse James (similar to Stanley Holmes, known as Big Time Crip).

Salt described Strawberry Russell and Julia as a husband-and-wife team with a vaudeville comedy act. Strawberry

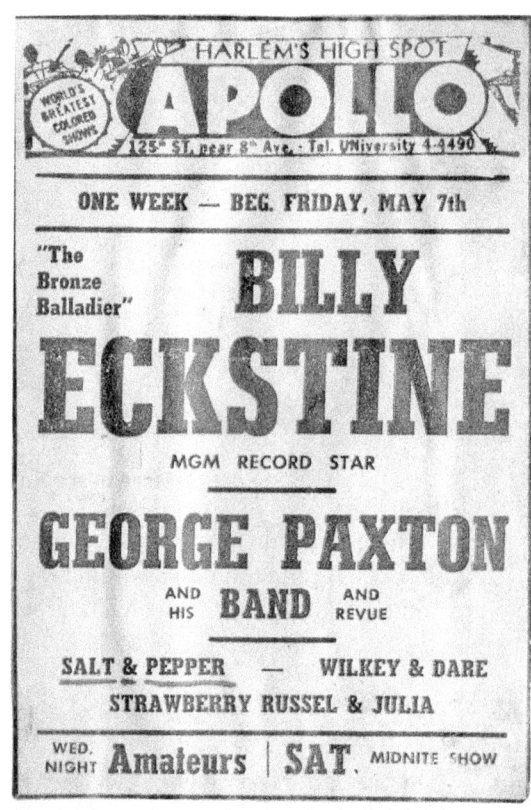

Singer/bandleader Billy Eckstine at the Apollo.

Strawberry Russell and Julia.

played the guitar, and Julia sang. At some point in the act, Strawberry would break off into a dance, and then Julia would break off into a song. They came back together into comedy. Salt thought they had a great act.

On the Bill with Billie

The week of December 5, 1952, was Salt and Pepper's last performance at the Apollo. It was led by Johnny Hodges and his band. Hodges was a saxophonist, who had worked often with Duke Ellington. The headliner was "Lady Day" Billie Holiday:

Johnny Hodges and His Great Band	Billy Holiday
The Checkers	Salt & Pepper
Lady Terry	Spo-De-O-Dee

The Checkers were an R&B group that included Bill Brown, David Baughan (Baughn), Charlie White, and John Carnegie. They were considered a supergroup that has remained somewhat in obscurity. "Checkmate" was the first CD reissue of Checkers' recordings to be taken directly from the original master tapes, complete with the hit song "A Friend in Need."[31]

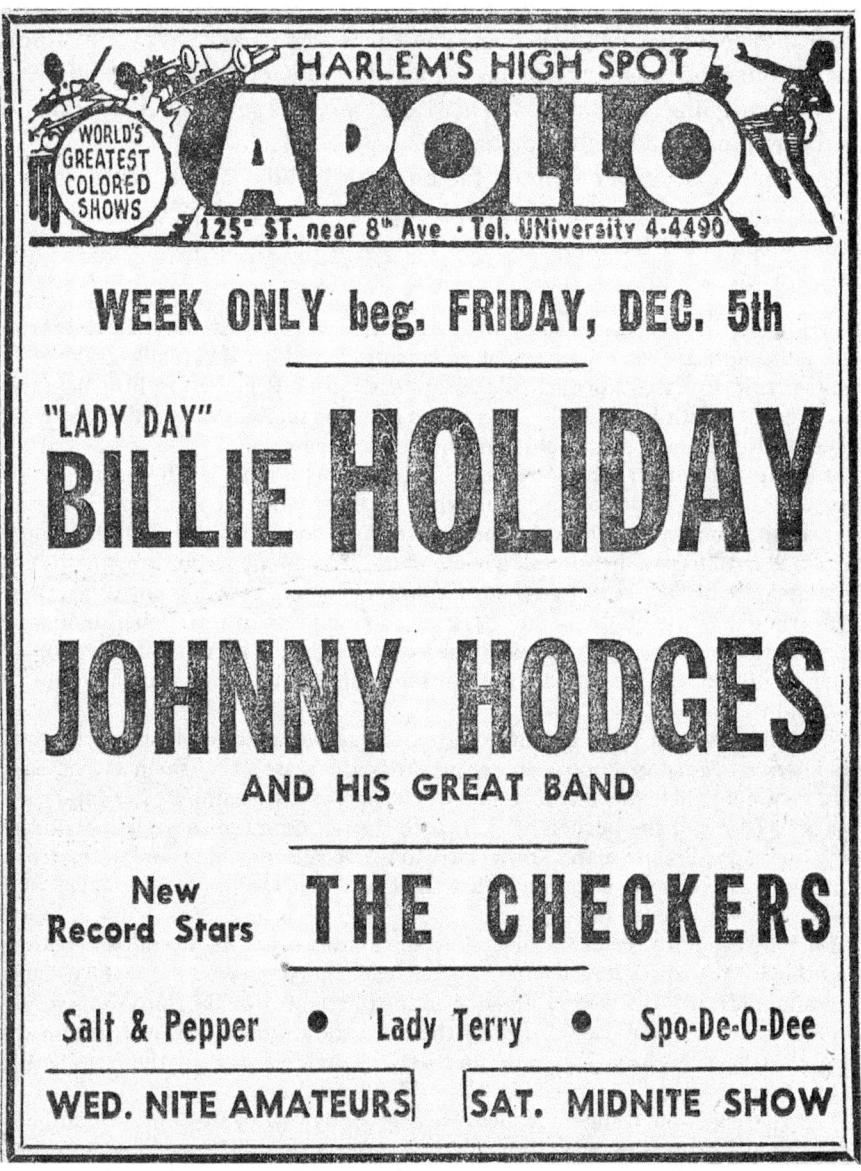

Salt and Pepper on the playbill with Billie Holiday.

Billie Holiday was the superstar of the show. In 1933, John Hammond discovered her when she was eighteen years old. Holiday became a legend in her own time. The illegitimate daughter of an illegitimate mother set the course for her own life. Holiday was raised by relatives, while her father, a banjo player and guitarist, was rarely part of her life. By twelve years of age, she had been molested and raped. She began working as a prostitute and earned extra money singing in Alice Dean's waterfront whorehouse.[32]

Holiday was tough, beautiful, and feminine. As an improvisational singer, she recorded with tenor saxophonist Lester Young, and they made beautiful music together. Holiday nicknamed Lester Young "Prez," and he called her "Lady Day." Together they recorded songs such as "The Year's Kisses" and "Why Was I Born?"[33] Among the hundreds of songs Holiday recorded were "God Bless the Child," "Strange Fruit," and "Lady Sings the Blues."[34] In her later years, she succumbed to drugs, which affected her career and finally took her life.

When Salt and Pepper were on the bill with Holiday at the Apollo, they were unnerved by her condition due to drugs. Salt gave two versions of the story. The original story displays Salt's humor and spontaneity, while at the same time a feeling of empathy for Ms. Holiday:

> [Ms. Holiday] was the star of the show. I think this was the last show she did before she died. Billie Holiday was a great, great, great singer. And her downfall was drugs. When we first came in in the morning, she always had a little Pekingese, a little dog, that she always carried with her and she always had this flowing mink. And the first show she would be dressed, and she would come in to the [theater].
>
> At the Apollo Theatre the star's dressing room was on the first floor, and the second floor was the next important act, and when you were one the top floor [laughter] you were the little man at the show. I think we had the second- or third-floor dressing room. We would have to pass her dressing room in order to get up to our dressing room. And the stairs were like fire escape stairs, you could see each other's dressing room, they were inside, though. We would pass her dressing room and many a-time her door would be open. And I don't know who she would be expecting, but in between shows people come to see you backstage, or friends come to see you, or sometimes you have your dinner brought in.
>
> She was known for having a white carnation [gardenia] in her hair, and that was her trademark. … I read in a book, on her life story, the reason that she had that carnation [gardenia] in her hair was that one time when she was just beginning her career, she was fixing her hair, and she burned her hair with the hot comb so severely that all her hair came out there. So she didn't know what to do because it didn't look attractive at all. Somebody gave her the suggestion that she cover that spot with a gardenia. And that was her trademark ever since.
>
> When we used to pass for the first show, she used to say, "Oh, hi Salt, hi Pepper. How's everything?" You know a nice greeting. "OK." Second show we'd come in. We come up the stairs, she said, "Hi," very subdued. And the third show, by the third show she'd really be looped, because she used drugs. By the third show, the door would just be cracked open a little bit, "Who's that going up there?" [laughter] And by the last show of the night, the door would be closed. And each show, she'd deteriorate.
>
> It was a trick of the trade there, because everybody was aware of her condition, musicians and all. She would sing all the old tunes, and everybody would wait for her. The Johnny Hodges' band, they were so aware of her condition that for the first two shows she would sing all of her recognizable numbers, the numbers that made her famous,

"God Bless the Child," "It Ain't Nobody's Business What I Do." So first show she would just be marvelous. And by the last two shows, when her condition was deteriorating, that's when she'd just sing a little bit and the band would take up most of the slack. But it was very cleverly done. It still received so much by her being there and singing a few choruses. She did her best work in the early part of the program. You had to improvise in show business, because anything could happen.

Yet, in the second version of the story, Salt cut out the details and ended by saying, "I think that was the beginning of her sickness and the last show that she did at the Apollo. And Pepper and I, we were very honored to be on the show with her. I want to keep her as great as she was, as far as her singing." Billie Holiday died on July 17, 1959.

Write-Ups

The Hazel Green Agency placed the names and accomplishments of Salt and Pepper in public view. As shown in the following extracts, both illness and future events were acknowledged in the newspaper (articles found in Edwina "Salt" Evelyn's scrapbook).

Salt, Pepper Stricken

New York—Jewell Welch and Edwina Evelyn, known as Salt and Pepper, were both stricken with an acute attack of grippe during their engagement at the Apollo Theatre here last week and were forced to cancel several engagements. The famous terpsichorean duo were ill most of the week but refused to leave the show, carrying on likewise in the fashion of truly great troupers. They are reported recuperating now and will resume their stage activities when they open at the fashionable Valdor Club in Montreal, Canada.

Hazel Green Variety 5 Act Unit

Hazel Green, Broadway agent, announced to members of the press last week that she has set Jewell Welch and Edwina Evelyn America's most outstanding femme dancing act for a new variety unit to be produced right after Christmas and which will feature a big band and at least five top-notch variety acts.

The two talented terpsichoreans who have the professional tag of SALT and PEPPER have just closed a weeks engagement at the Apollo Theatre in Harlem where they were dishing out some extra spicy seasoning in an unusually gay divertissement which featured other than themselves the very capable Scat Davis and orchestra, Canfield and Lewis, and Pvt. Cecil Gant.

Green acknowledged that Salt and Pepper performed with Davis and Gant, which was an established fact, but there was no evidence that their performance was at the Apollo. It could have been a mistake or an advertising ploy.

7

The Best Year of My Life

Touring with Earl Hines (1905–1983) was the greatest year in Salt's life. To understand the impact of Hines' knowledge, experience and accomplishments, it is necessary to travel back in the music world about 50 years.

The Chicago World's Fair of 1893 introduced the world to Ragtime music. Dance parties became all the rage as Ragtime ushered in the new syncopated sound. With the convenience of the railroad and the Great Migration of African Americans from southern states, the New Orleans jazz sound, with its many influences, was carried to Chicago.

As early as 1910–1912, New Orleans pianists Tony Jackson and Ferdinand Joseph LaMothe "Jelly Roll" Morton were in Chicago experimenting with improvisational styles. Following them between 1915 and 1918, Freddie Keppard, Emanuel "Manuel" Perez and Joseph "King" Oliver, who were also innovators of New Orleans jazz, made Chicago their home.[1]

The Great Migration spurred the establishment of the Bronzeville area, which nurtured a Chicago-style Harlem Renaissance. The movers and shakers of the period were Mississippi journalist and leader in civil rights movement Ida B. Wells, poets Gwendolyn Brooks from Kansas and Margaret Walker from Alabama, Mississippi author Richard Wright, Texas civil aviator Elizabeth "Bessie" Coleman, and New Orleans jazz artist Louis Armstrong. In the years that followed, other notables were acknowledged, such as Illinois dancer/choreographer Katherine Dunham, Kansas photographer/musician/film director Gordon Parks, Mississippi sociologist Horace R. Cayton, Mississippi Blues musician Muddy Waters and New Orleans Gospel singer Mahalia Jackson.

Earl Hines, born in Duquesne, Pennsylvania, on December 28, 1905, was classically trained in piano, and from childhood he could play by ear. Through the influence of singer Lois Deppe, Hines moved to Chicago in 1923. There he collaborated and created music with Louis Armstrong, was influenced by Joseph "King" Oliver, and learned from other significant musicians of early jazz.

By 1910, Chicago was already celebrating the Jazz Age. As thousands of workers from the United States and other countries were attracted to Chicago's industrial power. The demand escalated for cabarets, cafés, dance halls, movie houses, and amusement parks.[2] Chicago offered jazz at the Sunset Café, Dreamland Ballroom, the Royal Gardens, the Elite Club, and the Panama Club. By the early 1920s, before New York's Cotton Club, these Chicago clubs featured the legends of jazz, such as Joseph "King" Oliver, Louis Armstrong, Earl Hines, Johnny Dodds, Sidney Bechet, and Ethel Waters. In addition to the boom of jazz clubs, Chicago lured musicians and singers with the possibility of making records on the Okeh, Paramount and Vocalion labels.[3]

Although the crime subculture was present in Chicago as early as the 1850s, it wasn't until 1910 that the Mafia, Outfit, or Syndicate (as it was known) established a base in Chicago. With the passage of the Eighteenth Amendment, prominent bootleggers, racketeers and gangsters found the nightclub scene profitable. By the 1920s, crime ran rampant. Corruption was found throughout the legal and political systems, among judges, lawyers, politicians, and high-ranking policemen. Anyone could be bought off. Many businesses, nightclubs, bars, bankers, gamblers, and number runners gave kickbacks to the mobs for protection. Consequently, the syndicates owned numerous businesses, not to mention entertainers. Many famous entertainment stars found themselves in syndicate-controlled clubs, which regulated the length of the contract and what was played, sung, or danced.

Earl "Fatha" Hines.

Through the 1920s and 1930s, the impetus of bootlegging generated Irish, Italian and Jewish crime syndicates. These syndicates emerged from New York and other East Coast cities and spread to Chicago, Detroit, Boston, Cleveland, New Orleans, and other cities across the country. According to Lucky Millinder,

> The mob network was tied together like a musical triad: Madden controlled the East Coast's booze and beer distribution; Al Capone reigned over Chicago and its environs; Johnny Lazia controlled the police, liquor and gambling in Kansas City MO, and the Purple Gang dominated Detroit. Chicago, New York, and Kansas City housed a disproportionate percentage of all the great jazz talent in America during the 1920s and 30s. These cities were controlled by the Jazz Slave Masters and some of the very best black musicians were their serfs.[4]

The Jazz Slave Masters

In 1925, the Mafia boss Al Capone organized his mob in Chicago and generated a financial empire. If Capone said, "You can't work for anyone but me," that's exactly what he meant. The entertainer was obligated to stick with Capone or there could be an end to one's wages, reputation, or life. Many tried to escape to another club or city, but mob connections brought them back to Chicago.[5]

For many African Americans, there was a thin line between success as a performer and being owned by the jazz slave masters (a term used by Dempsey Travis). Jazz bandleaders Cab Calloway, Duke Ellington, Earl Hines, and others were threatened with violence for wanting or trying to pursue other venues.[6]

Chicago's Sunset Café was one of the most influential jazz clubs in the United States between 1917 and the late 1920s. In 1928, Ed Fox renamed the venue the Grand Terrace. Its theme was "The Planation," and it flourished with its grandiose plantation décor, service, and entertainment. From its beginning as the Sunset Café and continuing as the Grand Terrace, the club always integrated black, white, and other ethnic groups.[7]

In the 1920s and 1930s, Chicago was the center of the nation's radio broadcasting, the medium that popularized Chicago jazz. Radio had a stronger influence on the public than did records. By the 1930s, Earl Hines played his theme song twice a night over the airwaves from the Grand Terrace Ballroom. At 10:30 p.m., WMAQ broadcasted to the eastern half of the United States, and at 11:30 p.m. WENR relayed it to the western half. Hines' sound thus could be heard in the 48 states and Canada.

Dempsey Travis recalled:

> As young, aspiring musicians, my friends and I were Earl Hines listeners and Grand Terrace watchers. We used to hang out in the gangway next to the Terrace and listen to Hines through the open windows and watch the mink-draped white women and their tuxedoed companions in top hats glide from the back seats of chauffeur-driven cars to be entertained by our hero, Earl "Fatha." ... In contrast to the Cotton Club in New York's Harlem, the Grand Terrace would admit black millionaire policy men like the Jones Brothers and movie celebrities such as Eddie Anderson, who played Rochester, and Hattie McDaniel. The neighborhood folks never got closer to a table in the Terrace than the sidewalk or radio.[8]

Fox offered shows featuring the highest-caliber African American entertainers, such as Earl Hines and his band, Bill "Bojangles" Robinson, Buck and Bubbles, Ethel Waters and the Four Step Brothers. When the Grand Terrace became successful, Al Capone's gangsters took over. Hines reported that

> one man went to the cash register, one stood out front and one on either side of the building. The lieutenant went to the back. "We're going to take twenty-five percent," he said. "You must be losing you mind," Ed Fox said. "Well, you need protection." "I've been doing all right for two years and I don't need protection." "You're going to have protection. You have a nice family and you wouldn't want anything to happen to your boys, would you?" So they practically ran the place, and while they were there, the police never came in.[9]

The employees were told that no harm would come to them if they did their jobs and let the mob handle the operation. No one wanted to say anything to anybody about the situation, because then that person's picture would be in the paper, and the next day he would be found dead. Hines said that guns were often drawn at the Grand Terrace; even the waiters had guns. No gunshots were ever fired because of the innocent customers. Yet rival gangs would fight by throwing ice and bottles at each other.[10]

Although Capone dominated the Chicago scene with violence, Hines stated that Capone had some good traits, such as running a 24-hour restaurant for the poor, providing a place for them to live, and tipping big in a handshake or by sticking money in coat pockets. Capone, who had 30 bodyguards, appointed two bodyguards to protect Hines. Hines said it was because Capone thought of him as property in which he had invested money.[11]

Hines painted a picture of the times that included the abomination of Chicago's St. Valentine's Day massacre, the covert packages that were tossed his way while he was playing piano, and illegal racketeering. Eight hundred miles away, on the roof of New York's Cotton Club, the owner Owney Madden allegedly kept carrier pigeons for illegal mailing. These pigeons were so valuable that men guarded them with machine guns.[12]

Earl Hines had a contract for $150 a week with the Grand Terrace, an Al Capone–controlled club. Capone's lawyers had written the contract, which stated that if Hines attempted to leave the club, he would not be allowed to use his own name as a bandleader. The contract was also perpetual. If Ed Fox, the manager of the Grand Terrace, died, Hines would become the personal property of Fox's widow. Upon her death, the contract would be passed to Fox's oldest son, and if he died, it would be passed to the youngest son.

Bound by his contract, Hines remained at the Grand Terrace from December 1928 to 1941. He ultimately left the club with help from the National Federation of Musicians. The president of the federation, James (Jimmy) C. Petrillo, said the contract wasn't binding because of the way it was written. Hines then took his band to the Apollo Theatre. Fox procured an injunction to tie up the band's salary, but Petrillo stepped in and told Frank Schiffman, owner and manager of the Apollo, that if the salary wasn't released, Schiffman's Apollo show would not open. Schiffman immediately released the payroll.

Eventually, Fox lured Hines back to Chicago to perform in the New Grand Terrace that Fox now owned independently. Hines agreed to the contract if the band's salary was placed in escrow. Fox consented, but again he had an injunction placed on the funds. This time, Hines took Fox to court, and the judge decided in Hines' favor. He was freed at last.[13]

The "Fatha"

With his freedom from the syndicate, Earl "Fatha" Hines toured the country as an independent musician and bandleader, gaining national acclaim from his recordings and creating his music. Hines was an established pianist at the top of jazz scene and known throughout the country for his unique sound. He was acknowledged as

> one of the most influential pianists of the 1920s. Jazz took a revolutionary turn because of the recording he made with Louis Armstrong's Hot Five Combo and a few solo sides in 1928. They were called masterpieces then, as they are today.... "Earl could go on for 90 years and never be out of date," Count Basie said of Hines. "Hines' complex creations, his use of a single note line played in octaves in the right hand, and the cross-rhythms and counter melodies with his left, generated an influence still felt."[14]

Enthusiastically, Salt praised Earl Hines:

> He was a wonderful person. He was a wonderful musician.... He had a big band and played music and wrote songs. He was a great man! He was just marvelous.... We went all over with him. We toured all the Southern States.... Hines was known as Fatha. He was like a father. He treated you like family. He took care of us, told us he thought it was time for us to go home and to be in bed. He was like a father, a father image, you know.

In his biography, Earl Hines told the story behind his nickname "Fatha." He was broadcasting from the Grand Terrace in Chicago and used the theme song "Deep Forest." Hines' announcer and engineer Ted Pearson was wonderful at miking the sound for muted clarinets and trumpets, but Pearson's weakness was drinking too much Italian wine. The National Broadcasting Company (NBC), which sponsored the broadcasts, became dissatisfied with Pearson and threatened to fire him, but Hines and the band didn't want to lose him.

One night before the show, Hines talked with Pearson about his drinking problem. But during the first set, Pearson drank himself "under the table." During the fifteen-minute intermission, Hines and some of the musicians went to Pearson's table to revive him. They used ice and wet towels to bring him back to consciousness.

When Pearson was revived, he thought that Hines was reprimanding him and decided to get even. When Hines went on stage for the second set, Pearson went on the air saying, "Here comes Fatha Hines through the Deep Forest with his little children!"[15] NBC like the approach and decided to leave it in. Hines enjoyed the joke, but he was concerned because he thought he was too young to be called "Fatha." He always spelled it as *Fatha*, but the newspapers used the word *Father*. This caused him many problems, particularly when traveling in the South, where the word *Father* could mean the title of a priest or God the Father.[16]

Salt and Pepper on Tour

In December 1944, Salt and Pepper were on the playbill with Earl "Fatha" Hines at the Howard Theatre in Washington, D.C. Salt said that when a show was sensational, the bandleader would keep all the acts together to go on tour. It was probably here that Hines asked the team to tour with him and his band. Touring with Earl Hines, one of the jazz greats, had been beyond Salt and Pepper's expectations. The Howard was followed by the Royal Theatre in Baltimore on December 29, 1944. They continued to tour with Hines in theaters and clubs through many cities and states on the Chitlin' Circuit.[17] "It was one of the greatest, one of the greatest years of my life," Salt proclaimed.

Hines would choose performers not only for their achievements and potential but also for their ability to adapt to difficult traveling and working conditions. On occasion, he tried to feature a group of girl singers/dancers such as the Bluebonnets. However, he found such groups expensive and difficult because of their complaints about dressing rooms, costumes, and hotel reservations. In the 1930s, Earl Hines worked a four-week "Round the World" circuit, which at the time included Philadelphia's Pearl Theatre, the Lincoln and the Grand; New York's Harlem Opera House, the Lafayette and the Apollo; Baltimore's Royal Theatre; and Washington, D.C.'s

On the playbill with Earl Hines at the Howard.

Comedians Ford, Harris and Jones.

Howard Theatre. On that tour, Hines asked for the leader of the "Number One" Apollo chorus line Ristina Banks and comedian Dusty Fletcher to tour the entire trip.[18] These performers were good for the show and traveled easily.[19]

Between 1944 and 1946, Hines chose four acts for his tour that could adapt to the rigors of travel. These were Ford, Harris and Jones, the Mellow Tones, Salt and Pepper, and Arthur Walker. Other acts were occasionally added to the bill, depending on the length of the show, the availability of performers and the venue.

Touring with Hines was a most beneficial experience for Salt and Pepper. With over twenty years of professional experience as a creative pianist, bandleader, and manager, Hines welcomed them to his world of jazz and took these two young women under his wing. He coached Salt and Pepper with tips and rules for performing. Hines also introduced them to people who could make connections for them to perform in theaters and nightclubs, and he schooled them on the ins and outs of touring and how to travel safely as African American women. He instructed them on choosing housing and where to eat and shop. With Hines, Salt and Pepper were protected from the seamier side of nightclubbing and grew in awareness of lurking dangers and organized crime.

Meeting the Mark

Earl Hines was a stickler for being on time. Every contract was based on time, and Hines lived up to the contract. He had a system of rules that were supported by fines he imposed on his musicians and on the performers. In brief, the rules were as follows:

- Be on time. Punctuality meant almost as much as the quality of the performance. There was a $25 fine when a performer missed the curtain and a $5 fine for every minute afterward.
- When traveling by bus, there was a $5 fine if one was not ready when the bus was due to leave.
- The bus driver was fined $1 for every minute late.
- Different sections of the band had 25¢ fines for musical mistakes during a performance.
- All performers had to be in the theater a half-hour before showtime. This assured everyone that the show was ready to roll.[20]

With the emphasis on punctuality, Salt knew that Pepper would have a problem while working with Hines. During the week of August 17, 1945, Salt and Pepper performed at the Apollo Theatre in Chicago. After the supper show, which was the second show, most of the performers took a break. They were under Hines' rules, which they knew well. Instead of going out for dinner, many of the performers hung around the theater so they wouldn't be late for the next curtain call. Salt and Pepper decided that they would go out for a quick meal. Salt ate and returned to the theater, but she didn't keep track of Pepper. Fifteen minutes went by, and Pepper didn't show. A half-hour went by, and there was no Pepper. The show started, and still there was no Pepper. When it was time for their act, Salt went out with full energy and danced the entire musical piece alone. After Salt's performance, Pepper sauntered in backstage. Standing there to greet her was Fatha Hines. He was holding a late fine in this hand. It was most of her salary. Pepper, of course, looked surprised, as if she couldn't imagine that she was late, and said, "What? Mr. Hines?" Hines didn't want to hear her story and walked away. Pepper's salary was garnished. Salt said that Hines taught Pepper a valuable lesson, and she never again came in late for a performance.

Performance Tips...

Based on 20 years of experience in show business, Hines offered his performers the following tips:

- Appearance was half the battle for a band's performance. Hines' band had several uniforms. If there was no time for the costume valet to pack the uniforms, the musicians had to be extremely careful with hanging up their coats and not wrinkling their pants while sitting in the bus.[21]

(Salt already took great pride in the appearance of her team. She often spoke of how a third of the money that she earned was for buying costumes and costume upkeep. "Appearance was everything!")

- Never look at the audience; look over it. The audience will think you're looking at them. This was a method used to overcome fears, avoid distractions, and acknowledge the audience.
- A smile makes it look like you're having a ball.[22]
- For the singers, Hines told them that the higher they sang, the more they were singing from their heads; they should hold their heads back and look at the ceiling. This was a technique that Louis Armstrong used when hitting a high note on the trumpet.
- When singing in the low register, one had to control the abdominal muscles. These should be heavy and hard.[23]

Tap Dancers

Hines was quite knowledgeable about tap dancers. He was ready to work with Salt and Pepper, showcasing their rhythm and the highlights of their act. He was aware that the dancers set the tempo. They also had their own rhythmic riffs and licks that could be accentuated by the band.

Growing up in Duquesne, Pennsylvania, and playing in clubs around Pittsburgh, Hines became friends with Lovey Taylor, a great tap dancer. Taylor was very influential in Hines' move to Chicago and the big time. As a tap dancer, Hines said that Taylor "could do more with his feet than some people could do with their hands." Hines learned the rhythmic licks that Taylor was doing on the floor and played them on piano to enhance the dance and the music.[24]

A few years later, while playing at the Sunset Café, Buck and Bubbles often challenged Sammy Vanderhurst. Hines reported that when these great dancers had contests, one couldn't imagine what was going on. Their feet did things that looked impossible. Another influential team was a married couple named Brown and McGraw. She was cute in pretty dresses, and he was handsomely dressed in a uniform. They had a riff that became very famous: bomp-bomp-bomp-bu-bomp, bomp-bomp-bomp-bu-bomp. This rhythm, still used today, was associated with a sexy strut. Louis Armstrong played this rhythm with his trumpet while Brown and McGraw danced it. Later, most bands played the rhythmic riffs and licks that the tap dancers were doing with their feet.[25]

While at the Plantation Café, Joe Oliver showed Hines the tricks of playing the piano for tap dancers. In a room that didn't have good acoustics, Oliver taught Hines how to feel the tempo of the dancer, and when to play soft for the audience to hear the shuffle of the feet. Knowing when to crescendo and diminuendo prepared Hines to play for tap dancer Bill "Bojangles" Robinson and singer Ethel Waters.[26]

On the Road

The clippings in Salt's scrapbook indicate that Salt and Pepper were on the road with Earl Hines from late 1944 to early 1946. Salt said that they were hired and contracted as an act, which meant they traveled and performed together. Hines would often be booked to play alone or with his band without a revue-style show. On those occasions, Salt and Pepper performed in a nearby nightclub. For example, in September 1945, Hines was booked at El Grotto, 6412 S. Cottage Grove in the basement of the Pershing Hotel in Chicago. Salt and Pepper took a gig at the Rhumboogie Café, 343 East 55th Street, Chicago, a few blocks away.

At other times, the tour consisted of one-night gigs. The band arrived at the club or theater, played the gig, and traveled through the night by train or bus to the next booking. Salt indicated that sometimes she and Pepper were on the bus with the band, but it appears that they usually took the train and met the band at the next location.

According to the advertisements in the scrapbook, the tour included the following shows:

December 22, 1944	Howard Theatre, Washington, D.C.
Janie Moses, Lady of Song	Essix Scott
Ford, Harris and Jones	Four Mello-Tones
Salt and Pepper	Movie On Screen: *The Falcon Out West*
December 29, 1944	Royal Theatre, Baltimore, MD
"It's a Happy New Year Show":	
Salt and Pepper	Janie Moses
Arthur Walker	4 Mel-O-Tones
Ford-Harris-Jones	Movie: *Cry of the Werewolf*
January 5, 1945	Apollo Theatre,[27] Harlem, NY
Ford Harris & Jones	Salt and Pepper
Janie Moses	Arthur Walker
4 Mello-Tones	Lord Essex
Red Lyons	
February 2, 1945	National Theatre,[28] Louisville, KY
"Harlem Revue":	
Betty Roche	Jesse Perry
Mello Tones	Salt & Pepper*
Ford, Harris, Jones	Movie on Screen: *Enemy of Women*

*It appears that Salt and Pepper were not present for opening on February 2, which could have been due to weather conditions.

Earl Hines in Louisville, Kentucky.

May 4, 1945   Paradise Theatre, Detroit, MI
"Star Time":
Arthur Walker   Essex Scott
"Scoops" Carry, sax   Ford, Harris and Jones
Salt and Pepper   4 Mellow Tones
Movie on Screen: *The Broadway Big Shot*

    Featured Musicians: bass player Eugene Thomas; tenor Wardell Gray; guitar Rene Hall; trumpet Willie Douglas; and vocal Fats Palmer.

August 17, 1945	Regal Theatre, Chicago, IL

"Parade of Stars"
LeRoy Carrington, Prince of Taps
Salt & Pepper
Ford, Harris and Jones, Zany Comics
Stephany Stepherson and Palmer Davis, Dancers
Featured Musicians: Chick Booth, Billy Thompson, Bill Douglas
Arthur Walker, Kermit Scott,[29] Gus Chappell,[30] Palmer "Fats" Davis,[31] Bill
   Douglas,[32] Essix Scott[33] & Joe Ivy
George "Scoops" Carry[34] and Rhythm Quartette: Clifton Small (Piano),
   Rene Hall (Guitar), Billy Thompson (Vibraphone), Gene Thomas (Bass)
Movie on Screen: *Murder He Says*

August 24, 1945	Club Plantation,[35] St. Louis, MO
Four Melotones	Salt & Pepper
Ford, Harrison, Jones	Dick Montgomery
Red and Curley	
George Hudson and his Orchestra*	

*At times, Earl Hines was unable to perform due to previous commitments. In such situations, the houseband as George Hudson played the show.

September 21, 1945	Rhumboogie Café, Chicago, IL

Salt and Pepper at the Rhumboogie Café (8) while Hines was performing
   at El Grotto.

USO Shows

In 1945, Salt and Pepper were booked with Earl Hines and his band to perform in Russia on a USO (United Service Organizations) tour. They were thrilled for the chance of their lives. They visited Washington, D.C., where they received a security clearance. They filed for passports and applied for the USO shows. Everything had fallen into place. But as the time drew closer for the tour, Pepper, who was fearful of flying, made sure that Salt also became fearful. She'd say, "what if the plane crashes?" "what if we can't get home?" and a lot of other "what if's." About a month before the tour, Salt said that they just got chicken and backed out.

Since Salt was unable to afford college, one of her reasons for being in show business was to travel. She said that she always regretted the decision not to fly. She reminisced:

> It was nice to travel all over the United States and get paid for traveling. And that's why now I regret that we didn't go to Russia, because that would have given us an opportunity to expand our traveling and it would have been nice.... We could have gone over to Paris, Russia, and on the USO junkets over there in Europe. But we didn't want to fly, we would have both been afraid. I don't think Pepper would have flown all her life....
>
> So we lost a lot by not flying ... if we had flown to these places like most of the performers did, we would have been more prestigious. Like a lot of these musicians, they

had to go to Paris to become known, and then when they come back to the United States, they get the cream of the crop in jobs.... We could have gone.... That's the only thing I regret in show business that I didn't take a chance and travel.

Although she was heavyhearted about losing the opportunity, it appears that that particular trip fell through, and Earl Hines and his band did not perform in Russia until 1966. Salt was so impressed with Hines that she reminisced:

> Now this was the greatest year of our career to me—we toured one year with Earl "Fatha" Hines. He was a director for this whole show ... and just when I was going to see him around three years ago, right around the corner here at the Blue Note, he had a stroke. He was playing. I guess he was in his eighties, right around here on 3rd Street at the Blue Note. He had a stroke and he died. We toured one year with him. We went all over with him. We toured all the Southern states, and all. He was a great man, Earl "Fatha" Hines. He was a pianist. He was just marvelous. We toured all over with him.

8

All Aboard for the East Coast

Salt and Pepper headed for Grand Central Terminal and boarded the *Liberty Bell* to Philadelphia, which took them into their future. It was late 1945, and they were on their own.

The war years offered East Coast performers an abundance of entertainment venues. Salt and Pepper were ready to reap the benefits of playing nightclubs and theaters in Philadelphia, Atlantic City, Baltimore, New York, the Borscht Belt in the Catskill Mountains, and many cities in between.

Philadelphia

As the *Liberty Bell* came into Philadelphia's Pennsylvania Station, it was a going-home event for Pepper. She was eager to see Mother Welch and reconnect with some of her friends.

Salt described Mother Welch as a small, independent woman with a big bust. She had a neat, economical home with a cat in the backyard. Salt enjoyed meeting Mother Welch because she told jokes on herself and was as funny as Moms Mabley.

Mother Welch lived in a row house at 2458 Chadwick Street. The front door was open and welcomed everyone. In her generous style, Mother Welch helped people out and sometimes had abandoned children living with her. She enjoyed feeding the neighborhood by putting out a spread of ham and biscuits. Pepper explained that Mother Welch was a wonderful cook who specialized in real soul food: chitlins, chicken, greens, corn bread and fish. There was always plenty to eat, especially when they had friends over to play pinochle. Pepper clarified that pinochle was a game for the poor Black community, whereas the wealthy white community played bridge.

Pepper and Salt always stayed with Mother Welch when performing in Philly, and she was always happy to have Pepper home for a few weeks. Salt said, "She served us eggs and bacon for breakfast, dinner, and supper." But she would never take any money. Her reasoning was, "If I take your money, you could do what you want in my house, but if I don't take your money, I tell you what YOU want to do."

Salt told the following story repeatedly, roaring with laughter every time: Pepper would bring home her buddies at night. Mother Welch would call from upstairs, "Jewel, who's that with you?" Pepper answered, "It's a friend. He doesn't have a place to stay." Mother Welch replied, "Oh, yeah? Well, he still doesn't have a place to stay. Say good-bye."

Contrast in Class

According to Pepper, during the winter months Mother Welch was a domestic who cleaned houses for wealthy whites—"Jews and Italians." From Memorial Day to Labor Day, she and her sister Gertrude (Gertie) were cooks and housemaids at the New Jersey beach resorts in Asbury Park or Atlantic City. The area was bustling with tourists, the money was good, and all living expenses were paid.

Working as a domestic was a common job for African American women in the United States at that time. Yet African Americans in Philadelphia represented a wide range of socioeconomic levels unusual for the times.

Throughout the eighteenth and nineteenth centuries, an upper class of African Americans evolved in many large cities.[1] In Philadelphia, there were three distinct groups in the upper class: the original native Philadelphians, a second group of West Indians from the Dominican Republic and Haiti, and a third group of Southern fair-skinned, freeborn mulattoes.

African Americans descended from the original families of Philadelphia, such as Robert Bogle and James Le Count, found their fortunes in catering. Others pursued careers as physicians, pharmacist, attorneys, businessmen, and real estate investors. These families were leaders in cultural, religious and political life.[2] Although birth and family connections were important, the highest priority was education. These educated African Americans were known as the "Black Elite." They valued abstinence, sobriety, and high moral conduct, and they followed the sophisticated and polished etiquette of the well bred.[3] By the turn of the twentieth century, Philadelphia's Black Elite was attracted to W. E. B. Du Bois' philosophy of the "talented tenth," evidenced in private social fraternities that required college-degreed members. They regarded their place in life as being above skilled laborers and the uneducated, and intermingling with lower socioeconomic African Americans was discouraged. The Black Elite and middle-class Philadelphians found achievement as writers, bank developers, real estate brokers, and highly skilled laborers.[4]

Spurred by jobs related to World War I, tens of thousands of Southern Blacks moved to Philadelphia as part of the Great Migration. The gap for social contact widened among the Black Elite, the middle class, and the sizable proportion of African Americans who worked as domestics and laborers. It appears that entertainers were considered part of the middle class and were appreciated in both black and white communities. Yet Jim Crow laws affected every aspect of daily life and discrimination ran rampant, touching those in the middle and lower segments of the socioeconomic range.

During the Swing and Big Band eras, entertainment was nurtured in African American–owned theaters and clubs.[5] In 1914, African American John T. Gibson bought the Standard Theatre[6] on 1100 South Street. Gibson booked Black vaudeville and musical acts on the national Chitlin' Circuit. The Standard Theatre and the Dunbar Theatre[7] (also owned by Gibson) were a welcome haven for African American Philadelphians.[8]

Over the years, the audiences enjoyed shows and musical performances such as *My Friend from Kentucky: Darktown Follies* (1913); *Shuffle Along* (1921); *Chocolate Dandies* (1924); *Liza* (1922); *Struttin Time* (1924); *Dinah* (1925), which featured the famous dance Black Bottom; and *Runnin' Wild* (1923), which introduced the Charleston dance. Legendary performers graced the stages of Gibson's theaters, such as Mamie Smith, Bessie Smith, Alberta Hunter, Ethel Waters, Butterbeans and Susie, the Whitman Sisters, the Nicholas Brothers, and jazz bands led by Louis Armstrong and Duke Ellington. The Standard Theatre attracted multi-racial audiences until it closed in 1954.[9]

BORN TO SWING

As Salt and Pepper toured, Philadelphia offered them numerous opportunities in its many theaters and clubs. They often mentioned the Nixon Grand,[10] Lincoln Theatre,[11] Fans Theatre,[12] Pearl Theatre,[13] and the Standard Theatre.[14]

In 1945, Salt and Pepper were cast for the Irvin C. Miller[15] production *Born to Swing*. It opened at Philadelphia's Lincoln Theatre on Broad and Lombard Streets. Other performers in the show were comedian Tim Moore, dance team Joseph & Johnson, precision tap dancer Eddie Rector, and the Bronze Beauties chorus girls.

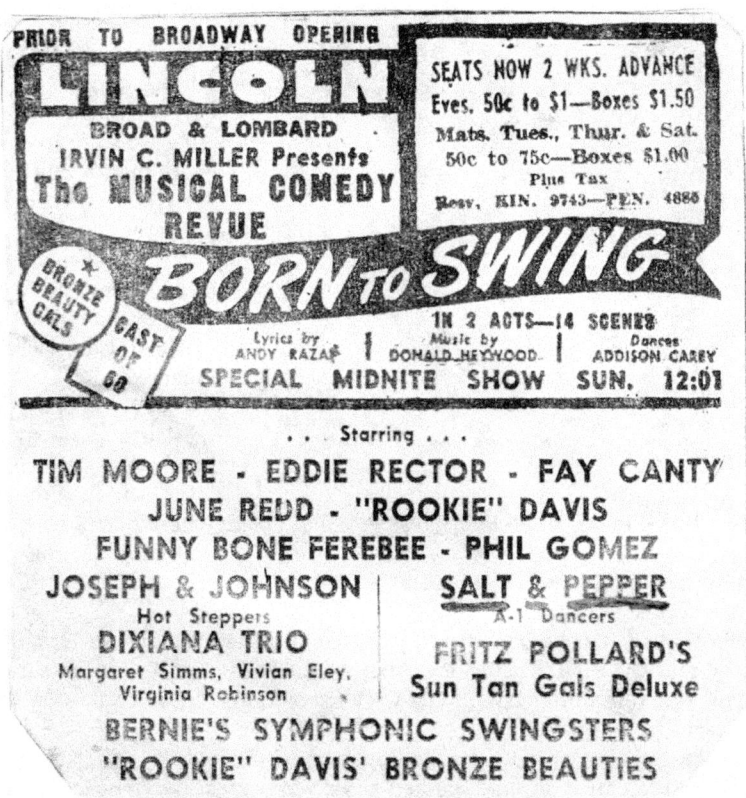

Lincoln Theatre, Philadelphia.

The show did not get good reviews. Newspaper critic Leonard Bushman attacked the show:

> The lush theatrical season continues at the unusual pace with Lincoln Theater when "Born to Swing" opened last night in a full staged production. Even in a "non-critical" year a few good specialties are not good enough to carry the burden of the show. The review needs plenty of rehearsal with the band, a tighter look and better chorus numbers to even enter the hit threat list.... In the first act, Jones and Joseph appear as clever dancers top the talent. Running them in close second is Eddie Rector, whose good foot work is lost in the confusion of a clumsy chorus.... Salt and Pepper sensational femme tappers, turn out to be the show stoppers. While it will probably never be another "Blackbirds," "Born to Swing" does show possibilities for entertainment.[16]

According to Bushman, Salt and Pepper's act was the show stopper, and they surpassed Eddie Rector and Joseph and Johnson. When asked if she was in competition with the male dancers, Salt hesitated. Then a smile came to her face and she admitted:

Salt and Pepper, spice of the program.

> I didn't want to say so. I didn't want to pat ourselves on the back. We didn't feel like we were in competition with them. Only thing we felt [was] that we could do whatever they could do. We could do it as well as they could do it. I'm sure they got more money than what the women got. And they worked more than we did.
>
> We worked constantly because of the era, the war, and a lot of the men were at war. And then they had all of these places [for] entertainment.... In one night you could go to five, or six, or seven places and always see a show, because they had that much entertainment around.
>
> If a manager had to make a choice of a team like "Coles and Atkins" or "Salt and Pepper," they would take the men. Even though they might not reveal it. But I'm sure that they would. No, [we were not angry] ... cuz we were working, so we could care less. It was quite different from today.
>
> Eddie Rector was supposed to be the star.... He was known for this dance called "The Sand." He used to dance on sand. Eddie Rector was a great tap dancer.... What I mean to say was, our name wasn't so big, but our act really showed what we could do. That's why we stayed so long in different places.

Eddie Rector was well known around the Northeast here. There were so many performers who were so great. But they never made the big times.... The only ones that know their greatness are performers who worked with them or who worked during the time or knew them. You have a few people who really made it ... Nicholas Brothers who made it into film. Because film was so limited then, you had to be the greatest to get into film. But how many of these performers who were qualified, they just never made it. So many of them made it after they got older, like Gregory Hines.

Harlem'z a-Poppin'

On November 2, 1945, the newly remodeled Fans Theatre opened with the show *Harlem'z a-Poppin'.* It offered a "colored newsreel" and the movie *The Fatal Witness*. It was the only "colored" stage show in Philadelphia,[17] and the theater promised to change the show every week, similar to the format of the Apollo Theatre.[18]

Harlem'z a-Poppin' starred Lillian Fitzgerald with her imitation of Betty Hutton, and the cast was filled out by Salt and Pepper, comedian John "Spider Bruce" Mason, exotic dancer Dolores Alvarado, Boyd and Chapman, soubrette Yack Taylor, world champion jitterbugs the Four Congaroos, singer/dancer MC Charles Ray, and twelve fast-stepping Dudleyettes. (The Fans Theatre was managed and produced by S. H. Dudley—thus the chorus girls were called the Dudleyettes.)

Lillian Fitzgerald from Philadelphia was a singer with Duke Ellington, a mistress of ceremonies, comedienne, soubrette, exotic dancer, producer, and choreographer.

Precision tap dancer Eddie Rector.

Dancer/singer Lillian Fitzgerald modeled for RC Cola.

Harlem'z a-Poppin', Fans Theatre, Philadelphia.

At seventeen years old, she started in show business at Harlem's Connie's Inn and the Cotton Club. Lillian, married to producer and tap dancer Chink Collins, was a very light-skinned African American woman with an exuberant personality.

Harlem'z a-Poppin' received an excellent critique from *Pittsburgh Courier*: "The orchestra under the direction of Willard (Chops) Thompson received part of the atomic applause from a mixed audience—white and Negro—men, women and children—society and the man-on-the street, from the reception it looks like a bright future for the Fans Theatre."[19]

Salt acknowledged the different African American newspapers of the time. The *Pittsburgh Courier*, printed on orange-colored paper, reviewed the shows and was distributed in the Midwest and New York areas. Another paper that reviewed the shows was New York's *Amsterdam News*. If a performer made it to the *Amsterdam News*, the quality of the act was critiqued, which could make or break performers.

Leaving Philadelphia, Salt and Pepper made a quick performance stop at the Roman Grill, and then on Friday, October 13, 1950, they crossed the Delaware River to the New Town Tavern in Delair, New Jersey. The critique read:

> It is gratifying that sepia artistes under the caption "Creole Burlesk" continue as the protracted attraction at Town Tavern over across the Delaware in Delair NJ. Philly's own Elsie Blow continues to head the precision prancing line. Among recent principals were Tondelayo and Calypso Boys; Wallace Brothers and "Salt and Pepper" (Edwina Evelyn and Jewell Welch) which has recently finished its 8th consecutive year of niterie engagements in the Midwest. Salt (Edwina) hails from our Quaker City.[20]

Atlantic City Was Entertainment

Chugging through the farms and Old World German-style cities, the *Quaker City Express* stopped at the New Jersey shore. Salt and Pepper headed to Kentucky Avenue, an area that would be swinging with the best in Black entertainment.

From the 1850s, Atlantic City grew, offering beaches and health resorts, as well as easy access from eastern cities. It soon became a vacation spot with enormous electric signs, luxurious hotels, the Boardwalk, and amusement piers. In 1921, the Atlantic City Pageant was established and later became an annual event known as the Miss America Contest. Boosted by the entertainment industry, the city grew and prospered, encompassing gambling, prostitution, and corruption. During World War II, the convention hall was converted to an army facility serving and training soldiers. Yet the lure of the city and its beaches captured both families and adults in search of a good time.[21]

The Atlantic City scene offered many nightclubs—namely, Daniel Stebbins' Babette's Supper Club[22] and Paul "Skinny" D'Amato's plush 500 Club. The 500 Club seated 1,000 people, housed prostitution and gambling, and fronted for several Mafia bosses.[23] The audience and performers were predominantly white; featured stars included Dean Martin and Jerry Lewis, Frank Sinatra, Jimmy Durante, Donald O'Connor and Sammy Davis, Jr.

Kentucky Avenue and the Curb

As early as 1870, African Americans began migrating to Atlantic City for jobs in hotels, resorts and recreation. The city offered a life of success rather than servitude. Yet after World War I, as the city prospered, racial lines were drawn. The city became segregated into the north side for blacks and the south side for whites. African Americans could only cross the lines for employment, which was limited to those working on the Boardwalk or in hotels on the south side.[24]

Thus, an African American area known as Kentucky Avenue and the Curb flourished on the north side, with its own brand of Black entertainment and nightclubs. It housed Grace's Little Belmont, the Wintergarden, the Paradise Club, and Club Harlem.[25]

Club Harlem, 32 N. Kentucky Avenue, was the premier nightclub for African American tourists visiting Atlantic City. It had matinees, nighttime shows, late-night shows, and breakfast shows. For thirty-four years, Crazy Chris Columbo led the orchestra at Club Harlem. Most famous Black musicians showed up to jam and develop their skills.

After the white clubs closed for the evening, Kentucky Avenue was jammed with celebrities, politicians, and tourists waiting to get into various clubs (providing a perfect example of who was permitted to cross racial lines). Club Harlem and the other Black clubs attracted top stars such as Louis Armstrong, Ella Fitzgerald, Count Basie, Ethel Waters, Nat "King" Cole, Lena Horne, Duke Ellington, Billie Holiday, Cab Calloway, Dinah Washington,[26] Sarah Vaughan, Moms Mabley, Slappy White, Billy Daniels, and Billy Eckstine.[27]

The Paradise

Paradise Club, 220 N. Illinois Avenue, Atlantic City, was a favorite club for Salt and Pepper. Their contracts were frequently renewed, and they were there for months at a time.

Paradise Club was owned by Harold "Hal" Paul Abrams, and he claimed it was "the oldest nightclub in America." According to Chris Columbo, "The Paradise was the first nightclub in the world. Before that you had cabarets and cafes, where entertainers would come right up to your table and sing risqué songs."[28] Abrams was also the general manager of the 500 Club[29] and the owner of Harold's Club and Basin Street Club.

The Paradise wasn't a plush club of 1940s, but resembled instead a Prohibition-era roadhouse. It was a dark room with a low ceiling and small tables surrounding a stage and dance floor. During the show, everything was bathed in white, amber, and blue spotlights. The waiters were well dressed and a camera girl wore a short skirt that showed her legs. Using a heavy Speed Graphic camera, the girl took souvenir photos of the guests.[30]

The performers were 90 percent African American and the clientele was 90 percent white, most of whom came from the Traymore Hotel.[31] Although white audiences enjoyed their experiences in Black clubs, segregation was clear and enforced in daily life. Salt explained:

> Club Harlem and the Paradise had black performers, but when it came time to go to the beach, there were certain sections of the beaches that were discriminatory. They had the big hotels on the Boardwalk like the Traymore Hotel. And if you were not a guest at that hotel, you couldn't go to a certain section of the beach. And that's how they were able to have a section of the beach sectioned off for the colored people. They had to go way down to the other end past the steel pier in order to ... use the beach. So ... that's the way it was in those days. In Jersey, which was Atlantic City not like today, VERY VERY prejudiced. They had Frank Sinatra down at the 500 Club. They used to come up to see

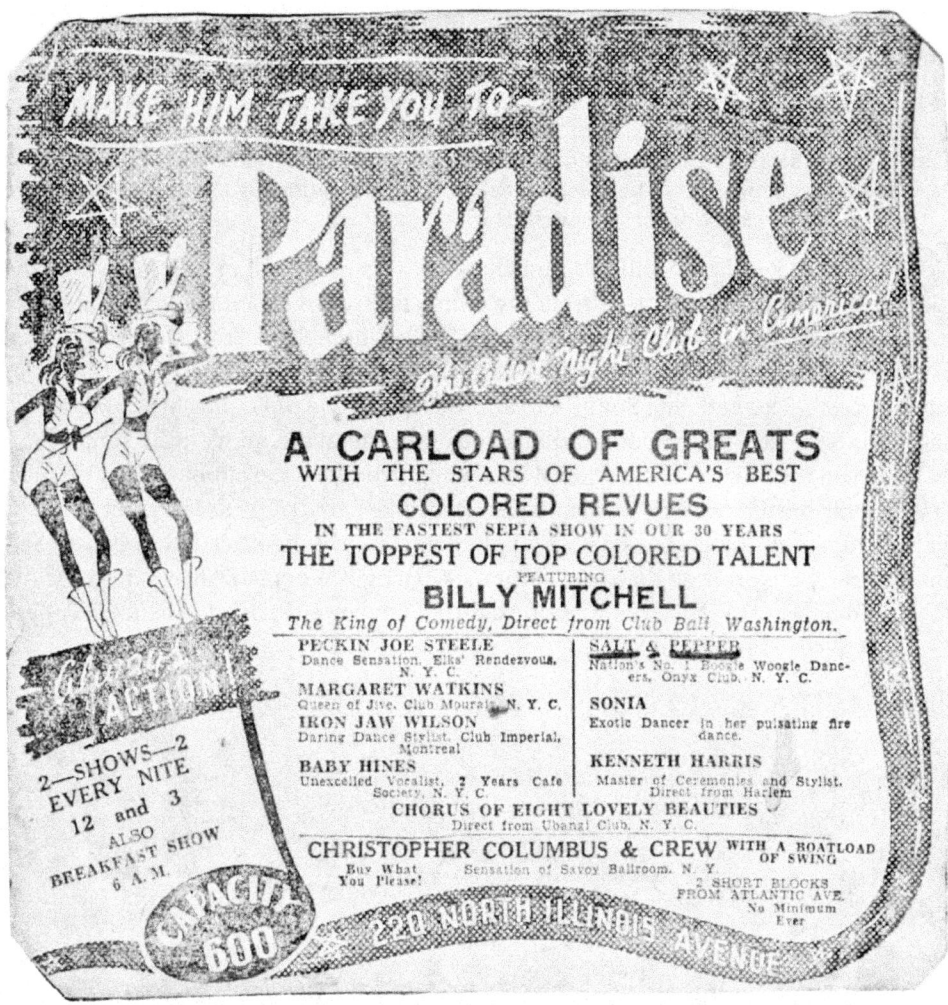

The Paradise in Atlantic City.

our shows, but we never went down to see their shows. So that's the way it was, and we had to accept it.... We were down there to do our job and to make a living. We did not go down there to try to change the Constitution.

The beach that Salt referred to was known as Chicken Bone Beach (1900–1964). The name evolved from the picnic basket lunches of fried chicken and the bones that were buried in the sand by Black beach-goers.[32]

In most interviews conducted with African American men and women from this period, their feelings were very similar to Salt's: Show business gave them a good life where they could make a living and enjoy doing a job that was respectable. No one wanted to cause racial or political problems. Everyone knew and had experienced racial discrimination and feared for their own lives at one time or another.

In 1944, Salt and Pepper were featured at the Paradise in a show called *Car Load of Greats* with the stars of America's best colored revues. It was advertised as "The

Fastest Sepia Show in Our 30 Years, The Toppest of Top Colored Talent." A small advertisement read:

> The Paradise claimed to be the oldest nightclub in America presents a good time for all at all times. Billy Mitchell king of the comedy is a popular MC for your sapient. A host of top flight sepia stars are featured nightly. Among which are Peckin' Joe Steele, Margaret Watkins, Iron Jaw Wilson, Babe Hines, Salt and Pepper nationally known boogie woogie dancers, Sonia exotic dancer, Kenneth Harris.

The show spotlighted Billy Mitchell, who "was a comedian and known as the King of the Nightclubs. At that time the comedians were called comics. The job of the comics was to keep the people laughing." Billy Mitchell was the Richard Pryor of his time. He had a collection of risqué songs that he performed, such as "I Can't Get Her Started," "The Bed-Bug Song," and another about two old maids in a folding bed. Salt said that Mitchell sang and did hilarious movements to go with the songs.[33]

Also on the bill was Peckin' Joe Steele, who introduced the famous Peckin' dance, in which his head moved forward and backward like a that of bird. Margaret Watkins was billed as the "Queen of Jive" and Baby Hines as the "Unexcelled Vocalist." Salt and Pepper were promoted as "the Nation's #1 Boogie Woogie Dancers, Onyx Club, N.Y.C." Sonia was advertised as an exotic dancer with her pulsating fire dance. Kenneth

The cast at Atlantic City's Paradise. *Top Row:* Baby Hines, Iron Jaw Wilson, Chris Columbo, Pepper, Billy Mitchell, Emory Joe, Salt (below), Margaret Watkins, Peckin' Joe Steele, and Sonia. *Bottom Row:* Jackie, Eva, Rudy, Hazel, Ann, Mimi, and Lulu.

Left: Margaret Watkins. *Right:* Iron Jaw Wilson.

Harris was the master of ceremonies and stylist. Originally he was part of the trio Ford, Harris, and Scott (Joe Scott continued to perform as a single). The driving force of the show was Chris Columbo and his orchestra, with the Atlantic City chorus girls filling out the entertainment.

One of Salt's favorite acts was Iron Jaw Wilson. She described the act as follows:

> Iron Jaw Wilson performed a novelty act. He picked up tables and chairs, picked [them up] with his mouth and danced. He'd even have somebody from the audience pick up the table to let them know the weight of the table and that there wasn't any trickery. He was marvelous. He did all kinds of turns and the people got really really excited because they thought that maybe the chairs or the tables would ... he would let them go. But he never missed, he never missed, he never missed. So it was quite a novelty act. He was marvelous.

Looking at the ad for the Paradise, "The Oldest Nightclub in America," Salt lamented, "Now it's just a parking lot. Every time I pass it, I almost cry."

Family and Friends...

Salt's family was able to come down to Atlantic City for her performances. She enjoyed the support of both family and friends.

> Oh yeah, you make friends. You go there so often that you actually know just where you're going to stay. You have friends there who give you such a great welcome, the ones who really put you over, because these are the ones that show up on opening night. They

send telegrams and they come, cuz they know you're coming in advance, because everything is advertised in advance. This is what makes it feel so good. You feel really at home. You're not hitting the stage cold. Cuz they're all there to applaud and wish you well. It's just a wonderful feeling. Homecoming. They would even follow you.

Atlantic City was a real performers' playground, "maybe we'll meet again next year." But that was so nice when you see each other again. It's like a family profession. We were always glad to see each other again. But I had many friends that were outside of show business who became real valuable friends, which is very important. It's a nice way to meet them.

A photograph taken at the Paradise displayed Salt and Pepper socializing with Mimi Johnson and Killer Johnson, a great basketball player. Mimi worked as a waitress at the gambling clubs where they played the dice game Twenty-One. Mimi was called a Twenty-One Girl; later in life, she was a correction officer.

Borscht Belt

Boarding the *Catskill Mountain Railroad*, Salt and Pepper were on their way to the Borscht Belt. The term *Borscht Belt* may bring to mind Sophie Tucker, Fanny Brice, Sid Caesar, and Jerry Lewis. Yet hundreds of comedians, dancers, and singers got their start in show business and/or performed on the Borscht Belt.

Mimi Johnson, Salt, Killer Johnson and Pepper.

A Little History

One might imagine the Borscht Belt to be similar to the Las Vegas Strip, with a large number of clubs and hotels in a given location, but it's quite the contrary. The Belt begins about 90 miles northwest of Manhattan and includes four to six counties (about four million acres).[34]

By the late 1870s, the Catskills Mountains were scattered with Jewish-owned farms and boarding houses. Gentile-owned hotels, cottages, and private clubs spread throughout the mountains and were used as vacationland from the cities. The attitude of many who owned these Gentile establishments was one of explicit discrimination against Jews, including refusing to allow them to enter the hotels and other facilities.[35]

By the late 1880s, about 80,000 German-speaking Jews were living in New York City. A huge influx of immigrants arrived in the United States at the turn of the twentieth century. The Jewish population in New York City alone grew from 1,250,000 in 1910 to nearly 2,000,000 by the mid–1920s.[36] With this growth, anti–Semitic attitudes intensified in the city. Jews were denied access to privately owned establishments while being deprived of their Jewish culture.

Over the years, some of the Catskills' Jewish farms evolved into boarding houses that served as vacation spots for Jews who were living in overcrowded cities and experiencing much discrimination. Boarding houses became a lucrative business, and many were converted into country resorts, small hotels, bungalow colonies and summer camps. These areas were not merely resorts but also places where Jewish culture was preserved.[37]

By the turn of the twentieth century, the Catskills served as a vacation spot for other ethnic groups, such as Italians, Germans, Lebanese, Armenians, and Syrians. Each ethnic group maintained its own cultures, and they segregated themselves from others.

Entertainment Filled the Catskills

The name *Borscht Belt* (or the *Jewish Alps*) evolved over time from the word *borscht*, which is a beet soup brought to America by Eastern European Jewish immigrants. This colorful (and quite tasty) meal, made of beets, carrots, cabbage, and tomatoes, was served as a basic stable.

Over the next fifty years the Borscht Belt region of the Catskills was the largest, richest and most densely populated area of hotels in the world.[38] According to the research of Phil Brown, the Borscht Belt included 926 hotels.[39] With the influx of vacation spots, the area became known for hosting the most renowned entertainers of the times. Jewish humor, music, and stars were nurtured and featured in the ballrooms, hotels, and country clubs. From the 1940s to the 1960s, entertainment flourished there, with stars such as Rodney Dangerfield, Madeline Kahn, Tony Martin, Jackie Mason, Bette Midler, Joan Rivers, Phil Silvers, Simon and Garfunkel, and Barbra Streisand.

Salt and Pepper on the Borscht Belt

Salt stated that she and Pepper often played the circuit in the Catskill Mountains. However, the only specific hotel she reported was the Premier Hotel in South Fallsburg. She did not relate the type of facilities and housing provided for them, given that the African American population of the Borscht Belt was small.

Verification of her performance is provided by a menu from Premier Hotel Music Hall. Salt said:

> This was July 14, 1945. I got the menu here.... It was like a dinner show, but after dinner they always had to have performers. In them days, we had live performers, live performers.... They always had full shows. You see at this time, they didn't have television. So everything was full shows, which was wonderful. You used to have to work there in order to be noticed. It was wonderful there.

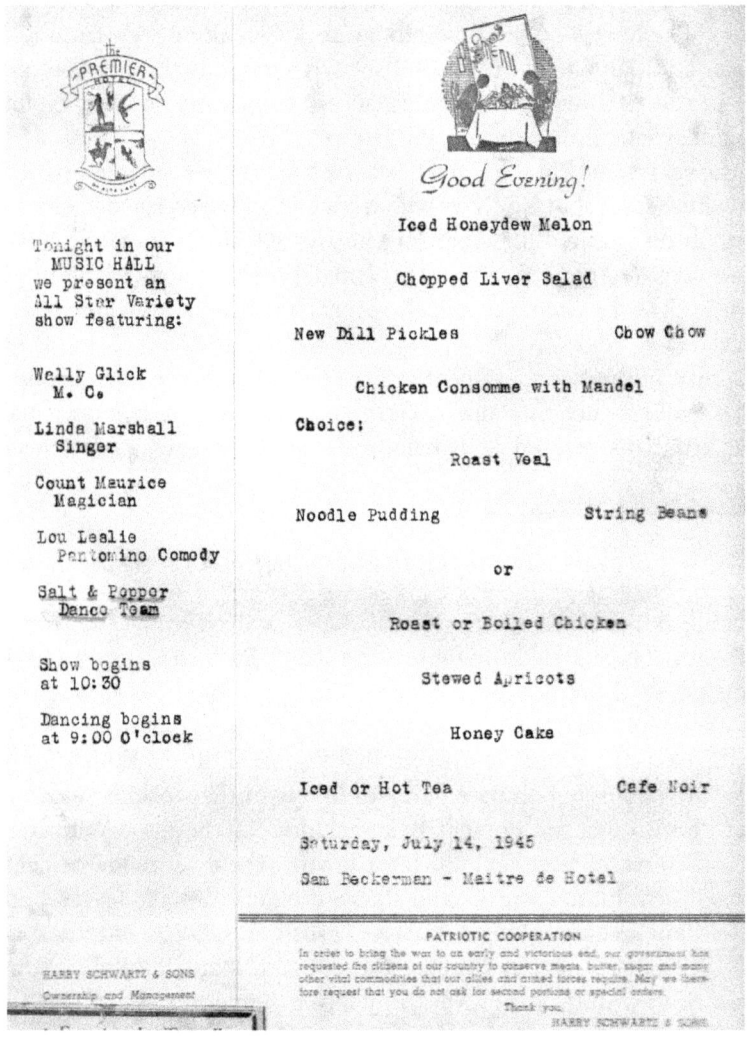

The Premier Hotel in the Catskills.

On the bill with Salt and Pepper were the MC Welly Glick, singer Linda Marshall, magician Count Maurice, and a novelty act by Lou Leslie.

Several times when Edwina was working on the Borscht circuit, there was no band or orchestra—only a small combo:

> Many a time when I was working alone, especially up in the mountains ... they didn't have big bands. And many a time if an accordion was on the show, you had to ask him to play something that he knows.... "What do you know? Give me a 4-bar introduction, give me 2 choruses, and then take me off with another 4 bars, with any good number or good beat that you know." And that's what he had to do. And I think that some of the dancers made them good accordion players.... They played things that they never thought they could play. But that's the way it was.... You show up with your whole portfolio of music and never take it out of the case. [laughter] ... That was the real show business. When you had to, the word is: you had to improvise. Whether you had music or not, you had to improvise. If there was no big band and there was an accordion player on the bill, then that would be the music. Tap dance and accordion music—unheard of.

The Tour Continued

The train traveled back to New York City, where Salt and Pepper were able to get weekend gigs and week-long engagements. Some of the clippings in the scrapbook included the Blue Mirror in Newark, New Jersey; The Boulevard on Long Island, New York; and Club 845 in the Bronx.

9

Crossing the Line

Boarding the *Keystone*, Salt and Pepper were carried below the Mason Dixon Line, the demarcation between liberty and repression. In the 1940s, Baltimore and Washington, D.C., both below the Mason Dixon Line, were considered part of the South. Although D.C. was the capital of the United States, attitudes of prejudice and discrimination were particularly evident.

With the driving force of being recognized for their talents, Salt and Pepper played the circuit. Washington, D.C.'s Howard Theatre, Gayety Theatre, and Lincoln Theatre and Baltimore's Royal Theatre produced full stage shows, complete with a movie. D.C.'s Club Bali and the Stardust Inn were two "hot spot" clubs with Swing bands and a full show. The area was jumping with excitement, and performing opportunities were plentiful. Salt and Pepper were there for several months at a time between 1944 and 1947, being held over week after week. Salt referred to D.C. as home.

Washington, D.C.

GAYETY THEATRE

The week of April 14, 1944, Salt and Pepper performed in *Harlem Follies* at the Gayety Theatre in Washington, D.C. It appears that many shows tried to carry the word *Harlem* because it suggested that the show had Swing music and Black entertainment.

On the subject of follies, *Ziegfeld Follies* used the French interpretation for the word *folly*, meaning a "revue" of popular theatrical entertainment with multi-acts of music, dance and sketches. However, in the case of African American entertainment, *folly* was connected to the art, entertainment and "blackness" of the period. In this context, it continued to carry the meaning from the minstrel period, which was a "lack of good sense and foolishness." Other derogatory titles from the minstrel acts were readily used to lure white audiences. For example, *Shuffle Along* was not "Cruising Along"; *Blackbirds* was not "Eagles" or "Swans"; *Chocolate Dandies* was not "Stylish Men" or "Affluent Gentlemen." Titles and imagery slowly changed over the second half of the twentieth century, as many African American performers and producers attempted to move away from the minstrel stereotypes.

9. Crossing the Line

On opening night at the Gayety Theatre for the *Harlem Follies*, large audiences were in attendance for each of the three shows. Seating in the mezzanine and orchestra sections was reserved for whites. Salt's family and friends took the *Nelly Bly* to D.C. to see the production. Upon their arrival, they were directed to the entrance for African Americans. Advertisements for the show indicated "First Balcony Reserved for Colored." Yet there were no reserved seats in the first balcony. A climb of several flights of stairs found them seats in the third balcony. From that location the performers looked very tiny.

Salt described the lay of the land at this time:

> Even though we were performers, we still couldn't sit in certain sections of the theater, because Washington was very, very discriminative. Washington was one of the worse discriminative places that I have ever been in ... I know it's changed now, but during the '40s, it was very very prejudiced.

GAYETY 9th Bet. E & F Met. 8662

TWO WEEKS STARTING FRIDAY, APRIL 14

Prior to N. Y. Opening
THE B'WAY PROD. CO. Presents

HARLEM FOLLIES

AN ALL COLORED REVUE

Staged and Conceived by S. H. Dudley, Jr.
with Lyrics and Music by Coleridge Davis
Dances by Helen Penn
featuring

**GLEN & JENKINS — BROWN & LEE
BATI & TUFFY — 4 CRACKERJACKS**

5 Cabineers — Jigsaw Jackson — Jessie James
Susie Brown — Pepper & Salt — Boogie & Woogie
Derby Wilson and Frenchy Lavada Snow
Winters and Morano

"Red" **ROSCOE SIMMONS**

And a Grand Supporting Cast

Entire First Balcony Reserved for Colored

2 PERFORMANCES DAILY
MATINEE, 2:30   EVENING 8:30
MID-NITE SHOW SATURDAY NITE—12:01 A.M.

The Gayety Theatre, Washington, D.C.

In one club, all performers were expected to use the back stairs to get into the club. The steps were steep and grated, similar to a fire escape. There was a performer named Big Time Crip. He only had one leg, like Pegleg Bates, but Crip danced on crutches. When he came and left the club, Crip's cane got caught in the grating, which cause him to fall. When the weather changed to snow, Crip, who was the star of the show, asked to use the front door. The manager told him that he was very sorry, but the back stairs was the only entrance for "Negroes." Big Time Crip quit the show.

That's what I'm saying about show business—it was so enlightening for you, cuz you go through these things that people never believed happened. That's because of the prejudice and ... the laws of Washington, D.C. But this is what makes you so open minded and so liberal, because you've been through so much and you know what it's all about.

Theater critics were extremely powerful at the time and could make or break a show or an act. During the performance of *Harlem Follies*, Salt could see the news reporters sitting in the first and second rows, writing their critiques. She stated that the difficult part of performing is you never know who will be in the audience; therefore, the performer's best possible work is a requirement at all times.

Harlem Follies was a two-act show featuring some of the best performers of the time. The show starred "Glenn and Jenkins," an African American comedy team from the vaudeville circuit. William H. Glenn and Walter Jenkins toured United States, Canada, and London, and they were very popular during the 1920s and 1930s. They were known for their blackface spoofs on stereotypical images of Blacks developed during the minstrel period. Their eccentric dancing was sparked by two of their acts: "The Broom Dance" and "Working for the Railway."[1] Their blackface style and imagery were still marketable to white audiences in the 1940s.

Framing the show were twenty-four tan-skinned chorus girls, known as the "Beauties of Harlem." The opening act was "Salt and Pepper," and also on the bill was Jesse James, a disabled dancer who performed on crutches, similar to Big Time Crip.

Derby Wilson was a great veteran tap dancer, who began his career in 1923 in the African American hit musical *Runnin' Wild*. Wilson, Pete Nugent, Chink Collins, and Sammy Dyer were chorus boys and billed as "The Dancing Redcaps." They performed an electrifying Rhythm Tap dance to music written by James Weldon Johnson, composer of the "Charleston."[2] Derby Wilson danced into the late 1960s.

The Crackerjacks were a variety act from the European tradition of acrobatics.

Below, left: "Glenn and Jenkins," William H. Glenn and Walter Jenkins. *Right:* Jesse James identified by Pepper Welch.

9. Crossing the Line

The Crackerjacks.

Archie Ware, the director of the group, said, "We had an acrobatic *variety* act—we tumbled in different costumes, we tapped, we sang, we danced, we featured lots of comedy—and our act was the fastest and *the first to do it in swinging rhythm*."[3]

THE HOWARD THEATRE

In the early 1900s, the major African American theater in Washington, D.C., and the largest African American theater in the world, was the Howard Theatre. It opened in 1910 at the corner of 7th and T Streets NW, in the area known as "Black Broadway." The theater was the home of the Lafayette Players and the Howard University Players. It also featured vaudeville, live theater, and talent shows. The *Washington Bee* dubbed the Howard Theatre "the Theatre for the People." It provided a place where color barriers were blurred and music unified the people.[4]

In the mid–1920s, the theater was sold to Abe Lichtman, a white theater owner of movie houses who catered to the African American audiences. By 1931, Shep Allen managed the theater, introducing amateur contests and helping launch the careers of Billy Eckstine, Ella Fitzgerald, and Pearl Bailey.[5]

On February 8, 1946, Salt and Pepper were on the bill at Lichtman's Howard Theatre with singing team 5 Red Caps (similar to the Ink Spots), two dancers/comedians Coke and Poke, and George Hudson and his Orchestra. At some point, Dick and Dot Remy were added to the program. The Remys' comic acrobats were later guests on television's *Ed Wynn Show*.

A write-up that was in Salt's scrapbook read as follows:

Salt and Pepper Click

WASHINGTON—Salt and Pepper, femme dancing duo, opens at the Howard Theatre here this Friday for a week's engagement prior to a tour of theatres and night clubs en route to California. The talented girl dancers are represented by Hazel Green and at present are being groomed for a musical comedy spot and a motion picture assignment for Paramount pictures.

Although the article mentions a possible motion picture contract, Salt was not aware of this prospect. Her scrapbook contained other newspaper documentation that was not totally accurate about other performers who were scheduled to appear on a bill and on a tour. A common marketing ploy by the newspapers, theaters, or clubs was to twist or exaggerate the truth to enhance the performer's credits. Some of the articles about Salt and Pepper could have been written by their agent Hazel Green as a means of keeping their names and accomplishments in the public eye. This type of advertising continues to be popular in the entertainment world of the twenty-first century.

Salt and Pepper found success in their own abilities as a performing duo, but they appreciated being promoted through the Hazel Green Agency. They were booked solid, and most of the shows were advertised in newspapers. Contract bookings varied in length. Club and theater bookings were between one and six weeks in length, with the option of renewal. Salt stated that they were held over (meaning that their contract was renewed) for months in the Club Bali in Washington, D.C., Club DeLisa in Chicago, and Rockheads' Paradise Café in Montreal.

Salt and Pepper were also held over at the Howard Theatre for several weeks. This entailed a different theme for the show, as well as new music and new choreography. In the process of making these changes, they performed three shows each evening and rehearsed for the new show in the mornings. New music and choreography demanded a lot of rehearsal and several days of creative work. In order to be creative, Salt stated, "You get loose."

Club Bali

Benjamin Caldwell opened Club Bali in the 1940s. This club, located at 1901 14th Street NW, featured live entertainment and a fourteen-piece orchestra in the bandstand behind the bar. The featured acts were the fabulous Cab Calloway, pianist Erroll Garner, and superstars Billie Holiday, Sarah Vaughan, and Dinah Washington. Of course, there were also many tap dancers and the chorus girls, known as the Baliettes.

The week of May 13, 1944, Salt and Pepper appeared in *Harlem's Poppin'* at Club Bali. The show presented the orchestra of Coleridge Davis and his Hardy Brothers Washingtonians, who were "dressed to the nines."

The show was led by the handsome MC Willie Bryant, who sang "Chicken Ain't

CLUB BALI

Washington's Finest Theatre Night Club
1901 14th Street, N. W.
DU. 7544

Washington's Newest Nite Club Revue Hit

Harlem's Poppin

Staged and Conceived by S. H. DUDLEY, JR.

DANCES BY HELEN PENN

STARRING

★ **WILLIE BRYANT**
Outstanding M. C.

★ APUS and ESTRELLITA

★ <u>SALT</u> and <u>PEPPER</u>

★ AUDRY THOMAS

★ JIGSAW JACKSON

★ **THE PENNETTES**

★ Coleridge Davis and his Hardy Bros. Orchestra

---

3 SHOWS—9:30, 11:30, 1:30 — SUNDAYS 8, 10, 12:30
Broadcast Every Tuesday and Thursday, 11 P.M.
Over WWDC   BENNY CALDWELL, Prop.

Admission $1.00 Sat., Sun. and Holidays. Ladies admitted free to the first show any night.
Coming Soon! The Revue Hit of All Times!

Harlem's Poppin'.

Nothing, but a Bird." Salt called Bryant the "Sweetheart of Show Business" and proclaimed that he was the "greatest master of ceremonies ever!" He started his career as a dancer with the *Whitman Sisters' Show* and appeared in *Chocolate Revue*, singing (with Bessie Smith) "Big Fat Ma and Skinny Pa." Bryant was a composer, conductor, singer, disc jockey, and MC. He appeared in two movies: *Keep Punching* (1939) and *A Fever in the Blood* (1961). Salt said, "You can see by his appearance that he could have been a great Hollywood star, but he wouldn't pass." Since Bryant refused to pass for white to get into Hollywood movies, he forfeited many opportunities for success.[6] The color bar and how one played the system determined one's success in life and within the African American community.

Also on the bill of *Harlem's Poppin'* were "Two of the smartest tap dancers of the stage today," Salt and Pepper; a comedy team using odd gestures and dancing, Apus and Estrellita; acrobatic act Jigsaw Jackson; and Helen Penn and her chorus line ("The Pennettes"). Singer Audrey Thomas backed up with "Minnie the Moocher."

After-hours

While Salt and Pepper were in Washington, D.C., Salt used her free time to go to museums and read. Yet Pepper's recollection of her free time went something like

Top: Singer Willie Bryant. *Bottom:* Comedians/dancers/singers Apus and Estrellita.

this: "We rehearsed a lot because I was so much into dancing. We went to a theater to see somebody else, because you learned from watching other performers. We never did much sleeping because at that time we didn't need much sleep. If they had some high jumpin' nightclubs, we'd go see some other performers."

After-hours spots were opened for musical jam sessions, with the intention of serving performers after the theater and nightclub shows closed. The after-hours spots opened at about 3:00 or 4:00 a.m. The performers would go out to various clubs to hear great music, dance, and "meet and greet." There were many after-hours spots that both Salt and Pepper enjoyed.

Salt and Pepper were loved wherever they went. Salt, with her gracious generous personality, and Pepper, with her bubbly, excited manner, won the hearts of their co-workers. After performing for 3 or 4 months at Club Bali, the performers gave them a chicken and chitlin' good-bye party that Salt really appreciated.

Curfew

During World War II, the public didn't have to look far to find a club or theater to lift their spirits. Club Bali had three shows nightly at 7, 9, and 11:00 p.m. But near the end of the war years, a midnight curfew was placed on the city by the Office of War Mobilization starting February 22, 1945. All amusement places, entertainment venues, movie theaters, bars, sports arenas and other such venues had to close by midnight. This had a huge effect not only on the economy of the clubs but also on the military and civilians who enjoyed the nightlife of the Swing Era. The following article, "Spotology" by Allen Drew,[7] encouraged the city to respond:

> Our cue to those who enjoy Night Clubs is make hay while the sun shines and only a small time thereafter as midnight has been made the zero hour for legitimate fun and sport for all Night Clubs, Dance Halls, Taverns, Sport Arenas and similar amusement businesses.... Best news of the week is that ou[r] top spot Casbah now is serving cocktails and that is a very good deal. Crowds there still hold with the curfew the spot will do a top business.... Look for Club Caverns to open at 6 and Bali at 5 (no official confirmation at this writing) but we feel sure you can put this down in your little black book....
>
> Club Bali starts Friday with the "Cats and the Fiddle" and the cats better jump over the moon before 12. Two other local favorites come to town with the show in the person of Salt and Pepper and dynamic Billy Mitchell. Bennie Cardwell, the proprietor has been doing some of the best booking of his career since he made the mistake of booking Jimmy Lunceford the week before Christmas and fate seems to give him a dirty deal with the new Curfew.... However, the public should realize that the recreational outlets in the Nation's Capital are limited and far inadequate and the type of entertainment they will receive will depend upon their support, so IF YOU WANT GOOD SHOWS AS FORMERLY—COME OUT EARLY and support your favorite spots if not stay away—then they will know that you will expect nothing, and that's what will get.... Allen Drew today as always.

Salt never mentioned the curfew, which may have had little effect on her work. She only expressed her admiration for the men and women in uniform who fought for the country. She was impressed that groups of WACs (Women's Army Corp) followed their shows and went to different towns to see them perform. Salt was a true

Top: Club Bali, Washington, D.C. *Bottom:* Salt and Pepper on stage at Club Bali.

patriot, and although African Americans were denied many of the privileges of white America, she felt that, as an African American woman, she had opportunities to succeed.

Baltimore, Maryland

THE ROYAL THEATRE

On the 1945 bill at the Royal Theatre were Anna Mae Winburn and the International Sweethearts of Rhythm, comedian Jackie "Moms" Mabley, Berne Hall, Salt and Pepper, singers the 6 Marvelettes, and singer Private Cecil Gant.

Private Gant had concluded his duty with the army and was welcomed back to the performing stage, where he popularized the song "I Wonder." It seems that in some of his performances, Gant dressed in starched khakis resembling his wartime apparel, complete with a black tie with his name spelled vertically in white block letters. "He played piano and rolled his eyes around like Fats Waller when he sang.... He had something in that voice, something catchy. He made you feel that he was trying to convey to you. He was terrific, he was beautiful."[8]

The International Sweethearts of Rhythm was a female band created as part of the Piney Woods Country Life School in Mississippi. The essence of the band was found in the diversity of its musicians: Mexican, Chinese, American Indian, African American and (later) white women. Consuella Carter laid the foundation for the group, but in 1941 the band severed its relationship with the school and turned professional.[9] A year later, "Edwina and Ana" toured with the International Sweethearts of Rhythm under the direction of Jean Sparks. As the band grew in popularity, leadership was entrusted to Anna Mae Darden Winburn. She was thin and beautiful, and she knew

The International Sweethearts of Rhythm, Baltimore.

music and how to direct it. Backed by female musicians playing full rhythm and brass sections, Winburn was the conductor and vocalist for the Sweethearts.[10]

Salt said that Winburn was a very nice person to work with on the show, but she was strictly business oriented. After all, she had an 18- to 20-piece band to keep on task. Salt proclaimed, "And they were just wonderful! It was a real novelty show that traveled the circuit."

Jackie "Moms" Mabley

Risqué humor of the 1930s and 1940s was usually subtle, Salt implied. The audience "got it." They were alert and didn't need to be slapped in the face with blatant jokes.

Jackie "Moms" Mabley (1894–1975) was "the first Black female comedian to gain widespread recognition."[11] According to Salt,

Anna Mae Winburn, bandleader of the International Sweethearts of Rhythm.

Moms Mabley's jokes were a little off color, but they were very, very funny. When I talk about comedians in our days, the comedians were funny without using four letter words. They were just naturally funny. You can do great things by being clean. Pigmeat and Moms Mabley, they were about the cleanest things. They would say things, and people would fall out their chairs.

Mabley was a personal friend of Salt and Pepper. Salt talked about Moms coming to her house, where her sister Edith cooked greens for them. They had good times laughing, talking, and playing card games.

Beginning her career in 1910, Moms performed on the Chitlin' Circuit through the Theater Owners' Booking Association (TOBA). As time went on, she developed her toothless old lady character with a baggy dress, stockings, a funny hat, and long shoes. She had a deep, gravelly voice and used her vocal and facial expressions to sell her comedy. Moms credits are extensive, as she performed at the Apollo Theatre as a regular, played in Broadway shows, worked in radio, and recorded her own comedy records. She later appeared on television, in film, and at the Copacabana, Carnegie Hall, and the Kennedy Center in Washington, D.C.

Pepper had a collection of Moms' comedy record albums that she had practically memorized. She paraphrased a few Moms jokes that she thought were really funny and said that people would fall out of their chairs laughing. Pepper related the following:

9. Crossing the Line

Advertisement for Jackie "Moms" Mabley.

Moms was on the Smothers Brothers TV show. She'd come out and just wave, "Hey Mom" and tell some, "Honey them jokes." I'm telling you, the people would fall down laughing.

Jackie Moms Mabley.... She tells a joke there, that she went to Philadelphia and went to a mental home to see a friend of hers…. She was in the waiting room and while she was sitting out there a fellow came out and walked over and starting listening to the wall. Then he'd sit down. After a few minutes he got up and went to listen to the wall. So she got curious and said, "Why do you go over there and listen to the wall? I don't hear anybody and I don't see anybody." And he said, "You know, it's been like that all day long."

Then she had one about what an old man could do for her is to lead her to a younger man. And then she'd pick a younger man in the audience. And then she'd say "that's the kind of man I like, cuz I don't want anybody who's as old as me or I don't want our ages to equal 100."

"Everybody tells the children to watch them red lights when they cross the street, those red lights never hurt nobody, they'd better watch them damn car lights." Now wasn't that funny, and the people would fall out.... She died a few years ago when she was in her late 70s.

Off the audiotape, Pepper talked about Moms Mabley's personal life. Moms performed a marvelous show on stage. But Pepper said that after the show Moms would take off her "Moms costume" and deck herself out in a white zoot suit and a big white fedora hat. She looked like a handsome man. She then strutted out the stage door into the alley, where women were screaming for her. According to Pepper, Moms would choose several girls, and off they went for the evening. Pepper implied that Moms was bisexual and preferred being with women. According to the documentary *I Got Somethin' to Tell You*, produced and directed by Whoopi Goldberg, Moms presented a masculine persona in her personal life and had a female life partner who usually accompanied her.[12]

Moms had a violent childhood: "She was raped at the age of 11 by an older Black man, and raped again two years later by the white town sheriff. Both rapes resulted in pregnancies; both babies were given away."[13] Moms never married, but she had four children: Christine, Yvonne, Bonnie, and Charles.[14] The performers interviewed over the years speculated that the father of Bonnie and Charles was Charlie Atkins (but only Moms and Charlie would know whether that was true, and they took the secret to their graves). Much of the information about Moms Mabley is about her professional life; her personal life is generally undisclosed.

Salt, Pepper, and many others from this era described a most fascinating sexual aspect of show business. Here people enjoyed the freedom to live without judgment. For example, sexual preference was a reality, not a verdict. In the theater world, a performer could be straight, gay, bisexual, married, or single. A girl could date a "John" (sugar daddy), or one could have several sexual partners simultaneously, or even be married and having affairs. Everyone knew the situation but didn't sit in judgment. The only judgments expressed were in situations where the husband/boyfriend was physically abusive and beat the woman.

Some of the biggest stars of vaudeville and the variety stage were gay, lesbian, bisexual, transgender, and so on, such as singers Ma Rainey, Bessie Smith, Gladys Bentley,[15] Josephine Baker,[16] Alberta Hunter, Ethel Waters,[17] and Tony Jackson.[18] Jackson, the pianist from New Orleans who brought jazz to Chicago, was one of the few men of the period to live an openly gay life. Homosexuality, bisexuality, adultery, and so forth were personal and separate from the stage world. Lifestyle choices did not appear to affect a person's career. But in the twenty-first century, technology gives the public access to the smallest detail of a performer's personal life. Judgment then comes down and can destroy a performer's career based on personal values and not on talent.

A Simple Good Time

Salt thought that the public had the idea that people in entertainment were fast, wild drinkers, and boozers. During her time as a performer, she was aware of drug attics and prostitutes; however, not everyone followed that lifestyle. Salt was in the entertainment field strictly for the traveling and to make a good living. She was proud to announce that she never had a reefer (marijuana cigarette), and that she wouldn't even know how to hold it. Salt wasn't into vices that could harm her. What she really enjoyed was telling jokes, laughing, playing and just having a good time.

The major backstage activity shared by many was the game of Tonk:

We had so much fun, just joking and seeing each other. In between shows, we used to play Pokeno. Or we'd play a show business card game that everybody knows called Tonk.... They know Tonk like the B.S. Chorus and the Shim Sham Shimmy. And we couldn't wait ... and I'm talking about the Bali down there with those same chorus girls ... we couldn't even wait to get off the stage to get in the dressing room to play Tonk.

Tuesday was payday. We'd play 10¢ a game. You'd have to keep the record because when you'd get paid on Tuesday, that's when you'd pay up the cards. [Laughter] So everybody had their own record. You had two columns there, "Owe Me" and "I Owe." And that's how we use to play cards, and you see now, that was a joy. One of the chorus girls down in Washington was so far ahead that she missed the show. She said, "her hand was worth more than the show." [Laughter]

You had to wait for a seat, too, because everybody wanted to play and no more than four can play at one time. It's five cards, and the object of the game is that the lowest hand wins. Some people, they call it Rummy. You can lower your hand by making spreads. Either three consecutive cards, like the 2, 3, 4 of clubs, or like 3 jacks. And you lay them down and lower your hand. When you think you have the lower hand you say, "Tonk." If you want to get in with the show people, you say, "How about a hand of Tonk?" and they'll go crazy. That's the show business delight.

And Jackie Mabley, oh my God, we used to play. I'll tell you an amusing story about her. We played Tonk with her all week long. Right after the show everybody beat it to the dressing room. That's how we killed our time: playing Tonk in between shows. We'd dress just five minutes before showtime, because we're too busy playing. If the game wasn't over and you had to go on the stage, the hand stays right there until you come back. [Laughter]

Well, the funny part about Jackie Mabley, she was a dear friend of all of ours. She was a Tonk player; she called a Tonk game. Everywhere, even during rehearsal, everywhere, you've got to play Tonk. So we used to play Tonk with her on credit. Come Saturday night, you might be in somebody's debt, you might owe 3, 4, 5 dollars. Come Sunday, you can't wait for the next day, because you want to get even. You want to get out of debt before payday, because every dollar, in those days, every dollar meant something. That's why everybody is so anxious, because you want to get even before payday.

Well, we all played Tonk ... I'll never forget, this was at the Royal Theatre, and in between, we were all playing Tonk. Well, Saturday night everybody owed Jackie Mabley; that was her week. Everybody owed her. Come Sunday, everybody was anxious to get started to play the game Tonk, in order to get even before Tuesday, which was payday. You know what she came up with: "[Moms] don't play on Sunday." [Laughter] Well, she almost got killed. [Laughter] She almost got killed. We said, "What are you talking about? You're so religious. You don't play on Sunday. We're all stuck here and we all want to get even before Tuesday." "I'm sorry, but Moms don't play cards on Sunday." [Laughter]

And so she wouldn't play and the game could not go on.... She's the one we wanted to get even with, because we didn't want to owe her 2 or 3 or 4 dollars. She's talking about, she don't play on Sunday. [Laughter] But that's the fun we used to have in show business. It was clean fun.... It was great. That's why it's so wonderful to reminisce. It really is wonderful.

It was the simple joys of life that made Salt happy. She had fun in a group of people who were "cracking jokes" and just having fun. Material things weren't important. Salt felt that happiness was in living, enjoying your life, and enjoying what you do.

> Those were the important things, and they cost nothing! You had more respect, you had more love for each other, you [had] more caring.... Those days were wonderful because living was a lot of fun just in itself.... We weren't concerned about cars or I gotta get this house in the country. Those things weren't important. We were joking and laughing.... We lived each day as it came. It was much better that way.

10

Down in Dixie

Performance opportunities for Salt and Pepper were abundant in the South, but with these opportunities came many challenges. The lack of pictures, information and advertisements in Salt's scrapbook from these experiences were noticeable. It was difficult to determine if the gigs were one-nighters, if Salt and Pepper were held over in a particular club or city, or even the exact itinerary traveled over the years. It could have been that they didn't stay long enough in any one place to collect the information, or perhaps the memory of these experiences were best forgotten. Yet a few stories were shared.

The Courts

Since the 1896 "separate but equal" ruling of Supreme Court, most states designed laws intended to keep races separate. In 1924, Virginia passed the "one-drop rule," which defined "colored" persons as those with any African or American Indian ancestry. A single drop of "black blood" put a person in the black category. Registration of parents at the time of a child's birth determined the child's race. This ruling was upheld in many states and later determined marriage rights, voting rights, property ownership, education, and where one could eat, sleep, sit, and so forth.

Of course, in the New World white men had impregnated women of African American and First Peoples (American Indian) descent for centuries, resulting in numerous children who were of "mixed blood." The reasons behind the rape of these women could have been a desire to increase the slave holdings of the master, to satisfy a man's own sexual desire, or to serve as an act of violence/punishment, or else it may simply have stemmed from the belief that those of African heritage or those who were not white were considered property and/or less than human (and thus undeserving of the consideration these men would accord women of their own race). Yet some men (like Thomas Jefferson) impregnated their mistresses in the "state of love." The conflicting condition is that laws against miscegenation were passed by a white society; yet white males raped African American women without consequences. If, however, an African American male approached a white female for any reason, it could result in torture and/or death for the man. The ironic aspect of this "one-drop rule" law is that today thousands of white Americans are discovering through the scientific study of DNA that they possess "black blood."[1]

Humiliating Jim Crow signs were erected across the country bearing a common message: "stay in your place." These signs targeted African Americans but were inclusive of other racial and ethnic groups. Moreover, touring in the Jim Crow South exposed Salt and Pepper not only to the reality of personal exclusion but also to the knowledge of nearby beatings, shootings, and lynchings.

On the Road

The situation for African American entertainers traveling in a bus or car seemed to be more difficult, as the attitude of local law enforcement toward African Americans was always one of suspicion. African Americans were often not allowed to drive on certain streets or in particular areas of a city. Law enforcement stopped them for no apparent reason other than race, which often resulted in beating, jailing, and killing. This situation can still be observed in various states in the twenty-first century as racial violence again rears its ugly head.[2]

Swing bands, that performed one-nighters, were on the road for several hundred miles a day. Upon arriving at the destination, the musicians set up the bandstand at the club or theater and rehearsed with the other acts. They performed one to three shows, packed up, and moved on to the next gig, usually driving through the night. The bus drivers would push through blizzards, rain, flooding, and bad roads to meet the looming deadlines. Accidents were not out of the ordinary, as drivers dozed off, got hit by oncoming trucks or cars, slid off the road, or experienced flat tires. Many musicians and entertainers were killed or critically injured in the course of their travels.[3]

In the 1940s, racial integration presented new challenges. Earl Hines hired the first white musician to play in his band in 1943, and Fletcher Henderson hired three white members shortly afterward. The mixing of races was considered breaking the color code. There were Jim Crow laws in effect that prohibited blacks and whites from sitting on the same bench, much less playing music on the same stage or traveling together on a bus, and even more so from flirting or dating each other. With integrated bands, the buses were often stopped and people were arrested, jailed, or threatened.[4]

The International Sweethearts of Rhythm (a women's band) toured with members who were African American, Mexican, Chinese and Native American. There seemed to be very few racial issues at first. However, when white women were hired, the bus was frequently stopped and searched. Firebombs were set in the dance halls where they were to play. Some girls had to hide their identities or were not allowed to play on stages in certain cities. In order to perform or travel together, the white women in the Sweethearts had to darken their skin with makeup while some Black women lightened theirs. Those with straight hair were curling, and those with curly hair were straightening. It was important for their skin and hair to look somewhat the same while having the band pass as international (international was acceptable as long as it did not include whites). Many of the musicians were arrested, and additional protection was needed for travel for the International Sweethearts of Rhythm.[5]

Jim Crow laws also affected the morale of soldiers during World War II. Not only were troops segregated, but USO entertainment also experienced the consequences of the law. Most USO shows were performed by whites, and African Americans were not allowed to attend. When Noble Sissle and Clarence Robinson's *Harlem on Parade* arrived at Fort Jackson, South Carolina, it was performed for white soldiers about a mile from the African American sector. After protest by the soldiers, "a special section of the theatre was being reserved for Negro troops. Over 1000 of these troops boycotted the show, holding that a colored show should at least be given in the colored sector so that colored troops might attend without being segregated."[6]

In another Jim Crow incident, white actor/comedian Jack Benny was not permitted to take African American Eddie "Rochester" Anderson on an overseas army tour. Benny and Anderson were performing partners, with Anderson playing the role of Benny's servant/stooge. Benny explained that Anderson was his friend and he didn't go anywhere Anderson couldn't go. If Anderson was not permitted to entertain the troups because of Jim Crow laws, Benny would not tour without him.[7]

Travel Accommodations

Hazel Green, the agent of Salt and Pepper, booked them in clubs or theaters throughout the United States. As agent, she received a 10 percent commission on all bookings (even if the performers got their own bookings through other means). The agent's task was to book the performances and advertise for them, and by all accounts Green did an outstanding job. However, Green was not responsible for travel or hotel accommodations, which was the more difficult part of the journey for most African Americans.

For Salt and Pepper, the experience was a constant adjustment to prejudice and the imposition of inequitable laws, even though they may have been the stars of a particular show. The most obvious predicament was in personal care, which included bathroom usage, food, and housing. In many clubs there were no dressing rooms for the performers, and costume changes were made in the kitchen. A rarely cleaned bathroom (toilet and sink) was provided for "Colored Only."

Finding food was huge problem. As they toured the South with Earl Hines and his orchestra, restaurants often refused to serve them. Salt said, "When they were doing one-nighters, we had 5, 6, 12 hundred dollars in our pockets, but we couldn't get a decent meal." They had to go behind the restaurant to a window where takeout food was sold to "Colored Only." They ate on the bus or sat on the ground or wherever else they could find a place to eat. Fettered by Jim Crow laws, eating in restaurants in the South was outlawed, and the concept of takeout food was an "outright degrading act of discrimination." However, in the twenty-first century, with the changing of the times, convenient fast-food chains serving through a back window are customary and appreciated by all with no memory of the affects of Jim Crow.

Salt, with her positive outlook on life, was able to adapt to many situations. But in order to deal with the frustration caused by discrimination, she said,

> We didn't feel any anger because we had an expression that we used: "We came down here to get the Yankee dollar, not to change to Constitution." And that's the attitude that

we took. It was hurting in some instances, but not enough to make me not perform. There were places in the South where we were treated like kings and queens. You have all these different experiences; everything is not alike.

Throughout the 1940s, Salt and Pepper toured as a performing duo with Earl Hines, Mantan Moreland, and Lockhart's "Hollywood Show." They knew the train system and usually traveled alone to meet their touring band. It was the safest means of transportation for two African American women in the Deep South.

The train rides from city to city, especially in the South, exposed Salt and Pepper to experiences of discrimination that were not as blatant on the Northeast Coast. Their rides mirrored the nation's prejudice through encroaching Jim Crow laws that were expanded in many states. Salt and Pepper were able to avoid precarious situations by following the rules for African Americans, doing their jobs, collecting their money, and quickly moving on to the next city. On the train, there was one passenger car for African Americans, which was behind the tender or coal-car. The tender carried the fuel (wood, coal, or oil) that created the steam used to operate the train.[8] The locomotive, which produced the necessary steam, emitted heat and smoke that was dirty and smothering for those riding behind it. Salt briefly described her pain:

> We used to have to ride in the back after the engine. They used to have the car for the colored people. And those are the cars you used to have to ride, I don't care who you were or what your purpose was. If you were a Negro, you just have to ride that car. It didn't bother me cause just as I said ... we were down there to make a living.
>
> We knew the South, the way it was down there at that time. So we just went along. But what hurt me was to see the servicemen. They had to ride on the same car. We couldn't believe it. They used to take off their jackets and they were in their T-shirts, but they were right behind the engine.
>
> But these were the experiences that made this business so great. Traveling, which I wouldn't have been able to do on my own because of the expense involved, traveling all through the South ... and the different cities ... and that's enlightening.[9]

Finding lodging was always a challenge. Large hotels, like the Traymore in Atlantic City, were usually out of the question because of the expense and discrimination. Nevertheless, a list of African Americans who owned and rented rooms to performers circulated within the Black community. Performers also asked other acts to give recommendations. Salt and Pepper searched for rooming houses that were safe and reasonably priced. Salt wanted a room for $5.00 a week, and Pepper's room was $7.00 because she liked a room with two windows. Most rooming houses provided a bedroom with a bathroom down the hall that was used by all residents.

Over the years, Salt met and fell in "like" with Larry, who worked as a cook on the train for the Pennsylvania Railroad. He often suggested train routes, hotels, and rooming houses. For years, he'd follow her from city to city to see her perform and be sure she was safe. Larry was crazy about her, and he used his employment to be close. Referring to the pictures of Larry and her, she said:

> Yeah, of course, this was me with one of my boyfriends at that time [showing a picture]. His name was Larry. He worked on the train at Penn Station Company. And he used to follow me all over. Wherever I went, he'd follow. He used to follow me. Come see me down in New Orleans, Chicago, Detroit, anywhere where he thought I was. He'd find

Edwina Evelyn and boyfriend Larry.

out where I was, he would come see the show. We'd be dancing and I'd look out there and there was Larry, out there, yeah. I was wondering how he got there, but he got there. Yeah. It was good, good. I was engaged to him too at one time. I lost the ring. I lost the ring in Philadelphia. But he swore I threw it away. [laughs] Yeah, yeah, but I really honestly truly lost it.

Louisville, Kentucky

Click-clacking on the *Kentucky Cardinal*, Salt and Pepper arrived in Louisville, Kentucky.[10] Larry had given them a recommendation for an African American rooming house. He warned Salt that, no matter what, "Don't tell the owner that you're in show business. If you tell him you're a performer, he's not going to accept you." Unfortunately, other show biz people who had stayed in the house were rowdy drinkers, gave lots of parties, and caused a lot of trouble. Upon arrival, Salt told the owner that she worked in a restaurant and that Pepper was a nurse who worked the night shifts. They would leave for their jobs in the late afternoon and return around midnight, keeping a very consistent schedule. They stayed there for a few weeks as the owners prepared their meals and got to know them a little.

One morning, as they came to the breakfast table, the owner put down the newspaper and said, "The jig is up." He had seen the advertisement that featured "Salt and

Pepper" in the newspaper. They looked at each other with an "oohhh, we got caught" look. As they waited for their eviction, the rooming house owners began to laugh. They were surprised by the news but realized that all people in show business were not irresponsible. They felt like Salt and Pepper were good decent women who only wanted to rent rooms for sleeping. Salt and Pepper stayed with those folks until their contract ended and left on good terms. They stayed friendly with them for a number of years afterward.

Kentucky Man

In Kentucky 1945, after Salt and Pepper performed, they went into the audience to meet the people. Kenneth A. Miller, a white man, had been in the club for every show during the week. Miller invited them to sit with him and ordered them sodas, because it was illegal to buy alcohol for Blacks. Salt thought that Miller was a politician or some kind of a big shot, because he seemed very rich.

Miller had a good time chatting and laughing with Salt and Pepper. Salt thought that either he was drunk or he felt like there were no color boundaries. Miller told them that if they should have any trouble while in the Deep South, they should call him. "If someone tries to stop you because you want to go somewhere, show the person my card, 'Kenneth A. Miller, Janitor.'" Miller said, "Negroes are my best friends. Right now, there's a Negro doing my jail time." Salt and Pepper were shocked by his confession.

It appears that Miller had killed someone or committed some other serious crime. Miller told them that as long as somebody served the jail time, he would be free. He accused an African American male of the crime. Salt remarked, "Miller bragged that the man was doing the jail time that he [Miller] should have served. Can you beat that?" Salt couldn't believe the story, but she took the card and the phony dollar certificate with his picture, "The United States of Aremica," dated February 7, 1945.

Ken's Negro Friendship.

St. Louis, Missouri

The *Dixiana* swayed down the tracks to St. Louis, Missouri. Salt and Pepper were bound for the Club Riviera.[11] They were on the bill with Lucky Millinder and his orchestra beginning the week of September 20, 1946. Also on the bill was the incredible team of Chuck and Chuckles (Charles "Chuck" Green and James Walker), who were outstanding tap dancers and comedians.

Club Riviera, St. Louis, Missouri.

While performing in St. Louis, a newspaper ad caught Salt's attention. On sale were the spectator shoes that she loved because she felt she looked so nice in them. These were dressy shoes with little heels, made in brown and white or black and white with black around the heel and toe. Salt said that St. Louis was known for making the best shoes at a reasonable price. In New York, the spectator shoes were $6.96, but they were half that price in St. Louis.

Salt wanted to go to the store to get the shoes. Pepper warned her that she would not be allowed in the store. However, Salt had strong feelings about the situation since she really wanted the shoes. She set out for the store. Her purpose wasn't to make trouble, but to get the shoes. She thought, "If the manager tells me to get out of the store, I'll leave."

She was neatly dressed and brought the ad from the paper. She was very hesitant as she walked into the store. But the salesman came right up to her as if he didn't see a color difference. He had her sit down, measured her feet, and brought out several pairs of spectator shoes. He treated her royally, and she bought several pairs.

The salesman also took her name and address, which was in the Bronx at the time. For years afterward, Salt received all the information on sales and new styles of spectator shoes. She thought he was a good salesman, and it ended up being a positive experience. She learned that there was a difference in people down south,[12] and she felt that a lot depended on how you presented yourself.

A quick 350-mile trip brought them to Mound City, Missouri, on the Kansas–Missouri–Nebraska border. There was no story, but there was a write-up in Salt's scrapbook that read:

> Chuck and Chuckles "The long and short of Buffoonery" scored sensationally in their first appearance at the Mound City joy spot. Also, on the bill were two band members Annisteen Allen (the shouter) and Bull Moose Jackson. "Salt and Pepper, a distinctively different two girl dance team, won themselves a place in the heart of local amusement seekers with their excellent hoofing and clothing."

New Orleans, Louisiana

Their journey on *The Rebel* took Salt and Pepper deep into Dixie. They were scheduled to perform at the Shadowland Club during the New Orleans Mardi Gras, February 7–18, 1947. Larry, Salt's boyfriend, arranged a place for them to stay. He said that it was cheap—only $5 a week. Larry often stayed there when he had layovers in New Orleans, and he made the reservations for them.

The story, as related by Salt and Pepper years later, went something like this: Feeling reassured by Larry's recommendation, they all jumped in a cab at New Orleans Union Station. It was getting late, and the cab seemed to drive and drive and drive for hours. It was actually only a few minutes, but it was dark and they were heading into the woods. Then the cab stopped, and before them was a spooky castle-like building. They were frightened, but Larry told them that it was a Catholic monastery.

They got their suitcases and walked up to the enormous doors. Larry touched a secret spot on the pillars, and the doors mysteriously went up on chains. Catholic nuns greeted them at the door. Pepper was shocked because she had never seen Black nuns. Larry introduced them as his friends and discussed the lodging reservations.

A sister led the way up the winding staircase. Larry followed close behind as Salt and Pepper walked arm-in-arm in sheer terror. All they could say was, "How did we get ourselves into this?" Pepper noticed a fire escape down the hall, which she thought would be a great getaway.

The sister walked quickly and quietly in a very direct manner. She stopped at the room that was chosen for Salt and Pepper. As the sister smiled gently, Pepper quivered and kept saying, "Yes, Mother, thank you, Mother." Larry went to his room.

Salt and Pepper opened the door to their room. There were no windows—just two beds. They were too scared to talk. Pepper jumped in the bed in the corner because she thought that was the safest place. Her biggest fear was that she might need to go to the bathroom and she would be afraid to go alone.

Pepper coughed and coughed. It could have been a cold, the New Orleans dampness, or the change of climate. Just as they were snuggling into their beds, the door burst opened and the lights popped on. The sister who had greeted them entered. She had a cup of something that looked like coffee and told Pepper to drink it. Pepper said, "Yes, Mother," and drank it down because she was too scared not to. Pepper said, "The cold started jumping around. Whatever the medicine was, it started to work and my cold was cured." Still, all Pepper wanted to do was to get out of there.

The next morning, when they needed to use the bathroom, they slowly opened the door and peeked out. They saw several nuns moving from room to room and then shut the doors. Salt and Pepper headed down to use the facilities. As the door opened, a cat screeched and ran around the bathroom. Pepper was sure it was a haunted house.

Pepper reported that they were both glad to get out of there. And when they were asked if they were coming back that night, Pepper replied, "No, I think we're supposed to meet our manager. We're gonna stay wherever we're going to work." Pepper claimed that she said those things because it was so frightening in there.

Salt's rendition of the story was similar, but she had a different spin at the end. She said that it was hard to find rooms in New Orleans because of the Mardi Gras, and the monastery was a safe place. According to Salt, they stayed at the monastery for the entire performance run and were treated royally. She chalked up the experience as another strange situation in trying to find accommodations.

Salt and Pepper performed three shows a night at the Shadowland Club. On Mardi Gras day (also known as Fat Tuesday), February 18, 1947, they left the monastery and headed for the club. There was an excitement in the air as all the revelers began their day. Salt recounted her experience:

> I'll never forget it as long as I live ... the show was on.... A group of Indians came in there and stopped the show. They came in and they started performing, doing their dances and everything like that. And everybody let them do just what they wanted to do ... it lasted about 15 or 20 minutes, and then they went out and the show continued.... Nobody made anything about it. No remark or anything [was said]. They left very peaceably. They couldn't serve them any liquor or nothing.... They weren't boisterous, they weren't

violent, they just came right in and did their dance number all over the floor. They actually stopped the show and they just left.

It appears that the Mardi Gras Indians were first organized in 1885 by Becate Batiste. His inspiration may have been Buffalo Bill's Wild West Show, which had performed as part of the World's Industrial and Cotton Exposition in New Orleans a year earlier. Batiste and a group of African American warriors made their debut on Mardi Gras and called their tribe Creole Wild West. Over the following century, other tribes or secret societies developed, such as the Wild Magnolias, the Golden Eagles, the Wild Tchoupitoulas, the Yellow Pocahontas, and the Black Eagles. Nevertheless, some believe that the African American tradition evolved and developed based on the friendships and marriages with Native Americans during the years of slavery. Many slaves had escaped and found refuge with the tribes living in the most southern areas of Louisiana.

The heritage was passed along as their costumes grew in magnificence. Throughout their marches, the Mardi Gras Indians would strut and perform their chants, songs and dances through the neighborhoods and into many clubs and bars. The tribes were originally reserved for men, but women are now included. Today, the Mardi Gras Indians continue to march and are a major attraction of the New Orleans Mardi Gras festivities.[13]

Moreland's Touring Company

In 1949, Salt and Pepper did a tour of one-nighters throughout the South with African American actor/comedian Mantan Morland, who was known especially for his role as the skittish chauffeur Birmingham in the *Charlie Chan* movies.[14]

Moreland's *Hollywood Revue* was a one-year tour. Part of the itinerary was as follows:

Nov. 30–December 1	Roosevelt Theatre, Centre Avenue, Pittsburgh, PA
December 11	Chattanooga, TN
December 12	Knoxville, TN
December 13	Nashville, TN
December 14	Montgomery, AL
December 15	Lincoln Theatre, Columbus, OH
December 16	Augusta, GA
December 17–20	Jacksonville, FL
December 25–28	National Theatre, Birmingham, AL
December 29–31	State Theatre, Cincinnati, OH

During the last two or three months of the year-long tour, Salt related that Moreland told the performers that the business wasn't doing well and he was stuck. But he wasn't the only one stuck! It appears that salaries were dependent on the success of the show. Their pay wasn't very good, and the cost of hotels, food, and travel was getting high.

As an unusual snowstorm blanketed the South, many of the theater dates were

On tour with Mantan Moreland, Birmingham, Alabama.

cancelled. Salt and Pepper continued to work with Moreland and performed four to eight weeks without pay. Salt wrote home and asked her parents to wire money for their expenses. Fortunately, Salt had sent home $50 or $100 every week as a safety cushion. Ultimately, the tour was cancelled and no one was paid. Salt felt that Moreland was a nice guy, and they left the show as his friend. With the wired money, Salt and Pepper arrived in New York for the biggest snowstorm Salt could remember. It was 1950.[15]

The following year, television became popular. Salt's mother, who was sick at this time, had one of the first General Electric television sets with a 10-inch screen. Salt remembered watching the Milton Berle and Ed Sullivan television shows. At midnight, when television programming went off, the stations ran old movies. Some of those movies featured Mantan Moreland. This was very annoying to Salt because they had worked without pay but Moreland was getting royalties for his movies on TV.

Salt and Pepper belonged to the American Guild of Variety Artists (AGVA), which was the mandated union for stage work. Salt said that if a person's membership card wasn't up to date, he or she wouldn't be allowed to perform in the next show. Salt and Pepper went to the AGVA on Broadway, where they received representation on their case. They brought their Mantan Moreland contracts and told their story of the money owed, the snowstorms, and how they were stranded without pay for months.

The AGVA agent instructed Salt and Pepper to document the title of Moreland's movie, the TV station on which it was played, and the time and day it aired. The union in turn had Moreland's royalties garnished until the women's back salaries were paid. Salt said,

> We got every dime that he owed us.... The other people who were on his show, they didn't know because they didn't go down to the agency and they let it slide. They said, "What? You got your money?" [laughter] It was like a whole thousand dollars, which was a lot of money in those days.... We told them we weren't college graduates, but we had a little common sense. Myrtle, who is LaZonda, Peggy Thomas, a singer, we told them and they went down to AGVA and did the same thing we did....
>
> I used to sit back and listen to people converse, and I never say anything because I've been through it. I know ... what happens down there. But it was all very enlightening and very, very informative. And after you go through it ... it was really an experience ... it's an education too that you couldn't get out a book.

11

Chicago

Hopping on the *Broadway Limited*, Salt and Pepper headed to Chicago to perform in some of the best clubs in the country. The Windy City's jazz scene had changed significantly by the 1940s: Prohibition had long been abolished; the country had found its way out of the Great Depression; the imprisonment of Al Capone terminated his control of the entertainment industry; and the war and postwar years enlivened the spirit of the people, creating an immediate desire for entertainment.

Bronzeville

The population growth of Chicago during the 1800s was staggering. In 1837, Chicago was chartered as a city of about 4,000 inhabitants. This grew to 109,000 in 1860. The 1880 census recorded 503,000 inhabitants, which doubled to over a million in 1890. Chicago passed Philadelphia to become the second largest city in the United States, and by 1910 the population had doubled again to 2.2 million.[1]

The city originally attracted business and professional people from New England and cities in the Northeast. By the 1840s, European migration to Chicago increased; first came the Irish, followed by Germans, British, and Scandinavians. The city later attracted Czechs, Lithuanians, Serbs, Croats, Greeks, and Chinese. It embodied an ethnic diversity.[2]

Industry in Chicago demanded workers in iron and steel, meatpacking, the clothing and garment industry, printing and publishing, railroading and electrical machinery. And by 1890, 79 percent of Chicago's population had been born abroad or were children of recent immigrants.[3]

Most African American migrants in the first group that moved to Chicago were small in number and arrived at a slower pace. They were financially established and able to buy homes. But between 1910 and 1930, the Great Migration brought an African American influx from the South. Differences between white-based culture and African American culture sharpened. Segregation of living space dominated as whites moved to suburbs. Racial conflict grew and intensified into race riots as early as 1919.[4]

Between 1910 and 1920, the African American population grew from 44,000 to 109,000. By 1930, a second wave of Black immigrants doubled the population to

234,000. The numbers of African Americans increased still more during World War II, and the population reached 337,000.

Migrants from the Deep South found housing in several small pockets outside the city's business district due to rental restrictions. The largest number of people settled on the south side of the city. This area is known as the "Black Belt," a strip of land seven miles in length and one and a half miles wide.[5] Most came seeking jobs, economic opportunities, social freedom, social justice, and a better life.[6] With a large influx of people and so little space, the area was soon considered a ghetto due to poverty, lack of education, exclusion, and subordination.

By the 1940s, the boundries of the Black Belt began to dissolve. African Americans created businesses in the Black Belt, and commerce boomed. Black-owned businesses stretched down South Park Boulevard, Michigan Avenue, State Street, 43rd Street, and 47th Street. This thriving community was self-sufficient, with banks, laundromats, churches, theaters, clubs, and restaurants. It became a city within a city. By 1945, the name "Bronzeville" emerged to represent the brown skin of most African Americans in the area. The term was needed to express the more positive image that people had about their community.[7]

Chicago's Regal Theatre

The Bronzeville area boomed as the Regal Theatre, Savoy Ballroom, the Rosenwald Complex, and South Center Building came into being. Headlining the *Pittsburgh Courier* on February 2, one article read:

47th Street and South Park Boulevard: Bronzeville's Downtown[8]
The Regal Theater, 47th and South Parkway, is scheduled to open February 4th [1928]. An elaborate program is planned for the opening week with Fess Williams, a Quintette from New York City, to do the stunts on the stage with a selected orchestra of 12 artists, while Dave Peyton will direct the orchestra in the pit. There will be several big loop acts on stage and first run pictures on the screen.

Its called the South Side's million dollar theater and a large force of our race will be in evidence as employees. The theater is next to the Savoy Ballroom. Just north of the theater will be a drug store and on the 47th Street side, a big department store. The Urban League is making an effort, with the assistance of Sheridan A. Bruseaux, to supply the department store with competent clerks and sales girls. Mr. Dorrell of Lubiner and Trintz is manager of the theater and Mr. Jordan, his assistant.

The Rosenwald Complex and the South Center Building brought a department store to the area with professional offices. Doctors, dentists, lawyers, and other black professionals were in residence on the second and third floors. The center thrived as residents attended movies and stage shows at the Regal Theatre. The patrons at the Savoy Ballroom danced to the sound of Count Basie, Duke Ellington and Jimmy Lunceford. During the week, The Savoy held skating and boxing matches.[9] Bronzeville grew as a center of jazz arts and provided jobs and financial stability.

The business complex in Bronzeville was owned by Brigadier General Harry Englestein. Richard "Dick" Jones was the manager. (Jones later became the ambassador to Liberia.[10]) Many felt that Englestein saw the area as a lucrative African American market. The reasons behind the development of the area are questionable; however, it did provide public facilities, jobs, charitable involvement, and promotion of black and white artists.

A state-of-the-art commercial and entertainment complex was constructed to serve the neighborhood. It included the South Center Department Store, the Chicago Savoy Ballroom, and the Regal Theatre. The South Center Department Store and Complex opened in 1928 and hired African Americans for nearly all job categories. The store's fifty-four departments occupied three floors and a basement. It was connected to Neisner Brothers' five-cent-to-a-dollar chain, Golde Clothes Shop, and Walk Over Shoe Company. The Savoy Ballroom opened in 1927 at 4733 South Parkway. The multi-million-dollar structure accommodated between 4,000 and 6,000 people.[11]

Across from the Savoy, the Regal Theatre opened at 47th South Parkway in 1928. It was built in an atmospheric style with a blend of Moorish, Spanish, and Far Eastern motifs. It sat 3,000 on leather-clad seats. In its luxurious style, a huge canopy with gilded columns, motifs of clouds and stars, and the large proscenium arch created the feel of an Oriental temple. The Regal had a state-of-the-art ventilation system, dressing rooms, an orchestra pit, and a Wurlitzer organ that could be hydraulically raised and lowered.[12] Opening night was an elaborate affair, with the women in long gowns and men in tuxedos. Flags waved all the way down the avenue, and the red neon sign flashing "Regal" could be seen from great distances. It was like an opening night in Hollywood.[13]

Before the Apollo Theatre in Harlem, there was the Regal, and its performers were the greatest in African American talent, such as Count Basie, Duke Ellington, Louis Armstrong, Billie Holiday, Lena Horne, and Ella Fitzgerald. The theater was also known for its popular Amateur Night contests and its charitable involvement in the community.[14]

In the early 1930s, Balaban & Katz acquired the theater. After a strong outcry from the African American community, the theater continued to operate through the Great Depression. The Regal produced great revues and movies until 1968, when it was closed due to bankruptcy.[15]

In Travis's *An Autobiography of Black Jazz*, Johnny Board, a tenor saxophonist, composer, and arranger, compared the Regal to other theaters on the circuit. He stated that the size and shape of a room affects a musician's performance. While playing the circuit, he found the Regal one of the most difficult venues to play because the audience there didn't applaud easily. He said they were polite and enjoyed the music, but it was hard to get them to clap. Board attributed this phenomenon to the distance between the orchestra pit and the audience. The Regal was larger than the Howard, the Royal, and the Apollo, and the audience was at least twenty rows back. At the Apollo, the audience was practically sitting on the band. The audience at the Apollo was generally quite responsive. If they didn't like something, they would boo the performers and throw rotten eggs.[16]

But according to Semmes's *The Regal Theater and Black Culture*, the audience cut across class and age, representing aesthetic norms through their expression of approval and disapproval in a call-and-response fashion. Although the Regal Theatre's primary market was the African American community, the audiences and performers were both black and white. The integration of cultural aesthetics was demanding on the performers when it came to capturing audiences. Music, song, dance, humor, and other forms of expression distinguish a community. Generally speaking, the African American values and responses are very different from those of a white community. These aspects of culture give a visible presence of a commonly held experience. The African American sound of the Swing Era was easily identified and appreciated at the Regal Theatre.[17]

Club DeLisa

During Chicago's 1933 World's Fair, two months after the repeal of Prohibition, the DeLisa brothers opened DeLisa Tavern at 5516 South State Street in Chicago's Bronzeville area. The brothers, Mike, Louie, and Jim DeLisa, Sr., were recent Italian immigrants. Mike and Louie were tailors, and Jim was a carpenter. When they arrived in the United States, they wanted to be part of the "fast action" in Chicago, and by 1923 they were involved in moonshining. For ten years, they had about six locations where they brewed moonshine and delivered it to several stops along State Street between 47th and 59th Streets where it was sold. As the business grew, the DeLisa brothers had both African Americans and Italian Americans distributing moonshine on foot and by cars. Money was so abundant that they were able to send $600,000 to their grandfather in Italy to build two churches.[18]

In 1934, the DeLisa brothers opened a nightclub one door south of the tavern, 5500 South State Street. Their attorney, John Comise, had contacts that ensured 24-hour-a-day nightclub and gambling operations without police interference.[19] The Club DeLisa was a 60' × 100' room with an 11' ceiling that had a continuous cloud of blue smoke. Three hundred and fifty people filled the room, but on Saturday nights five hundred were squeezed in.[20] The entertainment and gambling facility attracted celebrities such as comedian Bob Hope, singer Bing Crosby, singing cowboy Gene Autry, movie star George Raft, sex symbol Mae West, and African American singer/actor Paul Robeson.[21] Over the years, Club DeLisa played a major role in the promotion of jazz, Blues, R&B, and soul music.

The Club DeLisa's seating policy was determined by "eight Negro bouncers, captained by the 300 pound, six-foot-eight-inch Grover 'Big Boy' Chapman. The black bouncers seated you according to the tips they received and not according to your skin pigmentation."[22]

The club's advertisement read:

New Club DeLisa
4 NIGHTLY SHOWS
all colored revue
NO COVER OR MINIMUM CHARGE
Be sure to attend our Monday morning breakfast dance[23]

On Tuesday, February 11, 1941, Club DeLisa burned down. While smoke poured out of the top of the building, hustlers, cabdrivers, entertainers, and musicians were still gambling in the back, despite having been told several times that the building was on fire. The head chorus girl Freddie Cole, whose husband was part of the game, said that he didn't seem to hear what she was telling him. Freddie commented, "The only game where men become that single-minded is called 'sex.'"[24]

The New Club DeLisa was opened on April 27, 1941. The building of white glazed brick was built within three and a half months and was directly across the street from the old location. The $300,000 club seated 1,000 people comfortably, but they squeezed in 1,500 in a pinch. The club had air conditioning, a gas furnace and mellow red fluorescent lighting. The bandstand was at the end of the room, and the dance floor had a hydraulic lift for the stage shows.

On Saturdays and Sundays, people waited in very long lines to get into the club. There was no minimum fee and no cover charge, although patrons had to pay for set-ups of ice, water, ginger ale or Coke. Many brought their own liquor in a brown bag. The DeLisa brothers wanted everyone to get into the act and gave each patron a souvenir table knocker. Instead of clapping, the patrons would pound the table knockers to show their appreciation of the entertainment.[25]

The best African American performers made it to this "in" place in Chicago, which produced outstanding musical variety shows. Salt and Pepper performed in many of these shows, such as *Lime House Nite*, beginning August 17, 1946; *Flying Down to Rio* (date unknown); *DeLisa Bar-B-Q* (date unknown); and *Sweetheart Parade*, beginning January 27, 1951. The stars in each show represented the best talent of the day. (The exact dates and length of the shows' runs are unknown.)

Club DeLisa usually presented four shows nightly, as well as a Monday 4:00 a.m. breakfast show. From February 1946 through May 1947, while Salt and Pepper were performing at Club DeLisa, the Fletcher Henderson Orchestra was the house band. Other musicians, such as Count Basie, Joe Williams, Big Joe Turner, LaVern Baker, and Tiny Bradshaw, were also featured with their bands of 7 to 12 pieces. The variety-show format spotlighted singers, dancers, comedians and the chorus girls known as DeLisa Chorines.[26] Salt said that the club's regular was singer Joe Williams, who made the room explode with his rich baritone voice. The show usually ended with the chorus performing the B.S. Chorus followed by the entire cast in a rip-roaring tap dance (probably the Shim Sham), which "brought the house down." Freddie Cole was "last to leave the stage shaking her caboose to the rhythm of the drumbeat."[27]

Joe Williams (1918–1999), baritone singer with the Count Basie Orchestra, said that the Club DeLisa was unlike any other club in the world. He sang throughout the United States and Europe and found nothing comparable: "You could buy anything you wanted within the DeLisa compound in the 5500 block on South State Street. The DeLisa brothers owned the hotel, the gambling operation, the liquor store, and the dainty-looking girls who worked the bar stools inside the club. You could even buy Whiskey on election day."[28]

Salt and Pepper struck up friendships with many members of the cast. Salt befriended Mildred Cummings, known as Little Miss Cornshucks. She was a novelty act/comedian/singer advertised as Queen of the Blues. Cornshucks had a little girl persona fresh from the farm, complete with a straw hat with pigtails. She also sported

Salt and Pepper at Chicago's Club DeLisa.

old clothes, bare feet, and a basket on her arm.[29] As described by Salt, "When she finished her act, the basket was filled with money. People would put in 5- and 10-dollar bills and she use to pick them up with her toes. She was a real novelty. People would throw money up there just to see her pick it up with her toes. She picked it up, threw it in the basket and never missed a note."

    Willard Garner and Lurlean Hunter were singers. Hunter was hired to sing with

Fletcher Henderson at Club DeLisa.

the band at Club DeLisa and went on to record five albums.[30] Sonny Parker from Chicago sang the Blues. He was also a drummer and dancer.

Timmie Rogers and Freddie Gordon, "Timmie & Freddie," were a successful comedy dance team from about 1932 to 1944. Freddie doubled as the MC in DeLisa Bar-B-Q. Timmie Rogers (1915–2006) was revolutionary in Black humor. He refused to accept the standard "darky talk" or wear blackface. Rogers, like many of the performers of that time, took pride in clean humor. According to his daughter, Joy King, Rogers

Top: Singer/comedienne Little Miss Cornshucks. *Bottom:* "Timmie and Freddie": Timmie Rogers and Freddie Gordon.

thought the use of four-letter words showed a lack of creativity and originality. He became a stand-up comedian and songwriter, known for his catchphrase "Oh Yeah."[31]

According to Salt, George Kirby (a dishwasher at Club DeLisa) and Pepper used to ride bicycles every morning. His mother packed sandwiches for them, and they had picnics. Kirby was also a mimic, and Salt claimed that he could imitate anyone's voice: "Outside the dressing room, he would pretend that he was one of the chorus girl's boyfriend, [laughter] because he could do anybody's voice. And she'd say, 'Oh, I'll be right out.' And it wasn't who she expected. It was George and that was comedy. We all used to get a kick out of him."

Salt related that on the weekends, the shows were so crowded that there were usually extra performances. Monday nights (also called Dark Nights) were the slowest nights of the week, but the performers still had to be there because they worked seven days a week. One night, the performers decided to have a little fun and do what they called "bury the show." This was usually reserved for the last show of the season,[32] and it meant that the performers would switch up and do someone else's act. Two chorus girls would come out performing Salt and Pepper's act. Another dancer would perform the act of a singer, and so forth. That particular night, while the show was on, George Kirby came out of the kitchen and walked up to the microphone. He then proceeded to imitate all the performers. He was so good that people thought it was the actual person doing the act. He sang, danced and the M.C. Charlie Glen hired him that night, skyrocketing Kirby into a career as a singer, actor, and comedian. "George Kirby was great."

In *An Autobiography of Black Jazz,* Kirby related a similar story, albeit with a somewhat different take. It appears that Kirby went between Rhumboogie's Charlie Glenn and producer Joe "Ziggy" Johnson asking for a chance to perform but was denied. He left the Rhumboogie and got a job as a porter at Club DeLisa. Mike DeLisa had him chopping blocks of ice to make ice cubes. Simultaneously, he learned to bartend and was able draw attention to himself as a mimic. He finally asked producer Sammy Dyer for a chance to perform. Dyer said, "My, my! You're a mimic!" Kirby went home and looked up the word *mimic* because Dyer was gay, and Kirby didn't know what Dyer was calling him. Kirby was eventually allowed to do his act in the show while continuing to work as a porter and bartender. After nine months, he was allowed to just do the show.[33]

Referring to the August 17, 1946, critique in the *Chicago Defender*, an African American newspaper, Salt stated, "Every show that comes in, the critics are there, and the next day it's in the paper. And I mean their reviews were honest—if you were good, you were good; if you were not good, they'll let you know it. Just like I say, there was a lot of talent, but you had to be real talented in order to make it. There was a lot of talent out there, so in order to get these jobs you had to do well."

Making the Money

Salt and Pepper received a contract before they traveled to a city. Contracts could have been about $150 for a one-week show for the two of them. The patrons paid 35 or 47 cents, depending on the show and the club. Salt thought that she and Pepper made a lot of money for that particular time: "We used to keep up our appearance, which meant putting our clothes in the cleaners at all times. We had to pay our hotel expenses, our rooming house or whatever it was. We had to pay for our meals. We had to pay for our transportation. And then we used to have to save a little money because we never knew when the next gig was coming. So we did a lot with very little."

At Club DeLisa, the contract was for seven days a week, four shows a night, plus the Monday breakfast show. Salt and Pepper were usually held over for two or three weeks. At times they were in Chicago for six months at a stretch.

> [If] the people like you so much, then the managers from the other clubs would come and hire you. So you stayed in the city for a long time. Yeah, that's why I like Chicago so much. And that's why I knew so much about Chicago. Because these clubs the DeLisa, the Rhumboogie, and the Regal Theatre, and the Beige Room were all in Chicago.

Salt and Pepper earned additional money for "gangster shows." When the four shows of the evening were completed and the nightclub was technically closed, a small party of known gangsters or Mafia members would come to the Club DeLisa. The club was usually cleared upon their arrival. There was no sense of danger, but the DeLisa brothers hosted an entire show for this group. Salt and Pepper were

Salt and Pepper on Club DeLisa's stage.

amused when they looked out from the stage at the small party. There were only a few people in the audience, and yet they had to perform with full-out energy. At times, the performers were expected to socialize afterward with the "gangsters." This was an additional breakfast show. The performers and employees were paid extra for this work.

Pepper was impressed with the tips they received. She said that a white couple would call them to sit at their table and slip a tip in her pocket: "They said, 'Hi, girls, Salt and Pepper. Nice seeing you.' I looked in there [pocket], $100, or $200 or $300.

Naturally, Salt and I would split whatever we would get. People used to do that [give tips], if you did something and they enjoyed it ... you'd say, 'thank you.' Then you'd go up to your room and scream cuz there might be a $50 bill. People were great sports."

Salt reflected:

> The war in the '40s, everything was entertainment. Work was so plentiful that what we used to do, use the expression "we used to double." We used to work two nightclubs at a time. [In New York] we used to do a show here, go to Moraine's and do a show, then go to Small's Paradise and do a show. Go back and do the second show at Moraine's ... we used to do what they call double.
>
> The act ran 12 to 15 minutes. It was a lot of energy. We had a lot of energy at that time. Doubling! We used to do that in Chicago. After the show in the DeLisa nightclub (State Street) we used to do a midnight show downtown. People used to call it a Rambler.... After all the movies, after all the shows, the picture and everything, then they would have a stage show and call it a Midnight Rambler. And we used to make that.
>
> But those were the good days. The money seemed like nothing ... but it was the experience and the fun. Well, they say that we never received the recognition that we should have received. Just like I said before, we didn't care about recognition.... Now it's different. Money is the word. And money is the goal. We didn't want nothing like that. We were happy to be working.... We enjoyed what we did.... If we were seen and we got it, then it would have been something different. We were just happy working and traveling.
>
> Some people were in show business to make a name, to make a lot of money, had different goals, like one day to be in the movies. But Pepper and I, we weren't like that.... When we finished work, this was about 3 or 4 o'clock in the morning, most of the partygoers, they go from one cabaret to the other. They were getting out or because they were drinkers, so this was their pleasure. Our pleasure, we went home and got our rest. And the next day we were interested in the places of the city, the places of interest. We used to go to the movies. We used to go to the libraries. We used to go to the museum. To me show business was a chance to travel and make a living ... I wouldn't have been able to do it on my own, because it would be costly. It was a nice chance to make a living, and travel ... to travel while you were making a living.

Rhumboogie Café

Just five blocks east of Club DeLisa, Chicago's Rhumboogie Café, 343 E. Garfield Boulevard in Bronzeville, was opened in 1942. Charlie Glenn and Joe Louis, the world heavyweight boxing champion, owned the Rhumboogie.[34] The managers were Leonard Reed (tap dancer/producer) and Pat Brooks, Joe Louis' half brother. The club produced the best and most famous African American talent of the 1940s. It also attracted top names in the audience. Radio announcer Dave Garroway came to the show every night after his radio broadcast.[35]

A Chicago write-up stated:

> Three short years ago a new nightclub ... dedicated to the whole atmosphere of clean and decent entertainment ... opened in a blaze of glory on Garfield Boulevard. Today, from this same auspicious opening, the Rhumboogie Café has developed into the entertainment spot of the country. From every State in the Union have come guests to marvel at the high degree of entertainment and service perfection which permeates the spot....

Charlie Glenn's Rhumboogie Café in Chicago.

The present show, which is the last in a long list of "name" attractions, and which features the usual Charlie Glenn Beauty chorus, headline the names of T-Bone Walker, George Lane, Salt and Pepper, Snookie Marsh, Phyllis Smiley and Mildred Whitlow.[36]

Salt and Pepper were featured in many shows at the Rhumboogie Café. Each show ran for four weeks, and they were often held over for an additional four to eight weeks. The information in Salt's scrapbook acknowledged three of these shows: *New Autumn Revue*, *Broadway Revue*, and a show starring the Harlem Highlanders.

Salt raved about the stars in the *New Autumn Revue*: "T-Bone Walker—his famous song was, 'I wanna walk with you. I wanna talk with you ... I'm still in love with you.' That was his famous song, the song he made famous." Walker was a Blues shouter on guitar. Marl Young and his orchestra played for MC George Lane, who paced the show and sang with his outstanding baritone voice. Salt and Pepper were acclaimed as sensational tapologists, and singer Phyllis Smiley had sung with Duke Ellington. Other performers were comedian Snookie Marsh, and the Charlie Glenn's

Rhumboogie Belles highlighted chorus girls Ernestine Holloway and Mildred Whitlow. About the Rhumboogie Belles, Salt exclaimed, "Each one of them could do a show on their own, because they were so talented."

Broadway Revue was critiqued as the best show in the Rhumboogie's history, and the press stated that the line of those waiting to come in stretched round the corner. Marl Young's band supported the tunes of the show's star, Wynonie "Mr. Blues" Harris. Handsome "Mr. Blues" sang ballads, and the young women in the audience would swoon in response. Salt and Pepper, the classy dance team, performed moves with a tempo seldom matched (at least according to the press). Iron Jaw Wilson dazzled the audience with his tricks. Famed baritone George Layne and singer Phyllis Smiley from Chicago received rave reviews. Also on the bill were Mildred Whitlow and the Rhumboogie Chorus Boys and Girls. The press compared the costumes and performers of *Broadway Revue* with those of a Broadway show and stated that it was worthy of the $4.40 Broadway price.[37]

The third show advertised in Salt's scrapbook carried the name of the starring act: the Harlem Highlanders. According to the newspaper clippings, it appeared that Charlie Glenn was ready to the quit the nightclub business and return to his life as an automobile salesman. But, like a magician, Glenn added three of the nation's top attractions that helped his show surpass anything on the 1945 Billboard. The press gave high acclaim for the Rhumboogie shows and the efforts of Charlie Glenn. Some of Rhumboogie's write-ups mentioned the chef, bartender, secretary, and other behind-the-scenes employees. Each performer was introduced, alerting the public to their specialties. The lure for the public was emphasized, which included the pacing of the show, the contrasting styles, the achievements of the performers, and, of course, the chorus girls.

The playbill for *The Harlem Highlanders* show featured Walter Dyett and his Swing Orchestra, the greatest band in the Midwest; the "dancingest kids" in the business, Salt and Pepper; the interpretive dance duo of "Naki and Lida," who brought a South Sea environment to the show; and torchy songs by the alluring Delores Parker. Bobby Anderson had returned from the service to woo successive audiences with his mellow renditions, and the "Sing-Fionice," with four well-blended voices, were accompanied by a new bass and guitar combination. In the shows the chorus girls were called Rhumboogiettes.[38]

The Harlem Highlanders performed in kilts with a Scottish flavor. "Baby Laurence" Jackson was part of this act.[39] Laurence (1921–1974) later became a solo dancer/musician in the Bebop Era and a leader in Jazz Tap. He stated, "Tap dancing is very

Singer Delores Parker.

The Harlem Highlanders.

much like jazz music. The dancer improvised his own solo and expresses himself."[40] Laurence improvised solo lines and variations that made him almost as much of a hornman in the linear direction of his solos as he was a percussionist.[41] Laurence was not much of a showman, but his complex rhythmic patterns represented the jazz lines of Bebop artists Charlie "Bird" Parker, pianist Art Tatum, trumpeter Dizzy Gillespie, and drummer Max Roach.[42]

With each new show, Salt and Pepper changed their act. They worked for several days, and with a little rehearsal it evolved into a new act. Salt humbly said,

> We used to stay there [Rhumboogie Café] months at a time. And when the show changed every four weeks ... we were held over. If you were pretty good, they held you over for another show. Not putting any roses on us, but we could set up a new routine in the matter of two or three days. You just change your routine around and get loose.... You don't even have to use your regular music. You used standard music.... The music that we had written for our particular act was, of course, our major routine.... You'd change your routine, you'd get a different routine, and almost what they'd say: "You've found a home here." That's an expression they used to use.... That was one of our main stomping grounds. Chicago was like home. It was like home because we used to perform there every year.

Beige Room

Before World War II, Chicago's first-class dance halls were off-limits to African Americans on the south side of the city, even though the neighborhoods were predominantly African American. In 1939, the Medinah Club at 505 North Michigan Avenue cancelled a contract with Chicago Newspaper Guild. African American members of the Joint Council of Dining Car Employees who belonged to the same union as the Newspaper Guild were to be present at the club. A discrimination lawsuit was filed against the Medinah Club. This event triggered the Black community to demand access to many of the clubs and hotels in the area.[43]

The area was part of one of the most exciting jazz neighborhoods of all time. It encompassed the Savoy Ballroom, Pershing Hotel, and Regal Theatre, in addition to many smaller clubs, such as the Trianon Ballroom and White City Amusement Park Ballroom, that catered to white clientele.[44]

The Pershing Hotel at 64th and Cottage Grove was originally a white-only venue. In 1944, the basement of the hotel was leased, and the El Grotto Supper Club (1944–1947) at 6412 S. Cottage Grove opened and attracted Black audiences. Upon its closing in December 1947, the Beige Room opened.[45] In addition to the 200 residential rooms in the hotel, the building housed a 2,000-person-capacity in the ballroom and on the street-level lounge.[46] Later, the club featured Miles Davis and was known as Chicago's Birdland.[47]

Salt and Pepper were featured at the Beige Room November 5, 1948, in a revue called *Spellbound*. The first show was at 10:30 p.m. Salt said, "This was the Beige

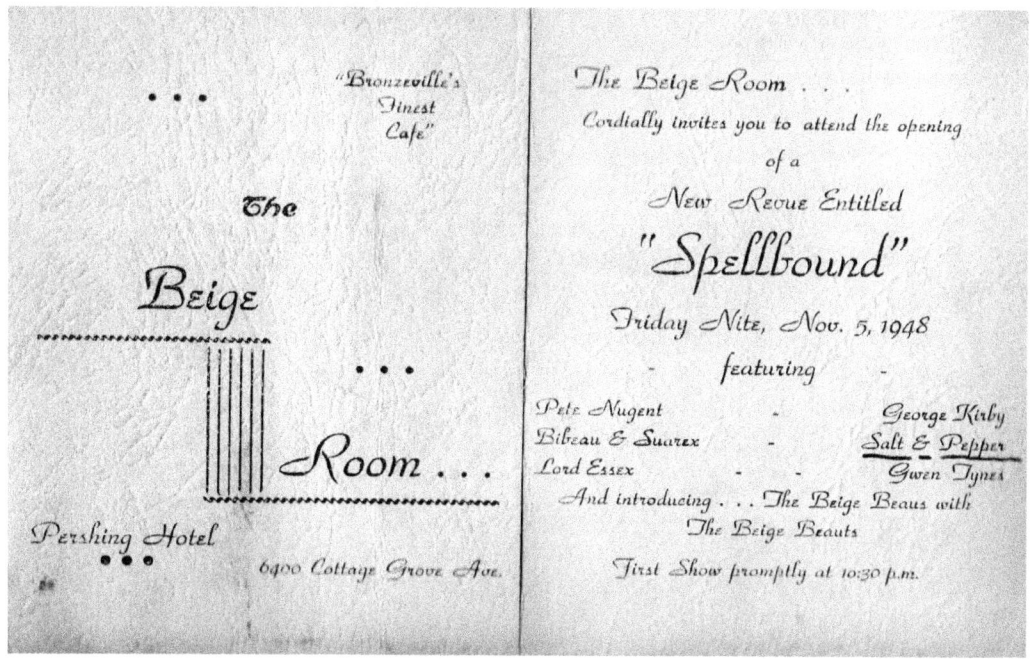

The Beige Room in Chicago.

Room in Chicago, where they had America's finest Harlem show. It was a fabulous nightclub and had the best of acts. Everyone that came to the club was well dressed."

Salt and Pepper were on the bill with comedian and mimic George Kirby, singer Gwen Tynes, tap dancer Pete Nugent, singer Lord Essex Scott, and dance team Bibeau and Suarez. It appears that Llon Bibeau of that team was the director of the show. There was also a chorus of male and female dancers called the Beige Beaus and Beauts.

Bibeau and Suarez.

Chicago Defender

In 1945, while Salt and Pepper were performing at the Regal Theatre with Earl Hines, they attended the Bud Billiken Parade, sponsored by the *Chicago Defender*. In 1929, Robert S. Abbott, founder of the paper, sponsored an outing for the young people who sold his newspapers. It was scheduled for the second Saturday in August at a South Side park in Chicago. It was called "Bud Billiken," a name inspired by a Chinese figurine that Abbott kept on his desk.[48] According to Chinese legend, Billiken was the guardian angel of little children. And the purpose of the Bud Billiken Parade was to serve as a charitable event on behalf of children.[49]

Salt recounted that the events took place in the park, and there was wonderful entertainment of top-name stars. She and Pepper attended several times over the years. The event was later expanded into the Chicago Defender Charities. The mission of the organization was to improve the quality of life for African Americans through educational, cultural and social programs. But its primary mission was to produce the Bud Billiken Parade, which continues to be the second largest annual parade in the United States, with over 150,000 marching units and floats. This cross-generational parade marches in the Bronzeville neighborhood on Chicago's South Side and concludes in Washington Park.[50]

A few years later, Salt and Pepper represented the Chicago Defender Charities in an event at the Parkway Ballroom. It was on February 5, 1951, that the Chicago Defender Charities sponsored a Mardi Gras ball. This charity event, "Swing with 'The Thing,'" brought together Duke Ellington, who appeared in afternoon concerts at Civic Opera House; Salt and Pepper, stars of Club DeLisa; Blues singer Lil Green; the Shelton Sisters dancers; and the Ink Spots, headliners of a Chicago stage show. Teddy Hale was featured with Louis Jordan from the Regal Theatre. Walter Dywett provided the dance music. The Mardi Gras theme had all the trimmings of New Orleans, complete with the crowning of a king and queen and prizes for best costumes.[51]

Daddy-O

In 1948, the Chicago Theatre Studio Party hosted a celebration for the fifteenth anniversary of the Ink Spots. The show was heard on "Stay-In-The-Know-With-Daddie-O," sponsored by Blatz Beer on WAIT radio station Monday, 5:15–5:45 p.m. The following guests from South Side clubs were included:

Ink Spots	Daddy-O Homes Daylie
Pete Nugent	Salt and Pepper
George Kirby	Rhythmites
Bibeau and Suarez	Benny Green
Joe Williams	Claude McLin, road band leader
Ivory Joe Hunter	Lord Essix Scott
Beige Beauts	

Daddy-O Holmes Daylee was a jazz disc jockey in Chicago on WAIT-AM, WMAQ-AM, WGN-AM and other radio and TV stations from the 1940s to the

1970s. His style was one of rhyme and upbeat chatter. He greeted his radio audience by announcing, "This is your musical host who loves you most." To introduce a news broadcast, he'd say, "And now, old midnight sun, don't run before we pay our musical dues. We wanna take you on a five-minute cruise through the world's latest news."

Daddy-O, the youngest of 12 children, was born in Covington, Tennessee, but orphaned when he was about 5 years old. He then moved to Chicago to live with an older brother. After high school, he briefly played basketball with the Harlem Globetrotters. He soon got a job at El Grotto Supper Club in the Pershing Hotel, bartending and entertaining customers with his tricks and rhyme: "'I'm as nice as a mother's advice,' he would say as he flipped ice cubes behind his back."[52] Through the advice of Dave Garroway, original host of the *Today* show, Daddy-O began working as a radio host. He combined his knowledge of jazz (which he had picked up in the clubs), his familiarity and experience with jazz stars, and his entertaining charm to become a sensational African American figure on the Chicago scene.[53]

12

On Midwestern Soil

All aboard for a whirlwind tour of the Midwest: Track #1—*The Wolverine*, stopping in Detroit, Michigan; Track #2—*The Iroquois* to Toledo, Ohio; Track #3—*Tippecanoe* to Indianapolis, Indiana. Now boarding from the Chicago Union Station!

Off and on trains from city to city, Salt and Pepper made their way through the Midwest. In each town they became aware of the musical gumbo that developed jazz. As the Dixieland sound traveled from New Orleans in the early 1910s and 1920s, it was influenced by the sounds of the Blues, Ragtime, Marches, classical, and ethnic influences. Each environment changed its beat, its feel and its emphasis. And it began to swing!

By 1920, Detroit's Motor Town, which became known as Motown in the 1960s, was awakened to the new sounds of thousands of African Americans who moved into industrial jobs and later to the auto industry. Add to this the music of bandleader James Reese Europe and the transported sound of "jook joints,"[1] and Detroit was open and ready for the sound of everything from Swing to Bebop, Rhythm and Blues (R&B) to Rock 'n' Roll.

Throughout the Great Migration, African Americans settled in the northeast area of Detroit, known at the Black Bottom. Detroit's Black Bottom was not related to the dance that appeared in the 1920s theatrical show *Dinah*, nor did it refer to the African American population that moved in during the Great Migration. The name instead evolved in the early 1700s from the French settlers that farmed the dark, fertile soil and low elevation—thus Black Bottom.[2]

Before the turn of the twentieth century there were fewer than 5,700 African Americans living in the Detroit area, most of them working as domestics. At first they were allowed into theaters and other public facilities. Yet, as the African American population rose from 5,700 in 1915 to 120,000 by 1930, so, too, did the rise of fear of the unknown. Over the years, segregation became shamefully obvious in the city. As African Americans arrived and gained industrial-class jobs, the social structure changed as well. Many who were represented as low-wage domestic workers rose to higher socioeconomic levels.[3]

With the huge influx of foreign and southern immigrants, and surrounded by blatant discrimination issues, most African Americans were confined to the Black Bottom area. Throughout the next thirty years, as the population grew, the housing issue in the Black Bottom turned into a crisis. With high rent and overcrowded con-

Salt and Pepper.

ditions, many found themselves living in a single room apartment with no cooking or indoor plumbing facilities.

Bordering the north side of the Black Bottom was Paradise Valley. This section of the city consisted of Black-owned businesses that welcomed African Americans. Nightclubs, restaurants and stores were established that welcomed both black and white clientele: "It was here that integration began in Detroit—where black and white first sat side by side for eating and entertainment. It was here that many politicians got their start—sowing seeds in the Black Bottom. It was here that ball players found a haven when they were ostracized from white hotels and restaurants."[4]

Detroit's Nightlife

In the early 1900s, with the Ragtime influence, social dance became the craze of Detroit. Ballrooms were built; bands were hired. The exquisite Graystone opened in 1922, complete with a doomed ceiling, marble staircases and hand-carved railings that led to a circular fountain. It had a capacity of 3,000–4,000. This ballroom, like many others at the time, was segregated. It encouraged dancing, but mixing of young couples was not permitted. The Graystone opened its doors to African Americans only on Monday nights. In his autobiography, Berry Gordy, Jr., wrote, "Graystone Ballroom and Graystone Gardens was where we went on Monday nights, the only night colored people could go. That was our night. Everybody who was anybody would be there, dressed to kill."[5]

Paradise Valley was ripe for African American nightlife. By the 1930s clubs, theaters and dance halls had cropped up and flourished. "Some of the popular clubs in the area included the Club Three Sixes, Club El Sino, Pendennies, 606 Horse Shoe, B&C Club, Congo Lounge, The Gay 90's Club, Royal Blue Bar, and the Bluebird Inn."[6]

In 1941, Orchestra Hall, which previously held the symphony, became the Paradise Theatre, 3711 Woodward and Parsons Streets. The theater was named for Paradise Valley. Under the new ownership of Ben and Lou Cohen, it opened on Christmas Eve with music by Louis Armstrong. It was an instant success. The audiences were predominantly African Americans.[7] It soon had the prestige of the Apollo in New York and the Regal in Chicago. Audiences paid 60¢ for the evening. Sunday shows and the entertainment included a movie segment, music and a floorshow. Weekday matinees were 40¢ during the war years.[8]

As mentioned earlier, on April 3, 1942, Salt performed at the Paradise Theatre with her early partner, Ann Baxter, as "Edwina and Ann." This fantastic show presented the music of Lucky Millinder and his orchestra, the Berry Brothers, and Sister Rosetta Tharpe. The week of May 4, 1945, while touring with Earl Hines, Salt and Pepper performed at the Paradise Theatre in *Parade of Stars*. Also featured in the show were the Three Maniacs of Rhythm: Ford, Harris and Jones; Arthur Walker; the Four Mellowtones; Essex Scott; and "Scoops" Carry. The movie was *Broadway Big Shot* with the *All-American News*.

In the 1940s, there was a steady change in nightclub ownership. The Plantation became the Club Congo and Club Sudan; the B&C changed to Club Owens and the El Sino.

In 1941, Club Three 666 or (the Three Sixes), at 666 E. Adams Street, was opened by Jap Sneed and managed by Richard King. It was a show bar with a chorus line, and it featured local and national acts.[9] King said:

> The building was originally built for a dance hall, and adjacent to the Club Three 666 was the Paradise Bowl.... We served terrific food, and our customers were a wonderful

group of people who worked in the downtown area. During this time, blacks couldn't eat just anyplace. People went to the YMCA, or some other business on St. Antoine, [and] usually came to the Club Three 666 for lunch. Our club was first class all the way, and out clientele was well dressed at all times.... During the week we'd average two hundred people per night and on Saturday we'd have a complete turnover.... When we lost the white business that we were getting, it was time to get out of the business. We sold the business in 1949.[10]

Detroit's Temperament

Tensions ran high in the nation. African Americans experienced daily discrimination while holding a job, and they were offered impoverished wretched living conditions. Jim Crow laws continued to be enforced as African Americans were denied the basic freedoms both in the North and the South. Moreover, since democracy was not experienced in the United States by all of its citizens, World War II's proposed concept of world democracy just added another futile promise for African Americans.

During World War II, Detroit's production plants mobilized the war effort. Detroit became known as "Arsenal of Democracy," despite not offering democracy to most Blacks in the city. Industrial employers hired African American laborers from the South who were ready to work. The plants provided jobs but not housing accommodations. Over 200,000 new Black residents were crammed into Paradise Valley, a 60-square-block area. With the overabundance of people in the Black Bottom, white communities aggressively guarded the city's segregated dividing lines.

On the evening of Saturday, June 20, 1943, racial tensions grew at an amusement park on Belle Isle. It appears that multiple fights broke out between black and white teenagers, aided by sailors stationed at the Naval Armory. As people tried to cross the bridge to return home, 5,000 whites blocked the exit and were ready to attack. The public heard two rumors that accelerated feelings through Paradise Valley. At the Forest Club in Paradise Valley, which catered to the Black population, a man who identified himself as a police sergeant announced that whites had thrown a black woman and her baby over the bridge at Belle Isle. Those at the club departed in a rage, looting and destroying white-owned stores and attacking anyone with white skin. Similarly, a second rumor, heard by white mobs, declared that a black man had raped and murdered a white woman on the bridge. The white mob encircled the downtown Roxy Theatre and assaulted the black movie-goers as they exited. White mobs also targeted streetcars carrying black laborers. When cars stopped, the passengers were likewise attacked. Black-owned cars were turned over and set on fire. Several hours later, more than 6,000 federal troops tried to calm the city. Nevertheless, fighting continued for many days, during which 25 black residents and 9 white residents were killed. White policemen were responsible for killing 17 of the 25 black residents. Approximately 700 were injured, and the property damage was over $2 million.[11]

A New Sound: Bebop

During the spring of 1947, Club El Sino opened at 1730 St. Antoine. A large dance floor with two floor shows per night showcased Larry Steele's dancers and singers. The club was at its height during its first year as a true Bebop haven. Bebop was the sound of El Sino, featuring pioneers in the field such as Charlie Parker, Dizzy Gillespie, Milt Jackson, Gene Ammons, and Illinois Jacquet. The Charlie Parker Quintet performed and recorded during the two last weeks of December 1947. Dizzy Gillespie's big band appeared June 5–19 and from November 21 to December 4, 1947.[12]

The Club Three Sixes presented *A Stellar Revue* for two weeks beginning October 16, 1947. Salt and Pepper were contracted for this show. They resided at the Norwood Hotel, Room 410, 550 East Adams, Detroit. Salt and Pepper replaced the male/female team Spic and Span for that week.

A Stellar Revue headlined the Four Notes: Gene Smith, Jimmy Sapp, Freddie Johnson, and Abie Levi. This singing quartet with one guitar traveled coast-to-coast and recorded on International Records. Also on the bill were Salt and Pepper, cited as "a fancy dancing duo and a crowd pleaser"; MC Johnny "Curley" Gardner; and the music of Leonard Morrison's orchestra.

Joe "Ziggy" Johnson was a renowned producer and choreographer in Detroit, but he moved on to produce shows at Paradise Club in Atlantic City. To boost excitement at Club Three Sixes, Ziggy returned to Detroit with his Atlantic City chorus line—the Ziggyettes.

Salt and Pepper featured at Club El Sino.

Salt and Pepper on stage at Club El Sino.

The girls were very good dancers, and their appeal was supported by their boiled shirts (stiff winged collars and starched front)[13] and low-cut gowns.

Beginning September 16, 1949, Salt and Pepper were also featured in Club El Sino's *Rocking Rhythm*, with music of Paul Bascomb and his Combo. Also appearing were singer Gwen Tynes, comedian and MC Sinclair Rogers, and the Goree Dancers.

With changing times reflected in the Bebop music and in Paradise Valley itself, white clientele who were supporters of the jazz entertainment became fearful. The attendance of the white population dwindled, affecting the financial stability of the Paradise Theatre and the nightclubs in the vicinity. Many clubs closed or moved to other areas of the city by the 1950s, but El Sino lasted until 1962.

Toledo, Ohio

By the 1940s, Toledo was known as the gambling mecca of the Midwest. It was saturated with illegal gambling spots, craps houses, and horse betting. In 1941, the city of Detroit, about 60 miles from Toledo, cracked down on illegal gambling. This action thrust thousands of gamblers to the gambling parlors in nearby Toledo. The people of Toledo had a system in place that kept down the violence associated with gambling, and if the system didn't work, the people could enforce a reform that would close down all gambling establishments. Toledo's Mafia worked within the system by keeping violence down while welcoming Detroit's gamblers to the city. Their goal, however, was to keep Detroit mobsters out of the illegal gambling action.[14]

In 1941, Club Devon, a first-class casino, was built on Benor Road at the Michigan/Ohio border. The American flag was hoisted in front of the building, and a legitimate business of superb dining, including prime rib and martinis, welcomed the guests. Yet the Club Devon was hailed as the largest illegal casino in America. The casino's main owners were three reputed gambling bosses of Toledo: Benny Aronoff, Joe Fretti, and Tony Paul. In the backroom, according to national gambling expert John Scarne, there were 53 gaming tables, roulettes, blackjack, and dice, as well as 20 booths for betting on the horses at the top tracks.[15]

In his book *Casinos*, Scarne reported:

> The largest number of illegal gaming tables in a single casino at one time in America were in operation during the early 1940s at the Club Devon, a sawdust joint in Toledo, Ohio. It catered largely to Detroit bettors who were transported the intervening 50 odd miles in Grayhound buses at the club's expense. The Devon had 20 banked craps tables, 25 blackjack tables, and 8 casino side games—53 gaming tables in all. Reports at the time claimed that the syndicate paid for all construction costs and was operating in the black at the end of the first day![16]

The club drew bettors from 400 miles away, which spurred a deal between the connection of Toledo and Detroit mobsters. Those in Detroit got a cut of the profits if they provided transportation to Club Devon. Buses and trucks would drop people off at different corners of the city; Club Devon drivers then picked them up and chauffeured them to the club. This was a diversion to keep the police from knowing the amount of action in the club. Gross profits of over a million dollars a week made Toledo the gambling center of the entire United States, with huge profits for the mob.[17]

From 1941 to 1956, according to newspaper accounts, the Toledo area was brimming with gambling clubs. Some of the most well-known gambling parlors were the Webster Inn and the Dixie Inn on North Detroit Avenue. All clubs paid homage to the local mob bosses:

> To manage the immense real estate holdings that belonged to the deceased Jimmy Hayes, Joe and Ben Fretti started the J&B Realty Company to complement their slot machine income.
> One-time assistants to Hayes, Joe and Pat Morrissey, opened the Dixie Inn just down the road. Over on Stickney Avenue near the old greyhound racetrack George Haddad, Al Jacobs, Charlie Bassett, and George Shamy opened the Academy Club. While at Detroit and Pasadena, the Chesterfield Club was run by Chalky Red and Louis "Paddock" Walker. Tom Worland still had his slot machines outside of Toledo, but he still partnered with Abe "Muzzler" Shapiro in the Victory Club.[18]

However, Toledo also had plenty of choices for "clean" entertainment. A movie on Saturday nights in the palatial theaters was a larger-than-life experience. The Loews, Rivoli, Palace, Princess, Royale, and many other theaters provided excellent entertainment. The Capital and Esquire also offered live entertainment and burlesque.

For many others, there were supper clubs such as Ka-See's Nite Club, the Bon Ton, Kin Wa Lows, Trianon Ballroom, and the Cherry Street Club. These clubs served very good food at reasonable prices, and they created top-notch and romantic atmospheres. Kin Wa Lows had a hydraulic stage upon which Ella Fitzgerald was presented, while Salt and Pepper were showcased at Ka-See's. It appears, however, that most clubs had white entertainment, such as Frank Sinatra, the Dorsey Brothers, Benny Goodman, Glen Miller, and Toledo's own Helen O'Connell. The Black jazz scene was rarely mentioned in the research.[19]

Cincinnati, Ohio

From the 1800s to the early 1900s, Cincinnati took a different path, as it became known for its taverns, bars, saloons, beer gardens, and cafés. Between 1840 and 1862, the number of breweries rose from 8 to 38. From 1870 to 1880, the production rose from 656,000 to 1,115,000 gallons of beer, with less than half exported. According to estimates in 1893, the national consumption of beer per capita was 16 gallons per year, but in Cincinnati, 40 gallons per year were consumed for every man, woman and child. In 1890, for a population of 297,000, there were 1,810 saloons, which averaged one saloon for every 37 men (since only adult males were allowed to enter).[20]

In 1901, Carrie Nation arrived in Cincinnati. Nation felt a calling from God to advocate for temperance. The image of her swinging a hatchet was downright terrifying. She described herself as "a bulldog running along at the feet of Jesus, barking at what he doesn't like." Between 1900 and 1910, she was arrested about 30 times after leading her followers in the destruction of multiple saloons with cries of "Smash, ladies, smash!"[21]

Upon hearing that Nation was arriving in Cincinnati, tavern owners ordered new window glass in preparation for the anticipated rampage. However, she didn't break any windows in Cincinnati. She was heard to say later, "My goodness, child, if I had undertaken to break all the windows of all the saloons on your Vine Street I would have dropped from exhaustion before I had gone a block."[22] With Prohibition enforced in 1919, Cincinnati's brewing industry came to an end by the late 1920s with the closing of the three most prominent breweries.

Cincinnati's economy grew as World War II stimulated industry. This, in turn, sparked the entertainment industry, with supper clubs, nightclubs, and theaters springing to life throughout Cincinnati and nearby Southgate, Kentucky.

In the African American community, Cincinnati's Cotton Club had historical significance for its role in booking and promoting Black entertainment.[23] The building was an ever-changing business establishment, from the ornate Carlisle House to a residence hotel, headquarters for a Jewish congregation, a hospital, and then back to a hotel. With the growth of the African American population in the area, the hotel opened to Black clients. At that time, the white hotel manager, Nathan Michelson, turned the previous club, the Grand Ballroom, into the Cotton Club. Michelson linked the name and entertainment reputation to that of Harlem's famous Cotton Club. Cincinnati's Cotton Club was a beautiful ballroom with Blues and jazz sounds that drew both black and white audiences. It was the only integrated nightclub in Cincinnati and featured hundreds of the greatest Black orchestras and celebrities of the era.[24]

Salt and Pepper performed at Cincinnati's Cotton Club in 1952. The club was filled to capacity with members from the Improved Benevolent and Protective Order of Elks of the World, who were celebrating their Golden Jubilee.[25] With music by Monty Morrison, the show featured MC Sonny Parker, vocalist Flint Moore, singer and comedian Mabel Hunter, Salt and Pepper, and Baby Washington. Washington was described by Don Moran as "(the body beautiful) who presents more that just a shake dance."[26]

One of the greatest stars to appear at Cincinnati's Cotton Club was Lincoln Theodore Monroe Andrew Perry (1902–1985), known as Stepin Fetchit. Perry, a star of the stage and 55 films, depicted the stereotypical coon character from the minstrel period. According to David Pilgrim at Ferris State University, Fetchit's style embodied the nitwit black man, scratching his head with eyes bulging. Film historian Donald Bogle commented:

Comedian Stepin Fetchit.

> His appearance, too, added to the caricature. He was tall and skinny and always had his head shaved completely bald. He invariably wore clothes that were too large for him and that looked as if they had been passed down from his white master. His grin was always very wide, his teeth very white, his eyes very widened, his feet very large, his walk very slow, his dialect very broken.[27]

Although he never won an Oscar, Lincoln Perry was the first African American movie star in the United States. In the mid–1930s, "Stepin Fetchit" was a millionaire and one of the highest-paid Black actors of the era. In 1976, Perry was awarded a special NAACP Image Award stating that, despite the stereotype, he had a trailblazing career without which many other Black film careers may not have existed. He was elected to the Black Filmmakers Hall of Fame in 1978. Although Perry has a star on the Hollywood Walk of Fame acknowledging his achievements, he was severely criticized by the Black community for propagating a stereotypical character.[28] It seems that Perry dealt with this criticism as he laughed himself all the way to the bank.

As an example of her fame, Mabel Hunter was featured in a film called *Burlesque in Harlem* (1954). It was reviewed by Paghat the Ratgirl as follows:

> [Mabel Hunter's] positioning after one of the show's chief babes is intentional, with the idea that a jolly big singer inherently parodies gorgeous dancing babes, & Mabel milks this expectation with some dancing too....

For Mabel's first appearance she's in a white evening gown as she does a "rap number" called "Fat Man Blues" which is very amusing, about how she likes men, even fat men can be thrilling, but how annoying it can be if some ugly-ass s.o.b. she's condescended to be interested in up & decides *she's* not good enough.

She returns later in a black evening gown to sing "I Wanna Rock" which is jump-jazz of the Louis Jordan school, with all the features of rock 'n' roll in place. She'll return a third time to sing another rockin' jump-jazz number, "He's Knocking But I Can't Let Him In." As this jump-jazz number develops, she unexpectedly lifts up her evening gown to reveal the most absurd striped pants, & spoofs a burlesque dance.

She's the only performer of the whole lot who gets three sets, undoubtedly because it was obvious she's just about the best on the bill. Damn but she should be better remembered as a great jazz singer & formative rocker, but this film seems to be the only chance to see how good she was.[29]

Indianapolis, Indiana

As Salt and Pepper traveled from New York to the Midwest in the 1940s, they found that the jazz scene had evolved similarly in many cities in the segregated United States. In cities where there was a large African American population, a center of social life, business and cultural activities evolved along a primary boulevard or "main stem": "In Los Angeles, it was Central Avenue; in Detroit, it was Hastings Street; in Harlem, it was 125th Street; and in Indianapolis—the city that bequeathed us jazz greats such as J.J. Johnson, Freddie Hubbard, David Baker, Slide Hampton, and Wes Montgomery—it was Indiana Avenue."[30]

Many jazz musicians learned their craft on the streets, in clubs, and in all-night musical "cutting contests" in which players tried to top each other's riffs and licks. These competitions and settings were part of the African American tap dance world from the birth of tap in the United States,[31] and many musicians admitted that they learned their improvisational licks from the tap dancers.[32]

Brothers Sea and Denver Ferguson, pioneering Black entrepreneurs in Indianapolis, ran a successful printing business around 1919, and they later made a fortune through the properties they acquired. Around 1931, they became interested in the local jazz community and began operating businesses that helped make Indianapolis a regional jazz center. The Ferguson brothers opened four important entertainment venues on the Avenue—the Cotton Club, the Trianon Ballroom on top of the Cotton Club, the Sunset Terrace Ballroom, and Royal Palm Gardens. They also owned the Ferguson Hotel and a booking agency for musicians. The Fergusons were recognized for making Indianapolis a major stop on the African American entertainment circuit.[33]

During the 1940s and 1950s, the height of the jazz club period, Indianapolis found itself a booming jazz scene. Crispus Attucks High School offered a nurturing music education environment for African American students. The school offered scholarships and an environment conducive for achievement, with legendary music teachers such as Russell W. Brown, Norman Merrifield, and Lavern Newsome. Indianapolis was filled with opportunities, as it was a crossroads in the United States that brought together tourists, musical styles, regional influences, and jazz music. The community exhibited an intergenerational passing down of the jazz tradition, supported by a close-knit African American community. This lifelong connection of musicians set the Indianapolis jazz community apart from other areas where the jazz population was transient.[34]

During its heyday, Indianapolis' jazz area was known as "Funky Broadway," "The Yellow Brick Road," and "The Grand Ol' Street." On Indiana Avenue, all of the Black community's needs were available, from doctors and lawyers to restaurants and shoe repair. The area also housed the city's Black newspaper, the *Indianapolis Recorder.* In addition, there was the Walker Theatre on Indiana Avenue, named for millionairess Madam C.J. Walker of the hair and cosmetic company. The building housed a beauty parlor, insurance office, doctor's office, drugstore, and the Missile Room, which was an after-hours club sponsoring Swing dances in the 1930s.[35]

The Cotton Club had a main floor featuring bands, a second floor for all-night jam sessions, and a third floor for revues with chorus girls, tap dancers, comedians, singers and novelty acts. The Sunset Terrace and the Walker Casino also provided live dance music. The Paradise played records instead of having a band perform, but there was a drummer who kept the beat. Henri's was a popular bar that specialized in the world's best jazz musicians. Moreover, Henri's, Georgia's Bar, and the Missile Room provided settings for cutting contests. Above Georgia's Bar was the Sky Club.[36]

Headliners Salt and Pepper found themselves at the Sky Club, 427 Indiana Avenue, for the club's opening night. The swanky glass- and leather-covered theater door invited the guests to a star-lined stairway and a sky-blue interior. Percy (Jackie P.) Saunders and Sonny Sebree, owners of the Sky Club theater and supper club, lavishly decorated the club for comfort and beauty. The meals were delectable and the decorum refined. At 10:00 p.m., multi-colored lights accented the stage. The covered tables and efficient waitresses set the tone for this exclusive restaurant.

Everyone was "dressed to the nines." Salt said, "It had a great, great show there with Pepper and I, and with Warren Haines. He was a singer, and Scatman [Max 'Mr. Blues' Bailey]. And of course, every show was full with a variety of performers, singers, dancers, and orchestration."

Also on the opening night playbill were Spo-De-O-De, a comedian and actor in the film *Caldonia*; a talented exotic dancer, Miss Suda; and a chorus of lovely fast-jumping girls, known as the Sky Rockets. These St. Louis chorus girls were trained and choreographed by Opal Brooks, and the music was provided by Jimmy Cole and his Jumpin' Jimmies Band.

The Sky Club was opened every night. The first show started at 10:00. Full shows were offered at the matinees on Sunday afternoon at 4:00 and 7:00, and patrons were encouraged to dance between shows. The Sky Club featured tap dancers, pantomimes and female impersonators. "You name it and it was happening."[37]

Salt was impressed with Indianapolis and the excellent treatment she and Pepper were given. She chuckled that a couple of interested fellows took them to the Indianapolis 500-mile car race.

Cicero, Illinois

The Italian Renaissance-style Palace Theatre in Cicero, 5242 W. 25th Street, opened in the 1920s. An ornate terra-cotta façade with a large arched window over the main entrance invited the crowds to live shows and popular movies. From 1951 to 2005, it was converted to a bowling alley. The building was later sold and demolished.[38]

The Palace Theater advertised a vaudeville-style show: MC and eccentric comedian Herbie Leon; xylophone wizard Phil Mika; singers the Three Kaye Sisters; the balancing act of Alwhite & Blue; and "speedy steppers, considered one of America's outstanding colored sister teams," Salt and Pepper. Buddy Shaw and his Orchestra provided the music. The 1948 featured movies were *Abbot & Costello Meet Frankenstein* and *The Strawberry Roan*, starring Gene Autry and Champion (his horse).

Milwaukee, Wisconsin

Wisconsin does not carry the title of the jazz capital of the United States, nor is it remembered for nationally known clubs famous during the Swing Era. Nevertheless, its wooded rural countryside had its own legend as a haven for Chicago-based gangsters.

The state often played host to infamous characters such as Al Capone and John Dillinger. In Manitowish Waters, the Little Bohemia Lodge was the location for a shootout between the Dillinger gang and the FBI in 1934. The restaurant still operates, and the property is preserved with Dillinger memorabilia. Babyface Nelson used Dillman's Bay Resort in Lac du Flambeau as a hideout from the FBI.

Chicago gang leader and speakeasy operator "Polack Joe" Saltis owned a 238-acre estate on Barker Lake near the town of Winter, not far from Al Capone's estate. Ralph Capone (Al's brother) made his home in northern Wisconsin. He settled in Mercer and operated the Rex Bar until 1974, when he died.

"During the Mafia's heyday, Milwaukee was home to some of the organization's most powerful men, including Frank Balistrieri, who was considered for head of the Commission: the Mafia's governing body." Known during Prohibition as the Lake Como Hotel, the French Country Inn in Lake Geneva was a hideaway for Al Capone, Bugs Moran, John Dillinger and Babyface Nelson.[39]

Ethnic groups from Scandinavian countries migrated to the Wisconsin area as early as 1839. Germans and Irish immigrants soon followed. African Americans populated the area by 1822; yet there were only 3,000 in the state by World War I. During the Great Migration, the African American population increased to 10,739 by 1930.[40]

Wisconsin was an agricultural state with owner-owned and -operated farms. There were some skilled jobs in industry, but earlier immigrants filled many of these jobs. As the Black population grew, so did the unabashed prejudice. In 1924, 2,000 members of the Ku Klux Klan paraded in Madison with 10,000–15,000 spectators.

By 1940, the African American population had grown to 12,158—these people came in search of industrial war jobs and stayed to raise their children. Yet racial discrimination and segregation continued, as the Milwaukee area was bonded by ethnicity and religion with rigidly established residential areas for over a century.[41]

In an attempt to trace their itinerary in Milwaukee, Pepper had a city entertainment magazine, *Goin' Places in Milwaukee and Racine.* The advertisements in the magazine provided insight into the interests of the community. There was news of the 1950 outboard marathon, the midget races at the State Fair Park, and a comment on bandleader Paul Whiteman, who was also a cattle rancher. Other promotions in the magazine were for restaurants, supper clubs, and nightclubs that presented white performers for white clientele. It appears that these may have had piano music and occasionally a singer. The Lakotas was the only club that featured Dixieland music. The Melody Room and Club 26 had full shows. Club Milwaukeean presented female impersonators. Club Terris had shows with a burlesque flair, and the Kilbourn Hotel featured an underwater burlesque-style show. The Capitol Pladium had a cocktail bar, entertainment and 16 bowling lanes. The Flame, where Salt and Pepper performed, was the only club that had Black entertainment:

> The best in Black and Tan entertainment is always on hand at the Flame, which is now under the direction of Derby Thomas. Floor shows and dancing are a nightly feature with the best of colored entertainers from eastern after-dark spots in the cast. Music for dancing pleasures is by Loretta Whyte and her swing orchestra.[42]

It appears that neither the memory of these clubs nor the actual buildings remain. The only evidence to support the existence of Club Terris and Tutz's Cocktail Bar

The Flame, Milwaukee, Wisconsin.

was on the Ebay website, where two matchbooks were found. Club Terris was advertised as "World's Most Unique Nite Club; Dancing and Floor shows nightly; No cover or minimum charge." The club also advertised, "Wrestling Shows Nightly at 'The World's Largest Bar' over 300 ft., 521–31 W. Wells St., Milwaukee, Wis" and "Elect Tom Terris Alderman 6th Ward in 1940, Authorized and paid for by Tom Terris, 621 N. North Ave., Milwaukee."[43] The second matchbook read, "Tutz's Cocktail Bar, 743 N. 3rd St., Milwaukee, Wis., Close cover before striking [the matchbook]; phone Broadway 9951, Fine Food Daily, Mixed Drinks and Cocktails, Entertainment, The Ohio Match Co."[44]

The Flame nightclub, where Salt and Pepper performed, is now the Blue Ribbon Brewery Lofts. With this little information on the Swing Era shows, Salt's scrapbook is the main evidence of their performance in Milwaukee during the summer of 1950.

13

"The Girls"

Cotton Club Girls, Apollo Rockets, Rendezvouettes, Dudleyettes, Baliettes, Roxyettes, Ziggyettes, Rockadets—the list of chorus girls goes on and on. By the 1930s and 1940s, most clubs and theaters across the country had their own "line of girls," who, in many cases, were the main draw of the show.

Chorus girls made their appearance in the British theater in the late 1800s. "*The Passing Show* (1894) produced by George Lederer, was considered the first successful American 'review.' ... It combined topical humor, a chorus of beautiful girls posing as 'living pictures' ... and an elaborate ballet."[1] Producer Florenz Ziegfeld's revue *Follies of 1907* was noted for the beauty of the chorus girls, first led by Ziegfeld's wife Anna Held. The Shubert Brothers and George M. Cohan followed shortly afterward with their chorus girl–style revues.[2]

Yet a forerunner to George Lederer's chorus girls came in 1890, when burlesque theater owner Sam T. Jack and stage director Sam Lucas produced *The Creole Show*. This production was revolutionary on the burlesque circuit, featuring 16 light-skinned African American teenage girls and a cast of women singers and comedians who "glorif[ied] the coloured girls." The shows moved away from the planation scene to an urban setting and acknowledged present-day African American themes of transition through the Great Migration to industrial jobs.[3]

Featuring African American women on stage was only a small part of the undertaking. Although music and dance made enormous contributions, overcoming and dissolving racial obstacles was the goal. Black theater found a place on Broadway, diminished blackface and the "Negro" stereotype, and changed the show format from that of the minstrels to a continuous storyline that addressed issues of African American education, military treatment, and the back-to-Africa movement. Furthermore, the influence of African Americans on the Broadway stage legitimized Ragtime music and dance, featured women in leading roles and as chorus girls, and brought world recognition to the genius of the culture.

Shuffle Along (1921) debuted African American chorus girls such as Florence Mills and Josephine Baker. The improvisational style of the chorus girls included tap and vernacular dance never before performed on Broadway.[4] Moreover, in 1924, dance director Charlie Davis added Rhythm Tap to the chorus line, making *Chocolate Dandies* the first Black Broadway musical in which the members of the chorus line danced so closely together with a rhythm that could really swing.[5]

Tap dance made a spectacular appearance in the Cotton Club. It was performed by male dancers exhibiting Rhythm Tap and Flash and by chorus girls performing Soft Shoe, Rhythm Tap and other vernacular dance styles. Chorus girls were also featured performing soubrette or specialty dances. Lavina Mack and Mae Barnes were considered excellent tap dancers of the 1920s, performing in such shows as *Runnin' Wild* (1923) and *Rang Tang* (1927).[6]

White audiences were lured to Harlem's nightclubs to enjoy the African American stars.

The cabarets expanded their musical entertainment to include chorus line production numbers with girls and boys. The performances of the chorus held the show's theme together with opening and closing acts. In time, the chorus numbers expanded to include a dance in the middle of the show.

In a Youtube segment titled "Red Hot 1930s Cotton Club Show," the singing and dancing of Cotton Club girls and boys were displayed. The women were glamorous, sexy, jazzy, suggestive and energetic while wearing revealing costumes that would have been considered shocking for the period. The men, in their white tuxedos, performed Flash tap in unison and displayed the large grins expected by white audiences. These spectacular performances obviously roused the audience, and a craze for the jazz spirit was born.[7]

The Choreographers

In the early years, many clubs and theaters hired producer/choreographers to come to the theater to organize and set the dances for the show. During the early years at the Apollo, the producers were Charlie Davis, Addison Carey, Leonard Harper, Teddie Blackman and Clarence Robinson. These producers had their own chorus lines, which traveled with them on the "Round the World" circuit.[8]

According to Leonard Reed, some of the producers didn't know how to dance, so they had the girls create the steps. Clarence Robinson, who had the ideas for the chorus numbers, would have Ristina Banks demonstrate the moves.[9] Although producers moved from club to club and from state to state, the names that generally appear in certain areas are Joe Johnson and Charlie Morrison in Chicago, Leonard Reed in Detroit, and Charlie Morrison in New York. Hortense "the Body" Allen Jordan, choreographer/dancer, was the first African American woman to put a chorus line on Broadway in the Paramount Theatre.[10]

Larry Steele is noted for his work as a producer, supporter, and mentor of African American musicians and dancers. Steele was known in Chicago as a singer, master of ceremonies, and bandleader. In the mid–1940s, he left Chicago for Kentucky Avenue in Atlantic City. There he helped organize African American entertainers on the Chitlin' Circuit and found himself as a producer at Club Harlem. In 1946, Steele produced *Smart Affairs*, a revue featuring the best in African American music and showcasing the most talented and beautiful African American showgirls. This show toured the country and was later produced in Miami, Florida. Steele also produced *Beige Beauties* and *Sepia Revue*.[11]

The Line

Chicago's Sunset Café (1921–1937), 315–17 E. 35th Street at South Calumet, and the Plantation Club (1924–1930s), 338 E. 35th Street, were simultaneously producing shows of the same caliber that popularized New York's Cotton Club (1923–1940).[12] These full shows featured an orchestra or Swing band, a solo act, dance teams, singers, comedians, exotic or shake dancers, and novelty acts. The chorus lines, ponies, and parade or showgirls were the glue that held the shows together.

The chorus lines often consisted of men and women, but as the years passed the line of girls became more popular. Different types of girls with similar coloring constituted a variety of lines. There was a line of girls of average height and stature who danced and sang. Another line of girls 5'2" or shorter were called "ponies," and they performed the more difficult dancing or movement work. (This may have been because they were closer to the floor, quicker, or able to do acrobatic stunts and Flash easier than taller girls.) According to Earl Hines, the chorus girls were such great performers that they "were the show."[13]

The parade or showgirls were tall beautiful young girls with light skin who wore alluring (sometimes revealing) costumes of sequins and feathers. Earl Hines remembered that at the Grand Terrace (originally the Sunset Café in Chicago), there were stairs on both sides of the bandstand. Six parade girls came down the stairs and posed "while the chorus line was tearing it up on the raised dance floor in front of the band." The role of the showgirls was to be attractive and create a picture by moving elegantly through the space. On stage, suggestive costumes were expected, sensual movement was applauded, and raw humor was enjoyed. Although these things may have been deemed obscene for the period, if delivered in good taste, Salt considered it, "making a living."

The number of girls in a chorus line ranged from 4 to 16, depending on the size of the club or theater's stage. These young beautiful girls had a uniform appearance of height, hairstyle and skin color, and they were 16 years of age and up, depending on beauty and talent.

The African American girls advertised as "sepia-skinned chorines" were biracial and could have passed for white. Their skin tones were very light and referred to as "high yella." For a performance, they were required to be tan. They achieved that goal by applying makeup to their faces and arms that lightened or darkened their skin, a process known as "make up or make down" ("make up" to lighten skin and "make down" to darken it).[14] The darkest girls at the Cotton Club were Lucille Wilson (medium brown skin), who was Louis Armstrong's first wife, and Edna May Holly (light brown skin), who was Sugar Ray Robinson's first wife.[15]

In interviews with many African American women, skin tone was always mentioned: "she had dark skin"; "she was as white as you and could pass"; "she had medium brown skin about my shade." These discussions not only acknowledged the physical differences but also confirmed that there were benefits to having light skin. Privately, a hierarchy of skin tone existed and was always mentioned as "s/he could have passed." But biased feelings about skin tone or the hierarchy of a color class were never discussed with the researcher.

Many of the "high yella" chorus girls could have passed in the white world. White male audiences were attracted to these women because they were young, beautiful, and, for many, a seductive taboo. From Pepper's point of view, the showgirls were there for the men to gloat over. She explained that the beautiful girls were not supposed to go home with the men. They were to sit, have cocktails, and flirt. Yet, often, a rich fellow called "Backstage Johnny" would shower a particular lady with flowers, and they'd have a relationship. On occasion, a "high yella" woman married a wealthy or not-so-wealthy white man.

The Girls Worked

By the late 1930s, most theaters hired their own chorus girls, called regulars, and employed them full-time with a dance captain. Next to the Cotton Club chorus line, the girls at the Apollo—tall, light-skinned, exceptional dancers—were acknowledged as the best chorus line in New York. Often, an excellent dancer came forward as a lead dancer. She was the soubrette who was framed by the other dancers.

At the Apollo, the show always started with a few musical arrangements by the orchestra to excite the audience. There were four to five shows a day at the Apollo, and the chorus girls performed three dances in each show: opening the show, the middle number, and closing the show with the finale. The girls tap danced and executed many dance forms, such as Hawaiian, Indian, and African.[16] In their spare time, they rehearsed for the following week's show and were fitted for costumes.

In the video *Been Rich All My Life*, the Apollo chorus girls Bertye Lou Woods, Marion Coles, Fay Ray, Cleo Hayes and Elaine Ellis reflected on working at the Apollo:

> You really lived here. You went to sleep. You got up in the morning and you came back there.... You didn't take a week off; if you wanted a job you didn't take it off, because when you came back somebody else would be working in your place. They had stars in the show, but we held those shows together because the audience came to see us. We got to know their faces. I first started working at the Apollo, I think, we were making $22.50, four, five, six shows a day. From 10 o'clock in the morning to 11 o'clock at night, rehearsal after the second and last show, that was every day. Opened on Friday morning with a brand new show every week. And then you'd be down there rehearsing til three o'clock in the morning. That's why they put beds upstairs.[17]

Chorus girl Daisy Richards performed at Club DeLisa in Chicago. She recalled that during World War II, the girls worked all night (five shows) and did a breakfast show on Sunday morning. At 5:00 a.m. on Sundays the chorus girls took a bus to Fort Sheridan to perform for the soldiers. They stayed there all day, returned to town with no sleep, and went back to the clubs to work that night.[18]

Bragging about the talent of the chorus line, Honi Coles said, "A dancing act could come into the Apollo with all original material and when they left at the end of the week, the chorus lines would have stolen many of the outstanding things that they did."[19] Ristina Banks, Bertye Lou Woods, and Yak Taylor were three of the chorus girls who learned and performed the routines of the male tap dancers.[20] Bertye Lou was the captain of the Apollo chorus girls. It appeared that the girls worked as a team and not competitively.

Apollo Chorus Girls: Bertye Lou Woods, Helen, Essie, Gert, Jeannette, Lyle.

At the Apollo, the band changed every Friday. There were particular dance numbers set to the music of a specific band and performed when the band appeared. These standard songs were used both because they were familiar to the audience and also because they meant less rehearsal for the band and the chorus. For example, a dance was choreographed to Duke Ellington's "The Creole Love Call," and it could be used every time he appeared.[21] Regarding Jimmie Lunceford's band, the Apollo girls said, "That was our band, a hell of a band, because they were swinging." Lunceford wrote a soft shoe number especially for them called "For Dancers Only." It was a complete Swing number, and the audience got into the music by clapping in time to the beat. It was so great that they could hardly get off the stage.[22]

Shows ended as the stars took their bows in ascending order of stardom. The most vig-

Saxophonist and bandleader Jimmie Lunceford.

Earl Bostic (possibly at New Smalls Paradise, New York).

orous dancing was saved until the top star had made his/her final appearance. Then everyone on the stage joined the chorus girls in a rip-roaring tap dance such as the Shim Sham or the B.S. Chorus that would bring the house down.[23]

Salt was quite impressed with the girls: "All of those chorus girls were so great; each one of them could have done an act on their own.... They were so talented that they could do everything. They could sing. They could dance. They could be a part of the comedy team. Anybody [performer] who was missing, they could fill in for them. So that made them extremely talented."

More Than Rehearsed

Freddie Cole Bates was the captain of the chorus girls at Club DeLisa in Chicago for twenty-one years. In 1934, when the DeLisa was a small tavern at 5516 South State, Freddie and two other girls were the chorus line. As special features, Freddie also performed toe-tap[24] and rhumba dances. She explained that during the 15-minute band intermission, the girls performed "ups," in which they took turns singing and dancing for tips at the patrons' tables. In show biz talk, they "worked the crowd." The girls would dance up to the table, lift their skirts and move flirtatiously, picking up the tip with their thighs or other parts of their anatomy. There were big tips in working "ups," and the money was supposed to be shared with the musicians who accompanied them as they worked the room. On one occasion, a chorus girl ran to the washroom to steal the money. Drummer Red Saunders suspected her and had one of the band members follow her to the washroom. He grabbed the door before she locked it and made her turn over the tips. There was a lot of money in "ups," and most dancers were willing to share with the musicians.[25]

Exotic Dancers

Exotic dancers appeared on most playbills; sometime they were headliners. Salt explained that an exotic dancer or shake dancer was tastefully alluring. She was provocative, but not as risqué as a stripper of today.

There was an art to being an exotic dancer. Chorus girls from the Cotton Club revealed that being an exotic dancer required covering one's private parts. This was done by the girl shaving herself and covering her genitalia with tape. Makeup was applied to the tape to match the skin color. The dancer then put on a G-string and wrapped herself in yards of fabric that could be removed for the act, although she always remained covered. There was a dignity and allure expressed by a high-quality exotic dancer.

Pepper seemed to have a large collection of exotic dancers and laughingly rolled her eyes when she discussed them. It is unclear whether she had any close friendships with these women.

Exotic dancer Sonia.

Glamor Was Part of the Deal

The Cotton Club, Apollo Theatre and Connie's Inn chose "their girls" according to talent, color, and beauty. Yet it was the ambience they created that was most important. Costumes were designed to accentuate the sexual—the captivating features of the women.

In the 1930s, the girls were given free training in ballet, tap dance, and singing, and they learned how to execute lines and sell a song. Madame Nijinska, a ballet and acting coach, taught them what lines were important and how to use their hands to

Dottie Adams.

express a song. An exotic dancer was taught to exaggerate her hands in order to cover her breasts and intimate space.

A Cotton Club girl was expected to look gorgeous when she entered the stage door entrance on Broadway and Lenox Avenue. When the show was finished and she left through the back door, the life of glamor was still mandatory. She had to enter and exit the club or theater looking glamorous; if not, she was fined.

When these "high yella" women worked on Broadway at the Cotton Club or any of the high society clubs, they were allowed to shop anywhere without having their credit checked. They could buy whatever they wanted on time, because the merchants wanted their clothing advertised by the stars. Backstage on payday, there was a string of merchants selling and collecting money for on-time purchases (similar to a credit card). The girls bought G-strings, perfume, shoes, and theatrical makeup called Mehron Cosmetics, which was blended to their skin tone. Machiavelli, whom they called the Prince, was there blending perfumes for them. They paid $1 or $2 to each merchant toward their bills, which gave them the opportunity to dress beautifully.

The girls went to work glamorous and hung out glamorous, but they didn't go into the clubs. Jim Crow laws were at work, and the girls were not allowed to walk in the front door.[26]

Another Moment to Shine

When the Swing Era came to an end, many of the chorus girls from the Apollo and Cotton Club took jobs as barmaids. Geri Kennedy was a bartender when the Cotton Club reopened in 1960. She became interested in the chorus girls and decided to showcase them. In 1986, Kennedy gathered the Cotton Club and Apollo Theatre dancers in a performing group called the Silver Belles. Her goal was to honor the women, give them a venue for performing, and preserve their legacies. The women were in their 70s and 80s, but still ready to dance. The Silver Belles performed at social events in New York and on short tours. Kennedy also produced a video that featured the Silver Belles, titled *Been Rich All My Life*.[27] The original Silver Belles danced until 2013.

14

Canadian Jazz

Stepping off the *Ambassador*, Salt and Pepper were just minutes away from the St. Antoine district of Montreal, Quebec, Canada, which was just below the railroad tracks. From the 1920s to the 1950s, Montreal boomed with the sound of jazz, nightclubs with Black entertainment, jam sessions, and after-hours spots. Clubs featured full shows of musicians, singers, dancers, comedians, and novelty acts that were popular in the jazz cities of the United States. Montreal was Canada's center of jazz, from the Swing bands of Duke Ellington and Cab Calloway to the Bebop sounds of Dizzy Gillespie and Charlie Parker.[1]

Salt and Pepper enjoyed Montreal and always spoke well of their performing experiences there. They performed six months at a stretch at Rockhead's Paradise Café and Café St. Michel in Montreal.

The Jazz City

Montreal, the center of jazz in Canada, popularized a Black art form. It is an amazing phenomenon, since in 1890 there were about 15,000 Blacks living throughout the Canadian provinces. A growth in population and a change in attitude contributed to the success of jazz in Montreal.

As early as 1628, West Indian slaves were imported to the Canadian colonies for the fur trading industry, but they worked mainly as domestics. During the American Revolution (1775–1783), Loyalists fled to Nova Scotia and brought their slaves with them. Freeman and rebellious enslaved people also arrived in Canada in search of land. This movement (1817–1862) became part of the Underground Railroad as thousands of those who were enslaved escaped to Ontario. After the Civil War and the abolition of slavery, a large number of African Americans returned to the United States.[2]

By the turn of the twentieth century, the railroad expanded its operations in Montreal, making it the center for hiring and training porters. Between 1900 and the late 1920s, Montreal's Black population increased from 300 to 3,000. During this time, many Black families established residences with a stable home life. Wealthier white Canadians who lived in the area moved away from the harbor and the railway terminal. Their homes were converted into apartments and rooming houses for Blacks who were in search of work as porters. As in most port cities, the transient population wanted short-stay housing and a "good time." Entertainment and "sporting" activities developed in this "other side of the tracks" area, known as the St. Antoine district. By the late 1920s, five Black cabarets were set up, which succumbed to prostitution, gambling, and horse race betting. Contrary to the stable Black families living in the area, the reputation of the whole became known for loose morals. The educational, social, and sanitation standards were low, with a death rate that exceeded the national average.[3]

Until this time, Canadians had very little experience with Black culture. However, Ragtime music seeped slowly into the Canadian air. In 1916, Englishman Harry Thomas and Canadian Willie Eckstein composed and recorded two rags with syncopation and complex melodic lines. Thomas was acknowledged as the first Canadian to record a Black American style of music based on Ragtime. The following year, New Orleans' "Original Dixieland Jazz Band" (all white musicians) arrived in New York, where they recorded two Dixieland tunes, bringing the sound of Dixieland—jazz—to world attention.[4]

Although foreign to Canadian ears, the new sound of marching bands was infused with the Black feel of Ragtime, Blues, and jazz. The sounds captured the attention of Canadians who loved to dance, and with the sounds came the dance craze of the Turkey Trot, the Grizzly Bear, and the Bunny Hug. Initially Canadians enjoyed the jazz sound when played by white musicians, who were welcomed into the Montreal ballrooms. But during the following years, New York African American stars began to make their appearance on the Canadian scene as well. The Four Harmony Kings, Florence Mills, America's Greatest Coloured Jazz Band, and the Broadway show *Shuffle Along* performed on Canadian stages.[5]

As the sound caught on, clubs featuring Harlem-style entertainment were opening in abundance in Montreal. Patrons enjoyed the dance bands, and slumming became popular. Clubs grew in popularity.[6] Not only had the sound caught on, but so did the jargon. In 1922, the Nemderoloc Club opened, which was "colored men" spelled backward. There was also the Orgen rooming house ("Negro" spelled backward), which housed the entertainers who performed at Café St. Michel.[7]

In the 1920s, when the United States suffered the results of Prohibition laws, Quebec's laws avoided total prohibition. Many flocked to Montreal to enjoy the pleasures of social drinking. The laws went through transition as gangster organizations, smuggling operations, and narcotics consumption rose. But within three years, the government decided to take control of the sale and distribution of alcohol throughout the province. State liquor stores, nightclubs, and hotels were licensed to sell beer and wine. Montreal became a refuge and "developed a reputation for good times in an era when Prohibition was inhibiting nightlife everywhere else on the continent."[8]

Montreal's jazz scene also flourished in the 1920s, as Montreal was a haven for itinerant Black musicians. Although Blacks were barred from certain hotels and nightclubs, they were able to work on the same bandstand with white musicians, share a meal at the same table with whites, and enjoy the company of white women without the fear of lynching.[9]

Unfortunately, during the Great Depression, Blacks in Montreal faced many of the same discriminatory issues that they did in the United States: illegal mixed-race bands, denial of visas for musicians to enter Canada, refusal of membership in white musician unions, rejection of liquor licenses, and raids on clubs. Restrictions were placed on the neighborhoods where Blacks could live and worship. Certain hotels would not rent to Blacks, and stores would not hire them.[10] Black musicians were not hired to play in bands in white hotels and nightclubs on the west side of the city, nor could Blacks enter white clubs, dance halls and ballrooms.[11]

Slowly, by the mid–1940s, the Canadian doors opened to jazz musicians, bands were integrated, and interracial dancing was permitted in Black clubs. Some of the restrictions paralleling those in the United States were lessened in Montreal; thus, the jazz scene peaked![12]

Rockhead's

Standing at the top of the steps, dressed in a suit with a red flower in his lapel, stood Rufus Nathaniel Rockhead. He welcomed his guests, with flowers for the ladies and gracious greetings for the men. Rockhead provided some of the best entertainment in Canada. He supervised all acts, producing only high-quality shows.[13]

Rockhead moved to Canada from a community of fugitive slaves (and their offspring) in Jamaica. After serving in World War I, he worked at several jobs, including a shoeshine stand and as a railway porter, where he smuggled bootleg liquor into Al Capone's empire. Using the money he made from bootlegging, Rockhead applied for a liquor license. It took two years to obtain because the Montreal officials had an issue with Black-owned bars.

In 1928, Rockhead bought a building, which became Rockhead's Paradise Café at 1252 St. Antoine Street. Over the years, the building had a lunch counter on the ground floor and a hotel above with prostitutes and their clients. He eventually transformed the space into a cocktail lounge and beverage room. On the third level, he cut a hole in the floor that overlooked the stage below and created a two-story nightclub with seating for 400. To maintain the Harlem nightclub atmosphere, Rockhead brought in Black entertainers from the United States.[14]

Although the club relied financially on the business of white clientele, Rockhead's Paradise Café welcomed Black patrons and hosted many Black celebrities, such as Joe Louis, Louis Armstrong, and others. Entertainment in the club featured Black musicians and performers, but Rockhead also hired racially mixed musicians in the cocktail lounge on the ground floor. As a respected leader in the Black community, Rockhead tried to ease the hardships caused by the Great Depression by providing jobs. Amateur contests were held in the beverage room with prizes of a few dollars and bottles of wine and beer. Moreover, throughout the club's history he offered matinee shows for neighborhood children, serving them sandwiches and sodas. Rockhead was at the top of the game for many years.[15]

The Show at Rockhead's

Salt and Pepper received top billing at Rockhead's Paradise Café. They appeared for a long engagement in 1947 and again beginning February 24, 1950. An advertising clipping titled "Comedy Singer Tops in Rockhead's Show" read:

The duo tap team of Salt and Pepper are still on hand at Rockhead's going through some of the best dance routines we have seen around town for a long time now. The two girls have been here for some time and it is to be hoped they will be around for quite a time to come.

Salt and Pepper both talked of another dance routine they performed to Louis Jordan's song "Run Joe." A picture of them in the act was taken with RP (Rockhead's Paradise) on the bandstand. The Calypso song with a Jamaican accent was very famous in New York. Salt paraphrased the song during an interview: "The version of the song that we sang was about playing the numbers; it was illegal. Joe went to the grocery store to play the numbers and they would warn him that the police were coming. And they would tell him, 'Run, Joe, run as fast as you can. [laughter] Run, Joe, the police holdin' the man.... Run, Joe, don't let the man catch you. [laughter] Run Joe. [laughter] Yeah, those were good days. Yeah!'"[16] This music paralleled the Caribbean music of Lord Caresser, the "King of Calypso Singers," which was played downstairs in the cocktail bar.

An advertising clipping introducing the line-up read:

> Outstanding among Montreal's' night spots is the Paradise Café, the leading coloured club in town, run under the excellent supervision of its popular host, Mr. Rufus Rockhead.
>
> Margaret Watson, a delightful and talented singer, heads the show this week which also includes Darlene O'Day, an exotic dancer, Salt and Pepper, dance team, Teddy Cole, dramatic baritone, Warren Banks as M.C., and Alan Wellman with his Rhythm Boys. Of course the sparkling Rockadets are still satisfying customers with their routines. Downstairs in the cocktail bar Lord Careeser, the "King of Calypso Singers" entertains each night.
>
> You'll find Rockhead's

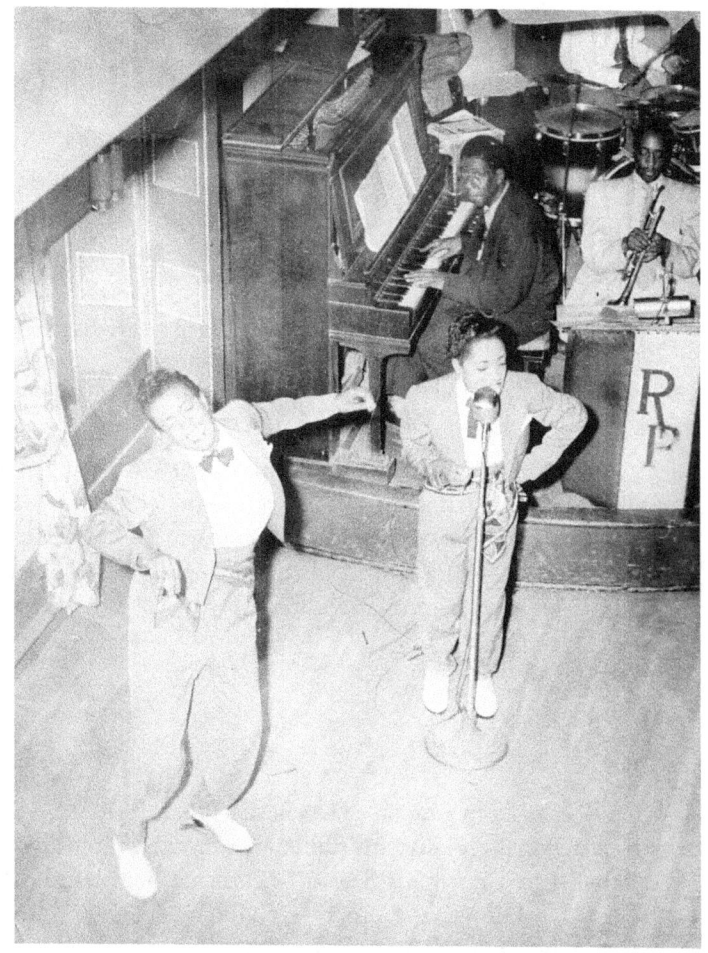

Salt and Pepper sing "Run Joe" at Rockhead's Paradise Café.

Cast at Rockhead's Paradise Café.

at 1252 St. Antoine St. right near Mountain. Don't pass by without dropping in for a visit.[17]

Margaret Watson was a strong singer with a bit of a risqué style. She was not vulgar, but she had a good-humored twinkle in her eye that amused the audience.[18] Over the years, there were other stars featured on the Canadian playbill with Salt and Pepper: the dancing feet of Little Papa, Iron Jaw Wilson, dramatic baritone singer Teddy Cole, exotic acrobat Wandra Mayo, exotic danseuse Princess Gomez, and Rose Lance.

Café St. Michel

Across from Rockhead's was the less formal Café St. Michel at 770 Mountain Street featuring Black entertainers from the United States. Yet the fame of Café St. Michel rested on Louis Metcalf's International Band. Metcalf had played trumpet with Duke Ellington, Fletcher Henderson, Jelly Roll Morton, and others. In 1947, Metcalf brought the Bebop sound to Canada. He "transformed an inelegant show club into the city's first jazz shrine.... Metcalf made the Café St. Michel a hallowed

Advertisement for Montreal's Café St. Michel.

name in jazz communities across Canada, and a required stop for musicians passing through town."[19]

With Louis Metcalf on the scene, the focus was music and improvisation. The sound was balanced by two shows nightly (three on Saturday) and standard music for audience dancing between shows. Metcalf let the patrons fill up on dancing segments, and gradually, by the third show, the Swing sound was replaced with new Bebop music. The musicians played as a band, soloed with licks and riffs, and explored the freedom that Bebop offered. Metcalf introduced a challenge dance where a musician played a brief solo for about four bars, and then a tap dancer would repeat the rhythm and add on to the phrase. The dancer challenged the musician, calling out, "Beat that!" They would continue the challenge back and forth until one was defeated. The audience was hooked on the sound and participated with cheers and laughter.[20]

The stage shows featured Salt and Pepper, who were advertised as a "comedy team of sepian dancers." One critique stated that "Salt & Pepper were an outstanding female dance duo dressed in male attire, who stole the show in two knockabout and tap routines." Others on the playbill were modern novelty singer and MC Rolbie Kirk, magician Yogie Chand, the Calypso Rhythms of Del Rio Trio, and, of course, Louis Metcalf on trumpet, with his band and pianist/singer Gene Cooper.[21]

Although Salt and Pepper were featured performers at Café St. Michel, the advertisement of "sepian" dancers didn't really seem to bother Salt. This description was often used to inform the public that it was a show of Black performers with entertainment of the same caliber as Harlem. The critique raved about their performance style and emphasized the male attire. It is uncertain whether women in Montreal wore pants at that time, but in order to have "knockabout" routines, Salt and Pepper were not going to be dainty. The focus of the show was on the Bebop music. Salt said that since there were only two nightly shows, it gave her and Pepper time to double at other clubs.

By 1949, Café St. Michel, with its Bebop flavor, and Rockhead's Paradise Café, with its outstanding Black entertainment, were drawing both black and white crowds of tourists from Canada and the United States. It was a passion for the music and the enjoyment of the moment that energized the musicians and the entertainers. Metcalf's musicians only received $50 a week, but the idea was to have fun and a steady job. Many musicians played 7 to 8 hours a night and didn't want to go home because they were having so much fun.[22]

The Swing Era affirmed the support that African Americans gave each other by finding joy in another's success. Performance in itself is competitive, but their attitude was not one of totally beating out the other person. Most entertainers take pleasure in performing. For Salt and Pepper and other African American performers of the Swing Era, having a job was the first goal. The fact that they had a job doing something they enjoyed was next to heaven. It was not that the dream of making movies, doing television, and having international fame was lacking, but for most African Americans of that time period such lofty goals appeared out of reach.

15

A Sweet Moment Slips Away

Everything has its time and place. The way of the world evolves; it builds on previous ideas, changes, and becomes anew. The Swing Era evolved from the call and response of enslaved peoples, the songs of the Blues, Marches, Ragtime, and Dixieland. It transformed through the Harlem Renaissance, the Great Depression, and World War II. It expressed the feeling of African Americans and the times. And by the early 1950s, the world had changed again, and so did its sound.

World War II provided an abundance of opportunities for African American entertainers to thrive. The public wanted relief from the sadness and anxiety of war, and live entertainment and movies provided a welcome distraction. Not only were performers hired for clubs and theaters, but many also had the opportunity to travel and become recognized through USO shows.

By the early 1950s, entertainment developed a different focus. The "full show" concept, where song, tap dance, comedy, music, exotic dance, and novelty were all held together by a theme or by a big-name band, dissolved. The idea of a concert in which the audience viewed only one genre or one star intrigued new audiences. As live entertainment in a full-show format came to an end, so did the fervor for tap dance. Although tap continued to be taught and performed, especially in the South, it was a symbol of Jim Crow for many African Americans. Public interest embraced modern jazz and social dances such as the jitterbug, the mambo, and the cha-cha. These dances became the new craze.

Music changed from Swing and Bebop to Rhythm and Blues, which evolved to Rock 'n' Roll (with a variety of cultural influences). Phonographs and records were affordable and marketed to teenagers. Record companies manufactured the 33-RPMs and 45s, which had better sound quality than 78s. The Big Band Era was dying out. Jukeboxes provided a variety of recorded music for a very low cost and were used in dance halls and private parties.[1]

The "song and dance" movies of early Hollywood dwindled. Other than *Singin' in the Rain* and a few Fred Astaire films, the style of dance in the movies changed to modern jazz and contemporary ballet. The movie industry used many innovative ideas to lure the public. As America fell in love with automobiles, drive-in theaters became popular. Wide-screen Cinerama and 3-D movies were introduced. There was even an attempt at Smellovision and Aromarama, where smells were released from theater seats to correlate with the setting of the movie scene.[2]

By 1955, nearly two-thirds of American households had a television.[3] This medium offered variety shows with musical numbers, comedy sketches, animal tricks, and so forth. With each TV show came stars from vaudeville, old Swing favorites, and movie stars. Some of the new television offerings included comedy-variety shows (e.g., *The Jack Benny Show*), personality-based shows (*Mr. Television*), Milton Berle's *Texaco Star Theatre*, Sid Caesar's *Your Show of Shows*, situation comedies (*I Love Lucy*), wild west shows (*The Lone Ranger*), news programs (Edward R. Murrow's *See It Now*), and children's programming (*The Howdy Doody Show*).[4]

Most tap dancers from the Swing Era blamed television for the end of their performing lives. But, with societal values changing so dramatically after World War II, nightclub and theater revue shows drew to an end. Audience attendance dwindled, and live entertainment funding was limited. The full show was reduced to a six-piece band or three-piece combo with one or two acts. Striving to hold audiences, nightclubs tried to feature Rock 'n' Roll entertainers, but these solo and group acts eventually filled stadiums. To stay alive, many nightclubs hired exotic/shake dancers. Thus, the clubs enabled a rise in strip shows, which started with partial nudity and provocative dancing and later progressed to unconcealed exhibition. Technology boomed, and in response to other changing views, the public chose to enjoy TV, which was less expensive and more of a family activity.[5]

By the early 1950s, the effects of the Government Issue Bill (GI Bill) were being experienced. Veterans Affairs (VA) loans were available, and the dream of homeownership became a reality for a predominantly white community. The suburban lifestyle surfaced, providing single-family housing with a private backyard, which had previously been a luxury reserved for the wealthy. It also became another segregation device as whites began to flee the cities. The automobile became a necessity as trolley cars were replaced by buses, and cars were needed to get to jobs from the suburbs. Between 1946 and 1964, 78.3 million babies were born and the American family structure changed. In many cases both parents worked, trying to provide their children with everything they were unable to have due to the Great Depression.

Even though African American newspapers from 1935 to the 1950s expressed pride in Joe Louis, Bill "Bojangles" Robinson, Duke Ellington, government leaders, and high society, the injustices experienced before, during and after World War II were mindboggling. While thousands of Black soldiers gave their lives for freedom in Japan, Germany and elsewhere throughout the world, the newspapers headlined murder, rape, and lynching in America. Despite the Emancipation Proclamation of 1862, the passage of the Thirteenth Amendment in 1865, and Roosevelt's New Deal in the 1930s, countless African Americans continued to live in poverty with little hope for the future. African American women experienced discrimination in the work force and continued to work mainly in agriculture, domestic service, and manufacturing.[6] The plight of the GIs and the poverty of the community sparked rage against white America. It was inevitable and justifiable.

The slavery and Jim Crow laws that camouflaged injustices for more than 300 years in the United States were finally abolished with the Civil Rights Act of 1964. Nevertheless, it wasn't until the late 1960s and 1970s that the effects of the civil rights movement started to be realized. African Americans were then allotted middle-class jobs with equal pay. Nonetheless, African American women, in particular, met barriers transitioning from domestic and menial positions with low salaries to jobs with a sustainable wage.

With the changes in entertainment, society, and values, many performers questioned their futures and struggled to find jobs in 1950s America.

The Effects of the Journey

The journey through the Swing Era with Edwina "Salt" Evelyn and Jewel "Pepper" Welch exemplified significant issues of the time—namely, the role of tap dance on the Swing Era stage, the status of African Americans, the role of women, and the effects of World War II. In addition to these broad historical issues, their story illuminated, often through their own words, how Salt and Pepper encountered these influences and created rewarding personal careers despite the injustices of the period.

Salt and Pepper, as African American women, looked daily into the ugly face of Jim Crow. They jumped the hurdles of racial discrimination, learning the tricks of moving in and out of white America without notice or personal harm. Throughout their travels, they were denied the right to eat, sleep, travel, and use public facilities allocated for white Americans. Though travel was usually by train or bus, the injustices observed and personally experienced were in themselves an education in humanity (or lack thereof). Nevertheless, both Salt and Pepper felt that travel was one of the greatest benefits of show business.

Based on their talent and determination, Salt and Pepper chose a life in show business and made a very good living from it. Without tap dance, however, they would never have had the opportunity, the money, or the right skin color to travel in the United States. In addition, there would have been many more obstacles for them to overcome without the sponsorship they received from agents and managers of the theaters and clubs in which they performed.

Through the many interviews that were conducted with African Americans who worked in show business during the Swing Era, it was evident that their relationships and mutual emotional support within their community were imperative for success. In responding to inquiries about opponents (such as "did you think you could dance better than so-and-so?" or "didn't you think you should have had top billing?"), their answers reflected an unexpected value system. Each performer was honest about his/her strengths and purpose. Each acknowledged those who were better or not so good, but never at the expense of another's character. Of course, every performer wanted to be at the top of the charts and enjoy stardom. But as African Americans, they supported each other and pooled their resources for the good of the community.

The bond in the African American community was strong, reflecting the history of Blacks in the United States. Many Swing Era performers had parents or grandparents who had survived enslavement; others had experienced the Great Migration. Socioeconomic backgrounds and education varied, and most developed their talents within their communities. The bond was essential to beat the system, for together they were all on the train for freedom, success, and the joys granted them in show business.

Salt and Pepper performed Rhythm Tap and Flash dance in what was considered a man's dance style, and they dressed accordingly. They were inspired by the rhythms of the Jazz Age and took the challenge of Flash movement reserved for men. The dance style, learned on the street, was based on friendly competition. A clever rhythm or a Flash step might beat others in the rivalry. Salt and Pepper knew that they could compete with the men and, in many cases, dance just as well (if not better). But the men usually received the higher billing. Edwina was not aware of the salaries of male tap dancers, nor did she expect to be paid equally. In the 1940s, all women were paid less than men and that has not changed much up to the present day.

As with many of the entertainers of the time, Salt and Pepper performed four to six shows a day. This was a matter of expending energy for a 15-minute full-out performance about every 60–90 minutes. Not only was this rise and fall of energy exhausting, but, as performers, their work also required flexibility in housing, travel, and working conditions.

In show business, private lives remained private, and many took the opportunity to explore their sexuality. Unless there was harm to another, different sexual lifestyles were accepted or ignored within the entertainment industry. It appears that sex did not have the same taboos for performers that it held in middle-class white America. For those African Americans who were gay or lesbians, show business was a haven from the judgment of their communities. The conflict was extremely intense. Homosexuality outside of show business was looked upon with disdain, since the stigma attached to it stunted efforts for liberty in a prejudiced America.

African American women appeared to be independent in show business. Their roles were determined by the degree of male dominance necessary for survival. For chorus girls, show girls, and exotic dancers, their purpose was to excite and sexually lure the male audience, which may have been a desired role for many. For Salt and Pepper, working as they did in a male-dominated art form, the skill and technique of the dance were their driving force. Also, as a female dance team, they were not subject to the constraints from male partners and/or choreographers.

A captivating point is that very few women tap dancers, whether married or single, had children. The reasons are probably as varied as each personality, but it is a phenomenon that has continued into the twenty-first century.

Tap dance and its performance were the factors that drove many dancers to accept a life on the road. Salt and Pepper were passionate about the dance form. They were not chorus girls. They were headliners, principals, featured performers. It was stardom! Their roles secured their self-worth and gave them the confidence necessary to take on the world. They enjoyed the simple pleasures of backstage life, which included laughter, playing tricks, card games, and the personalities of each unique performer.

Although drugs, alcohol, and "the wild life" surrounded them in the world of show business, Salt and Pepper remained focused on their work and connected with friends of similar values. That does not mean that they didn't enjoy the pleasures of show business. But Salt, in particular, had high standards and values, and she was able to save money, which prepared her for a stable life after show business.

Although white audiences delighted in Black entertainment and the freedom it appeared to offer, socializing with African Americans was prohibited. Moreover, whites took what they wanted from the African American community for their own benefit. This exploitation included (but was not limited to) talent, music, dance, and women. Many African Americans were suppressed and controlled in the world of entertainment. The white establishment, which was in control, functioned from the mindset of ownership, a remnant of the slavery system, which still shows its ugly head even today.

A theme for Salt and Pepper, as well as others who were interviewed, was one of "do what you have to do to make a living." If mugging[7] would excite a white audience, they mugged. If sitting for lunch on the grass was the only "restaurant" available, they ate on the grass. If moving through the world without drawing attention to themselves was required, they moved quietly. They were not sponsored by the NAACP (National Association for the Advancement of Colored People) to change viewpoints or laws. They were basically on their own. Edwina's philosophy was "We came down to make a living, not to change the Constitution." This is not to say that civil rights were not important, but, as two young women traveling together, they wanted to be safe because they knew the horrors that could result from a lack of caution.

As the sweet moments slipped away, the 1950s ushered in an era with new amusements, a new sound, and an aesthetic change in entertainment.

Epilogue:
What Do We Do Now?

Nightclub shows, theater productions, and the Big Band Era came to an end. Salt affirmed that she and Pepper stopped dancing in 1953. In Salt's scrapbook, there was an advertisement and write-up for a two-night-gig at the Zebra Lounge (one of their final mentions in print). The *New York Age*[1] stated, "Rhythmic Seasonings: That's the stuff winsome Edwina Evelyn (she is the little one) gives out with her dancing feet at the Zebra Lounge. Edwina, a half of the Salt and Pepper dance team, is holding down the fort while her partner, Jewell Welch, is recovering from a recent illness."

For Salt and Pepper, the major reason to terminate the partnership was Pepper's health. Salt said,

> Her heart began to fail. That's why we stopped dancing. I said, "Pepper, you're not going to be able to continue this grind traveling and dancing." She was a real trooper, but every so often she started going to the hospital. She was born with this hole in her heart. When her feet used to swell, every once in a while, we used to have to take perhaps six weeks off ... for the swelling to go down. We went to the hospital with her, her mother, all of us together. We'd say, "How can she do this dancing with a hole in her heart?" The doctor said, "[It's] because her heart is so accustomed to it that it doesn't affect it." But eventually as she got older it took its toll.

In the sweetest, most caring voice, Salt completed her thought: "You know, we had such a nice career together, and I didn't want to perform without Pepper. We had that kind of bondage and that togetherness. So I said it was a nice career, a very nice career. So that was enough."

Leaving show business was devastating for Pepper. It was a great job that gave her a good salary and the adulation she thrived on. It may have been one of the reasons that she appeared to live in the glory of the past.

For many of the chorus girls as well as for Pepper, barmaid jobs offered a decent salary and contact with the public, which had been part of their lives on stage. Pepper stayed in New York for three years, working as a barmaid at Hartie's MidWay Tavern, 458 E. 165th Street in the Bronx. (It was owned by Hartie and Johnny Pearson.)[2] She later returned to Philadelphia, where she worked on an assembly line in a lamp factory.

Pepper and Dollye Lewis shared an apartment in the Bronx. Pepper and Dollye were very good friends, but the nature of their relationship is not certain. Pepper had several women in whom she was interested, but no relationship lasted. Salt believed that Pepper had difficulty trusting others because of her troubled childhood. Unfortunately, Pepper didn't know that her mother gave her to relatives until very late in her life. She only knew that she was tossed from one relative to another as a young child. Therefore, her lack of trust in others could have stemmed from her earliest years.

It appears that Pepper and Candi acknowledged their sexuality as teenagers. They were interested and emotionally moved by other women. Edwina (Salt), however, didn't seem to have or didn't discuss interests in women. She dated and was engaged to Larry, who was the cook on the Pennsylvania Railroad. She seemed to have good relationships with men. Yet, when Edythe Robinson came into her life in the mid–1940s, they fell in love.

Edythe joined the Catholic Church with Edwina's mother in the role of godmother. Through this relationship, Edwina referred to Edythe as her sister or cousin. The two were life partners, but, because of the times, Edwina and Edythe lived closeted for 48 years.

Edythe, one of five children, was born September 21, 1916, in New Haven, Connecticut. Her relationships with men were devastating, as she was raped as a young girl and had a difficult association with Ed Brown. From the latter relationship, Edythe had one child, Bruce Nelson Robinson, born April 22, 1936, in New Haven. To care for her son, Edythe worked as a cook in a restaurant until she was 28 years old. She

Edwina Evelyn and partner Edythe Robinson.

and Bruce then moved to New York, where she got a job with the telephone company and worked for 30 years.

Edwina (Salt) and Edythe moved into a two-room apartment in a Harlem brownstone with a shared bathroom down the hall. Due to their lesbian relationship, Edythe's family pressured her to make a choice about Bruce's future. In the 1940s, homosexuality was considered immoral, a crime and/or a disease. Most gays and lesbians were closeted for their own protection. The family didn't want Bruce to live in that environment and thought it was best for him to live with his grandmother and his Aunt Lillian in New Haven. Edythe reluctantly let him go when he was about 10 years old. Giving up her son was a matter that she was never able to resolve.[3]

Edythe's son Bruce finished his high school education in the service. He went on to study at Dillard University and Xavier University in New Orleans, where he met his wife, Sylvia Ann Foucher. They had four children: daughter Pier Robinson and sons Dr. Kelly Robinson, Neil Robinson and Bruce Michael Robinson. Bruce completed his doctorate in economics, and he went on to teach and work as a member of several college boards in some of the most prestigious schools in the Philadelphia area. While serving as the associate director of the Peace Corps in Abidjan, Ivory Coast, West Africa, Dr. Bruce Robinson was killed in a car accident in February 9, 1970.[4]

When Edwina retired from show business in 1953, she got a job as an elevator operator, becoming the first African American to hold that job at the Fifth Avenue Hotel. She worked there until 1964. She then worked in the civil service for 20 years, operating an elevator in a federal court building in New York City. The job "elevator girl" required a uniform with white gloves. On the outside of the elevator were two steel doors, and on the inside was a brass grill accordion door. With her distinctive white gloves, the elevator girl would open both doors, announcing the floor number and what offices were on each floor. Edwina claimed that she was happy for the work and felt like she was paid a fair salary with a retirement fund. Her most impressive elevator rider was Angela Davis, a political activist during the civil rights movement. Edwina explained that it wasn't a joy ride for Davis, since she had been arrested and jailed. Based on Edwina's intelligence, knowledge, and experience, this employment would appear to be a humdrum job. Yet, despite the circumstances in which African American women found themselves, Edwina's attitude was always positive. She had a job, received the contracted money, and lived a peaceful, happy life.

Edwina had strong opinions about equality, and though there were long roads to travel, she felt that African Americans had made progress. She supported the civil rights movement but did not discuss her participation.

By working in the federal court building in New York, she became exposed to both the positive and the negative changes in society. She expressed some of her concerns:

> Those things, I think, are missing in this generation. We had respect for each other. We had respect for uniforms. We had respect for our neighbors. We had respect for our elders. We had respect for our teachers. It was different altogether. We were more afraid of our neighbors telling our mothers if we were sitting on the stoop after 10 o'clock.... It's a thin line between abuse and discipline.... What we use to call discipline they now call

abuse. And coming out of family court those are the worst cases in the world ... tragic cases because it involves a family.

Together, Edwina and Edythe did well financially. They moved to Greenwich Village and also owned two houses in upstate New York. Their time Upstate was spent with their family, as well as neighbors Mabel and her daughter Ruth. Edwina played the piano and sang while Edythe cooked for their company. They played cards, laughed, told stories, and played jokes on each other.

Edwina and her sisters Ivy and Edith Yvonne visited Atlantic City for dinner and playing the slot machines several times a month. Edwina said that they went for the exercise—"pulling the one-arm bandit" (the slot machine).

Edwina and Edythe were supporters of many who were in need. At times, relatives and friends stayed in their home until they were able to make it on their own. They seemed to always provide for the best interest of others both emotionally and financially. They were stable, loving and classy women.

Family Reunion

For more than 30 years, the Evelyns saluted their family with an annual reunion. Over 200 people met to share memories and keep their heritage alive. The document of the family history was called "The Whaler." Edwina's grandfather on her mother's side was Robert H. Coblins, a prominent man from St. Eustatius of the Dutch West Indies who arrived in New Bedford, Massachusetts, in 1881. Her grandmother was Elizabeth Rebecca Hall from the Virgin Islands, who moved to Washington, D.C., around 1884. Robert and Elizabeth married and had four daughters and one son: Florence Ramsey (1886–1943); Christina (1894–1963), who was Edwina's mother; Maria (1887–1955); Ethel Louise; and Victor (1899–1913), who was drowned in Westport, Massachusetts, on a fishing trip at 14 years old.

Christina Coblins married John Edward Eëvelyn, who came to the United States from Roseau, Dominica, in the French West Indies. When Eëvelyn came to the United States, he dropped the second "e" in his name as well as the umlaut. Thereafter, his name became John Edward Evelyn. He worked as the first African American sea captain off New Bedford, Massachusetts, and New London, Connecticut. Christina was a professional pianist, who spread her love of the arts to her children. The family was highly accomplished. At the reunions, they celebrated their many achievements in the United States.

Candi and Pepper

During the summer of 1990, Pepper made contact with Candi, her earlier dance partner. After having been separated for 47 years, they met in Elwood, New Jersey, where Candi lived with her sister Thelma and brother-in-law George Taylor.

After Candi and Pepper embraced, their conversation flowed as if there had been no passage of time. There were a few references to the good old days, but these women in their 70s mainly discussed their lives and their ailments. Candi had several bouts with breast cancer that were treated with radiation and a mastectomy. After her show business career ended, Candi had worked as a bartender, taking several odd jobs over the years, and she worked in the Atlantic City area as a dishwasher in 1990. She was in great spirits and had a positive, independent attitude.

Honors

In 1987, researcher Delilah Jackson produced *A Salute to the Harlem Opera House* in the Kaufmann Theatre, which honored Edwina and other stars for their contributions to the entertainment field. Edwina was thrilled—it was the first time since she had retired from show business 33 years earlier that she had been acknowledged. Regrettably, Pepper's name was not mentioned.

In September 1990, Geri Kennedy organized an elaborate tribute to honor the African American women who danced during the Swing Era, titled *For Dancers Only*. Kennedy was the manager of the Silver Belles, a reunited group of the original chorus girls of the Apollo Theatre and the Cotton Club. She acknowledged the Silver Belles and other women dancers of the period, including Edwina, Pepper, and Candi. (The event also celebrated Mother Hale, founder of the Hale House, which was a home for orphaned and unwanted children and those born addicted to drugs.)

For Dancers Only, which included a cocktail hour, dinner, and floor show, was held at the Marriott Marquis on 46th and Broadway in New York City. The doors opened to an elegant ballroom with several hundred people dressed in sequins, rhinestones, and the fineries of show business. The entertainment featured the Silver Belles, as well as Sister Sledge (the members of which were Geri Kennedy's nieces, Debbie, Kathy, Kim and Joni), who sang "We Are Family." Several tap dancers and comedians also performed. Edwina, Pepper, and Candi went on stage for the Shim Sham finale. The rest of the evening was spent taking pictures with Edwina's family; Sister Sledge; Sammy Davis, Jr.'s mother, "Baby Sanchez"; Marion Coles; and the Silver Belles.

Candi felt that this event honored the people who made it possible for other African Americans to move ahead in show business. They were the trailblazers. Candi and Pepper's hearts were filled with joy, laughter, and pride as they said their goodbyes and headed home.

Author's Notes—On a Personal Side

At the conclusion of my doctoral work, I presented a small lecture/demonstration at Temple University on October 4, 1991. Dianne Walker and Germaine Ingram were the featured tap dancers. In the audience were Swing Era dancers Jewel "Pepper" Welch, Edith "Baby Edwards" Hunt, Isabelle "Eleanor Byrd" Fambro, and Libby Spencer.

As Walker and Ingram discussed their roles in tap dance, the Swing Era dancers were called upon to answer questions and do a little performance. Pepper was so proud to have the opportunity to "strut her stuff." I presented a copy of my work to Pepper, Baby Edwards and Isabelle Fambro, who were subjects of my dissertation. Pepper embraced the book as if she had won an Academy Award. It was her final hurrah and, hugging the book, she danced herself up Broad Street.

After graduating from Temple University, I began my job search. Pepper enjoyed my company and the support I offered her as a friend. She definitely didn't want me to leave Philadelphia. Pepper insisted that she would go to the church to "light a candle" and pray for my job. I'm not sure what she prayed for, but I didn't get any of the jobs for which I interviewed. I finally had two interviews without telling Pepper and was offered a contract from each.

On Easter Sunday, Isabelle Fambro had a party. I offered to take Pepper to the gathering, but she said that she wasn't feeling well and didn't want to come. On Tuesday afternoon, Edwina called to say that Pepper had gone to the hospital on Sunday and passed away Tuesday morning, April 21, 1992. I was stunned. I knew she had a pacemaker, but I never realized how sick she was.

I went to the funeral home and asked to view her body. The lady escorted me down the cold hall and opened the door to where Pepper was lying. She took the sheet off Pepper's face, and I burst into tears. I said, "Her hair is white. Pepper didn't want anyone to know how old she was. That's why she dyed her hair with Grecian Formula." The lady apologized and chuckled at the same time.

It was the saddest and emptiest feeling I had ever had. I realized that Pepper was totally alone in her life and in her death. I sobbed for her for a long time. She was cremated the next morning.

There was a memorial service for Pepper on her birthday, May 23, 1992. It was held at Holy Child Catholic Church, 5200 N. Broad Street. Several friends and relatives attended the simple service. After memories and reflections by friends, Father Leone commented that he had known Pepper since she joined the Catholic Church. He said that she was quite a character, and he would remember her as the person who came to him every week asking for a few dollars to play the numbers for him. Father Leone added that he always knew when she had a hit, because he wouldn't see her for weeks. The ceremony concluded with an upbeat version of "When the Saints Go Marching In" sung by Sharon Powell Ross.

Pepper was quite a character with a big heart, an energetic laugh, and a free lifestyle.

Although I was unable to get her on the *Oprah Winfrey Show*, it is hoped that she will appreciate her memory and her stardom being honored in this work.

Candi

Candi Thorpe lived in Elwood, New Jersey, with her sister Thelma, who passed from cancer. George, Candi's brother-in-law, who was in a wheelchair, needed additional help. Candi, therefore, moved to a senior citizen apartment in Egg Harbor. She seemed happy with her new friends and visits from her godchild, Latesha Frazier. Candi had many bouts with cancer and developed problems with her heart.

Over the years, Candi and I talked often, and she wrote letters keeping me updated on her progress. A friend of mine who owned a rare bookstore found pictures of some women tap dancers, which she gave me. The photos were action shots of "Candi and Pepper" dancing. I had them blown up and sent to Candi. She had never seen the pictures and was thrilled to receive them. She said that she didn't have any pictures of herself from the years when she danced. We stayed close over the years; yet I didn't realize the importance of our relationship until many years after her passing.

Candi was so positive about life and passed that attitude on to everyone she met. One of her strongest characteristics was that she knew how to make all her stories hysterical! She could keep you laughing for hours.

Candi died on April 18, 1998.

Edwina

On November 13, 1993, Edwina lost Edythe Robinson, her beloved partner of 48 years. Edwina's life was turned upside down, but, in her usual private manner, she rarely discussed her pain. Nevertheless, she seemed lost for a while and focused on her sister Ivy, who had glaucoma. She walked to the Bowery daily to take care of Ivy's needs, especially after realizing that Ivy's caretaker of many years had been stealing Ivy's jewelry and other small but valuable items. Edwina's other sister, Edith, who lived in the Bronx, also started to decline, but, in her stylish manner, she drove a bright red scooter and hired a limo driver when she visited Edwina. By 2009, Edwina had lost most of her brothers and sisters, with whom she was very close. Her only remaining brother, Donald, died December 14, 2010, just a month before her. Edwina continued to live alone, but she had many friends, family members, and visitors.

Edwina was ultimately diagnosed with lung cancer. She then resided with Edythe's niece, Vernita McNeil, who cared for her. Edwina passed on Wednesday, January 26, 2011.

Tribute

This book is dedicated to Edwina "Salt" Evelyn. My intention is to represent Edwina's spirit and to add to her legacy as an African American woman tap dance star who performed during the Swing Era. Her pioneering spirit paved the way for a new generation of women tap dancers and performers. Edwina was independent long before the women's liberation movement of the 1960s. She ventured out as a dancer on the road of life, encountering new, frightening, and exciting situations. As an African American woman, she knew how to maneuver around racial obstacles to achieve her goals and make a successful living. She was intelligent, and, although financially unable to receive a college education as a young woman, she opened herself to learning and to knowing the world. Edwina had a wonderful life with Edythe Robinson during a time when the discussion of a lesbian lifestyle was taboo and disdainfully viewed by the African American community.

Edwina coped with loss and disappointment throughout her life but remained positive; experienced fame, yet remained humble; gave generously but anonymously; and possessed strong values but did not impose them on others. She was gracious and loving ... and she was my friend.

Appendix I

Schedule of Performances

This schedule of performances serves as a partial itinerary for Salt and Pepper as a team, performing both with other dance partners and as a solo act. It offers a general timetable of dates, cities, clubs and theaters in which they performed. The performers on the playbills are listed to preserve their legacies.

Jewel "Pepper" Welch

1937: Week of July 16, Irene's Café, 2200 Ridge Avenue, Philadelphia, PA, advertised as "Exclusively Colored Ownership"; Two Shows Nitely—Blue Matinee from 3 Until 8:00 p.m. (*Philadelphia Independent*, July 16, 1937, 16)
  Featuring **Pepper Welch** (Tap Dancer)   Bobby Bell
  Armstrong Melody Lads, Orchestra   Art, Rucker and Bowie at Bar
  Elease Hamilton

1939: Week of October 22, Hi-Hat Club, Lawnside, NJ (*Philadelphia Independent*, October 22, 1939, 16)
  Mable Furley, Lula Mae and **Pepper Welsh**

1940: Week of Friday, March 2, Apollo Theatre, 253 W. 125th Street, Harlem, NY (Advertisement from Jewel "Pepper" Welch's Collection)
  Staged by Leonard Harper and Sherman Dudley   Thomas Wilson
     Candi and Pepper
  Bardu Ali and his Orchestra   The Nortons
  Movie on Screen: *Gang War*

1940: Possibly weeks of April 14–May 4, O. V. Catto Lodge Auditorium No. 29, I. B. P. O. E. of W Downstairs Grille, 16th and Fitzwater, Philadelphia, PA (*Philadelphia Independent*, April 14, 1940, 17)
  Slappy and his Swingers   Dot Jackson
  Candy and Pepper   Lyle Smith
  Woodrow Wilson, Skate Artist   Bobby Vinson
  Franses Alexander, Torch Singer   Billy Johnson, emcee
  Helen Penn

1940: Buffalo, NY (Advertisement from Jewel "Pepper" Welch's Collection)
  Louis Satchmo Armstrong   **Candi & Pepper**
  Midge Williams   Big Time Crip
  Sonny Woods   Stump & Stumpy
  Luis Russell
  Movie on Screen: *Dr. Kildare's Strange Case*

1941: Week of Friday, January 3, Apollo Theatre, 253 W. 125th Street, Harlem, NY (Advertisement from Jewel "Pepper" Welch's Collection)
  Count Basie and his Band   **Candy and Pepper**—Prides of Philadelphia
  Jimmie Rushing   Henry Wessel–John Mason
  Helen Humes   Jimmie Baskette–Sandy Burns
  Happy, Pal and Pete—Two Men and a Mule   Beautiful Apollo Chorus
  Two Lucky Bucks—First Appearance a
   Dance Novelty

1941: Week of Friday, September 19, Apollo Theatre, 253 W. 125th Street, Harlem, NY (Advertisement from Jewel "Pepper" Welch's Collection)
    "Fats" Waller and his Great Band   **Candy & Pepper**—Superlative Tappers
    Apus & Estrelita—Fun, Melody, Dance   Sinclair & Leroy—Unrivalled Youngsters
    Myra Johnson—Great Blues Singer

1942: Week of Friday, January 17, Apollo Theatre, 253 W. 125th Street, Harlem, NY (*Chicago Defender*, January 17, 1942)
    Sweethearts of Rhythm   McGinty and Perkins
    Jackie Mabley   Six Abdullah Girls
    Brown Sisters   And a supporting Cast of Headliners
    Candy and Pepper

1942: Weeks of June 27–August 28, The New Small's Paradise in New Paradise Room, 13th Street and 7th Avenue, Harlem, NY (*Amsterdam News*, June 27; July 4, 11, 25; August 1, 8, 15, 22) Small's *Swings South*
    Jimmie Mordecal, MC   Tondelayo and Lopez
    Claudia McNeil   Dolores Brown
    Candy & Pepper   Earl Bostic and His Earls of Rhythm
    Otto Eason

1943: ca. March 28, Chicago, IL (*Chicago Defender*, April 3, 1943)
    Pepper Welch stopped on tour to West Coast

1943: Weeks of October 30–December 4, Elk's Rendezvous, Chicago, IL (*The New Amsterdam News*, October 30; November 6, 13, 20, 27; December 4, 1943) *Harlem to Hollywood*
    Ralph Cooper, MC   Manhattan Paul
    Gertrude Saunders   Willie Lewis
    Gwen Reid   **Pepper Welch**
    Neal & Hutchie   The Rendezvouettes Chorus
    Pauline Brtant   Herman Flintall's Orchestra

Edwina Evelyn and Ann (Anne) Baxter

1941: Beginning week of May 2 and 9, Harlem's Hollywood Cabaret, 105 W. 115th Street, Between 7th and Lenox Avenue, Harlem, NY 2 Shows: 12 and 2 a.m. Cont. entertainment Monday to Thursday (Advertisement from Edwina "Salt" Evelyn's Scrapbook)
    Becky Harding, Mistress of Ceremonies   Jewel Paige
    Lorenso Robernson   **Edwina & Anna**
    Claudia Wheeler   Jimmy Reynolds Band
    Yona

1942: Week of Friday, March 6, Apollo Theatre, 253 W. 125th Street, Harlem, NY (Advertisement from Edwina "Salt" Evelyn's Scrapbook)
    "Fats" Waller and his Band   Three Shades of Rhythm
    Burnham, Harris and Scott—one of the   Fred and his Football Dogs
        best trios in show business   **Evelyn and Ann**—cute tap duo
    Myra Johnson—blues singer   Leonard Harper's Dancing Girls and Boys
    Movie on Screen: *Public Enemies*

1942: Week of Friday, March 20, Royal Theatre, Baltimore, MD (Advertisement from Edwina "Salt" Evelyn's Scrapbook)
    International Sweethearts of Rhythm   The Co-Eds
        Orchestra—18 Queens of Swing   **Edwina and Anne**
    Jean Sparks—Dynamic Band Leader   Perkins & Mandy Lou
    5 Juggling Jules   Ann Lewis

1942: Week of Friday, April 3, Paradise Theatre, Detroit, MI (Advertisement from Edwina "Salt" Evelyn's Scrapbook)
    Lucky Millinder and his Recording   Sister Rosita Tharp—Recording Artist
        Orchestra   **Ann and Edwina**—Two girl novelty
    Trevor Bacon—Guitarist and singer   dancing team
    Berry Brothers—M-G-M *Lady Be Good*

Schedule of Performances

1942: Beginning July 18, Harlem's Hollywood Cabaret, 105 W. 115th Street, Between 7th and Lenox Avenue, Harlem, NY (Advertisement from Edwina "Salt" Evelyn's Scrapbook)
    Boots (Lee) Marshall—Comedian, MC
    Marion Hairsten—Sweet Singer
    Edwina & Anna—Dance Team
    Jean Daniels—Swing Songstress
    Claudia Wheeler

1942: Date Unknown, Harlem's Hollywood Cabaret, 105 West 116th Street, Harlem, NY (Advertisement from Edwina "Salt" Evelyn's Scrapbook)
    Lorenso Robernson
    Claudia Wheeler
    Boots Marshall
    Chiquita
    Edwina and Anna
    Jimmy Reynolds and Orchestra

Edwina Evelyn—Solo

1942: Weeks of October 17–29, Harlem's Hollywood Cabaret, 105 West 116th Street, Harlem, NY (*New York Amsterdam News*, October 17 and 24, 1942)
    Lee (Boots) Marshall, Comedian, M.C.
    Ann Brown
    Jewel Paige—Singer
    Delores Miner
    Gussie Washington
    Edwina

1942: Week of December 5, Kelly's Stables, 137 W. 52nd Street, New York City at the Gateway to Swing Lane (Advertisement from Edwina "Salt" Evelyn's Scrapbook)
    Shirley Lloyd—Former Singer of Ozzie Nelson's Orchestra
    Dorothy Manners—Up & Coming Personalty
    Iris Ray—Interpretations
    Edwina—"TAPS in RIFT"
    Jewel Granger—"Top Hat in Taps"
    The Nat Jaffe Trio
    Joan Lee
    Phyllis Arnold
    Julie Moss
    The Cotton Pickers

1943: Date Unknown, Hall's Savoy Nite Club, 1108 Springwood Avenue, Asbury Park, NJ (Advertisement from Edwina "Salt" Evelyn's Scrapbook)
    LaZonda—Exotic Dancer
    Edwina—Lady of Taps
    Baby Hines from Café Society
    Sam Theard—Master of Ceremonies
    Ruth Warner—Torch Singer
    Lacy Wharton and his Swing Band—Direct from Boston

1943: Date Unknown, Stardust, 4th and Virginia Avenue, SW, Washington, D.C. (Advertisement from Edwina "Salt" Evelyn's Scrapbook) *A New Show of Stars*
    Gertrude Saunders—New York Songbird
    Kay Hedgeman in her Versatile Style
    Johnnie Bragg, Singing M.C.
    Cheers and Jerrie in a Passion Dance
    Edwina—Sensational Tap Artist

1943: Date Unknown, Stardust, 4th and Virginia Avenue, SW, Washington, D.C. (Advertisement from Edwina "Salt" Evelyn's Scrapbook) *A New Show of Stars*
    Gertrude Saunders—Songbird
    Kay Hedgeman in her Versatile Style
    Cheers and Connie in Beach Coma
    Edwina—Sensational Tap Artist

1943: Tuesday, June 22, Stardust, 4th and Virginia Avenue, SW, Washington, D.C. (Advertisement from Edwina "Salt" Evelyn's Scrapbook) *A New Show of Stars*
    Cora Green—Singer
    Myrtle Hawkins—Shake Dancer Superb
    Billy Cheers—Everybody's Favorite
    Johnnie Bragg, Singing M.C.
    Kay Hedgeman in her Versatile Style
    Edwina—Tops in Taps

1943: Sunday, July 4, Amphitheatre, Washington, D.C., Special Service Office Presents: Gala All Star Afternoon Club Matinee (Advertisement from Edwina "Salt" Evelyn's Scrapbook)
    Clubs involved in the production:
    Music by Billy White
    Off Beat: Marshall Haley—Lyric Tenor, Marie Ricardo—"The Blues Lady," Ester Gardiner—Singer Deluxe
    Crystal Gardens: "Two queens of Swing" Bea Morton and Betty Logan
    Club Bali: Smith Sisters—Dance Team and Monette Moore—"Call the Police Girl"
    Club Stardust: **Edwina Evelyn**—Tap Dancer, Kay Hedgeman—Blues Singer, "Fats" Pinier
    Cocktail Clores Lounge: Doris Knighton and Geo. Kraft—Sensational M.C.
    Republic Gardes: "Toto" Ellington, Streamline Sue, Smitty & Dotty, and Jimmie Mordecai M.C. (Jazz Tap Dancer)

1943: Date Unknown: Talent Night: Moors Syncopators and the Stardust in Review, Washington, D.C, Manager Mr. Frank Moor, Courtesy of U.S.O. Rec. Center and Vivian Reynolds. (Advertisement from Edwina "Salt" Evelyn's Scrapbook)

    Johnnie Bragg, M.C.   Kay Hedgmon—Vocalist
    Miss Gertrude Saunders—Soloist   Johnnie Cheers—Comedian
    Jerry Martin—Dancer   **Edwina**—Dancer

1943: Weeks of September 18–October 24, Elk's Rendezvous, 133rd Street & Lenox Avenue, Harlem, NY (*Amsterdam News*, September 9; October 2 and 16, 1943)

    Ralph Cooper—Star of Stage, Screen Radio   Cousin Ida—Twentieth Century Comedienne
    Warren Evans—"Baby don't You Cry"   Manhattan Paul—Harlem's Glamour Boy
    Moore and Larry—Continental Favorites   **Edwina Evelyn**—Precision in Taps
    Jimmy Smith—A World Wonder   Copper Tan Rendezvouettes
    Ann Robinson—Hit star of "New Faces—1943"

Salt and Pepper

1944: Week of Friday, January 8, Apollo Theatre, 253 W. 125th Street, Harlem, NY (Advertisement from Edwina "Salt" Evelyn's Scrapbook)

    Erskine Hawkins and his Band   2 Swing Maniacs
    Jimmie Mitchell   **Salt and Pepper**
    Effie Smith   Tim and Vivian
    The Kimmys

1944: Week of Friday, January 15, Apollo Theatre, 253 W. 125th Street, Harlem, NY (Advertisement from Edwina "Salt" Evelyn's Scrapbook)

    Louis Jordan and his Typany Five   **Salt & Pepper**
    "Hot Lips" Page and his Band   And Other Headliners
    Gertrude Saunders

1944: Weeks of February 25–April 8, Elk's Rendezvous, 133rd Street & Lenox Avenue, Harlem, NY (Advertisement from Edwina "Salt" Evelyn's Scrapbook)

    Ralph Cooper   Joi-La-Joy
    Warren Evans   Manhattan Paul
    Salt & Pepper   Betty Mays
    Dolly Pembrook   The Rendezvouettes
    Baby Hines   Herman Flintall's Orchestra

1944: Week of April 14, Gayety Theatre, 513 9th Street, NW, Washington, D.C. (Advertisement from Edwina "Salt" Evelyn's Scrapbook) *Harlem Follies:* 2 act 20 scenes

    Glen & Jenkins   Susie Brown
    Brown and Lee   **Salt and Pepper**
    Bati & Tuffy   Boogie & Woogie
    Four Crackerjacks   Derby Wilson and Frenchy
    5 Cabineers   Lavada Snow
    Jig-saw Jackson   Winters and Morane
    Jessie James

1944: Week of May 13, Club Bali, 1901 14th Street, NW, Washington, D.C. Sherman Dudley Production (Advertisement from Edwina "Salt" Evelyn's Scrapbook) *Harlem's Poppin'*

    Willie Bryant—Unique style of singing "Chicken Ain't Nothing But a Bird"   Audrey Thomas—Singing of "Minnie the Moocher"
    Apus and Estrellita—Whose odd gestures and dancing are par excellent   Jigsaw Jackson—New act, rolling over like a hoop, head foremost
    Salt and Pepper—Dressed in white short coats and pants, tapping their way to thunderous applauses   Helen Penn and her Pennettes
        Coleridge Davis and His Hardy Brothers Washingtonians

1944: June 14, Club Bali, Farewell Party for **Salt and Pepper**, Washington, D.C. (Invitation from Edwina "Salt" Evelyn's Scrapbook)

    Farewell Party for "Salt and Pepper"
    That Great Act that stayed at the Bali so long. Solid!!
    At the Hole on 14th Street "Coolest Spot in Town!"
    On Sunday—June 4th, 1944

Schedule of Performances

From 10 til 2 Chicken & Chitterlings a Plenty
Entrée—A lovely way to Spend the evening

1944: Weeks of October 6–29, Rhumboogie, 343 E. Garfield, Chicago, IL (Advertisement from Edwina "Salt" Evelyn's Scrapbook) *New Autumn Revue*

Charlie Glenn's Rhumboogie is drawing all the raves since the arrival of "Salt and Pepper" to aid T-Bone Walker in make the show the hottest thing to reach the rialto in weeks.

- T-Bone Walker
- Marl Young and Orchestra
- George Layne—Singer deluxe
- Phyllis Smiley—Fine vocalizing
- **Salt and Pepper**
- Snookum Marsh—Comedian in song and dance

Rhumboogie Belles: Edith Bailey, Willa Harris, Stella Morrell, Ernestine Holloway, Juanita Hall, Sally Jones, Marie Clemons, Daisy Richards, Marian Green and Mildred Whitlow

1944: Week of November 17, Rhumboogie, 343 Garfield, Chicago, IL (This show appears to have run several times with slightly different casts.) (Advertisement from Edwina "Salt" Evelyn's Scrapbook)

- Wynonnie (Mr. Blues) Harris—The Hurry, Hurry Blues Man
- **Salt and Pepper**—Queens of Taps
- "Iron Jaw" Wilson—Table Lifting Dancer
- Phyliss Smiley—Song Stylist
- George Layne—Star Baritone
- Mildred Whitlow—Shake Dancer
- Marl Young's Orchestra
- 10—Dancing Girls—10
- 6—Dancing Boys—6

1944: ca. December 22, Howard Theatre, Washington, D.C. (Advertisement from Edwina "Salt" Evelyn's Scrapbook)

- Earl Hines—King of the Ivories and His Mighty Orchestra
- Janie Moses, Lady of Song
- Essie Scott—Personality Plus
- Ford, Harris and Jones
- Four Mello-Tones
- **Salt and Pepper**

Movie on Screen: *The Falcon Out West*

1944: Week of December 29, Royal Theatre, Baltimore, MD (Advertisement from Edwina "Salt" Evelyn's Scrapbook) *It's a Happy New Year Show:*

- Earl "Fatha" Hines and his Sensational Orchestra
- **Salt and Pepper**
- Janie Moses
- Arthur Walker
- 4 Mel-O-Tones
- Ford–Harris–Jones

Movie on Screen: *Cry of the Werewolf*

1945: Week of Friday, January 5, Apollo Theater, 253 W. 125th Street, Harlem, NY (Advertisement from Edwina "Salt" Evelyn's Scrapbook)

- Earl "Father" Hines and his Band and Revue
- Ford Harris & Jones
- **Salt and Pepper**
- Janie Moses
- Arthur Walker
- 4 Mello-Tones
- Lord Essex
- Red Lyons

1945: Weeks of February 2–8, National Theatre, Louisville, KY (Advertisement from Edwina "Salt" Evelyn's Scrapbook) *Harlem Revue*

- Earl "Fatha" Hines and his Orchestra
- Betty Roche
- Jesse Perry
- Mello Tones
- **Salt & Pepper***
- Ford, Harris, Jones

Movie on Screen: *Enemy of Women*

*It appears that Salt & Pepper were not present for opening on February 2, which could have been due to weather conditions

1945: Weeks of February 23–28, Club Bali, 1901 14th Street, NW, Washington, D.C. *Cats and the Fiddle*—No. 3 in 1945 Parade of Stars (Advertisement from Edwina "Salt" Evelyn's Scrapbook)

- **Salt and Pepper**
- Billy Mitchell
- Del St. John
- Lovi Lane
- Colerdige Davis and his Band
- The Baliettes

Starting February 26, All Clubs Close at 12:00 a.m., Every Night

1945: Discrepancy in Advertisements: Week of February 23, Club Bali, 1901 14th Street, NW, Washington, D.C. (Advertisement from Edwina "Salt" Evelyn's Scrapbook) *Jumpin At the Bali*, S. H. Dudley Production

- Baby Banks—Dancing doll
- **Salt and Pepper**—Ace Tap-Steppers

Lovi Lane—Exotic dancer
Del St. John—Jump songsters
Billy Mitchell—Comic Cut-up supreme

Balliettes—Nations Best Dressed Girls
Coleridge Davis and His Hardy Brothers
Washingtonians

1945: Date Unknown, Lincoln Theatre, Broad & Lombard Streets, Philadelphia, PA Staged by Leonard Harper and Sherman Dudley (Article from Edwina "Salt" Evelyn's Scrapbook) *Born to Swing*, an Irvin C. Miller Production

Tim Moore
Eddie Rector
Fay Canty
June Redd
"Rookie" Davis
Funny Bone Ferebee
Phil Gomez

Joseph & Johnson—Hot Steppers
Salt & Pepper—A-1 Dancers
Dixiana Trio, Margaret Simms, Vivian Eley, Virginia Robinson
Fritz Pollard's Sun Tan Gals Deluxe
Bernie's Symphonic Swingsters
"Rookie" Davis Bronze Beauties

1945: May 4, Paradise Theatre, 3711 Woodward at Parsons, Detroit, MI (Advertisement from Edwina "Salt" Evelyn's Scrapbook) *Star Time*

Earl Hines and his Orchestra
Arthur Walker
Essex Scott
"Scoops" Carry—on sax

Ford, Harris and Jones—Three Maniacs of Rhythm
Salt and Pepper—Tapping Twosome
4 Mellow Tones—Hot Harmony

Featured Musicians: Eugene Thomas, bass; Wardell Gray, tenor; Rene Hall, guitar; Willie Douglas, trumpet; and Fats Palmer, vocal
Movie on Screen: *The Broadway Big Shot* and All-American News

1945: Week of Saturday, July 14, Premier Hotel Music Hall Supper Club, South Fallsburg, Catskill Mountains, NY (Menu from Edwina "Salt" Evelyn's Scrapbook)

Welly Glick MC
Linda Marshall, Singer
Count Maurice, Magician

Lou Leslie, Pantomine Comedy
Salt and Pepper

1945: Week of August 17, Regal Theatre, Chicago, IL (Program from Edwina "Salt" Evelyn's Scrapbook) *Parade of Stars*

Earl "Fatha" Hines and his Orchestra
LeRoy Carrington—Prince of Taps
Salt & Pepper—Personality Plus in Taps
Essex Scott—Lord Essex

Ford, Harris and Jones—3 Maniacs of Rhythm
Stephany Stepherson and Palmer Davis—Dancers

Featured Musicians: Chick Booth, Billy Thompson, Bill Douglas, Arthur Walker, Kermit Scott, Gus Chappell, Palmer "Fats" Davis, Bill Douglas, Essix Scott & Joe Ivy
George "Scoops" Carry and Rhythm Quartette: Clifton Small (Piano), Rene Hall (Guitar), Billy Thompson (Vibraphone), Gene Thomas (Bass)
Movie on Screen: *Murder He Says*

1945: Week of August 24, Club Plantation, St. Louis, MO (Advertisement from Edwina "Salt" Evelyn's Scrapbook)

Four Melotones
Salt & Pepper
Ford, Harrison, Jones

Dick Montgomery
Red and Curley
George Hudson and his Orchestra*

*At times, Earl Hines was unable to perform due to previous commitments. The house band as George Hudson played the show.

1945: circa. September 21, Rhumboogie, 343 E. Garfield, Chicago, IL (This was a long running show with slightly different casts.) (Advertisement from Edwina "Salt" Evelyn's Scrapbook)

The Harlem Highlanders—Sensational Song and Dance Group
Walter Dyett's Band and His Swing Orchestra
Salt and Pepper—Return engagement By Popular Request!—America's Great Dancing Darlings

Naki and Lida—Interpretive duo Hawaii
Delores Parker—Songstress
Mildred Whitlow
Bobbie Anderson—Vocalist
Sing-Fionice
Rhumboogiettes in a Sizzling Revue!
The Bronze Beauty Chorus

While on tour with Earl Hines, this performance could have been performed during the week of Friday, September 21, 1945. Earl Hines was featured at El Grotto during this week.

1945: Beginning Friday, November 2, Fans Theatre, 40th and Market, Philadelphia, PA (Article and Program from Edwina "Salt" Evelyn's Scrapbook) *Harlem'z a-Poppin'*, S. H. Dudley management

Schedule of Performances

Lillian Fitzgerald
Spider Bruce
Dolores Alvarado—Exotic Dancer
Movie: *The Fatal Witness* and *Colored Newsreel*
Possibly two casts for *Harlem'z a-Poppin'*
John Mason, Comedian
Salt & Pepper, Spice of the program encores
Four Congaroos, Jitterbug
Delores Alvarado, Exotic dancer
4 Congaroos—Jitterbugs
Salt and Pepper
Yack Taylor, Soubrette
Charles Ray, Singer dancer
Boyd and Chapman
12 Dudleyettes, Chorus
Williard Chops Thompson and his 10 Swingsters

1946: Weeks of Friday, February 8–14, Howard Theatre, 620 T Street NW, Washington, D.C. (Advertisement from Edwina "Salt" Evelyn's Scrapbook)

Five Red Caps—Recording stars
Salt and Pepper—"Terpsichors Personified"
Coke and Poke—Inimitable funsters
Movie on Screen: *Jungle Captive*
Dick and Dot Remy—Act packed with vim and variety
George Hudson and Orchestra

1946: Week of Friday, April 5, Royal Theatre, Baltimore, MD (Advertisement from Edwina "Salt" Evelyn's Scrapbook)

International Sweethearts of Rhythm Orchestra
Anna Mae Winburn
Berne Hall
On Screen: Jinx Falkenburg in *The Gay Senorita*
Salt and Pepper
6 Marvelettes
Jackie (Moms) Mabley
Private Cecil Gant

1946: Week of Friday, August 16, Club DeLisa, 5521 South State Street, Chicago, IL (Advertisement from Edwina "Salt" Evelyn's Scrapbook) *Lime House Nites*

Little Miss Cornshucks—Queen of the Blues
George Kirby, Man of a 1000 voices
Beachcombers—Betty and Abdeen Ali
Lurlean Hunter
Willard Garner—singer
Hi-De-Ho Boys
Dot Adams—Shake Dancer
Salt and Pepper
Nick and Virgie—Roller Skate Dance Thrill on 16 Wheels
Fletcher Henderson and his Band featuring George Floyd
DeLisa Chorines
Charles Isom—MC

1946: Week of Friday, September 20, Club Riviera, St. Louis, MO (Advertisement from Edwina "Salt" Evelyn's Scrapbook)

Tony Parker Production
Lucky Millinder and his Orchestra
Anisteen Allen—Songstress
Chuck & Chuckles—Riot Team
Salt and Pepper—Queens of Dance
8—Rivierettes—8
Marcellus Wilson—MC

1946: Week of Friday, November 22, Apollo Theatre, 253 W. 125th Street, Harlem, NY (Advertisement and Article from Edwina "Salt" Evelyn's Scrapbook)

Ernie Fields and his Band
Wynoni Harris—King of the Blues
4 Step Bros.—Greatest Dancing Quartette
"Pigmeat"
Sybil Lewis
John Bunn
Salt & Pepper
Mel Moore

In the collection of Jewel "Pepper" Welch, the following itinerary from 1946–1947 was found. It appears that 1947 may be somewhat consistent with other performing events.

January 10	Lyric Theatre, Louisville, KY
January 12	c/o James E. Derrick, 806 E. Vine Street, Knoxville, TN
January 14–15	Frolic Theatre, Birmingham, AL
January 18–24	Palace Theatre, 324 Beale Street, Memphis, TN
January 25	c/o M.K. Allen Majestic, Little Rock, AR
January 28	Laurel, MS
January 29	Star Theatre, Hattiesburg, MS
January 30	ACE Theatre, Natchez, MS
January 31	Silver City Theatre, Alexandria, LA
February 2–8	Pike Theatre, Mobile, AL
February 9	Shadowland Club, 1921 Washington Ave., New Orleans, LA
February 11–12	Pekin Theatre, Montgomery, AL

1947: ca. May 30, Club DeLisa, 5521 State Street, Chicago, IL (Article from Edwina "Salt" Evelyn's Scrapbook)
    Salt and Pepper replaced Son and Sonny

1947: Fall, Café St. Michel, 770 Mountain Street, Montreal, Canada (Advertisement and Article from "Le Canada—Montreal, Mardure, 1947")
    Rolbie Kirk—MC and novelty singer
    Salt and Pepper—Comedy team of sepian dancers
    Yogie Chand, Suave Sepia Magician
    Del Rio Trio—2 boys and a girl, Calypso vein
    Louis Metcalfe and his Famous International Band
    Gene Cooper—Pianist/Singer

1948: Week of Friday, May 7, Apollo Theatre, 253 W. 125th Street, Harlem, NY (Advertisement and Article from Edwina "Salt" Evelyn's Scrapbook)
    Billy Eckstine—MGM Record Star
    George Paxton and his Band and Revue
    Salt and Pepper—Girl tap dancing act
    Strawberry Russel & Julia—Singing and talking comedians
    Wilkey & Dare—Comedy acrobats
    Jesse James—Handicapped acrobatic
    Dick Merrill—Vocalist

1948: ca. Week of Saturday, May 22, Club Savoy, Miami, FL[1] (Possibly on tour with Rosita Lockhart's "Hollywood Show"; Advertisement from Edwina "Salt" Evelyn's Scrapbook)

1948: Week of Saturday, October 16, Club Three Sixes, 666 East Adams, Detroit, MI (Advertisement from Edwina "Salt" Evelyn's Scrapbook)
    The Four Notes—Gene Smith, Jimmy Sapp, Freddie Johnson and Abie Levi
    Salt and Pepper—Dance Duo
    Ziggy Johnson's Atlantic City Beauties
    Cheri Morris—Singer
    Clara Bolden—Singer
    Johnny (Curley) Gardner—"All-American Half-Wit"
    Leonard Morrison's Orchestra

1948: Date Unknown, RKO Capitol (Advertisement from Edwina "Salt" Evelyn's Scrapbook)
Harlem Follies
    Bob Howard—The Nation's No. 1 Jive Bomber
    Salt and Pepper—Over-Seasoned with Rhythm
    Movie on Screen: *Woman in White*
    The Tampa boys—Lenox Avenue Cut-Ups
    Hawkins & Starr—All in fun
    Frank Radcliffe—Café Singing Sensation

1948: Week of Friday, November 5, Beige Room Pershing Hotel, 64th & Cottage Grove, Chicago, IL (Advertisement from Edwina "Salt" Evelyn's Scrapbook)
    Salt and Pepper
    George Kirby
    Gwen Tynes—Singer
    Lord Essix MC
    Pete Nugent—Dance
    Bibeau & Suarez
    The Beige Beaus with the Beige Beauts

1948: circa. November, Chicago Theatre Studio Party—Daddy-O. A celebration for the 15th Anniversary of the Stay-in-the-Know (Advertisement and Article from Edwina "Salt" Evelyn's Scrapbook)
    Ink Spots
    Daddy-O Homes Daylie—MC
    Pete Nugent
    Beige Beauts
    Salt and Pepper
    George Kirby
    Rhythmites
    Bibeau and Suarez
    Benny Green
    Joe Williams
    Claude McLin—Road Band Leader
    Ivory Joe Hunter
    Lord Essix Scott

1948: Date Unknown, New Club DeLisa, 5521 State Street, Chicago, IL, Sammy Dyer Production (Advertisement from Edwina "Salt" Evelyn's Scrapbook) *A DeLisa Bar-B-Q*
    Red Saunders and his great band with "VI" kemp
    Willard Garner
    Wallace Brothers
    Sonny Parker
    Hi De-Ho Boys
    Delores Alvarado
    Flink Moore
    12 Delisa Chorines
    Salt and Pepper
    Freddie Gordon, M.C.

Schedule of Performances

1948: Date Unknown, New Club DeLisa, 5521 South State St., Chicago, IL, Sammy Dyer Production (Advertisement from Edwina "Salt" Evelyn's Scrapbook) *DeLisa Flying Down to Rio*
    McCain & Alicia
    Honey Brown
    Nehi Berry
    Salt & Pepper
    Willard Garner
    Hi-De-Ho Boys
    12 DeLisa Chorines
    Freddie Gordon, M.C.
    Red Saunders and His Great Band with "VI" Kemp

1948: Date Unknown, Palace Theatre, 5242 W. 25th Street, Cicero, IL (Advertisement from Edwina "Salt" Evelyn's Scrapbook)
    Buddy Shaw and the Palace Theatre Orchestra
    Herbie Leon—MC/Comedian
    Hil Mika—Xylophone
    Three Kaye Sisters—Singers
    Al White and Blue—Poetry in Motion, Hand to Hand Balancing
    Salt and Pepper—"Speedy Steppers considered one of America's outstanding colored sister team."

1949: Friday, September 16, Club El Sino, 1730 St. Antoine, Detroit, MI (Advertisement from Edwina "Salt" Evelyn's Scrapbook) *Rocking Rhythm*
    Gwen Tynes
    "Mad Kitty" Baby Dee—singer—bombshell
    Marti Saylor
    Salt and Pepper
    Polly Goree Dancers
    Sinclair Rogers—MC
    Paul Bascomb and Orchestra
    Four Sinoettes

1949: circa. Week of July, Hawaii Klub, Schenectady Road, Albany, NY (Advertisement from Edwina "Salt" Evelyn's Scrapbook)
    Lee Noble—Broadway comic
    Marlane—Dancer
    Salt & Pepper—Direct from Apollo Theatre, N.Y. City
    Tommy Reed—Vocalist
    Rush Holden Dancers—featuring Mickey and Mary
    Doc Circe
    Jim and Tillie Gerard
    Charlie Randell
    Pete Bertasso
    Wally Overman—Symphony in Colors

1949: Week of October 30, Hawaii Klub, Schenectady Road, Albany, NY (Advertisement from Edwina "Salt" Evelyn's Scrapbook) Bid Farewell Party—Completing 17 Weeks of Fun
    Vic Earlson—comedy
    Del Markee
    Salt and Pepper
    Runa Rae
    Angela
    Ann Powell
    Doc Circe
    Evelyn Darlene
    Charlie Randell's Orchestra
    Gene Odyall
    Bob & Al
    Sheila Ryan

1948: January 7–8, Centre Avenue Theatre, Pittsburgh, PA (Advertisement from Edwina "Salt" Evelyn's Scrapbook)
    On tour with Rosita Lockhart's "Hollywood Show" top box theaters in Dixie

1949–1950: Moreland's *Hollywood Revue* was a one-year tour but not played consecutively. (Article from Edwina "Salt" Evelyn's Scrapbook)
    Part of the tour's itinerary included:
    November 30–December 1, Roosevelt Theatre, Centre Avenue, Pittsburgh, PA
        Mantan Moreland, Joe Morris, La Zonda, Ester Gardner, Melrose Colbert, **Salt and Pepper**, Raymond Griffin
    ca. December 10, Palace Theatre, Memphis, TN
        Mantan Moreland, Johnny Gardner, Joe Morris' Decca Recording Orchestra, Peggy Tomas, Zig and Zag, **Salt and Pepper**, LaZonda
    December 11, Chattanooga, TN
    December 12, Knoxville, TN
    December 13, Nashville, TN
    December 14, Montgomery, AL
    December 15–16, Lincoln Theatre, 771 East Long Street, Columbus, OH
        Joe Morris and Orchestra, Peggy Thomas, **Salt and Pepper**, LaZanda, Hollywood Beauty Chorus
    December 16, Augusta, GA
    December 17–20, Jacksonville, FL
    December 25–28, National Theatre, Birmingham, AL

Mantan Moreland, Peggy Thomas, **Salt and Pepper**, Johnny Gardner, Zig and Zag, LaZonda, Joe Morris Recording Band, Sammy Dyers Dancing Beauties Movie on Screen: *Roseanna McCoy*

December 29–January 2, 1950, State Theatre, 15th E. Central Avenue, Cincinnati, OH
    Mantan Moreland, Peggy Thomas, Joe Morris, LaZanda, **Salt and Pepper**, Hollywood Beauty Chorus
    Resided at Manse Hotel, 1004 Chapel Street, Cincinnati, OH, and the Sterling Hotel, 601 Mound Street, Cincinnati, OH

1950: Week of February 24, Rockhead's Paradise Café, 1252 St. Antoine Street, Montreal, Canada (Advertisement from Edwina "Salt" Evelyn's Scrapbook)

Maragret Watson—Charming Chanteuse, risqué	Allen Wellman Orchestra
Salt and Pepper—Terrific Tap Team	Downstairs: Lord Caresser—bar—King of Calypso Singers
Little Papa—Dancing Feet	Resided at Hotel Alberta, 1086 Osborne Street, Montreal
The Rockadets	

1950: ca. July 7, The Flame, 1315 North 9th Street, Milwaukee, WI (Advertisement from Edwina "Salt" Evelyn's Scrapbook)

Salt and Pepper	Loretta Whyte's Dance Band
Baby Scruggs—Queen of Disrobe	

Resided in Blue Spruce Tourist Rooms, Mrs. Beatrice Child's Proprietor, 1622–24 N. 5th Milwaukee 12, WI

1950: ca. October 14 and October 20, New Town Tavern, 7921 River Road, Delair, NJ (Advertisement from Edwina "Salt" Evelyn's Scrapbook)

Elsie Blow—head of precision prancing line	**Salt and Pepper**
Principal: Tondelayo and Calypso Boys	Ruth Baker
Wallace Bros.	

ca. 1951: Date Unknown, Rockhead's Paradise Café, 1252 St. Antoine Street, Montreal, Canada (Advertisement from Edwina "Salt" Evelyn's Scrapbook)

Margaret Watkins—Sensational Singer	The Rockadets
Wandra Mayo—Exotic acrobatics	Warren Banks MC
Salt and Pepper—Terrific Tap Team	

Downstairs: Lord Caresser—bar—King of Calypso Singers

ca. 1951: Date Unknown, Rockhead's Paradise Café, St. Antoine Street, Montreal, Canada (Advertisement from Edwina "Salt" Evelyn's Scrapbook)

Salt and Pepper	Rose Lance and Rockadets
Princess Gomez—exotic danseuse	

Downstairs: Lord Caresser—bar—King of Calypso Singers

1951: June 26–July 1, Rockheads's Paradise Café, St. Antoine Street, Montreal, Canada (Advertisement from Edwina "Salt" Evelyn's Scrapbook)

Margaret Watson	The Rockadets
Salt and Pepper	Allen Wellman Orchestra
Iron Jaw Wilson	

Resided at The Hotel Alberta, 1059–1061 Windsor, Montreal 3, Canada

1951: July 3–July 10, Rockhead's Paradise Café, St. Antoine Street, Montreal, Canada (Advertisement and Article from Edwina "Salt" Evelyn's Scrapbook)

Margaret Watson	Warren Banks, MC
Salt and Pepper	Alan Wellman with his Rhythm Boys—Orchestra
Darlene O'Day—exotic dancer	
Teddy Cole—dramatic baritone	Rockadets

Downstairs: Lord Caresser—bar—King of Calypso Singers
Resided at The Hotel Alberta, 1059–1061 Windsor, Montreal 3, Canada

1951: Week of January 27, Club DeLisa, 5521 State Street, Chicago, IL (Advertisement from Edwina "Salt" Evelyn's Scrapbook) *Sweetheart Parade*

Red Saunders and Band	Willard Garner
Salt and Pepper	Leon Oden
Joe Williams	Lonnie Simmons
Bob and Earl	Delisa Chorines
Gloria Howard	

Schedule of Performances

1951: Week of February 2, Club DeLisa, 5521 S. State Street, Chicago, IL (Advertisement from Edwina "Salt" Evelyn's Scrapbook) *Sweetheart Parade*
    Red Saunders and Band
    Salt and Pepper
    Joe Williams
    Bob and Earl
    Gloria Howard
    Willard Garner
    Leon Oden
    Lonnie Simmons
    DeLisa Chorines

1951: Week of February 5, A Night at the Mardi Gras, Sponsored by *Chicago Defender* at the Parkway Ballroom (Advertisement and Article from Edwina "Salt" Evelyn's Scrapbook)
    Louis Jordan
    Salt and Pepper
    Lil "In the Dark" Green
    The Sheldon Sisters
    Duke Ellington
    Ink Spots
    Teddy Hale
    Daddio Dailey

1951: Week of February 12, Club DeLisa, 5521 S. State Street, Chicago, IL (Advertisement from Edwina "Salt" Evelyn's Scrapbook) *Sweethearts Parade*
    Salt and Pepper
    Joe Williams
    Bob and Earl
    Gloria Howard
    Willard Garner
    Leon Oden
    Lonnie Simmons
    DeLisa Chorines

1951: Week of April 14, Hal Singer's Band and Helen Humes (Article from Edwina "Salt" Evelyn's Scrapbook)
    Article declares that **Salt and Pepper** would begin a coast to coast tour

1951: Monday, December 21, Chicago Theatre Studio Party for Daddy-O (Article from Edwina "Salt" Evelyn's Scrapbook)
    Ink Spots
    Daddy-O Homes Daylie
    Pete Nugent
    Beige Beauts
    Salt and Pepper
    George Kirby
    Rhythmites
    Bibeau and Suarez
    Benny Green
    Joe Williams
    Claude McLin, Road Band Leader
    Ivory Joe Hunter
    Lord Essix Scott

1951, Date Unknown, The Sky Club Supper Club, 427 Indiana Avenue, Indianapolis, IN (Advertisement and Article from Edwina "Salt" Evelyn's Scrapbook)
    Warren Banks—MC
    So-De-O-Dee
    Salt and Pepper
    Scatman "Mr. Blues Baliey"
    Suda, Talented Exotic Dancer
    The Sky Rockets

1952: Date Unknown, The Boulevard, 9405 Queen Boulevard, Elmhurst, Long Island, NY (Advertisement from Edwina "Salt" Evelyn's Scrapbook)
    Lew Nelson, MC
    Salt and Pepper
    Fred & Ann Carroll
    Ann Bebe
    Bill Henry's Orchestra

1952: Date Unknown, The Boulevard, 9405 Queen Boulevard, Elmhurst, Long Island, NY (Advertisement from Edwina "Salt" Evelyn's Scrapbook)
    Lew Nelson
    Salt and Pepper
    The Seldens
    Sandra Kiraly
    Bill Henry Orchestra

1952: Beginning Week of Saturday, June 13, New Zebra Lounge, 866 Longwood Avenue, NY (*New York Age*, June 14, 1952)
    Lou Mell Morgan—Trio
    Dennie Roberts, M.C.
    Exotic Dancer Tanya
    Tap Dancer **"Edwina"** Held over by Demand (Pepper is recovering)
    Hattie Green—Atlas Recording Blues Singer
    Frank (Floorshow) Culley and His Boys

1952: August 16, Cotton Club in The Sterling Hotel, only integrated nightclub in Cincinnati, 6th and Mount, Cincinnati, OH (Advertisement from Edwina "Salt" Evelyn's Scrapbook)

Sonny Parker MC
Flint Moore
Mabel Hunter

Salt and Pepper
Baby Washington—The Body Beautiful
Monty Morrison and orchestra

Fall: Year Unknown, KaSee's Theatre Nite Club, 4014 Lagrange St., Toledo, OH (Advertisement from Edwina "Salt" Evelyn's Scrapbook)

Paul Gilbert—M.C., Sensational new comedian
Salt and Pepper—Dancing Stars of Stage and Screen
Alice Morehouse—Distinctly Different Acrobatics

Lee Sheehan—Lovely Singing Star
Muriel Kretlow Dancers
Artie Kane, His Piano and His Orchestra

1952: Week of December 5, Apollo Theatre, 253 W. 125th Street, Harlem, NY (Advertisement from Edwina "Salt" Evelyn's Scrapbook)

Johnny Hodges and His Great Band
Billy Holiday
The Checkers

Salt & Pepper
Lady Terry
Spo-De-O-Dee

Date Unknown: Blue Mirror, 275 Clinton Avenue, Newark 2, NJ (Advertisement from Edwina "Salt" Evelyn's Scrapbook)

Marty Scott & His Orchestra—Formerly with Lou Prima
Peck & Peck—Comedians formerly with Erskine Hawkins Band
Salt & Pepper—Rhythmic Rhyms in Tap Dancing

Lora Pierre—Vocalist and Mistress of Ceremonies
Leonardo & Zola—Authentic Afro-Cuban Dancers

In the collection of Jewel "Pepper" Welch was a list of additional venues in which she performed solo, as part of "Candi and Pepper," or as part of "Salt and Pepper":

Juana Club, 2725 Woodward Avenue, Detroit, MI
The Zana Bar, 1001 E. Calfox, Aurora, CO
Club Carousel, Mr. Frank Norelle, Elmont, Long Island, NJ
Sportsman's Club, Lee Rainy, 330 Central Avenue, Newport, KY
Dew Drop Inn, Mr. Frank Painia's, 2836 LaSalle Street, New Orleans, LA
Moonglow Club, Mr. Shaeffler, corner of Willis and Michigan, Buffalo, NY
Rose Room, Mr. Teddy Blackman, Majestic Hotel, Cleveland, OH
Royal Peacock Club, Mr. Samuel A. Slaughter, 186½ Auburn Avenue NE, Atlanta, GA
Club Congo, Slim Jones, 550 E. Adams, Washington, D.C.
The Bill Robinson's Mimo Professional Club, Inc., 2237–2243 7th Avenue, New York, NY
Colonial Theatre, Woodward at Sibley Streets, Cincinnati, OH

Appendix II

In Memory of a Generation Who Performed

This appendix aims to shine a light on African Americans who performed from the late 1800s to the mid–1950s and who were not discussed in the text. This information is not intended to serve as biographies, but it makes available tidbits and notes that have been gathered from interviews and secondary research.

Dolores Alvarado, in addition to being an exotic dancer, was a showgirl at Chubby's in Allentown, Pennsylvania.[1]

Charles "Cholly" Atkins (1913–2003) was from Pratt City, Alabama, and he danced as part of "Coles and Atkins." This team was known for its elegant style and intricate rhythms. See: Charles "Honi" Coles. Cholly Atkins later became choreographer for Motown Recording Studios, creating precision choreography and vocal movement for singing groups such as the Temptations, the Four Tops and the Supremes. In 1989, he was awarded a Tony Award as co-choreographer for Broadway's *Black and Blue*.[2]

Bill Bailey (1912–1978), from Philadelphia, was the brother of Pearl and Eura Bailey. According to Marshall and Jean Stearns, Bailey's father was a Holy Roller preacher. While the congregation members stamped their feet and clapped their hands, young Bill sat there using his heels in an off-beat rhythm, creating a lot of Swing.[3] Bill Bailey and Derby Wilson, who became dance partners for several years, were protégés of Bill Robinson, with his flat-footed dance style (although Robinson forbade them from doing his tap dance steps and his famous Stair Dance). Bailey also appeared in several films, such as *Going Native* (1936), *Cabin in the Sky* (1943) and *Harlem Variety Revue* (1955). In 1955, Bill Bailey executed the first recorded version of the Moonwalk at the Apollo Theatre (although Bailey called this step the "Backslide"). This step was later copied by some of the greatest performers in the music industry, such as James Brown and Michael Jackson.[4]

Bibeau and Suarez: Mary Suarez Baird grew up in Spanish Harlem and the Bronx. She pursued dance at 9 years of age. Mary later received a 4-year French scholarship to City University while she pursued her dance career. She excelled in dance and became the founder of the African-Brazilian duo "Bibeau and Suarez." Llon Bibeau, her dance partner, was a dancer and director. Baird danced professionally for seven years and studied under Martha Graham and Katherine Dunham as well as African dance instructors. Mary Suarez Baird began teaching in 1968 and founded the Venettes, a performing dance group. Her work focused on connecting dance to everyday life, developing the Venettes Cultural Workshop and providing education/counseling support to the community. Her daughter, Vanessa Baird-Streeter, continues her mother's work.[5]

Bunny Briggs (1922–2014): In 1931, Briggs started his performing career at eight years old with Charles "Luckey" Roberts and his orchestra in the homes of society's Four Hundred, the Wanamakers, the Hitchcocks, and the Vincent Astors. He also performed with Charley Barnett and Tommy and Jimmy Dorsey. He can be heard in Duke Ellington's recording "Concert of Sacred Music." He likewise performed on television shows, such as *Motown Tribute of the Apollo*, Public Broadcasting Station's (PBS) *On Stage America*, and *Dance in America*. He was featured in the Broadway musicals *My One and Only* and *Black and Blue*, as well as the movie *Tap*. Briggs performed with Baby Laurence, from whom he learned a great deal about Jazz Tap. He was also influenced by Walter Green from Chicago, who specialized in Paddle and Roll. Briggs captivated audiences with his charm. His dance style adapted the Paddle and Roll, added pantomime (such as skating across the stage or galloping on a horse), employed eccentric accents, inserted vernacular dance steps such as the Suzie-Q, and concluded with a series of splits.[6]

Butterbeans and Susie: Jodie "Butterbeans" Edwards (1895–1967) and Susie Hawthorne Edwards (1896–1963) were a husband-and-wife song, dance and comedy vaudeville team. Susie sang and danced the Cakewalk, and Butterbeans performed eccentric dances. He was famous for the dance known as "Heebie Jeebies." Butterbeans wore tight pants and kept his hands in his pockets, acting as if he were itching to death. When he took his hands out of his pockets, he scratched his body in syncopated rhythms—thus heebie jeebies (based on a traditional African dance). The comedy bits of Butterbeans and Susie were based upon mutual marital insults, such as the following:

> Butterbeans sang, "I'd fight all the animals in the jungle or even in the zoo, I'd grab a lion and smack his face and tear a tiger in two!"
> Susie responded, "Yeah."
> Butterbeans continued: "If that aint' love, it'll have to do."
> Susie asked, "Till when, till when?"
> Butterbeans answered, "Till another fool come along."[7]

Billy and Eleanor Byrd (1917–2003): Isabelle Hankins Fambro was half of the song and dance team known as Billy and Eleanor Byrd. Fambro was born in South Carolina with Trinidadian and Shoshone Indian heritage; however, she lived most of her life in Philadelphia. As a child, she started singing and dancing in bars to pick up some nickels, and then she performed in the Lincoln Kiddie Hour. At 16 years old, she took the stage name Eleanor Joyce and later married Italian Lorenzo Fambo. They had two children, Sonny and Joyce. After they divorced, she teamed with Billy Byrd, who wrote their songs and tap danced. Fambro was the song stylist. They performed around the United States from 1944 to 1962 but never married.[8]

"Scoops" Carry (1915–1970): George "Scoops" Carry was featured as an alto sax and clarinetist with Earl Hines' band. Coming from the University of Iowa, Hines discovered this native Chicagoan in 1940. "Scoops" was the band's rehearsal leader, and he assumed Hines' place when he stepped off the bandstand.[9]

Nat "King" Cole (1919–1965): Singer and pianist Nathaniel Adams Cole was born in Montgomery, Alabama, and moved to Chicago as a child. He learned to play piano in the style of Earl Hines. His style of music was orchestrated ballads. The King Cole Trio was an innovative drummerless swinging jazz trio that performed from 1937 to 1955. They recorded songs such as "Straighten Up and Fly Right" (1943), "(Get Your Kicks on) Route 66" (1946), "Nature Boy" (1948), "Mona Lisa" (1950), "Too Young" (1951), "Ramblin' Rose" (1963) and "Those Lazy-Hazy-Crazy Days of Summer" (1964). In 1956, Cole made television history when he became the first African American host of a variety television series. After a short, successful career, Nat "King" Cole died from lung cancer.[10]

Charles "Honi" Coles (ca. 1911–1992) partnered with "Cholly" Atkins" to form the team "Coles and Atkins." This team was known for its elegant style and intricate rhythms. They performed a six- or seven-minute routine of fast, attention-getting steps; a precision dance; and their famous soft shoe, which was extremely slow, precise, and lyrical. This was followed by a challenge dance in which each dancer performed his own specialty. Coles stated that in their solos they worked entirely with the drummer and ignored the melody. Their goal of Rhythm Tap was swinging rhythmic complexity. They ended the act in precision steps and walked off together.[11] Coles was a member of the Copasetics and the Hoofer's Club, and he starred in Broadway's *Gentlemen Prefer Blondes*, *My One and Only*, and *Bubbling Brown Sugar*. He was likewise featured in films such as *The Cotton Club* and *Dirty Dancing*. Coles was also the Apollo Theatre's stage manager for many years.[12]

Chris Columbo (1902–2002), also known as Joseph Christopher Columbo Morris, was a jazz drummer and musician who was born June 17, 1902, and was actively drumming into his late 90s. He had the house band at New York's Cotton Club and Savoy Ballroom and in Atlantic City's Club Harlem, where he played for "Larry Steele's Smart Affairs." He toured the United States with his band, "Chris Columbo and the Sweet Gentleman of Jazz." He died in New Jersey on August 20, 2002, at 100 years old.[13]

Billy Daniels (1915–1988), also known as William Boone Daniels, performed in the United States and Europe from the 1930s to 1988.

Sammy Dyer performed in *Runnin' Wild* with the Dancing Red Caps, which also included Derby Wilson, Pete Nugent, and Chink Collins. The team stopped the show with stomping, clapping and stepping to James P. Johnson's "The Charleston."[14] Dyer was a choreographer and staged shows for the Sunset Café, Club Morocco, the Royal Theatre, Bennie Skoller's Swingland Café at 343 East Garfield (55th Street), and Chicago's Club DeLisa, where he spent eighteen years.[15] Dyer established the Sammy Dyer School of Dancing in May 1933. In 1950 he created the Dyerettes, a female dance troupe known to be the only chorus act of its kind. The Dyerettes toured internationally with some of the greatest entertainers of the twentieth century, including Nat "King" Cole, Sammy Davis, Jr., and Sarah Vaughan.[16]

Baby Edwards (1922–2000), also known as Edith Hunt, was a legendary tap dancer in her own time, as proclaimed by LaVaughn Robinson. She was born July 3, 1922, in Philadelphia. Starting at 3 years old, Baby Edwards competed in amateur contests and by 5 was on the Kiddie Hour at the Standard Theatre, Lincoln Theatre Kidding Hour, and the Horn and Hardart Children's Hour, where she was the only African American on the show. She sang, danced and did some acting spots. Edwards' mother taught her acrobatic stunts, and her brother Harry "Karry" Edwards taught her to tap dance. In 1933, she won first prize in the Children's Dance Contest at the Chicago World's Fair, with its "Century of Progress" theme. She was in *Swingin' a Dream* in November 1939 at the Centre Theatre in New York City. Throughout the years, Baby Edwards danced as part of several tap dance teams: "Pops and Baby" (partner unknown), "Taps and Baby" with Taps Miller, and "Spic and Span" with Willie "Span" Joseph. Spic and Span performed on black and white circuits and in USO shows until the 1960s. Afterward, Edwards performed as a solo act well into the 1990s. Her credits and legendary reputation are extensive. Although appearing shy, when Baby Edwards walked out on the stage, she was a dynamic tap dancer, and her jazz style singing was powerful and from the soul. She passed away on November 10, 2000.[17]

"Dusty" Fletcher (ca. 1897–1954), born Clinton Fletcher, was a comedian on the vaudeville circuit. He was known for his sketches "Open the Door, Richard" and "Here Comes De Judge." He performed regularly at the Apollo Theatre—a lean, handsome man who wore a large top hat and a thin, tattered black coat and trousers with long crumpled shoes. He worked black vaudeville and burlesque and apperared in the Mamie Smith revue of 1926. Fletcher worked on Tim Moore's roadshow *Southland Revue* (1927) and then took his own show, *Harlem Strutters*, on the road in the same year. Fletcher and John "Spider Bruce" Mason co-starred in *Bamboola* (1929) and wrote a spoof sketch of Eugene O'Neill's "Strange Interlude." They also wrote "The Suicide" and "The Wall Between." For the next twenty years, Fletcher wrote and appeared in revues and created musical short films. He worked with the top stars of the day, such as Jackie "Moms" Mabley, Ethel Water, Tim Moore, Hamtree Harrington, and Timmie Rogers, and he introduced the six-year-old Sammy Davis, Jr. By 1947, he was considered the most famous Negro comedian. The song "Open the Door, Richard" was a hit novelty tune between 1946 and 1947. Fletcher performed the sketch as part of the Cab Calloway short *Hi-De-Hi* (1947). It was also released as a one-reeler in *Open the Door, Richard*. Soon, *Richard's Answer* was released with Stepin Fetchit as the Richard who does not want to get out of bed to open the door. After legal battles, both Fletcher and Mason received credit for the lyrics while Jack McVea and a fictitious music publisher received credit for the music. By the late 1940s, Fletcher's style of comedy had faded, and he was replaced with new comedians of the 1950s.[18]

Ford, Harris and Jones, famed as the "Three Maniacs of Rhythm," "paced the show with whirlwind dancing, singing and comedy routine which bounces over the foot lights with a solid click."[19]

Charles "Chuck" Green (1919–1997) was born in Fitzgerald, Georgia. As a child, he stuck bottle caps on his bare feet and tap danced on the sidewalk for money. Chuck Green danced with the Chintz and Ella B. Moore Show. From 1930 to 1944, he toured with James Walker as "Chuck and Chuckles." Green was a protégé of "John Bubbles" Sublett and performed a melody of graceful Rhythm Tap that appeared effortless.[20] In 1969, Chuck Green led a tap revival, reassembling the tap dancers from Harlem's Hoofers Club for a series of "Tap Happenings." He has been featured in the George Nierenberg film *No Maps on My Taps*, the PBS special "*About Tap*," the movie *Tap*, and the Broadway musical *Black and Blue*.[21]

Cora Green, at the age of 14, with a rich contralto voice, started her vaudeville career as part of "Green and Pugh." She later joined Florence Mills and Ada "Bricktop" Smith to form the Panama Trio, which included legendary pianist Tony Jackson. The trio performed at the Panama Club in Chicago until it closed. The Panama Trio then toured the Pantages Circuit (a white venue) from 1916 to 1919. For many years, Green partnered with James Carl "Hamtree" Harrington, and they toured as "Harrington & Green" on vaudeville's Keith-Albee Circuit (a white venue). Their act was a medley of song, dance and comedy. Green appeared in *Put and Take* (1921), *Strut Miss Lizzie* (1922), the Lew Leslie production of *Dixie to Broadway* (1924), *Nobody's Girl* (1926) and *Vaudeville at the Palace* (1927). Following her Broadway run, she toured in Europe. In addition, she starred in *Ebony Showboat* (1929) and on Broadway in *Policy Kings* (1938). Green also starred in two films by Oscar Micheaux: *Swing!* (1938) and *Moon Over Harlem* (1939).[22]

Walter Green: Little is documented about Walter Green. But it appears that in 1937, Green arrived in New York from Chicago. He introduced the step called Paddle and Roll. While working at Elk's Rendezvous, he placed a sign out front in capital letters inviting all dancers to drop in and "be shot down by his unique foot work." According to Leroy Meyers, "Ralph Brown, Freddie James, Albert Gibson, and Chuck Green went over one night and clobbered him."[23] The Stearnses described the Paddle and Roll as "staccato taps with the toe and heel in a rocking motion ... [with] intermittent accents varying the steady roll."[24]

Teddy Hale (1926–1959) was one of the greatest tap dancers of the era. Not much is written about him, but everyone of the period mentioned his name. He was an improvisational dancer with close-to-the-ground rhythms.

In 1931, at five years old, Teddy Hale was in Black vaudeville. By the mid-1940s, he had worked with Luckey Roberts, with Ethel Waters' troupe, and at Harlem's Connie Inn, and he had made movie shorts dancing with various bands. Around 1947, Hale performed at New York's Paramount. Pete Nugent, who had seen the act with Derby Wilson, reported:

> Hale opened with three terrific choruses of a waltz before anybody realized what was happening. A routine to "Begin the Beguine" followed [which became Hale's trademark]. Then he threw in five lightning choruses of tap using transitional steps that only another dancer could appreciate. As a finale Hale sat down in a chair and danced to an up-tempo

two-to-a-bar, a very difficult feat, and then closed the act with a breathtaking assortment of spins, flips, and splits. Derby Wilson's only comment was a reverent "Sweet Jesus."[25]

LaVaughn Robinson recalled that Teddy Hale was a beautiful tap dancer and for 10 years danced the role of the shadow in Ted Lewis' act "Me and My Shadow." Robinson exclaimed, "Finesse! People missed an artist!"[26]

According to Constance Valis Hill, Teddy Hale died in 1959.[27]

Billie Holiday and Lester Young recorded songs such as "Your Mother's Son-in-Law," "Good Morning Heartache," "I Wished On the Moon," "Oh, Lady Be Good," "Fine and Mellow," "Trav'lin' All Alone," "He's Funny That Way," "Back in Your Own Backyard," and the list goes on.[28] Eleanora Fagan Gough changed her name to Billie Holiday because of her admiration for Billy Dove. She was born in Philadelphia on April 7, 1915, and died July 17, 1959, in New York City.[29]

Lena Horne (1917–2010) joined the Cotton Club as a chorus dancer at the age of 16. She was soon recognized for her singing talent. Horne sang with Noble Sissle's orchestra and appeared in Lew Leslie's *Blackbirds of 1939*. She was later hired to sing with Charlie Barnet's orchestra. Barnet was a white Swing bandleader and one of the first bandleaders to integrate. Horne was one of the first Black women to successfully work on both sides of the color line. She was featured at the Café Society and Savoy-Plaza Hotel nightclubs in the 1940s, and she appeared in *Life* magazine, becoming the highest-paid Black entertainer at the time. She was the first African American to sign a seven-year contract with MGM Studios, where she filmed movies like *Stormy Weather* and *Cabin in the Sky*. Because of her light-colored skin, Horne was difficult to cast. She refused to accept stereotypical roles of maids, butlers, and African natives. Horne sang at Carnegie Hall, worked in television, and later appeared in *The Wiz* (1978). She was also known for her work with civil rights.[30]

Alberta Hunter (1895–1984) headed for Chicago at 12 years old to become a cabaret singer. By the 1920s, she was writing and recording her own Blues songs. Her fame and talent were rewarded while singing at the Dreamland Café. Hunter toured most of her career and was a success in Europe, with "her suave, attractive body draped in satin and singing songs that ranged from sultry and smoldering to the ribald." She had a popular radio show and recorded on Black Swan, Paramount, Okeh, RCA Victor and numerous other labels. After World War II, Hunter, who spoke several languages, retired from show business to care for her mother. Later she lied about her age to enter nursing school, and she had a 20-year nursing career. She retired from nursing in 1977 and started performing again at the age of 82. Her singing style was unique: she had spoken ad libs as well as a sound that moaned and cried, all contrasted with sexy innuendoes. Some of her songs were "Down Hearted Blues," "Chirping the Blues," "You Shall Reap Just What You Sow," and "Amtrak Blues." In later years, Hunter was known as "Alberta Grandmama of the Blues."[31]

Germaine Ingram was born 1947 in Philadelphia. She studied and performed tap with her mentor, LaVaughn Robinson. Ingram has performed and taught workshops throughout the United States, Europe and the Caribbean. In the early 1990s, she began working with the Philadelphia Folklore Project, through which she produced *Stepping in Time*, which reflected the shows of the 1920s–1940s, and co-directed the video documentary *Plenty of Good Women Dancers*.[32]

Ludie Jones was born in New York City in 1916. By eleven years old, Ludie taught tap dance for Ms. Emma Kemp. At seventeen, she toured Europe with Lew Leslie's *Blackbirds of 1934*. With Peggy Wharton and Marion Worthy Warner, Ludie formed "The Lange Sisters." The team toured the Lowe's circuits and performed with Fats Waller, Louis Armstrong and Louie Russell's band. Later, Ludie formed "The Three Poms" with Sylvia Warner and Geraldine Ball (Pom-Pom was Geri's nickname). Sylvia Warner was a fast Buck and Wing dancer from Canada; Geraldine Ball performed acrobatics in a novelty style; and Ludie Jones was the Rhythm Tap dancer. For many years, the Three Poms toured with Cab Calloway. They received train accommodations that usually included a reserved car and sleepers, and they had the same hotel accommodations as the members of Calloway's band. The Three Poms toured USO shows throughout the Pacific and the United States. They were on the playbill with some of the greats of the era, such as Bill Bailey, Pearl Bailey, Stump and Stumpy, and Chuck and Chuckles. By the 1950s, when jobs became scarce, Ludie worked 23 years for the Bell Telephone Company. After retirement, she returned to tap dancing, her first love. In 1984, Ludie was featured on the television special *Motown Returns to the Apollo* alongside African American male dancers such as Sammy Davis, Jr., Bunny Briggs, Chuck Green, Jimmy Slyde, Sandman Sims, and Harold Nicholas. This was followed in 1984–1985 by a show called *Shades of Harlem*, which was based on the Cotton Club revues. Ludie Jones, Juanita Bossieau, and Ruby Reilly were the "Renaissance Ladies" who represented the seniors and were challenged by the "Renaissance Dancers," who were younger women dancers. This show traveled to Perugia, Italy, in 1986, where they performed in the Jazz Festival and for three weeks in Monte Carlo. During this period, Jones did radio show advertisements for *Shades of Harlem* and appeared on several television talk shows with Cab Calloway, such as *Regis in the Morning*. From 1986 to 2010, Ludie was also a member of "The Swinging Seniors," who performed at benefits and other entertainment functions. In addition, Ludie Jones taught tap dance classes at the Joseph Kennedy Center in Harlem until 2013. She's now semi-retired in New York City.[33]

Sissieretta Jones (1868–1933): Matilda Sissieretta Joyner Jones was born in Virginia and grew up in Rhode Island. She was a soprano singer of classical songs and operatic arias, lauded for her brilliant performances as she traveled throughout the world. Sissieretta sang at Covent Garden in London, Madison Square Garden in New York, the National Conservatory of Music (under the baton of the famous classical composer Antonin Dvorak), and even the White House for President Benjamin Harrison. She is said to be the first African American woman to sing at Carnegie Hall. Yet, because of the racism in the United States, all doors seemed closed to her. Her roadshow, *Black Patti's Troubadours*, was organized by her white managers in 1895. The "Black Patti" title referred to Italian opera singer Adelina Patti. This show was intended to serve as a bridge between minstrelsy and vaudeville. Sissieretta disdained the idea of blackface minstrel songs and "coon" songs that featured acrobats and comedians. Yet she needed to promote the roadshow in order to perform. The show supported many performers who went on to fame: Bob Cole, who wrote and produced the first full-length, all-Black musical comedy, *A Trip to Coontown* (1898); the tap dancers "King Rastus" Brown and Aida Overton Walker; and the first African American producer Ernest Hogan, who also starred on Broadway in the show *The Oyster Man* (1907). During the *Black Patti's Troubadours* show, the first act closed with a Buck Dance contest. It was followed by an olio, which featured specialty acts and ended with a Cakewalk. The show closed with an "Operatic Kaleidoscope" that featured Black Patti (Sissieretta Jones) accompanied by the entire cast. This show toured until 1915.[34]

William Henry Lane, known as Master Juba (c. 1824–1852) was the only African American known to participate with great success in the white American minstrels. Juba was coached by Uncle Jim Lowe, an African American jig and reel dancer. In 1848, Lane joined Pell's Ethiopian Serenades in London, England. He received national and international acclaim for the dance that he performed, which incorporated Black rhythmic characteristics with Irish jig dancing. Marian Hannah Winter states that "because of the vast influence of one Negro performer, the minstrel show dance retained more integrity as a Negro art form than any other theatrical derivative of Negro culture…. In America it was Juba's influence primarily which kept the minstrel show music in touch with the integrity of Negro source material." It was through Master Juba that one of the major characteristics of American tap dancing was recognized, which is that the dancer is equivalent to a musical instrument.

This concept of the dancer/musician became most apparent when the tap dancers performed during the Jazz Age.[35]

The Mellow Tones were a harmonizing singing group, similar to the Temptations of the 1960s. It was difficult to track this group because the spelling of the name was rarely the same, and it is assumed that they didn't record any music as a group.

Jelly Roll Morton (1890–1941) was born Ferdinand Joseph LaMothe in New Orleans. He promoted himself as the "inventor of jazz." Jelly Roll was considered the first jazz musician to score his arrangements in writing. His first published work in that genre was "Original Jelly Roll Blues." He was a Creole American ragtime musician and an early jazz pianist, bandleader and composer.[36]

Nicholas Brothers (Fayard and Harold) came to stardom out of Philadelphia. They used a combination of Rhythm Tap and Flash, which led them to become one of the most popular dance teams of the Swing Era. These brothers starred at Harlem's Cotton Club in 1932 (at the ages of fourteen and eleven years old, respectively) and went on to great success on the Broadway stage and the movie musicals. Their movie career included films such as *Big Broadcast* (1936), *Down Argentina Way* (1940), *Choo Choo Sing* (1943), and *Carolina Blues* (1944).[37]

Pete, Peaches & Duke: Pete Nugent, Irving "Peaches" Beaman, and Dukan "Duke" Miller constituted the tap team known as "Pete, Peaches & Duke." This team seems to have followed in the rhythmic path of John Bubbles and the style of Eddie Rector. "Pete Peaches & Duke" were also known for their clean, clear taps. Nugent prided himself on the choreography of movement and rhythm. He felt that all hoofers can execute steps, but the class act includes the way in which one moves his body and travels through space. "Pete, Peaches & Duke" opened their act with a military drill, dancing very close together; then, as each danced solo, the tempo was increased. Peaches danced to a slow four-to-a-bar, Pete to a moderate two-to-a-bar, and Duke to a fast two-to-a-bar. Duke Miller later became part of the team "The Miller Brothers and Lois."[38]

"Ma" Rainey (1886–1939), born Gertrude Pridgett, was known as the "Mother of the Blues." Her parents performed in minstrel shows, and Rainey started singing and dancing in minstrels and vaudeville at the age of 14. She married William "Pa" Rainey, who was a minstrel show manager. Thus, she was known as "Ma" Rainey. Together they performed Blues and popular songs while touring the country as part of Tolliver's Circus, the Musical Extravaganza, and the Rabbit Foot Minstrels. By the 1920s, Rainey was a solo star, and in 1923 she signed a recording contract with Paramount Records, where she recorded over 100 songs. Rainey retired in 1935 with enough money to build two theaters and buy her own home. She died of a heart attack in 1939.[39]

Eddie Rector (1890–1962) appeared in the role of Red Cap Sam in *Darktown Follies* in 1914, and he danced throughout the 1940s. Rector was known for his innovative approach to dance, which was called "a class act." He performed the Cakewalk, Charleston, Waltz Clog, and Sand Dance in a graceful, gliding manner. In his top hat and tails, Rector was known for introducing tap dance that traveled across the floor rather than remaining center stage.[40] John Hart remembered that Rector, a quiet man who kept to himself, had a wooden block upon which he danced up and down, did a cartwheel during his performance, and also danced on sand.[41]

Bill "Bojangles" Robinson (1878–1949) was classified by Jack Schiffman as "the first black superstar," a title by which he was known at the Cotton Club, the Apollo Theatre, Broadway's Palace Theatre, and Hollywood's movie musicals.[42] Robinson's style revolutionized tap dance on the Broadway stage and in movie musicals. His style, "Up On Your Toes," was an imitation of the Irish jig. He shifted his weight to the front of his foot and created a style of Buck and Wing with simple but clear rhythmic dancing. He used rhythms that were precise and versatile. Bill Robinson was known for dancing in wooden or split soles, instead of metal taps. These shoes were a combination of leather and wood that provided some flexibility. Wooden and leather soles, as opposed to metal taps, were worn for dance until the early 1920s.[43] Robinson's dance style reflected the verticality of white dancers of that time, and his mannerisms conformed to the Uncle Tom image appreciated by white audiences. Although his intention was to create clear rhythms, he emphasized personality. Robinson charmed the audiences with his large grin, the rolling of his eyes, and his controlled, delicate mannerisms. Musician Chris Columbo stated that Robinson "had all kinds of little gimmicks ... [Robinson said,] 'This is the way I walk when I'm happy ... and this is the way I walk when I'm sad.'" Columbo added, "I know a lot of dancers who could outdance him but they couldn't sell it like he could."[44] Robinson was the first African American tap dancer to gain success in show business, but he was criticized by many for pandering to the interests of white audiences. "Bojangles" Robinson was most noted for his tap dance movie roles with child star Shirley Temple. The popularity of the Stair Dance is linked with Robinson, who was the first African American to perform this dance on Broadway in Lew Leslie's *Blackbirds of 1928*.[45]

Timmie Rogers (1915–2006) was revolutionary in Black humor, as he refused to accept the standard "darky talk" or wear blackface. In one of Rogers' first solo shows, he wore a "tuxedo and sang a song that mocked segregation, 'I've Got a Passport From Georgia.' The stage manager hollered at him after the set to put on the sloppy clothes like the other colored comedians or he'd be fired. Rogers told the manager: 'I'm sure going to miss you.'" Rogers appeared on the *Jackie Gleason Show* and *The Melba Moore–Clifton Davis Show* in the 1970s.[46]

Essex or Essix Scott (1922–1960), also known as Lord Essex, was billed as "Personality Plus." In 1946 Scott was a tenor singer for Earl Hines; he recorded "Margie" and later "Rosetta," among others. Essex harmonized with Dolores Parker and Arthur Walker on "Margie." In the 1950s, Essex was part of the Ink Spots and later the Fabulous Ink Spots. He died in a boating accident in 1960.[47]

Sandman Simms (1917–2003), with his unique style of tap dancing on sand, was a mentor to Gregory Hines. Sandman was a regular at the Apollo Theatre.

Jimmy Slyde (1927–2008), a.k.a. Dr. Jimmy Slyed, was born James Godbolt in Atlanta, Georgia. He partnered with Jimmie Mitchell, whose stage name was "Sir Slyde." Together they appeared in clubs and on New England's burlesque circuit as the Slyde Brothers. Jimmy Slyde was known as an improvisational dancer because sound was his driving force. He said, "I'm not a routine man. Cause dancing is a translating thing, especially if you're tapping. You're making sounds yourself ... different dancers have different sounds.... I'm strictly sound-oriented.... Tap dancing fits with the music—it's like a summation there." Jimmy Slyde moved to Paris, where he taught and performed, appearing in *Black and Blue* (1985) at the Chatelet Theatre. Slyde received a Tony Award nomination for his role in the Broadway production of *Black and Blue* (1989). He also appeared in several films and TV programs, among them *Cotton Club* (1984), *Round Midnight* (1986), and *Tap* (1989). He was featured in the video *About Tap* (1985) with Chuck Green and Steve Condos. Slyde also opened Jacob's Pillow Summer Dance Festival (1996). Among his many teaching gigs, he taught a series of tap workshops, spreading his style throughout the United States and other parts of the world. Slyde died in Hanson, Massachusetts.[48]

Bessie Smith (1894–1937) was born in Chattanooga, Tennessee, and is considered the greatest Blues singer who ever lived. By 18 years old, she worked the theater circuit of minstrel shows and cabarets. Smith started her career as a dancer on the playbill with Ma Rainey. With large audiences, Smith created her own extravagant shows, starring as a Blues singer with 40 people in the cast. Due to segregation, Smith had her own railroad car in which she took her show around the country. She was extremely successful, bringing in $2,000 a week. Smith understood the blues because she lived the Blues. She recorded about 160 songs for Columbia Records, such as "Tain't No Body's Business If I Do" and "Back Water Blues." Smith's music influenced Rhythm and Blues and Rock 'n' Roll. Bessie Smith was killed in an automobile accident at the age of 42.[49]

Mamie Smith (1883–1946) was a singer, dancer, and pianist on the vaudeville stage. While starring in the musical revue *Maid of Harlem*, she was approached to record her songs. The General Phonograph's Okeh studio recorded Smith singing "That Thing Called Love" and "You Can't Keep a Good Man Down." The songs were a huge success, and Okeh quickly recorded her rendition of "Crazy Blues." Mamie Smith changed the course of show business history, making the first Blues recording by an African American singer. She was known as "The First Lady of the Blues."[50]

"Race records" had been in use from the 1920s, when Mamie Smith had a best-selling Okeh record of "Crazy Blues." The term "Rhythm and Blues" (R&B) came into use in the late 1940s, after *Billboard* magazine substituted it for "race records." R&B stemmed from a rich, indigenous African American folk tradition. It was "good time" dance music that "came roaring out of the churches of black America, the black bands of the swing era, and the segregated ghettos of big cities."[51]

"Libby" Spencer (1920–1998) was born Mary Olivia Hill in St. Petersburg, Virginia. Spencer was an Apollo chorus girl dancer and the dance captain of the Apollo Theatre chorus line from 1940 to 1948. She performed regularly in nightclubs and in Atlantic City with Hortense Allen's revue. Spencer also taught tap dance in the City of Philadelphia's Recreation Department, where she founded and directed the City of Philadelphia's Performing Arts Camp.[52]

"Spider Bruce" (1895–1952): Born in Winston-Salem, North Carolina, John "Spider Bruce" Mason was a comedian whose career spanned from the minstrel period to the Apollo Theatre. He was one of the few who performed in blackface into the 1940s. Along with Dusty Fletcher and Pigmeat Markham, Mason's comedy was most popular in the 1930s and 1940s. He also performed the routine "Open the Door, Richard" that was associated with Dusty Fletcher.[53]

Stump and Stumpy were originally the team of James Cross and Eddie Hartman, who combined singing, comedy and tap dance for a well-known act. Later Harold Cromer took on the role of Stumpy.[54]

John "Bubbles" Sublett (1902–1986) and his partner Ford Lee "Buck" Washington (1903–1955) were a comedy-song-dance team known as "Buck & Bubbles." John Bubbles was considered by many the greatest tap dancer of his time and was called "The Father of Rhythm Tap" because of his inventive musicality and low-to-the-ground style. He divided each measure into four beats and slowed the tempo, leaving more time for rhythmic sounds. Bubbles executed steps such as double over-the-top and backward trenches, but his performance accentuated a relaxed, casual style. Buck and Bubbles were the first African American team to perform at the Palace Theatre on Broadway and traveled west on the Orpheum Circuit. They were also the first African American artists to perform at Radio City Music Hall and probably the first to appear on television in a broadcast from London. Buck and Bubbles were featured in the *Ziegfeld Follies of 1931*, and Bubbles sang and danced in George Gershwin's *Porgy and Bess* in 1935. Buck and Bubbles appeared in several motion pictures, including *Varsity Show*, *Cabin in the Sky* and *A Song Is Born*.[55]

Yack Taylor was a woman known for novelty songs of the 1920s–1940s, such as "Knockin' Myself Out," "Hard Lovin' Blues," and "Whip It to a Jelly."[56]

Sophie Tucker (1887–1966): "The Last of the Red Hot Mamas" was a Jewish singer performing comical risqué songs such as "I Don't Want to Be Thin," "Nobody Loves a Fat Girl, But Oh How a Fat Girl Can Love," "My Yiddishe Momme," and "Some of These Days." She began her career using blackface in vaudeville, followed by the Ziegfeld Follies, radio and movies such as *Honky Tonk* (1929), *Broadway Melody of 1938* (1937), and *The Joker Is Wild* (1957).[57]

Sarah Vaughan (1924–1991) received her first singing job in 1942 from Earl Hines. She was loved for her "perfect pitch and rhythmic sense, her sophisticated ear for chord changes, and her astonishing voice—she could sing everything from soprano to baritone. The audience liked her devil-may-care spirit, too, and eventually dubbed her 'Sassy.'" To her admirers, Vaughan was known as "The Divine One."[58]

Arthur Walker was a singer discovered by Earl Hines in a small nightclub in Los Angeles in 1944. He was featured as the band's baritone singer and trumpeter with a wonderful, unusual style.[59]

Dianne Walker was born in 1951 in Boston, Massachusetts. She studied with tap masters Leon Collins and Jimmy Slyde. Walker is a teacher and mentor to the new generation of tap dancers, including Savion Glover. She performed in the Broadway revue *Black and Blue* (1997), the film *Tap* (1989), and television documentaries *Tap Dance in America* (1989), *Honi Coles: The Class Act of Tap*, and *JUBA: Masters of Tap & Percussive Dance* 1998.[60]

Ethel Waters (1896–1977), referred to as "Mother of Us All," had an early life that made her tough and resilient. She was born in Chester, Pennsylvania, as the result of rape to a mother about thirteen years old. The family moved often for work, and Waters was often alone and suffered a series of accidents and illnesses. She soon befriended whores, sporting men, gamblers and pimps. In 1917, she made her debut as a shimmy dancer and singer on the Theater Owners Booking Association (TOBA) vaudeville circuit and was billed as "Sweet Mama Stringbean." Her style was softer and delicate, producing a contrast to that of Ma Rainey and Bessie Smith. In a clear, light voice Ethel Waters sang the Blues. By 1925, she played white vaudeville, singing songs as "My Man" and "He's Funny That Way." "She became the first black woman to headline at the Palace Theatre in New York, starred at the Plantation and Cotton Clubs, and went to Hollywood." At the Cotton Club, she introduced "Stormy Weather," composed for her by Harold Arlen, which reflected her life. She was the first African American star of a national radio show and the first on Broadway. Ethel Waters was featured in such movies as *Cabin in the Sky*, *The Sound and the Fury*, and *Rufus Jones for President*, as well as television shows such as *The Jackie Gleason Show* and *Beulah*.[61]

Slappy White (1921–1995), born Melvin Edward White in Baltimore, was an actor and comedian. He worked with Redd Foxx on the Chitlin' Circuit. White also appeared in the films *Amazing Grace* (1974), *Amazon Women on the Moon* (1987), and *Mr. Saturday Night* (1992), as well as the television shows *Sanford and Son*, *That's My Mama*, *Blossom*, and *Cybill*.[62]

The Whitman Sisters (1900–1943), a team of four sisters (Essie, Mable, Alberta, and Alice), produced their own Black vaudeville show. This show toured the United States on various theater circuits and was known as the "Royalty of Negro Vaudeville." The troupe was a great incubator of dancing talent. Through the Whitman Sisters, hundreds of tap dancers received their first break into show business. The sisters "not only employed comedians who were Buck Dancers in the old style tent show tradition, they also featured dancers as dancers a hint of what was to come on Broadway and sold the show to the public largely on the strength of this dancing." The Whitman Sisters changed with the times and featured the finest dancers. They were known for identifying young talent, and, with the parents' permission, they literally raised and educated the children in their family troupe. Many great tap dancers, such as Bunny Briggs, Groundhog, and Joe Jones of the team "Three Little Words," performed with the Whitman Sisters.[63]

Chapter Notes

Chapter 1

1. "Research Resources on Chicago, Jazz, and the Great Migration," *Chicago Jazz Archive*, University of Chicago Library, last generated April 4, 2012, accessed January 2, 2015, http://www.lib.uchicago.edu/e/su/cja/greatmigration.html.

2. In 1868, the Fourteenth Amendment to the U.S. Constitution was ratified, ensuring that "all persons born in the United States ... excluding Indians not taxed" were citizens and were to be given "full and equal benefit of all laws." However, in 1892, Louisiana passed a Separate Car Act that legalized segregation in common carriers, such as railroads. The Citizens' Committee of New Orleans recruited John Plessey (a seven-eighths white person) to challenge the ruling. Plessey was a Creole of color, a term used to refer to black persons in New Orleans who traced some of their ancestors to the French, Spanish, and Caribbean settlers of Louisiana before it became part of the United States. Plessey was arrested for sitting in a first-class "whites only" train car of the East Louisiana Railroad. The case eventually appeared before the U.S. Supreme Court, where Plessey's lawyers argued that the Separate Car Act was unconstitutional according to the Fourteenth Amendment. But Judge Henry Brown wrote that the Fourteenth Amendment implied a legal distinction between the white and "colored" races but did not eradicate a color distinction, nor did it enforce the mingling of the two races. Thus, the 1896 Supreme Court decision set the precedent of "separate but equal" manifested in the Jim Crow laws. These laws imposed on the two races "separate" public facilities, such as restaurants, theaters, restrooms, hotels, theaters and public schools. Trains and buses were also segregated, and in many states marriage between whites and colored people was prohibited. The reality for African Americans was that all public facilities were "separate" but unquestionably inferior to those enjoyed by whites. Justice John Harlan, the lone dissenter on the Plessy case, argued, "Our Constitution is color-blind, and neither knows nor tolerates classes among citizens. In respect of civil rights, all citizens are equal before the law.... The present decision, it may well be apprehended, will not only stimulate aggressions, more or less brutal and irritating, upon the admitted rights of colored citizens, but will encourage the belief that it is possible, by means of state enactments, to defeat the beneficent purposes which the people of the United States had in view when they adopted the recent amendments of the Constitution." Library of Congress, "U.S. Congressional Documents and Debates, 1774–1875, 39th Congress, 1st Session, 358," *A Century of Lawmaking for a New Nation*, accessed September 21, 2011, http://memory.loc.gov/cgi-bin/ampage?collId=llsl&fileName=014/llsl014.db&recNum=389; and Richard Wormser, "The Rise and Fall of Jim Crow: Plessy V. Ferguson (1896)," Public Broadcasting Service, Oregon Public Broadcasting Corporation, 2002, accessed September 21, 2011, http://www.pbs.org/wnet/jimcrow/stories_events_plessy.html.

3. Jo Tanner, "Shuffle Along: The Musical at the Center of the Harlem Renaissance," *Drop Me Off in Harlem*, accessed December 30, 2013, http://artsedge.kennedycenter.org/interactives/harlem/themes/shuffle_along.html.

4. Jim Haskin, *The Cotton Club* (New York: New American Library, 1977), 18.

5. Minstrelsy, or the minstrel show, was a form of American entertainment popular from 1830 into the 1950s. It consisted of song, dance, music, and skits performed by white people who wore blackface makeup made of burnt cork. The thrust of the show was to create a buffoonish image of Negroes. The irony was that these shows began with enslaved people mocking the movement and dance styles of their white owners. In turn, the white performers, unaware of the spoof, mocked the Negroes who were mocking the whites.

6. *Shuffle Along* featured songs that became the popular tunes of the day, such as "Love Will Find a Way," "Shuffle Along," "Gypsy Blues," "Bandana Days," and "I'm Just Wild About Harry."

7. Tanner, "Shuffle Along."

8. See Marshall Stearns and Jean Stearns, *Jazz Dance: The Story of American Vernacular Dance* (New York: Schirmer Books. 1968), 145–47, 195; and Grant Harper Reid, *Rhythm for Sale* (North Charleston: CreateSpace Independent Publishing Platform, 2013), 119.

9. Constance Valis Hill, *Tap Dancing America: A Cultural History* (Oxford: Oxford University Press, 2010), 101.

10. Stearns and Stearns, *Jazz Dance*, 338.

11. *Ibid.*, 212–14.

12. Ted Gioia, *The History of Jazz* (New York: Oxford University Press, 1997), 94.

13. "The Volstead Act," *Alcohol Problems and Solutions*, accessed December 30, 2012, http://www.alcoholproblemsandsolutions.org/Controversies/Volstead-Act.html; and "The Volstead Act: October 28, 1919," *History, Art & Archives: United States House of Representatives*, accessed December 30, 2012, http://

history.house.gov/Historical-Highlights/19011–950/The-Volstead-Act/.

14. Kathy Weiser, "Speakeasies of the Prohibition Era," *Legends of America*, page 2, updated March 2010, accessed December 30, 2012, http://www.legendsofamerica.com/ah-prohibitionspeakeasy2.html.

15. Haskin, *The Cotton Club*, 15.

16. Other African American theaters in New York City were the Renaissance Theatre, the Alhambra Theatre, the Douglas Theatre, and the Odeon Theatre.

17. Cab Calloway and Bryant Rollins, *Of Minnie the Moocher & Me* (New York: Thomas Y. Crowell, 1976), 88.

18. The Cotton Club attracted the most affluent guests: columnists Ed Sullivan, Walter Winchell, Mark Hellinger, and Louis Sobol; stars Jimmy Durante, Milton Berle, Lillian Roth, George Raft, Eddie Duchin, Ray Bolger, Bert Lahr, Irving Berlin, Cole Parter, Marlene Dietrich, Ed Wynn, Eddie Cantor, Al Jolson, and Bing Crosby; political figures Mayor Jimmy Walker of New York, J. Edgar Hoover, Clyde Tolson (associate director of the FBI), Boston's Mayor Zimmerman, and Franklin D. Roosevelt, Jr.; Dutch Schultz the gangster; and Warden Lawes of Sing Sing Prison. Haskin, *The Cotton Club*, 89, 149.

19. Truckin': This dance movement consists of short slides forward on alternating feet; the shoulders sway in opposition to the foot as the index finger wiggles at shoulder height. Stearns and Stearns, *Jazz Dance*, 41.

20. The Suzy-Q (or Susie-Q): This vernacular dance step was performed in many styles of dance, including tap. One version of this dance is to clasp the hands inverted and hold them straight down in front of the body. Place the right heel next to the left foot in a parallel position, and turn the right foot outward as the left foot steps to the side. This is performed three times; then step right and kick the left. Reverse the combination.

21. Shorty George: This was a step well known in Harlem and used as part of the breakaway or improvisation during the Lindy Hop. See Stearns and Stearns, *Jazz Dance*, 323–24. A version of this step is still executed in tap dance. It is performed on the balls of the feet with the knees bent. As the dancer takes a small step forward on the right foot, the knees sway to the right and are then reversed. The arms are bent and the index fingers point downward. The right arm is extended downward as the dancer steps on the right foot and is then reversed with the left foot.

22. Haskin, *The Cotton Club*, 22–23.

23. Kamri M. Owens, "Website #2 Harlem Gangs (1920–1930)," *Scoop.it!* (part of "Crime of the 1930's"), January 16, 2013, http://www.scoop.it/t/crime-of-the-1930-s/p/3995074712/2013/01/16/website-2-harlem-gangs-19201-930.

24. Calloway and Rollins, *Of Minnie the Moocher & Me*, 71.

Chapter 2

1. All formal interviews with Edwina "Salt" Evelyn were held between April 26, 1990, and June 1, 1990. Informal interviews and telephone conversations continued until her death on January 26, 2011. Most direct quotes from Edwina found throughout this manuscript are not noted or dated.

2. Many children went to dancing schools in the Harlem area. Some of the noted dance teachers were Phil Simmons, Grace Charles, Ella Gordan, Mary Bruce, Ruth Williams and Alice Garrett.

3. Between 1910 and the late 1970s, Nedick's had a chain of over 100 hot dog stands throughout New York City. According to the website *Warm Muh Weenah*, Nedick's produced great-tasting hot dogs as well as its famous orange drink. See http://loop48.com/bump/good-like-nedicks/.

4. Falling Off the Log: This step travels sideways. One version of this step is to jump to the right on the right foot, jump on the left foot slightly behind the right, lift the right foot while crossing it in front of the left, jump to the right on the right foot, jump on the left foot in front of the right, and lift the right foot while crossing it behind the left. Repeat combination. Quarter turns and the height of the crossing foot enhance the style.

5. Interview by author in Atlantic City, NJ, with Chris Columbo, August 1, 1990.

6. Calloway and Rollins, *Of Minnie the Moocher & Me*, 72.

7. Judy Pritchett, with Frank Manning, "Shorty George Snowden," *Archives of Early Lindy Hop: Biographies of the Original Lindy Hoppers*, copyright 1995–2006, accessed September 24, 2013, http://www.savoystyle.com/shorty_george.html.

Chapter 3

1. Ted Fox, *Showtime at the Apollo* (New York: Holt, Rinehart and Winston, 1983), 107.

2. *Ibid.*

3. *Ibid.*, 13.

4. Stride piano is a rhythmic style of jazz piano playing, developed in the 1920s. The right hand plays a syncopated melody, while the left hand plays an alternating bass note, bass octave or tenth followed by a chord. It gives an "oom-pah" feel. The music has embellishments and improvisations.

5. Stanley Dance, *The World of Earl Hines* (New York: Charles Scribner's Sons, 1977), 57.

6. Gene Fernett, *Swing Out: Great Negro Dance Bands* (Midland, MI: Pendell, 1970), 151.

7. Dance, *The World of Earl Hines*, 259.

8. Philip Berrigan and Rusty E. Frank, "Berry Brothers," *American National Biography Online*, updated January 2002, accessed April 2, 2015, http://www.anb.org/articles/18/180–3672.html.

9. Frank Cullen, with Florence Hackman and Donald McNeilly, *Vaudeville Old & New: An Encyclopedia of Variety Performers in America*, Vol. 1 (New York: Routledge, 2007), 104–5.

10. Robin D. B. Kelly, *Thelonious Monk: The Life and Times of an American Original* (New York: Free Press, 2009), 42–43.

11. Gunther Schuller, *The Swing Era: The Development of Jazz, 1930–1945* (New York: Oxford University Press, 1989), 390.

12. Seasons of Change, "African Americans and Death," *Caring and Sharing Through Every Season*, 2015, accessed May 20, 2015, http://www.caringseasons.com/african-americans-and-death/.

13. Kelly, *Thelonious Monk*, 86–87.

14. Lee Mortimer, "Night Clubbing with Lee Mortimer," *The Sunday Mirror*, April 14, 1946, accessed May 21, 2011, available at http://sites.google.com/site/newyorkcityapril1946/in-progress/newspapers/the-sunday-papers-on-april-14/the-sunday-mirror/the-columnists/night-clubbing-with-lee-mortimer.

15. Patrick Burke, *Come In and Hear the Truth: Jazz and Race on 52nd Street* (Chicago: University of Chicago Press, 2008), 113.

16. In the late 1800s, James A. Bradley bought 500 acres of land on the New Jersey coast as a place of rest and relaxation. Bradley developed this area, which was named Asbury Park in honor of Bishop Francis Asbury. By the mid-1900s, Asbury Park was a resort with hotels and homes, and it claimed to have "the finest boardwalk in the world." Christopher Clay, "History of Asbury Park," *Asbury Park, "Then & Now"*, February 8, 2011, accessed July 13, 2011, available at http://www.drakkar91.com/ap/asbury9.htm.

17. Knight, "Spotting Capital Nite Spots," *Baltimore Afro-American*, June 5, 1943.

18. Dance, *The World of Earl Hines*, 27–28.

19. Eugene Chadbourne, "Jack Gee," *All Music*, accessed April 1, 2015, http://www.allmusic.com/artist/jack-gee-mn0000127224/biography.

20. Knight, "Spotting Capital Nite Spots."

21. Jimmie Mordecai was a tap dancer and actor. He performed in *St. Louis Blues* with Bessie Smith (1928) and *Yamekraw* (1930) with music by James P. Johnson. See https://www.youtube.com/watch?v=PmnNXkubRx4 and https://www.youtube.com/watch?v=k2sFvb_Aygs.

Chapter 4

1. All formal interviews with Jewel "Pepper" Welch were held between March 1, 1989, and July 15, 1990. Informal interviews and phone conversations continued until her death on April 21, 1992. Most direct quotes from Pepper found throughout this manuscript are not noted or dated.

2. Between the 1920s and 1940s, Philadelphia had the following theaters that presented large Black vaudeville shows and musical stage shows featuring tap dance: the Nixon Grand, on the corner of Broad Street and Montgomery Avenue; the Lincoln Theatre on Broad and Lombard Streets; the Fans Theatre on 4th and Market Streets; and the Pearl Theatre on Broad and Oxford Streets.

3. *Philadelphia Independent*, August 30, 1936.

4. Ibid.

5. *Philadelphia Independent*, advertisement for Hi-Hat Club in Lawnside, New Jersey, October 22, 1939, 16.

6. *Philadelphia Independent*, advertisement for Irene's Café, June 16, 1940, 18.

7. All formal interviews with Mildred "Candi" Thorpe were held between August 16 and November 18, 1990. Informal interviews and telephone conversations continued until her death on April 18, 1998. Most direct quotes from Candi found throughout this manuscript are not noted or dated.

8. Stearns and Stearns, *Jazz Dance*, 69.

9. By the turn of the twentieth century there were tent shows called gillies or carnivals. Gillies traveled by wagon and performed "one nighters," which meant that the show performed in a town for one evening and then moved to another for the next night. Carnivals, which traveled by railroad, usually performed a week in each locale.

10. John Kenrick, "A History of the Musical: Minstrel Shows," *Musicals 101.com: The Cyber Encyclopedia of Musical Theatre, Film, & Television* (rev. ed. 2003), accessed September 11, 2011, http://www.musicals101.com/minstrel.htm.

11. *Philadelphia Independent*, "The Stroller," July 16, 1937.

12. Octavius Valentine Catto (1839–1871) was an African American educator and civil rights activist. See V. Chapman Smith, "The Triumph and Tragedy of Octavius V. Catto," *UShistory.org*, accessed November 15, 2014, http://www.ushistory.org/people/catto.htm.

13. *Philadelphia Independent*, "Erskine Hawkins at O.V. Catto," April 28, 1940, 17.

14. Wings: There are many variations of the wing, but the basic technique is a side shuffle on the supporting foot or simultaneously on two feet. The feet are in a parallel position and remain in this position as one foot (or both feet) is brushed out to the side and quickly brushed inward, and the dancer lands in the starting position. There are three sounds in this step: brush out, brush in, and step.

Through the Trenches, or Pulling Trenches: This is one of the earliest Flash steps, which made its appearance on the entertainment stage in 1914 courtesy of African American Toots Davis. One version of this step is executed as the dancer stands on the right foot and springs upward to the outside edge of the foot. The dancer pulls this foot backward in an arc pathway. Then the dancer steps on the left foot and reverses the movement. The body is on a forty-five-degree angle, and the arms reach for the floor in opposition to the foot. The step travels from side to side. (Interview by author in West Philadelphia, PA, with Edith "Baby Edwards" Hunt, 1990.)

15. *Philadelphia Independent*, May 5, 1940, 18.

16. *Philadelphia Independent*, "Brighter Lighter Banter," January 19, 1941, 16.

17. Discussions and terminology of homosexuality from that time period were provocative. Pepper referred to derogatory words like *queer, faggot, dykes* and *bulldykes*, but the euphemisms of the time seemed less hurtful, such as "that way," "a bit funny," "a member of the church" or "a friend of Dorothy." Gay men and lesbians lived closeted and/or bore the animosity of the public. For African Americans, the conflict was extremely intense and looked upon with disdain. As a people, African Americans were just attaining liberty after 400 years of enslavement. Many believed that the stigma attached to homosexuality diminished their efforts. Nevertheless, in the world of entertainment one's lifestyle was not an issue, and, for the most part, people were allowed to be who they were. It wasn't until the AIDS epidemic of the 1980s that America began openly discussing homosexuality.

18. *Chicago Defender*, April 3, 1943.

Chapter 5

1. Donald Bogle, *Heat Wave: The Life and Career of Ethel Waters* (New York: HarperCollins, 2011), 258.

2. Preston Lauterbach, *The Chitlin' Circuit and*

the Road to Rock 'n' Roll (New York: W. W. Norton, 2011), 159.

3. Fox, *Showtime at the Apollo*, 19.

4. An Eton jacket was a short jacket cut off just below the waist, worn as the school uniform of boys at Eton College until 1976, and also at other English schools.

5. B.S. Chorus is a dance routine performed by hoofers, usually at the end of a show. It consists of one chorus of music, thirty-two bars or four steps. One variation of the four steps follows: (1) Time Step. (2) Cross Over Step: Hop (left), shuffle step (right), back flap (left), shuffle (right), hop (left), ball heel (right) crossed over left, tap (left) to side. This step is reversed and repeated and followed by a break. (3) Wing Step: Shuffle step (right), brush (left), wing (right), Maxie Ford. This step is performed three times followed by a break. (4) Over the Tops performed in half-time music tempo, and Through the Trenches. (Interview by author with Buster Brown, who taught classes at the Colorado Dance Festival, Boulder, CO, 1990.).

6. Shim Sham Shimmy: According to the Stearnses, this dance became a standard routine in show business around 1931; yet its origin will always be in contention. It appears that Willie Bryant and Leonard Reed performed a comic dance when they were in the Whitman Sisters' vaudeville troupe. The dance team "Three Little Words" performed this routine (or a similar one) at Connie's Inn in Harlem. The dance became known as Shim Sham. (See Stearns and Stearns, *Jazz Dance*, 195–96.) It consists of one chorus of music, thirty-two bars, and four steps. The rhythm is syncopated and has a swing feel. One version of this dance follows: (1) Shim Sham Step: Shuffle step (right), shuffle step (left), shuffle ball change (right), shuffle step (right). Reverse and repeat combination. Honi Coles Break: Step (right), hit tip of left behind right, ball heel drop (left), ball heel drop (right), ball (left), step (right, left). (2) Push or Rock Step: Stamp (right), heel drop (left); repeat; ball heel drop (right and reverse), ball (right). Reverse and repeat combination. Break: ball heel drop (left and reverse), ball (left), ball heel drop (right and reverse), ball (right), step (left and right). (3) Tack Annie: Brush (right) inward, tap the ball (right), step (right apart from left); reverse; repeat; brush (left) inward, step (left), ball change. The combination is performed three times with a Honi Coles Break. (4) Half Break: Step (right, left), shuffle (right) ball change; repeat; Honi Coles Break. Repeat combination (4) without break and exit walk. (A version of the Shim Sham taught by Charles "Honi" Coles at the Colorado Dance Festival, 1986.) Note: In *The World of Earl Hines*, Hines acknowledges that in Chicago during the mid-1920s, there was a woman named Tack Annie. She had a couple of girlfriends who looked after her. It appears that Tack Annie was the roughest woman he had ever seen in this life, so tough that it took several men to hold her down (Dance, *The World of Earl Hines*, 35).

7. A tag is a four- or eight-bar phrase added to the end of the musical score and/or the dance. The last performer closes the routine with an exciting or comical movement.

8. George Nierenberg (director), *About Tap* [VHS], Direct Cinema Limited, June 1, 1985.

9. The Shorty George was the signature step of "Shorty George" Snowden. Barely five feet tall, Shorty George parodied his height in this step. The maneuver was also well known in Harlem and used as part of the breakaway or improvisation during the Lindy Hop. It is performed on the balls of the feet with the knees bent. As the dancer takes a small step forward on the right foot, the knees sway to the right and are then reversed. The arms are bent and the index fingers point downward. The right arm is extended downward as the dancer steps on the right foot and is then reversed with the left foot. See Pritchett, "Shorty George Snowden," and Stearns and Stearns, *Jazz Dance*, 323–24.

10. The Struttin' step can be found in many West African dances. During the slavery period in the United States, this step evolved to a stylized walk as slaves imitated and exaggerated the dances of their masters. These humorous styled struts were demonstrated in the Cakewalk, Truckin' and other finale dances.

11. The Stearnses describe Over the Top as a Flash step: a "bending forward, springing up, and bringing each leg, in turn, around from the back and across the front of the other leg figure-eight pattern that had previously been performed flatfooted giving the impression of elaborate and energetic self-tripping" (Stearns and Stearns, *Jazz Dance*, 190). Today this step might be described as one foot jumping over the opposite leg. There is usually an inward circling of the leg in which the foot scrapes the floor before it is jumped over.

12. Toots Davis is credited with introducing Trenches or Pulling Trenches in 1914 in the Broadway show *Darktown Follies*. As one of the first Flash steps, it referred to being in the trenches of World War I. One version of this step is executed as the dancer stands on the right foot and springs upward to the outside edge of the foot. The dancer then pulls this foot backward in an arc pathway. Subsequently, the dancer steps on the left foot and reverses the movement. The body is on a forty-five-degree angle, and the arms reach for the floor in opposition to the foot. The step travels from side to side. (Interview by author in West Philadelphia, PA, with Edith "Baby Edwards" Hunt, 1990.)

13. Kazatskys is a move in which one squats to the ground and leans back on the right hand while thrusting the left leg high forward and then back to the starting place; as the legs return, the action is reversed. The movement is usually done four to eight times.

Chapter 6

1. Jack Schiffman, *Uptown: The Story of Harlem's Apollo Theatre* (New York: Cowles Book Company, 1971), 2.

2. Jack Schiffman, *Harlem Heyday* (Buffalo, NY: Prometheus Books, 1984), 14.

3. *Ibid.*, 15.

4. Schiffman's choreographers included Charlie Davis, Addison Carey, Leonard Harper, Teddie Blackman, Clarence Robinson and Leonard Reed.

5. Schiffman, *Uptown*, 27.

6. *Ibid.*, 30.

7. Schiffman, *Harlem Heyday*, 14.

8. Schiffman, *Uptown*, 16.

9. *Ibid.*, 29.

10. *Ibid.*, 28.
11. Fox, *Showtime at the Apollo*, 131.
12. Schiffman, *Uptown*, 16.
13. Fox, *Showtime at the Apollo*, 104.
14. Fox, *Showtime at the Apollo*, 18.
15. Schiffman, *Harlem Heyday*, 110–11.
16. *Ibid.*.
17. *Ella Fitzgerald: The Official Site of the First Lady of Song*, accessed January 8, 2015, http://www.ellafitzgerald.com/about/index.html.
18. Stearns and Stearns, *Jazz Dance*, 155.
19. Karl Stark, *Inquirer* staff writer, "The Essence of Pearl Bailey: The Singer/actress/good-will Ambassador Brought a Love of Folks to the Many Stages of Her Life," Phillywww, August 20, 1990, accessed September 30, 2011, http://articles.philly.com/19900-82-0/news/25932475_1_pearl-bailey-lump-sum-talent-contest.
20. Jimmy Mitchell, whose stage name was "Sir Slyde," studied at the Stanley Brown dance studio in Boston. There he met and partnered with Jimmy Godbolt, calling the team "the Slyde Brothers." Jimmy Godbolt was later known as Jimmie Slyde.
21. Eugene Chadbourne, "Effie Smith," *All Music*, accessed December 10, 2013, http://www.allmusic.com/artist/effie-smith-mn0000177570.
22. Jim Lowe, "Tim Moore," *Vot Der Dumboozle?*, 2000, accessed December 1, 2013, http://www.yodaslair.com/dumboozle/tmoore/tmoordex.html; and "Tim Moore, Biography," *IMDb*, accessed September 30, 2013, http://www.imdb.com/name/nm0601953/bio?ref_=nm_ov_bio_sm.
23. "Louis Jordan," *BBC Music*, accessed December 10, 2013, http://www.bbc.co.uk/music/artists/b8b30 6997-8144-fd1-ab756-f22f5da0fac.
24. "Oran Thaddeus Page [Hot Lips]," Texas State Historical Association, accessed April 3, 2015, http://www.tshaonline.org/handbook/online/articles/fparx.
25. Eugene Chadbourne, "Ernie Fields," *All Music*, accessed January 15, 2015, http://www.allmusic.com/artist/ernie-fields-mn0000203516/biography.
26. Schiffman, *Harlem Heyday*, 122, 207.
27. Rusty Frank, *Tap! The Greatest Tap Dance Stars and Their Stories, 1900–1955* (New York: William Morrow, 1990), 298, 312–15; Schiffman, *Harlem Heyday*, 175; and "The Four Step Brothers," *Footnotes on Tap*, accessed September 30, 2012, http://www.footnotesontap.com/LegendBiosPhotos/FourStepBrothersPage.html.
28. Fox, *Showtime at the Apollo*, 95.
29. "Sybil Lewis, Biography," *IMDb*, accessed September 29, 2013, http://www.imdb.com/name/nm 0507783/bio?ref_=nm_ov_bio_sm.
30. "Melvin Moore," Living Legends Foundation, Inc., accessed December 9, 2013, http://www.livinglegendsfoundation.com/melvin-moore.
31. Tony Rounce, "Checkmate: The Complete King Recordings 1952–55: The Checkers," *Ace Records*, accessed December 12, 2013, http://acerecords.co.uk/checkmate-the-complete-king-recordings-19525-5.
32. Geoffrey C. Ward, *Jazz: A History of America's Music*, based on documentary film by Ken Burns (New York: Alfred A. Knopf, 2000), 206.
33. "Prez & Lady Day: The Story of Billie Holiday and Lester Young," *The Jim Cullum Riverwalk Jazz Collection* (Stanford University Libraries), accessed March 1, 2015, http://riverwalkjazz.stanford.edu/program/prez-lady-day-story-billie-holiday-and-lester-young; and *Billie at 100: A Century of Lady Day*, accessed March 1, 2015, http://www.billieholiday.com.
34. Ward, *Jazz: A History of America's Music*, 269–70.

Chapter 7

1. James R. Grossman, Ann Durkin Keating, and Janice L. Reiff, eds., *Encyclopedia of Chicago* (Chicago: University of Chicago Press, 2004), 433.
2. *Ibid.*
3. *Ibid.*, 433–34.
4. The term *jazz slave masters* was used by some to describe the situation that many musicians and entertainers endured during the 1920s and 1930s in connection to the Mafia. Dempsey J. Travis, *An Autobiography of Black Jazz* (Chicago: Urban Research Institute, 1983), 41.
5. *Ibid.*, 39.
6. *Ibid.*, 39, 43.
7. Dance, *The World of Earl Hines*, 45.
8. Dempsey J. Travis, "Where the Jazz Was Super-Hot," *Chicago Tribune*, March 26, 1985, accessed May 24, 2015, http://articles.chicagotribune.com/19850-32-6/news/8501170148_1_dance-floor-radio-band.
9. Dance, *The World of Earl Hines*, 58.
10. *Ibid.*, 61.
11. *Ibid.*
12. *Ibid.*, 61–62.
13. Travis, *An Autobiography of Black Jazz*, 45–46.
14. From Earl "Fatha" Hines' obituary, died April 22, 1983, in *The Day* (New London, CT), April 24, 1983.
15. Travis, *An Autobiography of Black Jazz*, 75.
16. *Ibid.*, 74–76.
17. Chitlin' Circuit: Chitterlings are the smaller intestines of a pig, cooked for food. Originally eaten by enslaved Africans in the Southern states, chitterlings or chitlins were a symbol of poverty. In the minstrel era, African Americans were portrayed as naïve buffoons who sang, danced, stole watermelons and ate "chitlins." John Kenrick, "A History of the Musical: Minstrel Shows," *Musicals 101.com: The Cyber Encyclopedia of Musical Theatre, Film, & Television* (rev. ed. 2003), accessed September 11, 2011, http://www.musicals101.com/minstrel.htm#Throng.

During the days of vaudeville and big bands, theaters that featured African American entertainers were known to be part of the Chitlin' Circuit. It wasn't an organized circuit, but rather a collection of theaters throughout the South, East and upper Midwest. The Chitlin' Circuit developed between the 1930s and existed to the 1960s and featured jazz, blues, and soul music. These theaters provided African American entertainment in a safe and acceptable environment during a time of racial segregation. Preston Lauterbach, in *The Chitlin' Circuit and the Road to Rock 'n' Roll*, listed the theaters on the Chitlin' Circuit, such as the Royal Peacock in Atlanta, Georgia; the Carver Theatre in Birmingham, Alabama; the Cotton Club, Small's Paradise and the Apollo Theatre in New York City; Robert's Show Lounge, Club DeLisa and the Regal Theatre in Chicago; the Howard Theatre in Washington, D.C.; the Uptown Theatre in Philadelphia; the Royal Theatre in Baltimore; the Fox Theatre in Detroit; the Victory Grill in Austin, Texas; the Hippodrome Theatre in Richmond, Virginia; the Ritz Theatre in Jacksonville, Florida; and the Madam C. J. Walker Theatre on Indiana Avenue in Indianapolis. See also "The Chitlin Circuit," *Official R&B Music Hall of Fame Museum* (website), accessed October 23, 2013, available at http://www.rbhalloffame.com/the-chitlin-circuit/.

18. Dance, *The World of Earl Hines*, 70.
19. *Ibid.*, 98.
20. *Ibid.*, 85.
21. *Ibid.*
22. *Ibid.*, 88.
23. *Ibid.*, 92.
24. *Ibid..*, 32.
25. *Ibid.*, 48.
26. *Ibid.*, 54–55.
27. Wardell Gray, *A Chronology*, "Earl Hines Orchestra," January 5, 1945. http://wardellgray.org/Wardell%20Gray%20Chronology%201945%20(master).htm.
28. *Ibid.*, "16-piece orchestra...," February 2, 1945. http://wardellgray.org/Wardell%20Gray%20Chronology%201945%20(master).htm.
29. Kermit Scott played bass with the Earl Hines band.
30. Gus Chappell played trombone with the Earl Hines band.
31. Palmer "Fats" Davis from Philadelphia joined Hines in 1943. He played trumpet and sang. See Dance, *The World of Earl Hines*, 285.
32. Bill Douglas was a trumpet player "who was *really* something else. He had his own style and was just phenomenal." *Ibid.*, 269.
33. Essex or Essix Scott (1922-1960) also known as Lord Essex was billed as Personality Plus. In 1946 Scott was a tenor singer for Earl Hines recorded *Margie* and later *Rosetta* among others. Essex harmonized with Dolores Parker and Arthur Walker on *Margie*. In the 1950s, Essex was part of the Ink Spots and later the Fabulous Ink Spots. He died in a boating accident in 1960. *Ibid.*, Dance, 287-88.
34. George "Scoops" Carry was featured as alto sax and clarinetist with Earl Hines Band. Out of the University of Iowa, Hines discovered this native Chicagoan in 1940. "Scoops" was the band's rehearsal leader and assumed Hines' place when he stepped off the bandstand. Ibid., Dance, 286.
35. Gray, "Plantation Club, St. Louis" August 24, 1945. http://wardellgray.org/Wardell%20Gray%20Chronology%201945%20(master).htm

Chapter 8

1. Some of these cities included Boston, New York, Washington, D.C., Philadelphia, Cleveland, Chicago, Atlanta and New Orleans.
2. Willard B. Gatewood, *Aristocrats of Color: The Black Elite, 1880–1920* (Indianapolis: Indiana University Press, 1990), 96–103.
3. *Ibid.* 10–11.
4. *Ibid.*, 234–35.
5. Evangeline Holland, "The Black Elite in America," *Edwardian Promenade*, February 25, 2012, accessed September 8, 2013, http://edwardianpromenade.com/society/the-black-elite-in-america/.
6. The Standard Theatre opened in 1888. It was originally a white-owned and operated theater that discriminated against its black clientele. But when John T. Gibson bought the theater, he turned it into a thriving business with 1,325 seats in the heart of Philadelphia's black community. Gibson owned and operated the theater from 1914 to 1931. During the Great Depression, Gibson, who had been heavily invested in real estate, lost both the Dunbar and the Standard theaters, which became movie houses. In 1945 the Standard was bought by Wax Theatres. The Standard Theatre closed in 1954, and it was torn down in 1957. "The Arts, Popular Culture and Sports, 1644–1965," Pennsylvania Historical and Museum Commission, accessed September 8, 2013, http://www.phmc.state.pa.us/bhp/blackhistory/arts-popular-culture-sports-1644-to-1965.pdf, and "Standard Theatre Historical Marker," *Explore PA History*, accessed September 8, 2013, http://explorepahistory.com/hmarker.php?markerId=1-A-62.
7. On December 29, 1919, the Dunbar Theatre on South and Broad Streets opened. It was constructed by E. C. Brown and Andrew Stevens, Jr. The Dunbar was the first black-built, black-owned theater in Philadelphia. It was owned by black entrepreneur John T. Gibson and was home to the Lafayette Players, popular vaudeville entertainers. Later bought by white interests, the Dunbar was renamed the Lincoln. It hosted major Black performers from the 1920s into the 1940s. "The Dunbar Theatre Historical Marker," *Explore PA History*, accessed September 15, 2013, http://explorepahistory.com/hmarker.php?markerId=1-A-152.
8. "Standard Theatre Historical Marker," *Explore PA History*.
9. "The Arts, Popular Culture and Sports, 1644–1965," 223–24.
10. In Philadelphia 1888, the Grand Opera House on N. Broad Street and W. Montgomery Avenue opened with 3,000 seats. It was owned by Nixon-Nirdlinger and was renamed the Nixon Grand in the early 1920s. In 1930, Warner Brothers operated the theater, which functioned as an African American cinema between 1925 and 1940, when it was demolished. Mike Rivest, "Philadelphia Movie Theatres," *Rivest's Ultimate List of Movie Theatres and Drive-Ins*, January 1, 2012, accessed August 30, 2013, http://movie-theatre.org/usa/pa/philadelphia/main.html.
11. The Lincoln Theatre at Broad and Lombard Streets operated between 1919 and 1955. The owners were the Stanley Theatre Company (1920), Cities Theaters Corporation (1935–1940), and Wax Theaters (1945). Rivest, "Philadelphia Movie Theatres."
12. The Fans Theatre at 4032 Market Street opened as the Knickerbocker in 1914 with 1,826 seats. It was renamed Fays in 1919. Between 1935 and 1945 it was owned by C. & F. Theater Company. In 1948, it was christened the Fans Theatre under Reo Amusements Company, and it was sold in 1950. It functioned as the Fans until 1963, when it closed and was demolished. Rivest, "Philadelphia Movie Theatres."
13. The Pearl Theatre (1927–1963), with 1,400 seats, was located at 1600 North Broad Street and designed by J. K. Long. In the 1942 *Film Daily Year Book*, the Pearl is listed as one of eleven "Negro Theaters" in the Philadelphia area. The other theaters were the Dixie, Nixon Grand, Royal, Joy, Douglas,

Strand, New Garden, Standard, Rex, and Globe. Alan Kraus, "Pearl Theatre: 2047 Ridge Avenue, Philadelphia, PA 19121," *Cinema Treasures: Your Guide to Movie Theaters*, accessed August 30, 2013, http://cinematreasures.org/theaters/9485.

14. The Standard Theatre at 1126 South Street operated from around 1935 to 1955. It was an African American theater with 1,325 seats, and in 1945 it was owned by Wax Theaters. Rivest, "Philadelphia Movie Theatres."

15. "A graduate of Fisk University in Nashville, Tennessee, Irvin Miller was an actor, writer, playwright, director and producer on both stage and screen for nearly a half-century. He was best known for his annual stage review, the *Brownskin Models*." "Irvin C. Miller, Biography," *IMDb*, accessed August 15, 2013, http://www.imdb.com/name/nm0588498/bio. See also "The Arts, Popular Culture and Sports, 1644–1965."

16. Leonord Bushman, "'Born to Swing,' Harlem Revue, in Lincoln Bow," poss. *Pittsburgh Courier*, c. 1945 (clipping from Evelyn's scrapbook).

17. Joe Woods, "Spider Bruce Steals Show as Fans Theatre Reopens," poss. *Pittsburgh Courier*, November 3, 1945 (clipping from Evelyn's scrapbook).

18. "Fans' Theatre Set to Reopen Friday," *Pittsburgh Courier*, November 2, 1945.

19. "Fans Opening Show Acclaimed; Rated Greatest Show in Years," *Pittsburgh Courier*, November 3, 1945.

20. "Seaboard Express by Cholly," *Philadelphia Independent*, October 14, 1950.

21. Leo Champion, "History of the Atlantic City Boardwalk," *USA Today*, accessed August 3, 2013, http://traveltips.usatoday.com/history-atlantic-city-boardwalk-20055.html.

22. Babette's was located at 2211 Pacific Avenue and owned by Daniel Stebbins. It was initially called the Golden Inn; however, Stebbins changed its name to Babette's after his marriage to a showgirl named Blanche Babbett. Babette's, with its bar in the shape of a ship, catered to high-class (and very well-dressed) clientele. Backroom card tables were available for the guests. "Early Atlantic City Nightclubs," *Monopoly City*, accessed August 3, 2013, http://www.monopolycity.com/ac_earlyclubs.html.

23. "500 Club, Atlantic City, NJ," *Robert Eisenstadt's Antique Gambling Chips & Gambling Memorabilia*, accessed August 5, 2013, http://www.antiquegamblingchips.com/500Club.htm.

24. Christine Salvatore-Smith, "Broken Promises: Atlantic City and Its African-American Population," *Academia*, August 17, 2007, accessed July 31, 2013, http://www.academia.edu/1783523/Broken_Promises_Atlantic_City_and_Its_African-American_Population, 2–3.

25. "Kentucky Avenue Magic," *The Atlantic City Experience*, accessed July 31, 2013, http://www.atlanticcityexperience.org/index.php?option=com_content&view=article&id=28&Itemid=27.

26. Ibid.

27. Archie Black, "The Black Side of the Five," *JFK-COUNTERCOUP₂*, February 1, 2013 accessed July 30, 2013, http://jfkcountercoup2.blogspot.com/2013/02/the-black-side-of-five.html.

28. Misty Kammerman, "This Side of Paradise," *Atlantic City Press*, June 12, 1977.

29. "Harold P. Abrams Collection," Atlantic City Free Public Library, accessed July 30, 2013, http://encore.acfpl.org/iii/encore/record/C%7CRb1052438%7CSabrams%7CP0%2C1%7COrightresult%7CX5?lang=eng&suite=pearl.

30. The Speed Graphic camera was engineered for the purpose of commercial photography. Ken Vail, *Count Basie: Swinging the Blues, 1936–1950* (Lanham, MD: Scarecrow Press, 2003), 98.

31. Kammerman, "This Side of Paradise."

32. Until 1900, blacks and whites enjoyed the Atlantic City beaches together. But as Atlantic City grew, hotel owners pushed black beach-goers from the front of their establishments down to Missouri Avenue. The Chicken Bone Beach served the working class of Atlantic City while parents worked in the tourist industry. Ronald J. Stephens, "Chicken Bone Beach, Atlantic City, New Jersey (1900–)," *BlackPast.org: Remembered & Reclaimed*, accessed May 1, 2015, http://www.blackpast.org/aah/chicken-bone-beach-atlantic-city-new-jersey-1900.

33. Travis, *An Autobiography of Black Jazz*, 404–5.

34. Phil Brown, *Catskill Culture: A Mountain Rat's Memories of the Great Jewish Resort Area* (Philadelphia: Temple University Press, 1998), 23.

35. David Stradling, *Making Mountains: New York City and the Catskills* (Seattle: University of Washington Press, 2007), 104.

36. "New York—Migration," *City Data*, accessed June 15, 2013, http://www.city-data.com/states/New-York-Migration.html.

37. Stradling, *Making Mountains*, 11.

38. Borscht Belt Hotels in the Catskills, accessed June 15, 2013, https://www.google.com/maps/d/viewer?mid=zYwliaOmM5ak.kAmW_uIQWEGg&hl=en_US

39. Edwina seemed familiar with the following hotels: Grossinger Hotel, which was the main hotel in Grossinger; the Premier Hotel in South Fallsburg; the Concord Hotel in Kiamesha Lake (formerly known as Ideal, Overlook, and Gluck's); the Raleigh Hotel; Nevele Country Club in Ellenville; Brown's Hotel in Loch Sheldrake (formerly Black Apple Inn, and now the Grandview Palace condominiums) or Brown's Lake View in Black Lake; Kutcher's or Kutsher's Country Club in Monticello, and Nevele Grand Hotel in the Town of Wawarsing. Brown, *Catskill Culture*.

Chapter 9

1. Stearns and Stearns, *Jazz Dance*, 145, and William H. Glenn, "Glenn and Jenkins Scrapbook," Schomburg Center for Research in Black Culture, New York Public Library, accessed June 8, 2013, http://archives.nypl.org/scm/20861.

2. Stearns and Stearns, *Jazz Dance*, 145.

3. *Ibid.*, 265 (emphasis in original).

4. Howard Theatre Rebirth and Restoration, Inc., Historical Images Collection, accessed June 2, 2013, http://www.howardtheatre.org/Historic_Images.html.

5. "Howard Theatre, African American Heritage Trail," *Cultural Tourism DC*, accessed September 30, 2013, http://www.culturaltourismdc.org/portal/howard-theatre-african-american-heritage-trail#.Vi6QvH6rTIU.

6. Scott Yanow, "Willie Bryant," *All Music*, accessed May 20, 2013, http://www.allmusic.com/artist/willie-bryant-mn0000961904.

7. Allen Drew, "Spotology," poss. *Pittsburgh Courier* (aticle found in Edwina "Salt" Evelyn's scrapbook).
8. Lauterbach, *The Chitlin' Circuit*, 142.
9. Antionette Handy, *Black Women in American Bands and Orchestras* (Lanham, MD: Scarecrow Press, 1998), 49.
10. *Ibid.*, 62.
11. Anne Commire and Deborah Klezmer, eds., *Women in World History: A Biographical Encyclopedia*, "Jackie Mabley," Vol. 10 (Waterford, CT: Yorkin Publications, 2002), 4.
12. Whoopi Goldberg, *I Got Somethin' to Tell You* (comedy/documentary film), 2013.
13. Leslie Bennetts, "The Pain Behind the Laughter of Moms Mabley," *New York Times* (Theatre section), August 9, 1987, accessed February 14, 2013, http://www.nytimes.com/1987/08/09/theater/theater-the-pain-behind-the-laughter-of-moms-mabley.html.
14. Commire and Klezmer, *Women in World History*, 4.
15. Daphne Duval Harrison, *Black Pearls: Blues Queens of the 1920s* (New Brunswick, NJ: Rutgers University Press, 1990), 14 and 104.
16. Anne Collinson, "Baker, Josephine," in *Encyclopedia of Lesbian, Gay, Bisexual and Transgender History in America*, Vol. 1, edited by Marc Stein (New York: Charles Scribner's Sons/Thomson/Gale, 2004), 56.
17. Donald Morton, "Cultural Studies and Cultural Theory," in *Encyclopedia of Lesbian, Gay, Bisexual and Transgender History in America*, Vol. 1, edited by Marc Stein (New York: Charles Scribner's Sons/Thomson/Gale, 2004), 275.
18. Secret Histories Project, "Tony Jackson, c. 1884–1921," December 31, 2012, accessed February 12, 2013, http://secrethistoriesproject.tumblr.com/post/39297110201/21-tony-jackson-ah-the-dawning-of-the-jazz-age.

Chapter 10

1. Louis Henry Gates, Jr., "Exactly How 'Black' Is Black America?" *The Root*, February 11, 2013, accessed April 7, 2015, http://www.theroot.com/articles/history/2013/02/how_mixed_are_african_americans.3.html.
2. Mike Brunker, Monica Alba, and Bill Dedman, "Hate Crime in America, by the Numbers," *NBC News*, June 18, 2015, http://www.nbcnews.com/storyline/jewish-center-shootings/snapshot-hate-crime-america-numbers-n81521; Jane Predergast, "2001 Riots Led to Top-Down Change for Cincinnati Police," *Cincinnati Enquirer*, April 3, 2011, http://usatoday30.usatoday.com/news/nation/20110–40–3-cincinnati-riots-anniversary_N.htm; Kate Randall, "Toledo, Ohio: Neo-Nazi March Sparks Riot," *World Socialist Web Site*, October 17, 2005, https://www.wsws.org/en/articles/2005/10/ohio-o17.html; Ewen MacAskill, "Oakland Riots after Verdict in Police Shooting of Oscar Grant," *The Guardian*, July 9, 2010, http://www.theguardian.com/world/2010/jul/09/oakland-riots-oscar-grant-shooting-verdict; "Michael Brown's Shooting and Its Immediate Aftermath in Ferguson," *New York Times*, August 25, 2014, http://www.nytimes.com/interactive/2014/08/12/us/13police-shooting-of-black-teenager-michael-brown.html?_r=0#/#time348_10366. All sites accessed April 7, 2015.

3. Dance, *The World of Earl Hines*, 69–70.
4. Sherrie Tucker, *Swing Shift: "All-Girl" Bands of the 1940s* (Durham, NC: Duke University Press, 2000), 147.
5. *Ibid.*, 147–56.
6. "Discrimination Hits USO Stage Show; Soldiers Boycott Theatre," *Baltimore Afro-American* (Theatre section), April 11, 1942.
7. "Jim Crow Prevented Rochester from Making Overseas Army Tour without Jack Benny: Orson Welles's Tells of Talk with U.S. General," *Afro-American*, November 8, 1945.
8. Interview by author in Quartzsite, AZ, with O.P. Van Auken (a railroad telegrapher), November 25, 2012.
9. Interview by author in Greenwich Village, NY, with Edwina Evelyn, April 26, 1990.
10. Based on the schedules of Salt and Pepper, as well as Earl Hines, it appears that Louisville, Kentucky, was the destination. "List of Named Passenger Trains of the United States," *Wikipedia*, accessed January 2, 2012, https://en.wikipedia.org/wiki/List_of_named_passenger_trains_of_the_United_States_(I%E2%80%93M)#K.
11. Jordan W. Chambers owned Club Riviera, which was a meeting place for many prominent politicians and celebrities. In 1963 he was elected constable and Democratic committeeman of the 19th Ward of St. Louis, becoming the first black Democratic committeeman in St. Louis. Chambers was involved in politics and civil rights for his entire life. Connie Nisinger, "Jordan W. Chambers," *Find a Grave*, accessed October 14, 2013, http://findagrave.com/cgi-bin/fg.cgi?page=gr&Grid=22625.
12. During the American Civil War (1861–1865), several slave states did not secede from the United States. Thus, these states were considered border states. Kentucky and Missouri had both Confederate and Union sympathizers. Race relations in St. Louis were more complex than in many other places because the city was located in the border state of Missouri. "A Preservation Plan for St. Louis, Part I: Historic Contexts, Page 8—The African-American Experience," *The City of St. Louis, Missouri* (website), accessed October 14, 2013, https://www.stlouis-mo.gov/government/departments/planning/cultural-resources/preservation-plan/Part-I-African-American-Experience.cfm.
13. James Gill, *Lords of Misrule: Mardi Gras and the Politics of Race in New Orleans* (Jackson: University Press of Mississippi, 1997), 140.
14. "Mantan Moreland, Biography," *IMDb*, http://www.imdb.com/name/nm0603646/bio.
15. In reporting on the tremendous snowfall of 2006, one reporter made reference to the snowstorm of 1947: "A total of 26.9 inches fell in Central Park, the most since record-keeping began in 1869, the National Weather Service reported. In what weather experts called a remarkable and relentless fall that began late Saturday afternoon and ended late yesterday, it eclipsed the legendary blow of December 26–27, 1947, which dropped 26.4 inches and killed 77 people." Robert D. McFadden, "A Record Snow: 26.9 Inches Fall in New York City," *New York Times*, February 13, 2006; see also Chris Togneri, "1950's 'Big Snow' Remains Etched in Memory," *TribLive News*, November 24, 2013, accessed April 7, 2015, http://triblive.com/news/allegheny/49843377–4/inches-snow-storm#axzz3We4Fwv97.

Chapter 11

1. Walter Nugent, "Demography," *Encyclopedia of Chicago*, 2005, accessed December 27, 2013, http://www.encyclopedia.chicagohistory.org/pages/962.html.
2. *Ibid.*
3. *Ibid.*
4. *Ibid.*
5. Clovis E. Semmes, *The Regal Theater and Black Culture* (Basingstoke: Palgrave Macmillan, 2011), 48.
6. *Ibid.*, 47–48.
7. Elizabeth Schroeder Schlabach, *Along the Streets of Bronzeville: Black Chicago's Literary Landscape* (Chicago: University of Chicago Press, 2013), 8.
8. "Regal Opens This Week," *Pittsburgh Courier*, February 4, 1928 https://www.newspapers.com/image/40008119/?terms=opening%2Bof%2Bthe%2Bregal.
9. Charles Walton. "47th Street and South Park Boulevard: Bronzeville's Downtown." Jazz Institute of Chicago, 2002–2013. Available at http://www.jazzinchicago.org/educates/journal/articles/47th-street-and-south-park-boulevard-bronzevilles-downtown.
10. *Ibid.*
11. Semmes, *The Regal Theater and Black Culture*, 1–21.
12. Ray Martinez and Bryan Krefft, "Regal Theatre: 4710 S. Dr. Martin Luther King Jr. Drive, Chicago, IL 60615," *Cinema Treasures: Your Guide to Movie Theaters*, accessed September 30, 2013, http://cinematreasures.org/theaters/992.
13. Semmes, *The Regal Theater and Black Culture*, 25.
14. Martinez and Krefft, "Regal Theatre."
15. *Ibid.*
16. Travis, *An Autobiography of Black Jazz*, 217.
17. Semmes, *The Regal Theater and Black Culture*, 9.
18. Travis, *An Autobiography of Black Jazz*, 124–25.
19. *Ibid.*, 130.
20. *Ibid.*, 124.
21. *Ibid.*, 131.
22. *Ibid.*, 43.
23. *Ibid.*, 122.
24. *Ibid.*, 131.
25. *Ibid.*, 135, 138.
26. David W. King, producer, "Spanning Over 100 Years of Cinematic History, Chitlin' Circuit: Club DeLisa," *Jaxon Film Fest Retrospective*, accessed October 18, 2012, http://jaxonfilmfest.wordpress.com/?s=club+DeLisa.
27. Travis, *An Autobiography of Black Jazz*, 143.
28. *Ibid.*, 472.
29. Erik Hage, "Little Miss Cornshucks," *All Music*, accessed October 18, 2012, http://www.allmusic.com/artist/little-miss-cornshucks-mn0000299107/biography.
30. Travis, *An Autobiography of Black Jazz*, 134; and Eugene Chadbourne, "Lurlean Hunter," *All Music*, accessed October 18, 2013, http://www.allmusic.com/artist/lurlean-hunter-mn0000207183/biography.
31. Denise M. Watson, "Timmie Rogers: Revolutionary for a New Black Comedy," *Virginian-Pilot*, February 3, 2008, accessed May 1, 2015, http://hamptonroads.com/2008/02/timmie-rogers-revolutionary-black-comedy#.
32. Kammerman, "This Side of Paradise."
33. Travis, *An Autobiography of Black Jazz*, 425–33.
34. Joe Louis (Joseph Louis Barrow, May 13, 1914–April 12, 1981) held the title of boxing's world heavyweight champion from 1937 to 1949.
35. David Cunningham ("Dave" Garroway, 1913–1982) began his career as a radio announcer and premiered on the *Today* show in 1952. Garroway hosted the show until 1961. Sally Bedell, "Dave Garroway, 69, Found Dead; First Host of 'Today' on NBC-TV," *New York Times* July 22, 1982, accessed April 1, 2015, http://www.nytimes.com/1982/07/22/obituaries/dave-garroway-69-found-dead-first-host-of-today-on-nbc-tv.html; and Travis, *An Autobiography of Black Jazz*, 246.
36. "Top Show Spots: Charlie Glenn Pilots Café into Midwest's Finest," poss. *Chicago Defender* (clipping from Evelyn's scrapbook).
37. "Call Present Boogie Show Finest," poss. *Chicago Defender* (clipping from Evelyn's scrapbook).
38. "Glenn Scores Again with Surprise Acts," poss. *Chicago Defender* (clipping from Evelyn's scrapbook).
39. The Harlem Highlanders were a group from the mid–1930s. They were originally "The Four Buds," who sang, danced and played a string instrument called a tipple. Baby Laurence Jackson was part of the group. They joined an act called "The Three Gobs," and the group was subsequently billed as "The Six Merry Scotchmen." They wore kilts and were soon billed as the Harlem Highlanders. They danced and sang the arrangements of Jimmie Lunceford in six parts. Stearns and Stearns, *Jazz Dance*, 339.
40. Schiffman, *Harlem Heyday*, 175.
41. *Baby Laurence World's Premier Tap Dance Dancemaster*, Classic Jazz Records (vinyl records), USA, 1976.
42. Constance Valis Hill, "'Baby Laurence' Jackson (1921–1974)," *American Tap Dance Foundation: Tap Dance Hall of Fame*, accessed April 1, 2015, http://www.atdf.org/awards/laurence.html.
43. Travis, *An Autobiography of Black Jazz*, 88.
44. Michael Jackson, "Brilliant Corners: The Pershing Hotel, Chicago," *Rhythm & News*, Issue 417 (2008), 6, accessed July 16, 2013, http://delmark.com/pdfs/rn714-all.pdf.
45. *Chicago Jazz*. http://guides.lib.uchicago.edu/c.php?g=297184&p=1983832
46. Jackson, "Brilliant Corners."
47. "Researching Chicago Jazz Venues."
48. Naomi Nix, "Crowds Take in 84th Annual Bud Billiken Parade," *Chicago Tribune News*, August 10, 2013, accessed 14 September 2013, http://articles.chicagotribune.com/20130–81–0/news/chi-crowds-take-in-84th-annual-bud-billiken-parade-20130810_1_jesse-jackson-sr-marching-band-chicago-defender.
49. Semmes, *The Regal Theater and Black Culture*, 53.
50. Nix, "Crowds Take in 84th Annual Bud Billiken Parade."
51. "Entertainment Boasts Top Talent," *Chicago Defender*, ca. February 4, 1951 (clipping from Evelyn's scrapbook).
52. Travis, *An Autobiography of Black Jazz*, 263–65.
53. Sufiya Abdur-Rahman, "Holmes 'Daddy-o' Daylie, 82: Pioneer Radio Personality," *Chicago Tribune News*, February 14, 2003, accessed September 14, 2013, http://articles.chicagotribune.com/20030–21–4/news/0302140188_1_bartender-radio-host-broadcast-communications.

Chapter 12

1. In Katrina Hazzard-Gordon's *Jookin',* jook joints are described in depth. At one point, Hazzard-Gordon quotes Zora Neal Hurston in defining the word *jook* as "the world of a Negro pleasure house. It may mean a bawdy house. It may mean the house set apart on public works where men and women dance, drink, and gamble. Often, it is a combination of all these." Jook joints were generally owned by blacks. In these locations, African Americans came together to share culture, play music, and dance the movements that could be traced back to Africa. See Hazzard-Gordon, *Jookin': The Rise of Social Dance Formations in African-American Culture* (Philadelphia: Temple University Press, 1990), 77–116.

2. Cathy MacDonald, "Detroit's Black Bottom and Paradise Valley Neighborhoods," Walter P. Reuther Library, Wayne State University, May 4, 2012, accessed October 1, 2013, http://www.reuther.wayne.edu/node/8609.

3. Lars Bjorn, with Jim Gallert, *Before Motown: A History of Jazz in Detroit, 1920–1960* (Ann Arbor: University of Michigan Press, 2001), 4.

4. MacDonald, "Detroit's Black Bottom."

5. Dan Austin, "Graystone Ballroom," *HistoricDetroit.org,* 2013, accessed August 19, 2013, http://historicdetroit.org/building/graystone-ballroom/.

6. "Eyes That Burn: The Vanished Neighborhood of Black Bottom," *PmWiki,* accessed August 19, 2013, http://wiki.stryck.com/EyesThatBurn/TheVanishedNeighborhoodOfBlackBottom.

7. The Paradise Theatre brought in the best talent of the 1940s, such as Duke Ellington, Louis Armstrong, Earl Hines, Jimmy Lunceford, Bill "Bojangles" Robinson, Lena Horne, and Pearl Bailey. "Paradise Theatre," *The Concert Database,* accessed August 21, 2013, http://www.theconcertdatabase.com/venues/paradise-theater.

8. Bjorn, *Before Motown,* 70.
9. Ibid., 65.
10. Ibid., 65–66.
11. "Detroit Race Riots 1943," *PBS: American Experience,* accessed September 15, 2013, http://www.pbs.org/wgbh/americanexperience/features/general-article/eleanor-riots/.
12. Bjorn, *Before Motown,* 97.
13. "The Full-Dress 'Boiled Shirt,'" *The Fedora Lounge,* accessed October 23, 2013, http://www.thefedoralounge.com/threads/the-full-dress-boiled-shirt.52367/.

14. Michael D. Sallah, "Midwest's Gambling Mecca," *The Blade* (Toledo, OH), October 6, 1996, Section A, 8–9, accessed September 15, 2013, http://news.google.com/newspapers?nid=1350&dat=19961006&id=mDQxAAAAIBAJ&sjid=cgMEAAAAIBAJ&pg=6564,1354747.

15. Ibid.
16. Clint Mauk, "Entertainment: The Good and the Bad," *Toledo.com,* March 24, 2009, accessed July 22, 2013, http://www.toledo.com/index.php?src=news&srctype=detail&category=intoledo&refno=143.
17. Ibid.
18. Kenneth R. Dickson, "Part 13: Games of Chance Thrive during War Years," *The Blade* (Toledo, OH), October 27, 2013, accessed July 22, 2014, http://www.toledoblade.com/frontpage/2008/12/19/Part-13-Games-of-chance-thrive-during-war-years.html.

19. Mauk, "Entertainment."
20. "Taverns," *Greetings from Cincinnati,* accessed July 21, 2013, http://www.cincinnativiews.net/taverns.htm.
21. "Carrie Nation," *PBS: American Experience,* accessed September 20, 2013, http://www.pbs.org/wgbh/amex/1900/peopleevents/pande4.html.
22. "Taverns."
23. Steven C. Tracy, *Going to Cincinnati: A History of the Blues in the Queen City* (Urbana: University of Illinois Press, 1993), 89.
24. Ibid.
25. The Improved Benevolent and Protective Order of Elks of the World began as a small militant group of men who formed what was in 1952 the most powerful fraternal order of Negro Elks in the world. It started on the banks of the Ohio River with less than 50 members, but at the time of the Golden Jubilee celebration it had more than 550,000 active members.
26. S. Don Moran, "The Avenue Breakdown," Cincinnati, 1952 (clipping from Evelyn's scrapbook).
27. Donald Bogle, *Toms, Coons, Mulattoes, Mammies, & Bucks: An Interpretive History of Blacks in American Films* (New York: Continuum, 1989), 41.
28. Roy Hurst, "Stepin Fetchit, Hollywood's First Black Film Star," *NPR Books,* March 6, 2006, accessed September 15, 2013, http://www.npr.org/templates/story/story.php?storyId=5245089.
29. Paghat the Ratgirl, review of *Burlesque in Harlem,* accessed April 1, 2015, http://www.weirdwildrealm.com/f-burlesque-in-harlem.html.
30. David Brent Johnson, "The Once-Thriving Jazz Scene of … Indianapolis?" *NPR Music,* March 28, 2012, accessed September 30, 2013, http://www.npr.org/blogs/ablogsupreme/2012/03/27/149474702/the-once-thriving-jazz-scene-of-indianapolis.
31. David Brent Johnson, "Along the Avenue: The Legacy of Indianapolis Jazz," *Night Lights,* September 18, 2007, accessed September 30, 2013, http://indianapublicmedia.org/nightlights/indianapolis-jazz-indiana-avenue/.
32. Dance, *The World of Earl Hines,* 48.
33. "The Avenoo: Clubs and Ambience of Indiana Avenue," *Indiana Avenue and Beyond,* accessed September 30, 2013, http://jazzindianaavenue.wordpress.com/the-avenoo-clubs-and-ambience-of-indiana-avenue/; and "Ferguson, Denver and Sea (brothers)," *Notable Kentucky African Americans Database,* University of Kentucky Libraries, accessed September 30, 2013, http://nkaa.uky.edu/record.php?note_id=2292.
34. Johnson, "Along the Avenue."
35. "Black History: Indiana Avenue," IndyStar.com, February 1, 2013, http://archive.indystar.com/article/99999999/NEWS06/110125028/Black-History-Indiana-Avenue.
36. David Brent Johnson, "The Basics of David Baker: A Conversation," *Night Lights,* August 28, 2007, accessed September 30, 2013, http://indianapublicmedia.org/nightlights/the-basics-of-david-baker-a-conversation/; Johnson, "Along the Avenue.
37. Johnson, "The Basics of David Baker."
38. Bryan Krefft, "Palace Theatre: 5242 W. 25th Street, Cicero, IL 60804," *Cinema Treasures: Your Guide to Movie Theaters,* accessed August 18, 2013, http://cinematreasures.org/theaters/4533.
39. "Wisconsin's Gangster Tour," TravelWisconsin.com, April 24, 2009, accessed August 20, 2013, http://

www.travelwisconsin.com/article/things-to-do/wisconsins-gangster-tour.
40. "Wisconsin—Ethnic Groups," *City Data*, accessed August 19, 2013, http://www.city-data.com/states/Wisconsin-Ethnic-groups.html.
41. "Black History in Wisconsin," *Wisconsin Historical Society*, accessed October 20, 2013, http://www.wisconsinhistory.org/topics/blackhistory/#after.
42. *Goin' Places in Milwaukee and Racine*, June 30, 1950.
43. "Club Terris & Elect Tom Terris Alderman 1940 Milwaukee WI 40 Strike Match-book," *Ebay*, accessed October 21, 2013, http://www.ebay.com/itm/Club-Terris-Elect-Tom-Terris-Alderman-1940-Milwaukee-WI-40-Strike-Matchbook/300950474097?pt=LH_DefaultDomain_0&hash=item46120bcd71.
44. "Tutz's Cocktail Bar Matchbook Milwaukee Wisconsin Low Number," *Ebay*, accessed October 21, 2013, http://www.ebay.com/itm/tutzs-cocktail-bar-matchbook-milwaukee-wisconsin-low-number-/221269361512?pt=LH_DefaultDomain_0&hash=item3384ae8368.

Chapter 13

1. Don B. Wilmeth, with Tice L. Miller, eds., *The Cambridge Guide to American Theatre* (Cambridge: Cambridge University Press, 1996), 324.
2. *Ibid.*.
3. Jayna Brown, *Babylon Girls: Black Women Performers and the Shaping of the Modern* (Durham, NC: Duke University Press, 2008), 92–93.
4. Tanner, "Shuffle Along."
5. Hill, *Tap Dancing America*, 75–76.
6. Stearns and Stearns, *Jazz Dance*, 145, 195; Haskin, *The Cotton Club*, 22–23.
7. "Red Hot 1930s Cotton Club Show—Censored Reel Survives of Dancers Orgy!," YouTube, uploaded by 2reelerApril 17, 2010, accessed April 8, 2015, https://www.youtube.com/watch?v=cLBz3tW3kBI.
   16 mm reel found of censored black dancers orgy! It's Cotton Club Girls Gone Wild! Best scenes are at the end! Meant for the trash, and never meant to be seen! Elegant black showgirls ditch Opera for Jazz as they get seduced by a hot jazz tune. ... It is so slickly produced that it almost passed the Hays Code, but not the "dancers orgy" at the end."
8. Fox, *Showtime at the Apollo*, 77.
9. *Ibid.*
10. "Hortense Allen Jordan (September 17, 1919–March 15, 2008)," Philadelphia Folklore Project, last modified December 17, 2010, accessed March 20, 2013, http://folkloreproject.org/artists/hortense-allen-jordan.
11. "Larry Steele," *The Atlantic City Experience*, accessed March 21, 2013, http://www.atlanticcityexperience.org/index.php?option=com_content&view=article&id=29%3Ala.
12. "Key to Map of Chicago South Side Jazz c.1915–c.1930," *Chicago Jazz Archive*, University of Chicago Library, last generated April 4, 2012, accessed March 1, 2013, http://www.lib.uchicago.edu/e/su/cja/mapkey.html.
13. Dance, *The World of Earl Hines*, 58.
14. "Daisy Richards," Houston Area Digital Archives, November 1, 1989, accessed December 1, 2011, http://digital.houstonlibrary.org/cdm/singleitem/collection/Interviews/id/11/rec/1.
15. Interview by author in Philadelphia, PA, with Jewel "Pepper" Welch.
16. Heather Lyn MacDonald, *Been Rich All My Life* (Toots Cracking Production, 2006). Featuring the Silver Belles: Marion Coles, Elaine Ellis, Cleo Hayes, Fay Ray, Bertye Lou Wood, and manager Geri Kennedy.
17. *Ibid.*
18. "Daisy Richards," Houston Area Digital Archives.
19. Fox, *Showtime at the Apollo*, 77.
20. Schiffman, *Uptown*, 65.
21. "Daisy Richards," Houston Area Digital Archives.
22. MacDonald, *Been Rich All My Life*.
23. Travis, *An Autobiography of Black Jazz*, 143.
24. Toe-tap was a rhythm dance executed on ballet pointe shoes with metal taps on the tip of the shoe.
25. Travis, *An Autobiography of Black Jazz*, 125, 127, 130.
26. Fitzgerald, Lillian. Interviewed in West Philadelphia, PA, April 10, 1992.
27. Wendy R. Williams, "Harlem's Legendary Silver Belles," *New York Cool*, accessed September 13, 2013, http://www.newyorkcool.com/archives/2006/August/feature.html.

Chapter 14

1. Niki Lambros, "Montreal: Emerging Jazz Capital of the World," *Le Panoptique* (Publié le 1 février, 2009), accessed November 2, 2013, http://www.doc4net.fr/doc/1491700693958?cn=11.
2. The National Park Service begins the Underground Railroad chronology in 1817, with Andrew Jackson's war with the Seminole Indians and the runaways in Florida, and ends it with the conclusion of the Civil War in 1865. See "The Underground Railroad," *Traveling Through Time: Archived Articles of Shelby County People, Places and Events*, accessed November 1, 2013, http://www.shelbycountyhistory.org/schs/blackhistory/undergroundrr.htm; and John Gilmore, *Swinging in Paradise: The Story of Jazz in Montreal* (Montreal: Ellipse Editions, 2011), 20–22.
3. Gilmore, *Swinging in Paradise*, 22–23.
4. *Ibid.*, 18–19.
5. *Ibid.*, 19, 28.
6. Clubs grew in popularity in Montreal. Some of these included Rockhead's Paradise Café, the Kit-Kat Cabaret, Café St. Michel, the Washington Club, the Cosy Grill, the Boulevard, the Blue Sky, Connie's Inn, the Montmartre, the El Morocco, the Esquire, the Downbeat, the Savoy, and the Terminal Club.
7. Gilmore, *Swinging in Paradise*, 23, 49, 157, 160.
8. *Ibid.*, 30.
9. *Ibid.*, 29.
10. Rosemary Sadlier, "Equity and Human Rights," *Black History Canada*, 2008, accessed November 2, 2013, http://blackhistorycanada.ca/theme.php?id=5.
11. Gilmore, *Swinging in Paradise*, 55, 77.
12. *Ibid.*, 53–54.
13. *Ibid.*, 163–65.
14. *Ibid.*, 164.
15. *Ibid.*
16. Interview by author in Greenwich Village, NY, with Edwina Evelyn, July 7, 2005.
17. "Rockhead's Paradise Café," Montreal, Canada (clipping from Evelyn's scrapbook).

18. H.W., "Comedy Singer Tops in Rockhead's Show," Montreal, Canada (clipping from Evelyn's scrapbook).
19. Gilmore, *Swinging in Paradise*, 115.
20. *Ibid.*, 128.
21. "Le Canada—Montreal, Mardure, 1947, Montreal, Canada" (clipping from Evelyn's scrapbook).
22. Gilmore, *Swinging in Paradise*, 128.

Chapter 15

1. "The 1950s: Happy Days: 53c. Land of Television," *U.S. History: Pre-Columbian to the New Millennium*, accessed August 12, 2013, http://www.ushistory.org/us/53c.asp.
2. "The History of Motion Pictures" (lecture), University of Washington, accessed August 12, 2013, http://faculty.washington.edu/baldasty/JAN13.htm.
3. "The 1950s: Happy Days."
4. Richard F. Taflinger, "Sitcom: What It Is, How It Works: A History of Comedy on Television: Beginning to 1970," Washington State University, 1996, accessed August 12, 2013, http://public.wsu.edu/~taflinge/comhist.html.
5. Gilmore, *Swinging in Paradise*, 200–201.
6. National Women's History Museum, "A History of Women in Industry," 2007, accessed August 15, 2013, http://www.nwhm.org/online-exhibits/industry/womenindustry_intro.html.
7. "Mugging" indicates facial expressions used by a performer to indicate a joyful and playful mood. Many African Americans thought mugging was perpetuating a racist stereotype.

Epilogue

1. Leslie Matthews, "Bronx Limited," *New York Age*, June 14, 1952.
2. *New York Age*, February 18, 1950.
3. Interview by author in West Orange, NJ, with Vernita McNeil (Edythe Robinson's niece), May 26–27, 2012, and April 25–26, 2015.
4. Peace Corps Volunteer—Peace Corps (Volunteer, Volumes 8–9, page 44), Office of Public Affairs, Peace Corps, 1970; "The Orrin Benjamin Hawley Family of Woodbury, Connecticut: Information about Bruce Nelson Robinson," Genealogywww, updated July 5, 2012, accessed October 21, 2013, http://www.genealogy.com/ftm/h/a/w/Charles-B-Hawley-MD/WEBSITE-0001/UHP-0399.html; and interview by author in West Orange, NJ, with Vernita McNeil (Edythe Robinson's niece), May 26–27, 2012.

Appendix I

1. Billy Eckstine, "Doings at Club Savoy," Saturday, May 22, 1948.

Appendix II

1. Ron Devlin, "Pearl Bailey Keeps On Doin' in Allentown Visit, 71-Year-Old Singer Dishes Up Wisdom," *The Morning Call*, December 3, 1989, accessed January 2, 2015, http://articles.mcall.com/19891–20–3/news/2713779_1_pearl-bailey-drummer-georgetown-university-class.
2. "Charles 'Cholly' Atkins," *American Dance Legends*, accessed April 15, 2015, http://www.theatredance.com/legends/atkins.html.
3. Stearns and Stearns, *Jazz Dance*, 37.
4. "The First Moonwalk—Bill Bailey—The Apollo Theatre—New York—1955," YouTube, uploaded December 12, 2010, accessed April 1, 2015, www.youtube.com/watch?v=y71njpDH3co.
5. "Venettes History," *Venettes Cultural Workshop*, accessed September 20, 2013, http://www.venettesculturalworkshop.org/v_History.asp.
6. Stearns and Stearns, *Jazz Dance*, 352; and Bruce Weber, "Bunny Briggs, Tap Dancing Virtuoso, Dies at 92," *New York Times*, November 26, 2014, accessed April 2, 2015, http://www.nytimes.com/2014/11/27/arts/dance/bunny-briggs-tap-dancing-virtuoso-dies-at-92-.html?_r=0.
7. Stearns and Stearns, *Jazz Dance*, 242–43.
8. Interview by author in Philadelphia, PA, with Isabelle "Eleanor Byrd" Fambro, August 14 and September 20, 1990.
9. Dance, *The World of Earl Hines*, 286.
10. "Nat 'King' Cole Biography," *Rock and Roll Hall of Fame Museum*, accessed December 20, 2013, http://rockhall.com/inductees/nat-king-cole/bio/.
11. Stearns and Stearns, *Jazz Dance* 307–8.
12. Constance Valis Hill, "Charles 'Honi' Coles (2 April 1911–12 November 1992," *American Tap Dance Foundation: Tap Dance Hall of Fame*, accessed April 15, 2015, http://www.atdf.org/awards/honi.html.
13. Interview by author in Atlantic City, NJ, with Chris Columbo, August 1, 1990.
14. Jacqui Malone, *Steppin'on the Blues: The Visible Rhythms of African American Dance* (Urbana: University of Illinois Press, 1996).
15. Semmes, *The Regal Theater and Black Culture*, 85.
16. "Legacy: Sammy Dyer (1933–1960)—Founder/Director," Sammy Dyer School of the Theatre, accessed April 10, 2015, http://www.sammydyerschoolofthetheatre.com/legacy.
17. Interview by author in West Philadelphia, PA, with Edith "Baby Edwards" Hunt, August 15, 1990.
18. Cullen, *Vaudeville Old & New*, 388–89.
19. *Nebraska State Journal* (Lincoln), February 28, 1943, 33.
20. Stearns and Stearns, *Jazz Dance*, 246.
21. Constance Valis Hill, "Chuck Green (6 November 1919–7 March 1997)," *American Tap Dance Foundation: Tap Dance Hall of Fame*, accessed April 1, 2015, www.atdf.org/awards/green.html.
22. Cullen, *Vaudeville Old & New*, 288; Lean'tin L. Bracks and Jessie Carney Smith, eds., *Black Women of the Harlem Renaissance Era* (Lanham, MD: Rowman & Littlefield, 2014), 93; and Bernard L. Peterson, Jr., *Profiles of African American Stage Performers and Theatre People, 1816–1960* (Westport, CT: Greenwood Press, 2000), 111.
23. Stearns and Stearns, *Jazz Dance*, 351.
24. A popular version of Paddle and Roll is as follows: heel dig or place the right heel on the floor; spank or brush the right foot backward; place the ball of the right foot on the floor slightly behind the supporting foot; drop the right heel to the floor. This four-sound step is then executed on the left foot; it is usually performed in a series. A variety of accents and syncopation can be employed.
25. Stearns and Stearns, *Jazz Dance*, 349–50.

26. Interview by author in Philadelphia, PA, with LaVaughn Robinson, September 14, 1988, and September 5, 1990.
27. Hill, *Tap Dancing America*, 76.
28. "Prez & Lady Day: The Story of Billie Holiday and Lester Young," *The Jim Cullum Riverwalk Jazz Collection* (Stanford University Libraries), accessed March 1, 2015, http://riverwalkjazz.stanford.edu/program/prez-lady-day-story-billie-holiday-and-lester-young.
29. *Billie at 100: A Century of Lady Day*, accessed April 1, 2015, http://www.billieholiday.com.
30. "Biography," *Lena Horne* (website), accessed April 1, 2014, http://www.lena-horne.com/biography_lena_horne.htm; and "Lena Horne: In Her Own Words," *PBS: American Masters*, May 14, 2010, accessed April 1, 2015, http://www.pbs.org/wnet/americanmasters/episodes/lena-horne/about-the-performer/487/.
31. Harrison, *Black Pearls*, 199–217.
32. "Germaine Ingram," Philadelphia Folklore Project, accessed November 6, 2013, http://www.folkloreproject.org/artists/germaine-ingram.
33. Interview by author in New York, NY, with Ludie Jones, July 20 and September 24, 1990.
34. Stearns and Stearns, *Jazz Dance*, 77–78, 85; and Gerard Heroux, "Sissieretta Jones: American Opera Pioneer (1869–1933)," *Rhode Island Music Hall of Fame Historical Archive*, accessed April 3, 2015, http://www.ripopmusic.org/musical-artists/musicians/sissieretta-jones/.
35. Marian Hannah Winter, "Juba and American Minstrelsy," in *Chronicles of the American Dance: From the Shakers to Martha Graham*, edited by Paul Magriel (New York: Henry Holt, 1948), 42–53.
36. "Jelly Roll Morton, Biography: Pianist, Songwriter (1890–1941)," Biographywww, accessed April 29, 2014, http://www.biography.com/people/jelly-roll-morton-9415945.
37. Frank, *Tap!*, 301–12.
38. Stearns and Stearns, *Jazz Dance*, 301–2.
39. N. Lee Orr, "Gertrude 'Ma' Rainey (1886–1939)," *New Georgia Encyclopedia*, May 9, 2003, accessed March 29, http://www.georgiaencyclopedia.org/articles/arts-culture/gertrude-ma-rainey-18861-939; "Gertrude 'Ma' Rainey (1886–1939)," *Red Hot Jazz Archive*, accessed March 29, 2013, http://www.redhotjazz.com/rainey.html.
40. Schiffman, *Harlem Heyday*, 147.
41. Interview by author in West Philadelphia, PA, with Edith "Baby Edwards" Hunt, August 15, 1990.
42. Schiffman, *Harlem Heyday*, 147.
43. Telephone interview by author with Marion Coles, January 1991.
44. Interview by author in Atlantic City, NJ, with Chris Columbo, August 1, 1990.
45. Stearns and Stearns, *Jazz Dance*, 155.
46. Watson, "Timmie Rogers"; "Stars of Vaudeville #737: Timmie Rogers," *Travalanche*, accessed October 15, 2013, http://travsd.wordpress.com/2013/07/04/stars-of-vaudeville-737-timmie-rogers/.
47. Dance, *The World of Earl Hines*, 287–88.
48. "Jimmy 'Slyde' Godbolt," National Endowment for the Arts: NEA National Heritage Fellowships, accessed April 1, 2015, http://arts.gov/honors/heritage/fellows/jimmy-slyde-godbolt; and "Biography," Tap Legacy Foundation: Jimmy Slyde Tribute Website, accessed April 15, 2015, http://jimmyslyde.taplegacy.org/biography/.
49. "Bessie Smith, Biography: Singer (1894–1937)," Biographywww, accessed December 21, 2013, http://www.biography.com/people/bessie-smith-9486520.
50. Harrison, *Black Pearls*, 42–49.
51. Arnold Shaw, *Honkers and Shouters: The Golden Years of Rhythm & Blues* (New York: Collier Books, 1978), xvi.
52. "Libby Spencer," Philadelphia Folklore Project, accessed November 6, 2013, http://www.folkloreproject.org/artists/libby-spencer.
53. "Died John (Spider Bruce) Mason," *Jet: The Weekly Negro News Magazine* II, no. 11 (July 10, 1952), 21.
54. Hill, *Tap Dancing America*, 103–4.
55. Jenai Cutcher, "John Bubbles," *DanceTeacher*, September 29, 2011, accessed November 30, 2013, http://www.dance-teacher.com/2011/09/john-bubbles.
56. "Yack Taylor," *All Music*, accessed April 5, 2015, http://www.allmusic.com/artist/yack-taylor-mn0000683526/songs.
57. Susan Ecker and Lloyd Ecker, *I Am Sophie Tucker: A Fictional Memoir* (Westport, CT: Prospecta Press, 2014); see also http://www.sophietucker.com.
58. Ward, *Jazz: A History of America's Music*, 449.
59. Dance, *The World of Earl Hines*, 285.
60. "Dianne Walker," Contemporary Black Biography, Encyclopediawww, 2007, accessed November 6, 2013, http://www.encyclopedia.com/doc/1G22-687800053.html.
61. Bogle, *Heat Wave*, 3–35; Ward, *Jazz: A History of America's Music*, 109; "Ethel Waters, Biography," *IMDb*, accessed April 1, 2015, http://www.imdb.com/name/nm0914083/bio.
62. "Slappy White, Biography," *IMDb*, accessed December 19, 2013, http://www.imdb.com/name/nm0925463/bio?ref_=nm_ov_bio_sm#mini_bio.
63. Stearns and Stearns, *Jazz Dance*, 85, 91.

Bibliography

Books and Articles

Abbott, Lynn, and Doug Seroff. *Ragged but Right: Black Traveling Shows, "Coon Songs," and the Dark Pathway to Blues and Jazz (American Made Music).* Jackson: University Press of Mississippi, 2012 (reprint).

Anderson, Jervis. *This Was Harlem: A Cultural Portrait, 1900–1950.* New York: Farrar Straus Giroux, 1982.

Bedell, Sally. "Dave Garroway, 69, Found Dead; First Host of 'Today' on NBC-TV." *New York Times*, July 22, 1982. Available at http://www.nytimes.com/1982/07/22/obituaries/dave-garroway-69-found-dead-first-host-of-today-on-nbc-tv.html.

Bennett, Lerone, Jr. *Before the Mayflower: A History of Black America.* Chicago: Johnson Publishing Company, 1988.

Bjorn, Lars, with Jim Gallert. *Before Motown: A History of Jazz in Detroit, 1920–1960.* Ann Arbor: University of Michigan Press, 2001.

Bogle, Donald. *Heat Wave: The Life and Career of Ethel Water.* New York: HarperCollins, 2011.

_____. *Toms, Coons, Mulattoes, Mammies, & Bucks: An Interpretive History of Blacks in American Films.* New York: Continuum, 1989.

Bracks, Lean'tin L., and Jessie Carney Smith, eds. *Black Women of the Harlem Renaissance Era.* Lanham, MD: Rowman & Littlefield, 2014.

Brown, Jayna. *Babylon Girls: Black Women Performers and the Shaping of the Modern.* Durham, NC: Duke University Press, 2008.

Brown, Phil. *Catskill Culture: A Mountain Rat's Memories of Great Jewish Resort Area.* Philadelphia: Temple University Press, 1998.

Burke, Patrick. *Come In and Hear the Truth: Jazz and Race on 52nd Street.* Chicago: University of Chicago Press, 2008.

Calloway, Cab, and Bryant Rollins. *Of Minnie the Moocher & Me.* New York: Thomas Y. Crowell, 1976.

Collinson, Anne. "Baker, Josephine." In *Encyclopedia of Lesbian, Gay, Bisexual and Transgender History in America*, Vol. 1, edited by Marc Stein. New York: Charles Scribner's Sons/Thomson/Gale, 2004.

Cullen, Frank, with Florence Hackman and Donald McNeilly. *Vaudeville Old & New: An Encyclopedia of Variety Performers in America.* Vol. 1. New York: Routledge, 2007.

Dance, Stanley. *The Night People: The Jazz Life of Dicky Wells.* Washington, DC: Smithsonian Institution Press, 1991.

_____. *The World of Earl Hines.* New York: Charles Scribner's Sons, 1977.

Ecker, Susan, and Lloyd Ecker. *I Am Sophie Tucker: A Fictional Memoir.* Westport, CT: Prospecta Press, 2014.

Elam, Harry J., Jr. and Davie Krasner. *African American Performance and Theater History.* Oxford: Oxford University Press, 2001.

Emery, Lynne Fauley. *Black Dance from 1619 to Today.* Princeton, NJ: A Dance Horizons Book, 1988.

Fernett, Gene. *Swing Out: Great Negro Dance Bands.* Midland, MI: Pendell, 1970.

_____. *Thousand Golden Horns. Midland.* Midland, MI: Pendell, 1966.

Frank, Rusty E. *Tap! The Greatest Tap Dance Stars and Their Stories, 1900–1955.* New York: William Morrow, 1990.

French, Ellen Dennis, and Anne Commire, ed. *Women in World History: A Biographical Encyclopedia* Vol. 10. Detroit: Yorkin Publications, 2002.

Fox, Ted. *Showtime at the Apollo.* New York: Holt, Rinehart and Winston, 1983.

Gatewood, Willard B. *Aristocrats of Color: The Black Elite, 1880–1920.* Indianapolis: Indiana University Press, 1990.

Gill, James. *Lords of Misrule: Mardi Gras and the Politics of Race in New Orleans.* Jackson: University Press of Mississippi, 1997.

Gilmore, John. *Swinging in Paradise: The Story of Jazz in Montreal.* Montreal: Ellipse Editions, 2011.

Gioia, Ted. *The History of Jazz.* New York: Oxford University Press, 1997.

Grossman, James R., Ann Durkin Keating, and Janice L. Reiff, eds. *Encyclopedia of Chicago.* Chicago: University of Chicago Press, 2004.

Handy, D. Antoinette. *Black Women in American Bands and Orchestras.* Lanham, MD: Scarecrow Press, 1998.

_____. *The International Sweethearts of Rhythm.* Metuchen, NJ: Scarecrow Press, 1983.

Harrison, Daphne Duval. *Black Pearls: Blues Queens of the 1920s.* New Brunswick, NJ: Rutgers University Press, 1990.

Haskin, Jim. *The Cotton Club.* New York: New American Library, 1977.

Hazzard-Gordon, Katrina. *Jookin': The Rise of Social Dance Formations in African-American Culture.* Philadelphia: Temple University Press, 1990.

Hill, Constance Valis. *Tap Dancing America: A Cultural History.* Oxford: Oxford University Press, 2010.

Hill, Errol G., and James V. Hatch. *A History of*

African American Theatre. New York: Cambridge: Cambridge University Press, 2003.
Kammerman, Misty. "This Side of Paradise." *Atlantic City Press*, June 12, 1977.
Katz, William Loren. *Black Indians: A Hidden Heritage*. New York: Atheneum, 1986.
Kellner, Bruce, ed. *The Harlem Renaissance: A Historical Dictionary for the Era*. New York: Methuen, 1984.
Kelly, Robin D. B. *Thelonious Monk: The Life and Times of an American Original*. New York: Free Press, 2009.
Knowles, Mark. *Tap Roots: The Early History of Tap Dancing*. Jefferson, NC: McFarland, 2002.
Lauterbach, Preston. *The Chitlin' Circuit and the Road to Rock 'n' Roll*. New York: W. W. Norton, 2011.
Malone, Jacqui. *Steppin'on the Blues: The Visible Rhythms of African American Dance*. Urbana: University of Illinois Press, 1996.
Morton, Donald. "Cultural Studies and Cultural Theory." In *Encyclopedia of Lesbian, Gay, Bisexual and Transgender History in America*, Vol. 1, edited by Marc Stein. New York: Charles Scribner's Sons/Thomson/Gale, 2004.
Peace Corps Volunteer—Peace Corps (Volunteer, Volumes 8–9, page 44). Office of Public Affairs, Peace Corps, 1970.
Peterson, Bernard L., Jr. *The African American Theatre Directory, 1816–1960: A Comprehensive Guide to Early Black Theatre Organizations, Companies, Theatres, and Performing Groups*. Westport, CT: Greenwood Press, 1997.
——. *A Century of Musicals in Black and White: An Encyclopedia of Musical Stage Works By, About, or Involving African Americans*. Westport, CT: Greenwood Press, 1993.
——. *Profiles of African American Stage Performers and Theatre People, 1816–1960*. Westport, CT: Greenwood Press, 2000.
Placksin, Sally. *American Women in Jazz: 1900 to the Present Their Words, Lives, and Music*. New York: Wideview Books, 1982.
Reid, Grant Harper. *Rhythm for Sale*. North Charleston: CreateSpace Independent Publishing Platform, 2013.
Riis, Thomas L. *Just Before Jazz: Black Musical Theater in New York, 1890–1915*. Baton Rouge: Louisiana State University Press, 1989.
Scaruffi, Piero. *A History of Jazz Music, 1900–2000*. Silicon Valley: Omniware, 2007.
Schiffman, Jack. *Harlem Heyday*. Buffalo, NY: Prometheus Books, 1984.
——. *Uptown: The Story of Harlem's Apollo Theatre*. New York: Cowles Book Company, 1971.
Schlabach, Elizabeth Schroeder. *Along the Streets of Bronzeville: Black Chicago's Literary Landscape*. Chicago: University of Chicago Press, 2013.
Schuller, Gunther. *The Swing Era: The Development of Jazz, 1930–1945*. New York: Oxford University Press, 1989.
Semmes, Clovis E. *The Regal Theater and Black Culture*. Basingstoke: Palgrave Macmillan, 2011.
Sengstock, Charles A., Jr. *That Toddlin' Town: Chicago's White Dance Bands and Orchestras, 1900–1950*. Urbana: University of Illinois Press, 2004.
Shaw, Arnold. *Honkers and Shouters: The Golden Years of Rhythm & Blues*. New York: Collier Books, 1978.
Stearns, Marshall, and Jean Stearns. *Jazz Dance: The Story of American Vernacular Dance*. New York: Schirmer Books, 1968.
Stradling, David. *Making Mountains: New York City and the Catskills*. Seattle: University of Washington Press, 2007.
Tracy, Steven C. *Going to Cincinnati: A History of the Blues in the Queen City*. Urbana: University of Illinois Press, 1993.
Travis, Dempsey J. *An Autobiography of Black Jazz*. Chicago: Urban Research Institute, 1983.
Tucker, Sherrie. *Swing Shift: "All-Girl" Bands of the 1940s*. Durham, NC: Duke University Press, 2000.
Vail, Ken. *Count Basie: Swinging the Blues, 1936–1950*. Lanham, MD: Scarecrow Press, 2003.
Ward, Geoffrey C. *Jazz: A History of America's Music*. Based on documentary film by Ken Burns. New York: Alfred A. Knopf, 2000.
Willis, Cheryl M. *Tap Dance: Memories and Issues of African American Women Who Performed Between 1930 and 1950*. Temple University (Ann Arbor: UMI Dissertation Services, 1991).
Wilmeth, Don B., with Tice L. Miller, ed. *The Cambridge Guide to American Theatre*. Cambridge: Cambridge University Press, 1996.
Winter, Marian Hannah. "Juba and American Minstrelsy." In *Chronicles of the American Dance: From the Shakers to Martha Graham*, edited by Paul Magriel. New York: Henry Holt, 1948.
Wolf, Robert. *Crazeology: An Autobiography of a Chicago Jazzman: Bud Freeman*. Chicago: University of Illinois Press, 1989.
Zinn, Howard. *A People's History of the United States*. New York: Harper Perennial Modern Classics, 2003.

Newspapers and Magazines

Baltimore Afro-American. Known as the *Afro*, this weekly newspaper was founded in 1892 by John H. Murphy, Sr., a former slave. It is the longest-running African American family-owned newspaper in the United States. Searched 1944–1947.
Chicago Defender. Weekly newspaper founded by Robert S. Abbott for African American readers. 1905–present. Searched 1940–1950.
The Day (New London, CT). 1881–present.
Down Beat (Chicago, IL). American magazine focused on jazz and blues. 1934–present.
Goin' Places in Milwaukee and Racine. June 30, 1950.
Jet: The Weekly Negro News Magazine (Chicago, IL). Founded by John H. Johnson of Johnson Publishing Company. 1951–2014 (then became a digital magazine).
Nebraska State Journal (Lincoln, NE). February 28, 1943.
New Amsterdam News (New York, NY). Founded in 1909. Searched 1940–1952.
Philadelphia Daily News. Interstate General Media, tabloid newspaper. 1925–present. Searched 1940–1945.
Philadelphia Independent (billed itself as "The World's Greatest Negro Tabloid"). 1931–1971. Searched 1937–1945.
Pittsburgh Courier. May 10, 1910–October 22, 1966.
Variety. Penske Media Corporation, American enter-

tainment trade magazine. Founded in 1905; last daily printed edition was March 19, 2013.

Online Sites

"500 Club, Atlantic City, NJ." *Robert Eisenstadt's Antique Gambling Chips & Gambling Memorabilia*. Available at http://www.antiquegamblingchips.com/500Club.htm.

"The 1950s: Happy Days: 53c. Land of Television." *U.S. History: Pre-Columbian to the New Millennium*. Available at http://www.ushistory.org/us/53c.asp.

Abdur-Rahman, Sufiya. "Holmes 'Daddy-o' Daylie, 82: Pioneer Radio Personality." *Chicago Tribune News*, February 14, 2003. Available at http://articles.chicagotribune.com/2003-02-14/news/0302140188_1_bartender-radio-host-broadcast-communications.

Albertson, Chris. *1925–27: Lesbianism in the Life of Bessie Smith*. Available at http://xroads.virginia.edu/~ug97/blues/katz.html.

"The Arts, Popular Culture and Sports, 1644–1965." Pennsylvania Historical and Museum Commission. Available at http://www.phmc.state.pa.us/bhp/blackhistory/arts-popular-culture-sports-1644-to-1965.pdf.

Austin, Dan. "Graystone Ballroom." *HistoricDetroit.org*, 2013. Available at http://historicdetroit.org/building/graystone-ballroom/.

"The Avenoo: Clubs and Ambience of Indiana Avenue." *Indiana Avenue and Beyond*. Available at http://jazzindianaavenue.wordpress.com/the-avenoo-clubs-and-ambience-of-indiana-avenue/.

Bennetts, Leslie. "The Pain Behind the Laughter of Moms Mabley." *New York Times* (Theater section). August 9, 1987. Available at http://www.nytimes.com/1987/08/09/theater/theater-the-pain-behind-the-laughter-of-moms-mabley.html.

Berrigan, Philip, and Rusty E. Frank. "Berry Brothers." *American National Biography Online*. Updated January 2002. Available at http://www.anb.org/articles/18/18-03672.html.

"Bessie Smith, Biography: Singer (1894–1937)." Biographywww. Available at http://www.biography.com/people/bessie-smith-9486520.

Billie at 100: A Century of Lady Day. Available at http://www.billieholiday.com.

"Biography." Lena Horne (website). Available at http://www.lena-horne.com/biography_lena_horne.htm.

"Biography." Tap Legacy Foundation: Jimmy Slyde Tribute Website. Available at http://jimmyslyde.taplegacy.org/biography/.

Black, Archie. "The Black Side of the Five." *JFK COUNTERCOUP₂*, February 1, 2013 Available at http://jfkcountercoup2.blogspot.com/2013/02/the-black-side-of-five.html.

"Black History: Indiana Avenue." IndyStarwww, February 1, 2013. Available at http://archive.indystar.com/article/99999999/NEWS06/110125028/Black-History-Indiana-Avenue.

"Black History in Wisconsin." *Wisconsin Historical Society*. Available at http://www.wisconsinhistory.org/topics/blackhistory/#after.

Borscht Belt Hotels in the Catskills. Available at https://www.google.com/maps/d/viewer?mid=zYwliaOmM5ak.kAmW_uIQWEGg&hl=en_US.

Brunker, Mike, Monica Alba, and Bill Dedman. "Hate Crime in America, by the Numbers." Available at http://www.nbcnews.com/storyline/jewish-center-shootings/snapshot-hate-crime-america-numbers-n81521.

"Carrie Nation." *PBS: American Experience*. Available at http://www.pbs.org/wgbh/amex/1900/peopleevents/pande4.html.

Chadbourne, Eugene. "Effie Smith." *All Music*. Available at http://www.allmusic.com/artist/effie-smith-mn0000177570.

———. "Ernie Fields." *All Music*. Available at http://www.allmusic.com/artist/ernie-fields-mn0000203516/biography.

———. "Jack Gee." *All Music*. Available at http://www.allmusic.com/artist/jack-gee-mn0000127224/biography.

———. "Lurlean Hunter." *All Music*. Available at http://www.allmusic.com/artist/lurlean-hunter-mn0000207183/biography.

Champion, Leo. "History of the Atlantic City Boardwalk." *USA Today*. Available at http://traveltips.usatoday.com/history-atlantic-city-boardwalk-20055.html.

"Charles 'Cholly' Atkins." *American Dance Legends*. Available at http://www.theatredance.com/legends/atkins.html.

"The Chitlin Circuit." *Official R&B Music Hall of Fame Museum* (website). Available at http://www.rbhalloffame.com/the-chitlin-circuit/.

Clay, Christopher. "History of Asbury Park." *Asbury Park, "Then & Now"*, February 8, 2011. Available at http://www.drakkar91.com/ap/asbury9.htm.

"Club Terris & Elect Tom Terris Alderman 1940 Milwaukee WI 40 Strike Matchbook." *Ebay*. Available at http://www.ebay.com/itm/Club-Terris-Elect-Tom-Terris-Alderman-1940-Milwaukee-WI-40-Strike-Matchbook/300950474097?pt=LH_DefaultDomain_0&hash=item46120bcd71.

Cutcher, Jenai. "John Bubbles." *DanceTeacher*, September 29, 2011. Available at http://www.dance-teacher.com/2011/09/john-bubbles.

"Daisy Richards." Houston Area Digital Archives, November 1, 1989. Available at http://digital.houstonlibrary.org/cdm/singleitem/collection/Interviews/id/11/rec/1.

Davis, James F. "Who Is Black? One Nation's Definition." *PBS: Frontline*. Available at http://www.pbs.org/wgbh/pages/frontline/shows/jefferson/mixed/onedrop.html.

DeFerrari, John. "Lost Washington: The Gayety Theatre." *Greater Greater Washington*, January 26, 2011. Available at http://greatergreaterwashington.org/post/8960/lost-washington-the-gayety-theater/.

"Detroit Race Riots 1943." *PBS: American Experience*. Available at http://www.pbs.org/wgbh/americanexperience/features/general-article/eleanor-riots/.

Devlin, Ron. "Pearl Bailey Keeps On Doin' in Allentown Visit, 71-Year-Old Singer Dishes Up Wisdom." *The Morning Call*, December 3, 1989. Available at http://articles.mcall.com/1989-12-03/news/2713779_1_pearl-bailey-drummer-georgetown-university-class.

"Dianne Walker." Contemporary Black Biography, Encyclopediawww, 2007. Available at http://www.encyclopedia.com/doc/1G2-2687800053.html.

Dickson, Kenneth R. "Part 13: Games of Chance Thrive during War Years." *The Blade* (Toledo, OH),

October 27, 2013. Available at http://www.toledo blade.com/frontpage/2008/12/19/Part-13-Games-of-chance-thrive-during-war-years.html.
"The Dunbar Theatre Historical Marker." *Explore PA History*. Available at http://explorepahistory.com/hmarker.php?markerId=1-A-152.
"Early Atlantic City Nightclubs." *Monopoly City*. Available at http://www.monopolycity.com/ac_earlyclubs.html.
Ella Fitzgerald: The Official Site of the First Lady of Song. Available at http://www.ellafitzgerald.com/about/index.html.
"Ethel Waters, Biography." *IMDb*. Available at http://www.imdb.com/name/nm0914083/bio.
"Eyes That Burn: The Vanished Neighborhood of Black Bottom." *PmWiki*. Available at http://wiki.stryck.com/EyesThatBurn/TheVanishedNeighborhoodOfBlackBottom.
"Ferguson, Denver and Sea (brothers)." *Notable Kentucky African Americans Database*, University of Kentucky Libraries. Available at http://nkaa.uky.edu/record.php?note_id=2292.
"The Four Step Brothers." *Footnotes on Tap*. Available at http://www.footnotesontap.com/LegendBiosPhotos/FourStepBrothersPage.html.
"Frank Sinatra, Biography: Film Actor, Singer (1915–1998)." Biographywww. Available at http://www.biography.com/people/frank-sinatra-9484810.
"The Full-Dress 'Boiled Shirt.'" *The Fedora Lounge*. Available at http://www.thefedoralounge.com/threads/the-full-dress-boiled-shirt.52367/.
Gates, Louis Henry, Jr. "Exactly How 'Black' Is Black America?" *The Root*, February 11, 2013. Available at http://www.theroot.com/articles/history/2013/02/how_mixed_are_african_americans.3.html.
"Germaine Ingram." Philadelphia Folklore Project. Available at http://www.folkloreproject.org/artists/germaine-ingram.
"Gertrude 'Ma' Rainey (1886–1939)." *Red Hot Jazz Archive*. Available at http://www.redhotjazz.com/rainey.html.
Glenn, William H. "Glenn and Jenkins Scrapbook." Schomburg Center for Research in Black Culture, New York Public Library. Available at http://archives.nypl.org/scm/20861.
"Good Like Nedick's." *Warm Muh Weenah*, March 14, 2012. Available at http://loop48.com/bump/good-like-nedicks/.
"The Great Migration: Bronzeville Is Born." Available at http://cuip.net/~swyatt/The%20Great%20Migration/bronzeville_is_born.htm.
Hage, Erik. "Little Miss Cornshucks." *All Music*. Available at http://www.allmusic.com/artist/little-miss-cornshucks-mn0000299107/biography.
"Harold P. Abrams Collection." Atlantic City Free Public Library, Atlantic City, NJ. Available at http://encore.acfpl.org/iii/encore/record/C%7CRb1052438%7CSabrams%7CP0%2C1%7COrightresult%7CX5?lang=eng&suite=pearl.
Heroux, Gerard. "Sissieretta Jones: American Opera Pioneer (1869–1933)." *Rhode Island Music Hall of Fame Historical Archive*. Available at http://www.ripopmusic.org/musical-artists/musicians/sissieretta-jones/.
Hill, Constance Valis. "'Baby Laurence' Jackson (1921–1974)." *American Tap Dance Foundation: Tap Dance Hall of Fame*. Available at http://www.atdf.org/awards/laurence.html.

———. "Charles 'Honi' Coles (2 April 1911–12 November 1992)." *American Tap Dance Foundation: Tap Dance Hall of Fame*. Available at http://www.atdf.org/awards/honi.html.
———. "Chuck Green (6 November 1919–7 March 1997)." *American Tap Dance Foundation: Tap Dance Hall of Fame*. Available at www.atdf.org/awards/green.html.
"The History of Motion Pictures" (lecture). University of Washington. Available at http://faculty.washington.edu/baldasty/JAN13.htm.
Holland, Evangeline. "The Black Elite in America." *Edwardian Promenade*, February 25, 2012. Available at http://edwardianpromenade.com/society/the-black-elite-in-america/.
"Hortense Allen Jordan (September 17, 1919–March 15, 2008)." Philadelphia Folklore Project, last modified December 17, 2010. Available at http://folkloreproject.org/artists/hortense-allen-jordan.
"Howard Theatre, African American Heritage Trail." *Cultural Tourism DC*. Available at http://www.culturaltourismdc.org/portal/howard-theatre-african-american-heritage-trail#.Vi6QvH6rTIU.
Howard Theatre, Rebirth and Restoration, Inc., Historical Images Collection. Available at http://www.howardtheatre.org/Historic_Images.html.
Hurst, Roy. "Stepin Fetchit, Hollywood's First Black Film Star." *NPR Books*, March 6, 2006. Available at http://www.npr.org/templates/story/story.php?storyId=5245089.
"Interview: Sid Caesar." *Archive of American Television*. Available at http://www.emmytvlegends.org/interviews/people/sid-caesar.
"Introduction to researching Chicago jazz venues: Bronzeville, South Shore, and Woodlawn Clubs." University of Chicago Library, accessed July 15, 2013. http://guides.lib.uchicago.edu/c.php?g=297184&p=1983832.
"Irvin C. Miller, Biography." *IMDb*. Available at http://www.imdb.com/name/nm0588498/bio.
Jackson, Michael. "Brilliant Corners: The Pershing Hotel, Chicago." *Rhythm & News*, Issue 417 (2008). Available at http://delmark.com/pdfs/rn714-all.pdf.
"Jelly Roll Morton, Biography: Pianist, Songwriter (1890–1941)." Biographywww. Available at http://www.biography.com/people/jelly-roll-morton-9415945.
"Jerry Lewis, Biography: Film Actor, Theatre Actor, Television Actor, Comedian, Philanthropist (1926–)." Biographywww. Available at http://www.biography.com/people/jerry-lewis-9381122?page=2.
"Jim Crow Prevented Rochester from Making Overseas Army Tour without Jack Benny: Orson Welles's Tells of Talk with U.S. General." *Afro-American*, November 8, 1945.
"Jimmy 'Slyde' Godbolt." National Endowment for the Arts: NEA National Heritage Fellowships. Available at http://arts.gov/honors/heritage/fellows/jimmy-slyde-godbolt.
Johnson, David Brent. "Along the Avenue: The Legacy of Indianapolis Jazz." *Night Lights*, September 18, 2007. Available at http://indianapublicmedia.org/nightlights/indianapolis-jazz-indiana-avenue/.
———. "The Basics of David Baker: A Conversation." *Night Lights*, August 28, 2007. Available at http://indianapublicmedia.org/nightlights/the-basics-of-david-baker-a-conversation/.
———. "The Once-Thriving Jazz Scene of ... Indi-

anapolis?" *NPR Music*, March 28, 2012. http://www.npr.org/blogs/ablogsupreme/2012/03/27/149474702/the-once-thriving-jazz-scene-of-indianapolis.

Kenrick, John. "A History of the Musical: Minstrel Shows." *Musicals 101.com: The Cyber Encyclopedia of Musical Theatre, Film, & Television.* Copyright 1996, revised 2003. Available at http://www.musicals101.com/minstrel.htm.

———. "A History of the Musical: Minstrel Shows: Part II." *Musicals 101.com: The Cyber Encyclopedia of Musical Theatre, Film, & Television.* Copyright 1996, revised 2003. Available at http://www.musicals101.com/minstrelb.htm.

"Kentucky Avenue Magic." *The Atlantic City Experience.* Available at http://www.atlanticcityexperience.org/index.php?option=com_content&view=article&id=28&Itemid=27.

"Key to Map of Chicago South Side Jazz c.1915–c.1930." *Chicago Jazz Archive*, University of Chicago Library. Available at http://www.lib.uchicago.edu/e/su/cja/mapkey.html.

King, David W. "Spanning Over 100 Years of Cinematic History, Chitlin' Circuit: Club DeLisa." *Jaxon Film Fest Retrospective.* Available at http://jaxonfilmfest.wordpress.com/?s=club+DeLisa.

Kraus, Alan. "Pearl Theatre, 2047 Ridge Avenue, Philadelphia, PA 19121." *Cinema Treasures: Your Guide to Movie Theaters.* Available at http://cinematreasures.org/theaters/9485.

Krefft, Bryan. "Palace Theater, 5242 W. 25th Street, Cicero, IL 60804." *Cinema Treasures: Your Guide to Movie Theaters.* Available at http://cinematreasures.org/theaters/4533.

Lambros, Niki. "Montreal: Emerging Jazz Capital of the World." *Le Panoptique* (Publié le 1 février, 2009). Available at http://www.doc4net.fr/doc/1491700693958?cn=11.

"Larry Steele." *The Atlantic City Experience.* Available at http://www.atlanticcityexperience.org/index.php?option=com_content&view=article&id=29%3Ala.

"Legacy: Sammy Dyer (1933–1960)—Founder/Director." Sammy Dyer School of the Theatre. Available at http://www.sammydyerschoolofthetheatre.com/legacy.

"Lena Horne: In Her Own Words." *PBS: American Masters*, May 14, 2010. Available at http://www.pbs.org/wnet/americanmasters/episodes/lena-horne/about-the-performer/487/.

"Libby Spencer (1920–1998)." Philadelphia Folklore Project. Available at http://www.folkloreproject.org/artists/libby-spencer.

Library of Congress. "U.S. Congressional Documents and Debates, 1774–1875, 39th Congress, 1st Session, 358." *A Century of Lawmaking for a New Nation.* Available at http://memory.loc.gov/cgi-bin/ampage?collId=llsl&fileName=014/llsl014.db&recNum=389.

"List of Named Passenger Trains of the United States." *Wikipedia.* Available at https://en.wikipedia.org/wiki/List_of_named_passenger_trains_of_the_United_States_(I%E2%80%93M)#K.

"Louis Jordan." *BBC Music.* Available at http://www.bbc.co.uk/music/artists/b8b30699-7814-4fd1-ab75-6f22f5da0fac.

Lowe, Jim. "Tim Moore." *Vot Der Dumboozle?* Copyright 2000. Available at http://www.yodaslair.com/dumboozle/tmoore/tmoordex.html.

MacAskill, Ewen. "Oakland Riots after Verdict in Police Shooting of Oscar Grant." *The Guardian*, July 9, 2010. Available at http://www.theguardian.com/world/2010/jul/09/oakland-riots-oscar-grant-shooting-verdict.

MacDonald, Cathy. "Detroit's Black Bottom and Paradise Valley Neighborhoods." Walter P. Reuther Library, Wayne State University. May 4, 2012. Available at http://www.reuther.wayne.edu/node/8609.

"Mantan Moreland, Biography." *IMDb.* Available at http://www.imdb.com/name/nm0603646/bio.

Martinez, Ray, and Bryan Krefft. "Regal Theater: 4710 S. Dr. Martin Luther King Jr. Drive, Chicago, IL 60615." *Cinema Treasures: Your Guide to Movie Theaters.* Available at http://cinematreasures.org/theaters/992.

Mauk, Clint. "Entertainment: The Good and the Bad." Toledowww, March 24, 2009. Available at http://www.toledo.com/index.php?src=news&srctype=detail&category=intoledo&refno=143.

McFadden, Robert D. "A Record Snow: 26.9 Inches Fall in New York City." *New York Times*, February 13, 2006.

"Melvin Moore." Living Legends Foundation, Inc. Available at http://www.livinglegendsfoundation.com/melvin-moore.

"Michael Brown's Shooting and Its Immediate Aftermath in Ferguson." *New York Times*, August 25, 2014. Available at http://www.nytimes.com/interactive/2014/08/12/us/13police-shooting-of-black-teenager-michael-brown.html?_r=0#/#time348_10366.

Mortimer, Lee. "Night Clubbing with Lee Mortimer." *The Sunday Mirror*, April 14, 1946. Available at http://sites.google.com/site/newyorkcityapril1946/in-progress/newspapers/the-sunday-papers-on-april-14/the-sunday-mirror/the-columnists/nightclubbing-with-lee-mortimer.

National Women's History Museum. "A History of Women in Industry." 2007. Available at http://www.nwhm.org/online-exhibits/industry/womenindustry_intro.html.

"Nat 'King' Cole Biography." *Rock and Roll Hall of Fame Museum.* Available at http://rockhall.com/inductees/nat-king-cole/bio/.

"New York—Migration." *City Data.* Available at http://www.city-data.com/states/New-York-Migration.html.

Nisinger, Connie. "Jordan W. Chambers." *Find a Grave.* Available at http://findagrave.com/cgi-bin/fg.cgi?page=gr&Grid=22625.

Nix, Naomi. "Crowds Take in 84th Annual Bud Billiken Parade." *Chicago Tribune News*, August 10, 2013. http://articles.chicagotribune.com/2013-08-10/news/chi-crowds-take-in-84th-annual-bud-billiken-parade-20130810_1_jesse-jackson-sr-marching-band-chicago-defender.

Nugent, Walter. "Demography." *Encyclopedia of Chicago*, 2005. Available at http://www.encyclopedia.chicagohistory.org/pages/962.html.

"Oran Thaddeus Page [Hot Lips]." Texas State Historical Association. Available at http://www.tshaonline.org/handbook/online/articles/fparx.

Orr, N. Lee. "Gertrude 'Ma' Rainey (1886–1939)." *New Georgia Encyclopedia*, May 9, 2003. Available at http://www.georgiaencyclopedia.org/articles/arts-culture/gertrude-ma-rainey-1886-1939.

"The Orrin Benjamin Hawley Family of Woodbury, Connecticut: Information about Bruce Nelson

Robinson." Geneaologywww, updated July 5, 2012. Available at http://www.genealogy.com/ftm/h/a/w/Charles-B-Hawley-MD/WEBSITE-0001/UHP-0399.html.

Owens, Kamri M. "Website #2 Harlem Gangs (1920–1930)." *Scoop.it!* (part of "Crime of the 1930's"), January 16, 2013. Available at http://www.scoop.it/t/crime-of-the-1930-s/p/3995074712/2013/01/16/website-2-harlem-gangs-1920-1930.

Paghat the Ratgirl. Review of *Burlesque in Harlem*. Available at http://www.weirdwildrealm.com/f-burlesque-in-harlem.html.

"Paradise Theater." *The Concert Database*. Available at http://www.theconcertdatabase.com/venues/paradise-theater.

Predergast, Jane. "2001 Riots Led to Top-Down Change for Cincinnati Police." *Cincinnati Enquirer*, April 3, 2011. Available at http://usatoday30.usatoday.com/news/nation/2011-04-03-cincinnati-riots-anniversary_N.htm.

"A Preservation Plan for St. Louis, Part I: Historic Contexts, Page 8—The African-American Experience." *The City of St. Louis, Missouri* (website). Available at https://www.stlouis-mo.gov/government/departments/planning/cultural-resources/preservation-plan/Part-I-African-American-Experience.cfm.

"Prez & Lady Day: The Story of Billie Holiday and Lester Young." *The Jim Cullum Riverwalk Jazz Collection* (Stanford University Libraries). Available at http://riverwalkjazz.stanford.edu/program/prez-lady-day-story-billie-holiday-and-lester-young.

Pritchett, Judy, with Frank Manning. "Shorty George Snowden." *Archives of Early Lindy Hop: Biographies of the Original Lindy Hoppers*. Copyright 1995–2006. Available at http://www.savoystyle.com/shorty_george.html.

Randall, Kate. "Toledo, Ohio: Neo-Nazi March Sparks Riot." *World Socialist Web Site*, October 17, 2005. Available at https://www.wsws.org/en/articles/2005/10/ohio-o17.html.

"Researching Chicago Jazz Venues: Bronzeville, South Shore, and Woodlawn Clubs." *Chicago Jazz Archive*, University of Chicago Library. Available at http://guides.lib.uchicago.edu/content.php?pid=66937&sid=1002421.

"Research Resources on Chicago, Jazz, and the Great Migration." *Chicago Jazz Archive*, University of Chicago Library, last generated April 4, 2012. Available at http://www.lib.uchicago.edu/e/su/cja/greatmigration.html.

Rivest, Mike. "Philadelphia Movie Theatres." *Rivest's Ultimate List of Movie Theatres and Drive-Ins*. Available at http://movie-theatre.org/usa/pa/philadelphia/main.html.

Rounce, Tony. "Checkmate: The Complete King Recordings 1952–55: The Checkers." *Ace Records*. Available at http://acerecords.co.uk/checkmate-the-complete-king-recordings-1952-55.

Sadlier, Rosemary. "Equity and Human Rights." *Black History Canada*, 2008. Available at http://blackhistorycanada.ca/theme.php?id=5.

Sallah, Michael D. "Midwest's Gambling Mecca." *The Blade* (Toledo, OH), October 6, 1996, Section A, 8–9. Available at http://news.google.com/newspapers?nid=1350&dat=19961006&id=mDQxAAAAIBAJ&sjid=cgMEAAAAIBAJ&pg=6564,1354747.

Salvatore-Smith, Christine. "Broken Promises: Atlantic City and Its African-American Population." *Academia*, August 17, 2007. Available at http://www.academia.edu/1783523/Broken_Promises_Atlantic_City_and_Its_African-American_Population.

Seasons of Change. "African Americans and Death." *Caring and Sharing Through Every Season*. 2015. Available at http://www.caringseasons.com/african-americans-and-death/.

Secret Histories Project. "Tony Jackson, c. 1884–1921." December 31, 2012. Available at http://secrethistoriesproject.tumblr.com/post/39297110201/21-tony-jackson-ah-the-dawning-of-the-jazz-age.

"Slappy White, Biography." *IMDb*. Available at http://www.imdb.com/name/nm0925463/bio?ref_=nm_ov_bio_sm#mini_bio.

Smith, V. Chapman. "The Triumph and Tragedy of Octavius V. Catto." *UShistory.org*. Available at http://www.ushistory.org/people/catto.htm.

"Standard Theatre Historical Marker." *Explore PA History*. Available at http://explorepahistory.com/hmarker.php?markerId=1-A-62.

Stark, Karl, *Inquirer* staff writer. "The Essence of Pearl Bailey: The Singer/actress/good-will Ambassador Brought a Love of Folks to the Many Stages of Her Life." Phillywww, August 20, 1990. Available at http://articles.philly.com/1990-08-20/news/25932475_1_pearl-bailey-lump-sum-talent-contest.

"Stars of Vaudeville #737: Timmie Rogers." *Travalanche*. Available at http://travsd.wordpress.com/2013/07/04/stars-of-vaudeville-737-timmie-rogers/.

Stephens, Ronald J. "Chicken Bone Beach, Atlantic City, New Jersey (1900–)." *BlackPast.org: Remembered & Reclaimed*. Available at http://www.blackpast.org/aah/chicken-bone-beach-atlantic-city-new-jersey-1900.

"Sybil Lewis, Biography." *IMDb*. Available at http://www.imdb.com/name/nm0507783/bio?ref_=nm_ov_bio_sm.

Taflinger, Richard F. "Sitcom: What It Is, How It Works: A History of Comedy on Television: Beginning to 1970." University of Washington, 1996. Available at http://public.wsu.edu/~taflinge/comhist.html.

Tanner, Jo. "Shuffle Along: The Musical at the Center of the Harlem Renaissance." *Drop Me Off in Harlem*. Available at http://artsedge.kennedy-center.org/interactives/harlem/themes/shuffle_along.html.

"Taverns." *Greetings from Cincinnati*. Available at http://www.cincinnativiews.net/taverns.htm.

"Tim Moore, Biography." *IMDb*. Available at http://www.imdb.com/name/nm0601953/bio?ref_=nm_ov_bio_sm.

Togneri, Chris. "1950's 'Big Snow' Remains Etched in Memory." *TribLive News*, November 24, 2013. Available at http://triblive.com/news/allegheny/4984337-74/inches-snow-storm#axzz3We4Fwv97. Travis, Dempsey J. "Where the Jazz Was Super-Hot." *Chicago Tribune*, March 26, 1985. Available at http://articles.chicagotribune.com/1985-03-26/news/8501170148_1_dance-floor-radio-band.

"Tutzs Cocktail Bar Matchbook Milwaukee Wisconsin Low Number." *Ebay*. Available at http://www.ebay.com/itm/tutzs-cocktail-bar-matchbook-milwaukee-wisconsin-low-number-/221269361512?pt=LH_DefaultDomain_0&hash=item3384ae8368.

"The Underground Railroad." *Traveling Through Time: Archived Articles of Shelby County People, Places and Events*. Available at http://www.shelbycountyhistory.org/schs/blackhistory/undergroundrr.htm.

"Venettes History." *Venettes Cultural Workshop*. Available at http://www.venettesculturalworkshop.org/v_History.asp.

"The Volstead Act." *Alcohol Problems and Solutions*. Available at http://www.alcoholproblemsandsolutions.org/Controversies/Volstead-Act.html.

"The Volstead Act: October 28, 1919." *History, Art & Archives: United States House of Representatives*. Available at http://history.house.gov/Historical-Highlights/1901–1950/The-Volstead-Act/.

Walton, Charles. "47th Street and South Park Boulevard: Bronzeville's Downtown." Jazz Institute of Chicago, 2002–2013. Available at http://www.jazzinchicago.org/educates/journal/articles/47th-street-and-south-park-boulevard-bronzevilles-downtown.

Wardell Gray: A Chronology (1945). Available at http://wardellgray.org/Wardell%20Gray%20Chronology%201945%20(master).htm.

Watson, Denise M. "Timmie Rogers: Revolutionary for a New Black Comedy." *Virginian-Pilot*, February 3, 2008. Available at http://hamptonroads.com/2008/02/timmie-rogers-revolutionary-black-comedy#.

Weber, Bruce. "Bunny Briggs, Tap Dancing Virtuoso, Dies at 92." *New York Times*, November 26, 2014. Available at http://www.nytimes.com/2014/11/27/arts/dance/bunny-briggs-tap-dancing-virtuoso-dies-at-92-.html?_r=0.

Weiser, Kathy. "Speakeasies of the Prohibition Era." *Legends of America*, updated March 2010. Available at http://www.legendsofamerica.com/ah-prohibitionspeakeasy2.html.

Williams, Wendy R. "Harlem's Legendary Silver Belles." *New York Cool*. Available at http://www.newyorkcool.com/archives/2006/August/feature.html.

"Wisconsin—Ethnic Groups." *City Data*. Available at http://www.city-data.com/states/Wisconsin-Ethnic-groups.html.

"Wisconsin's Gangster Tour." TravelWisconsinwww, April 24, 2009. Available at http://www.travelwisconsin.com/article/things-to-do/wisconsins-gangster-tour.

Wormser, Richard. "The Rise and Fall of Jim Crow: Plessy V. Ferguson (1896)." Public Broadcasting Service, Oregon Public Broadcasting Corporation, 2002. Available at http://www.pbs.org/wnet/jimcrow/stories_events_plessy.html.

"Yack Taylor." *All Music*. Available at http://www.allmusic.com/artist/yack-taylor-mn0000683526/songs.

Yanow, Scott. "Willie Bryant." *All Music*. Available at http://www.allmusic.com/artist/willie-bryant-mn0000961904.

Film, Television, Video and Music

Baby Laurence World's Premier Tap Dance Dancemaster. Classic Jazz Records (vinyl records), USA, 1976.

"The First Moonwalk—Bill Bailey—The Apollo Theatre—New York—1955." YouTube, uploaded December 12, 2010. Available at www.youtube.com/watch?v=y71njpDH3co.

Goldberg, Whoopi. *I Got Somethin' to Tell You* (comedy/documentary film). 2013.

MacDonald, Heather Lyn. *Been Rich All My Life* [VHS]. A Toots Cracking Production, 2006.

Nierenberg, George, director. *About Tap* [VHS]. Direct Cinema Limited. VHS Release Date: June 1, 1985.

"Red Hot 1930s Cotton Club Show—Censored Reel Survives of Dancers Orgy!" YouTube, uploaded by 2reeler, April 17, 2010. Available at https://www.youtube.com/watch?v=cLBz3tW3kBI.

Interviews by Author

Brown, James "Buster." Interviewed and taught classes at Colorado Dance Festival, Boulder, CO, 1990.

Coles, Charles "Honi." Interviewed and taught classes at Colorado Dance Festival, Boulder, CO, 1986.

Coles, Marian. Telephone interview, January 1991.

Columbo, Christopher. Interviewed in Atlantic City, NJ, August 1, 1990.

Evelyn, Edwina "Salt." Interviewed in Greenwich Village, NY, April 26, May 10, July 15, 1990, and July 7–8, 2005. Informal interviews and telephone conversations continued until her death on January 26, 2011.

Fambro, Isabelle "Eleanor Byrd." Interviewed in Philadelphia, PA, August 14 and September 20, 1990.

Fitzgerald, Lillian. Interviewed in West Philadelphia, PA, April 10, 1992.

Hart, John. Interviewed in West Philadelphia, PA, August 15, 1990.

Henle, William. Interviewed in Quartzsite, AZ, November 25, 2012.

Hunt, Edith "Baby Edwards." Interviewed in West Philadelphia, PA, June 20, July 6 and 18, August 1 and 15, 1990, and informal interviews until 1992.

Jones, Ludie. Interviewed in New York, NY, July 20 and September 24, 1990.

McNeil, Vernita. Interviewed in West Orange, NJ, May 26–27, 2012, and April 25–26, 2015.

Robinson, LaVaughn. Interviewed in Philadelphia, PA, September 14, 1988, and September 5, 1990.

Thorpe, Mildred "Candi." Interviewed in Elwood, NJ, August 16, September 9, and November 18, 1990. Informal interviews and telephone conversations continued until her death April 18, 1998.

Van Auken, O.P. Interviewed in Quartzsite, AZ, November 25, 2012.

Welch, Jewel "Pepper." Interviewed in Philadelphia, PA, March 1 and 21 and July 15, 1989. Informal interviews and telephone conversations continued until her death on April 21, 1992.

Index

Abrams, Harold "Hal" Paul 98
Academy Club, OH 157
after-hours spot 112–113, 161, 174
Allen, Annisteen 128
Allen, Drew 113
Allen, Shep 109
Alvarado, Dolores 95, 201, 207
Alwhite & Blue 162
amateur contests 17, 19, 21, 36, 43, 52, 67, 68, 69, 109, 135, 176, 209
American Guild of Variety Artists (ABVA) 131
America's Greatest Coloured Jazz Band 175
Ammons, Gene 155
Amos 'n'Andy (television) 69, 70; see also Moore, Tim
Anderson, Bobby 145, 200
Anderson, Eddie "Rochester" 80, 123, 224
Anderson, Maceo 72; see also Four Step Brothers
Apollo Chorus Line, NY 65, 84, 165, 168, 169, 195, 215
Apollo Theatre, NY 1, 17, 19, 25, 37, 43, 44, 46, 52, 54, 64–77, 81, 87, 95, 116, 135, 166, 168, 169, 171, 173, 191, 195, 196, 198, 199, 201, 202, 203, 206, 207, 208, 209, 212, 213, 214, 215
Apus and Estrellita 112, 198
Armstrong, Louis 8, 44, 45, 65, 78, 81, 86, 93, 98, 135, 153, 167, 176, 195, 212
Aronoff, Benny 157
Asbury Park 19, 28, 92, 197
Atkins, Charles "Cholly" 8, 94, 118, 207, 209, 228; see also Coles, Charles "Honi"
Autry, Gene 136, 162

B&C Club, MI 153; see also Club El Sino; Club Owens
Babette's Supper Club, NJ 97
Baby Laurence see Jackson, Baby Laurence
Babyface Nelson 162
Badge, Laura 29
Bailey, Bill 39, 68–69, 207

Bailey, Eura 68–69, 207
Bailey, Pearl 17, 67, 68–69, 109, 207, 212
Baker, David 160
Baker, Josephine 8, 118, 165
Baker, LaVern 137
Balaban & Katz 135
Baliettes, D.C. 110, 165, 199
Balistrieri, Frank 162
Banks, Ristina 84, 166, 168
Banks, Warren 177, 204, 205
Barnes, Mae 166
Bascomb, Paul 156, 203
Basin Street, NJ 98
Baughan, David 75; see also The Checkers
Baxter, Ann 19–21, 24–25, 64, 153, 196
Beaman, Irving "Peaches" 8, 213; see also Miller, Duke; Nugent, Pete; "Pete Peaches & Duke"
Beauties of Harlem 108
bebop music 1, 5, 8, 30 145, 146, 151, 155–156, 174, 178, 179, 180, 181
Bechet, Sidney 78
Beige Beaus and Beauts 148, 149, 202, 205; see also chorus boys and girls
Beige Room, IL 141, 147–148, 202
Benny, Jack 123
Bentley, Gladys 118
Berle, Milton 131, 182, 218
Berry Brothers 17, 22–24, 153, 196, 218
Bibeau (Llon) and Suarez 148, 149, 202, 205, 207
Big Band Era 92, 181, 187
Big Time Crip 44, 47, 73, 107, 108, 195
Bill Robinson's Mimo Club 44, 206
Birdland, IL 147
Black Belt 134
Black Bottom 151–154, 226
Black Bottom (dance) 93
Black Elite 92, 222
Black Patti's Troubadours 40; see also Jones, Sissieretta
Blackberries of 1932 30

Blackbirds of 1928 (stage show) 8, 70, 214
blackface 8, 40, 108, 139, 165, 212, 214 215
Blackie 44
Blackman, Teddie 166
Blake, Eubie 8
Blow, Elsie 97, 204
Blue Mirror, NJ 19, 105, 206
Bluebird Inn, MI 153
Board, Johnny 135
"Bojangles" see Robinson, Bill "Bojangles"
Bon Ton, OH 157
Booth, Chick 89, 200
Born to Swing (stage show) 93–94, 200
Borscht Belt 102–105, 223; see also Catskills Mountains
The Boulevard, NY 105, 205
Boyd and Chapman 95, 201
Braddock Hotel and Grill 25, 66
Bradshaw, Tiny 137
Bragg, Johnny 30
Brecher, Leo 17, 64
Brice, Fanny 102
Briggs, Bunny 8, 61, 208, 212, 216
Bronze Beauties 93, 200
Bronzeville 78, 133–136, 143, 149
Brooks, Gwendolyn 78
Brooks, Opal 161
Brooks, Pat 143
Brown, Bill 75; see also Checkers
Brown, Buster 61, 220
Brown, James 17, 207
Brown and McGraw 86
Bryant, Willie 110–112, 198
B.S. Chorus (dance) 60, 119, 137, 170
Buchanan, Charles 13
"Buck and Bubbles" 8, 17, 80, 86, 215; see also Sublett, John "Bubbles"
Bud Billiken Parade 149
Bunn, John 71, 201
Bunny Hug (dance) 175
Burley, Mabe 37
Burnham, Harris and Scott 22, 196

237

Index

bury the show 140
Butterbeans and Susie 93, 208

Caesar, Sid 102, 182
Café St. Michel, QC 174, 175, 178–180, 202
Caldwell, Benjamin 110
call and response 66, 135–136, 181
Calloway, Cab 9–10, 14, 65, 69, 80, 98, 110, 174, 210, 212
Canfield and Lewis 77
Capone, Al 79–81, 133, 162, 176
Capone, Ralph 162
Cardwell, Bennie 113
Careeser, Lord 177, 204
Carey, Addison 166
Carlisle, Una Mae 46
Carnegie, John 75; *see also* The Checkers
Carrington, Roy 89
Carry, George "Scoops" 88, 89, 153, 200, 208
Carter, Benny 69
Carter, Consuella 115
Catholicism 13, 128, 188, 192
Cats and the Fiddle (floor show) 113, 199
Catskills Mountains 103, 104, 223; *see also* Borscht Belt
Cayton, Horace R. 78
Cha-Cha (dance) 181
challenge dance 11, 60, 62, 67, 68, 72, 86, 179, 180, 184, 207, 209, 212
Chand, Yogie 180, 202
Chapman, Grover "Big Boy" 136
Chappell, Gus 89, 200
Charleston (dance) 36, 93
Charlie Davis's Chorines 29
Charlie Glenn's Rhumboogie Chorus Lines 144, 145
The Checkers 75, 206, 221, 235; *see also* Brown, Bill; Baughan, David; White, Charlie;
Cheers (Billy) and Jerrie 30, 197
Cherry Street Club, OH 157
Chesterfield Club, OH 157
Chicago Defender (newspaper) 51, 141, 149, 196, 205
Chocolate Dandies (stage show) 93, 106, 165
Chocolate Revue (stage show) 112
chorus boys and girls 19, 65, 108, 145, 148; *see also* Beige Beau and Beauts
"Chuck and Chuckles" 128, 201, 210, 212; see also Green, Charles "Chuck"; Walker James
Church of God in Christ 24
circuits 19, 40, 82, 209, 212, 216; *see also* round the world
Civic Opera House 149
Civil Rights Act of 1964 182
classical music 78, 151, 212
Clores Cocktail Lounge, D.C. 33, 197

Club Bali, D.C. 33, 106, 110, 113, 114, 197, 198, 199
Club Congo, MI 44, 46, 153, 206
Club DeLisa, IL 110, 136–143, 149, 168, 170, 201, 202, 203, 204, 205, 209
Club Devon, OH 157
Club Eight Forty-Five (845), NY 105
Club El Sino, MI 19, 153, 155, 156, 203; *see also* B&C Club; Club Owens
Club Harlem, NJ 19, 98, 166, 209
Club Morocco, IL 209
Club Owens, MI 153; *see also* B&C Club; Club El Sino
Club Paradise, NJ 98, 155
Club Plantation, MO 89, 200
Club Riviera, MO 127, 201
Club Three Sixes, MI 153, 155, 202
Cohan, George M. 165
Cohen, Ben 153
Cohen, Lou 153
Cohen, Sidney 17
Coke and Poke 110, 201
Cole, Jimmy 161
Cole, Nat "King" 98, 208-209
Cole, Teddy 177, 178, 204
Cole Bates, Freddie 137, 170
Coleman, Elizabeth "Bessie" 78
Coles, Charles "Honi" vii, 3, 8, 39–40, 94, 168, 207, 209, 216
Coles, Marion vii, 168, 191
Collins, Chink 96, 108, 209
Colombo, Chris vii, 13, 65, 98, 100, 101, 209, 214
Comise, John 136
competition tap-style 2, 8, 50, 58, 94, 180, 184
Congo Café, PA 41
Congo Lounge, MI 153
Connie's Hot Chocolates 8
Connie's Inn, NY 9, 96, 171
Cooper, Al 13
Cooper, Gene 180, 202
Cooper, Ralph 17, 52, 53, 54, 196, 198
Copper Tan Rendezvouettes 52, 198
costume styles 1, 2, 38, 57–58, 180
Cotton Club, IN 160, 161
Cotton Club, OH 158, 159, 205
Cotton Club, NY 9, 10, 65, 72, 78, 80, 81, 96, 165, 166, 167, 168, 171, 172, 173, 191, 209, 211, 212, 213, 214, 216
Cotton Club Chorus Lines, NY 165, 166, 168, 171
Count Basie 1, 17, 46, 47, 48, 49, 64, 65, 70, 81, 98, 134, 135, 137, 195
Cousin Ida 52, 198
Crackerjacks 108–109, 198
Creole Show (stage show) 165

Criner, John L. 69
Crispus Attucks High School 160
Crosby, Bing 136, 218
Crystal Caverns, D.C. 33, 57, 113, 197
Cummings, Mildred *see* "Little Miss Cornshucks"

The Dancing Redcaps 108
Daniels, Billy 98, 209
Darktown Follies (stage show) 93, 213
Darktown Revue (stage show) 70
Davis, Charlie 29, 165, 166
Davis, Coleridge 110, 198, 200
Davis, Miles 147
Davis, Palmer "Fats" 71, 89, 200
Davis, Sammy, Jr. 97, 191, 209, 210, 212
Davis, Scat 77
Daylie, Daddy-O Homes 149–150, 202, 205
Delisa Chorines 137, 201, 202, 204, 205
Del Rio Trio 180, 202
Deppe, Lois 29, 78
Dillinger, John 162
Dinah (stage show) 93, 151
Dixie Inn, OH 157
dixieland jazz 7, 151, 163, 175, 181
Dobson's Comedy Dog Act 71
Dodds, Johnny 78
Dorsey Brothers 158, 208
Doubling 143
Douglas, William "Bill" 88, 89, 200
Dreamland Ballroom, IL 78, 211
Du Bois, W.E.B. 92
Dudley, S.H. 95, 195, 198, 199, 200
Dudleyettes 95, 165, 201
Dunbar Theater, PA 92
Dunham, Katherine 78, 207
DuPree, Reiss 44
Durante, Jimmy 97, 218
Dyer, Sammy 108, 141, 202, 203, 204, 209
Dyett, Walter 145, 200
Dywett, Walter 149

Eckstine, "Billy" 73, 98, 109, 202
Eckstine, "Willie" 175
Ed Small's Paradise, NY 9, 44, 52, 53, 143, 196
Ed Wynn Show (television) 110
Edwards Sisters 68
El Grotto, IL 87, 89, 147, 150, 200
Elite Club, IL 78
Elk's Rendezvous, NY 19, 52–54, 196, 198, 210
Ellington, Duke 10, 65, 70, 74, 75, 80, 93, 95, 98, 134, 135, 144, 149, 169, 174, 178, 182, 197, 205, 208

Index

Ellington TOTO 33, 197
Ellis, Elaine 168, 227
El Sino, MI 19, 153, 155, 156, 203; see also B&C Club, MI; Club Owens, MI
Englestein, Brig. Gen. Harry 134–135
Europe, James Reese 151
Evans, Warren 52, 54, 198

Fambro, Isabelle "Eleanor Byrd" vii, 191–192, 208
Fans Theatre, PA 93, 95, 96, 200
Ferguson, Denver 160
Ferguson, Sea 160
Fetchit, Stepin 159, 210, 226; see also Perry, Lincoln
Fields, Ernie 64, 71–73, 201
Fields, W.C. 70
Fifty-second (52nd) Street 25–26, 197
Fitzgerald, Ella 17, 36–37, 50, 67, 68, 98, 109, 135, 158
Fitzgerald, Lillian vii, 95–96, 201
Five Hundred Club, NJ 97, 98, 223
Five (5) Red Caps 109, 201, 209
The Flame, WI 163–164, 204
Flash (dance) 10, 41, 54, 61, 62, 63, 72, 166, 167, 184, 213
Fletcher, Clinton "Dusty" 10, 17, 84, 209
Flintall, Herman 54, 196, 198
Ford Harris & Jones 70, 84, 87, 88, 89, 101, 199; see also Three (3) Maniacs of Rhythm
Forty-second (42nd) Street (film) 13
Four Congaroos 95, 201
Four Harmony Kings 175
Four Mello-Tones 71, 84, 87, 88, 153, 199, 200, 213
Four Notes 155, 202
Four Step Brothers 24, 71–72, 80; see also Anderson, Maceo; McDonald, Rufus L. "Flash"; Walker, Red; Williams, Al
Fox, Ed 80, 81
Fretti, Joe 157
full show format 5, 19, 65, 104, 106, 161, 163, 167, 174, 181, 182; see also revue format

Gale, Moe 13
gambling 2, 8, 79, 97, 102, 136–137, 156–157, 175
gangsters 10, 25, 52, 79, 80, 141–142, 162, 175
Gant, Pvt. Cecil 77, 115, 201
Garcia, Lou 37, 38
Gardiner, Ester 33, 197
Gardner, Johnny "Curley" 155, 202
Garner, Erroll 110
Garner, Willard 138–139, 201, 202, 203, 204, 205

Garrett, Alice Dancing School 11
Garroway, Dave 143, 150
Gay 90s Club, MI 153
Gayety Theatre, D.C. 106–109, 198
Gee, Jack 30, 219
George Ward Orchestra 26, 28
Georgia's Bar, IN 161
Gibson, John T. 92–93, 222
gigs 14, 19, 46, 57, 60, 87, 105, 121, 122, 141, 187, 214
Gilliam, Anna Ree 18–19
gillies & medicine show format 40
Glen, Charlie 19, 140, 141, 143, 144, 145, 199
Glenn and Jenkins 108
Glick, Welly 104–105, 200
Goldberg, Whoopi 118
Goodman, Benny 158
Gordon, Freddie 139–140, 202, 203; see also Rogers, Timmie
Gospel 24, 78
Grace Hall's Chorus Girls 29
Grace's Little Belmont, NJ 98
Grand Terrace Ballroom, IL 22, 80, 81, 82, 167; see also Sunset Cafe
Gravens Moore, Vivian 69, 70, 198; see also Moore, Tim
Gray, Wardell 71, 88, 200
Graystone Ballroom, MI 153, 226
Great Depression 10, 12, 14, 17, 25 36, 133, 135, 175, 176, 181, 182
Great Migration 1, 5, 78, 92, 133, 151, 162, 165, 183
Green, Benny 149, 202, 205
Green, Chuck 8, 127, 128, 210, 212, 214, 228; see also Chuck and Chuckles; Walker James
Green, Cora 30, 32, 197, 210
Green, Hazel 56, 77, 110, 123
Green, Lil 149
Green, Walter 60, 61, 208, 210
Grizzly Bear (dance) 175

Haines, Warren "Max 'Mr. Blues' Bailey" 161
Hale, Teddy 8, 60, 61, 149, 205, 210, 211
Haley, Marshall 33, 197
Hall, Adelaide 8
Hall, Berne 115, 201
Hall, Rene 88, 89, 200
Hall's Savoy Nite Club, NJ 19, 28, 197
Hammond, John 71, 76
Hampton, Lionel 67
Hampton, Locksley Wellington "Slide" 160
Harding, Becky 24, 196
Harding, Buster 24, 196
Harlem Follies (stage show) 106–108, 198, 202
Harlem Highlanders 144–146

Harlem Opera House, NY 8, 82, 191
Harlem Renaissance 5, 7, 9, 78, 181
Harlem's Hollywood Cabaret, NY 24, 196, 197
Harlem's Poppin' (floor show) 110–112, 198
Harlem'z a-Poppin' (floor show) 95- 96, 200, 201
Harold's Club, IL 98
Harper, Leonard 22, 166, 195, 196, 200
Harrington, Keith "Hamtree" & Green 30, 210; see also Green, Cora
Harris, Kenneth 100
Harris, Wynoni "Mr. Blues" 71, 72, 145, 201
Hawkins, Coleman 26, 69
Hawkins, Erskine 41, 54, 55, 64, 69, 198, 206
Hawkins, Myrtle "LaZonda" 28, 29, 132, 197, 203, 204
Hayes, Cleo 168
Hedgeman, Kay 30, 33, 197
Henderson, Fletcher 60, 65, 73, 122, 137, 139, 178, 201
Henri's Bar, IN 161
Hi-Hat Club, NJ 37, 195
"high yella" 65, 167, 168, 173
Hines, Baby 28, 29–30, 54, 100, 197, 198
Hines, Earl "Fatha" 1, 22, 28, 29, 60, 61, 64, 65, 70, 78–90, 122–124, 149, 153, 167, 199, 200, 208, 214, 216
Hodges, Johnny 64, 74–76, 206
Holiday, Billie "Lady Day" 17, 26, 74–77, 110, 135, 206, 211
Holloway, Ernestine 145, 199
Holly, Edna May 167
Hoofers Club, NY 8, 210
Hope, Bob 136
Horne, Lena 10, 98, 135, 211
Hot Chocolates (stage show) 8, 22
Howard Theatre, D.C. 19, 29, 44, 57, 82, 83, 84, 87, 106, 109–110, 135, 199, 201
Howard University Players 109
Hubbard, Freddie 160
Hudgins, Johnny 8
Hudson, George 60, 89, 110, 200, 201
Hunt, Edith "Baby Edwards" vii, 191–192, 209; see also Spic and Span
Hunter, Alberta 93, 118, 211
Hunter, Ivory Joe 149, 202, 205
Hunter, Lurlean 138, 201, 225
Hunter, Mable 159–160, 201, 206

I Got Somethin' to Tell You (DVD) 118
improvisation 1, 7, 8, 41, 44, 60, 61, 62, 63, 76, 77, 78, 105, 146, 160, 165, 179, 210, 214

Indianapolis Recorder (newspaper) 161
Ingram, Germaine 191, 211
Ink Spots 73, 149, 202, 205, 214
Integration 67, 70, 73, 80, 93, 96, 98, 109, 112, 136, 152–154, 159, 175–176, 180
International Sweethearts of Rhythm 22, 46, 115–116, 122, 196, 201; *see also* Winburn, Anna Mae
Irene's Café, PA 38 41, 195
Ivy, Joe 89, 200

Jack, Sam T. 165
Jackson, Baby Laurence 8, 44, 60, 145–146, 208
Jackson, Bull Moose 128
Jackson, Delilah 191
Jackson, Mahalia 78
Jackson, Milt 155
Jackson, Tony 7, 30, 78, 118, 210
Jackson Five (5) 17, 207
Jacquet, Illinois 155
James, Jesse 73, 108, 202
Jazz Tap (dance) 8, 145–146, 197, 208
Jenkins, Tillie 51, 54, 56
Jigsaw Jackson 112, 198
Jim Crow Laws 7, 92, 121–124, 154, 173, 181, 182, 183
Jitterbug (dance) 181; *see also* Lindy Hop
Johnson, Budd 61
Johnson, James Weldon 108
Johnson, J.J. 160
Johnson, Joe "Ziggy" 141, 155, 166, 202
Johnson, Killer 102
Johnson, Mimi 102
Johnson, Myra 22, 196
Joi-La-Joy 54, 198
Jones, Ludie vii, 211–212
Jones, Richard "Dick" 134
Jones, Sissieretta 40, 212, 229; *see also* Black Patti
Jones Brothers 80
jook joints 151, 225
Jordan, Hortense "the Body" Allen 166, 215
Jordan, Louis 54, 64, 70, 71, 149, 160, 177, 198, 205
Joseph & Johnson 93, 200

Ka-See's Nite Club, OH 157, 158
Keith Circuit 19, 30, 210
Kelly's Stables, NY 19, 22, 26, 197
Kennedy, Geri 3, 173, 191
Keppard, Freddie 78
Kin Wa Lows, OH 157, 158
The Kinneys 69
Kirby, George 140–141, 148, 149, 201, 202, 205
Kirby, John 22
Kirk, Rolbie 180, 202
Knighton, Doris 33, 197

Knights of the White Camellia 40
Kraft, Geo. 33, 197
Ku Klux Klan 7, 40

Lacy Wharton and his Swing band 28, 197
Lady Terry 75, 206
Lafayette Players 109, 222
Lafayette Theater, NY 9, 17, 52, 82
Lance, Rose 178, 204
Lane (Layne), George 144- 145, 199
Lederer, George 165
Lenox Lounge, NY 52
Leon, Herbie 162, 203
Leslie, Lew 8, 210, 211, 214
Lewis, Jerry 97, 102
Lewis, Sybil 71, 72–73, 201
Lichtman, Abe 109
Lincoln Theatre, NY 9
Lincoln Theatre, OH 130, 203
Lincoln Theatre, PA 39, 93, 94, 200, 209
Lindy Hop (dance) 14, 218
Little Belmont, NJ 98
"Little Miss Cornshucks" 137–138, 140, 201; *see also* Cummings, Mildred
Little Papa 178, 204
Liza (stage show) 30, 93
Lockhart's Hollywood Show, NY 124, 202, 203
Logan, Betty 33, 197
Louis, Joe 143, 176, 182
Lucas, Sam 165
Lunceford, Jimmie 10, 113, 134, 169
Lyles, Aubrey 8
Lyons, Red 71, 87, 199

Mabley, Jackie "Moms" 17, 44, 91, 98, 115, 116–120, 201, 210
Mack, Lavina 166
make up—make down 167
male dominated dance form 2, 8, 10, 50, 94, 165–166, 168, 184, 212
marches 151, 175, 181
Marshall, Linda 105, 200
Madden, Owney 79, 81
Mae, Lula 37, 38, 195
Mambo (dance) 181
Manhattan Debs 58, 59
Manhattan Paul 52, 53, 54, 196, 198
Manning, Frankie 14
Mardi Gras Ball 149
Mardi Gras Indians 129–130
Markham, Dewey "Pigmeat" 17, 71, 72 , 116, 201, 215
Mason, John "Spider Bruce" 95, 201, 210, 215
Maurice, Count 105, 200
Mayo, Wandra 178, 204
Mays, Betty 52, 54, 198
McDaniel, Hattie 80

McDonald, Rufus L. "Flash" 72; *see also* The Four Step Brothers
McLin, Claude 149, 205
Medinah Club, IL 147
Merrill, Dick 73, 202
Metcalf, Louis 178–180, 202
Michelson, Nathan 158
Midnight Rambler 143
Mika, Phil 162
Miller, Duke 8, 213; *see also* Beaman, Irving "Peaches; Nugent, Pete; "Pete Peaches & Duke"
Miller, Flournoy 8
Miller, Glen 158
Miller, Irvin C. 93
Miller, Norma 14
Miller, Norman "Porto Rico" 67–68
Miller Brothers and Lois 34; 213; *see also* Miller, Duke
Millinder, Lucius "Lucky" 22, 24, 79, 127, 153, 196, 201
Mills, Florence 8, 30, 165, 175
minstrel format 8, 40–41, 165, 212, 213
Minton's Playhouse, NY 52
Miss Suda 161
Missile Room, IN 161
Mitchell, Billy 100, 113, 199, 200
Mitchell, Jimmie 69, 198, 214
Monk, Theolonius 22
Montgomery, Dick 89, 200
Montgomery, Wes 160
Moore, Flint 159, 206
Moore, Gertie 69
Moore, Melvin 73
Moore, Monette 34, 197
Moore, Tim 69, 93, 200, 210; *see also Amos 'n' Andy* (television); Gravens Moore, Vivian
Moore and Larry 52, 198
Moorerhy, Mel 71
Moraine's, NY 53, 54, 143
Moran, Bugs 162
Mordecai, Jimmie 33, 196, 197
Moreland, Mantan 69, 124, 130–132, 203, 204
Morrison, Charlie 166
Morrison, Leonard 155, 202
Morrison, Monty 159, 206
Morton, Bea 33, 197
Morton, "Jelly Roll" 7, 78, 178, 213
Moses, Janie 71, 87, 199
Moten, Bennie 70
Motown (Detroit's Motor Town) 151, 207, 208, 212
musical styles 151, 175, 181; *see also* classical music; Dixieland; gospel; marches; ragtime; rap; rhythm and blues (r&b); rock 'n' roll; swing
My Friend from Kentucky: Darktown Follies (stage show) 93

Naki and Lida 145, 200
National Association for the Ad-

vancement of Colored People (NAACP) 7, 185
National Federation of Musicians 81
National Theatre, AL 130
National Theatre, KY 87
Nemderoloc Club, QC 175
New Orleans Mardi Gras; *see also* Mardi Gras Indians
New Town Tavern, NJ 97, 204
New York Age (newspaper) 54, 187
New York Times (newspaper) 24
New York's *Amsterdam News* (newspaper) 73, 97, 196, 197, 198
Nicholas Brothers 10, 17, 93, 95, 213
Nixon Grand Theatre, PA 24, 37, 93
Nubin, Katie Bell 24
Nugent, Pete 8, 108, 148, 149, 202, 205, 209, 210, 213 *see also* Beaman, Irving "Peaches; Miller, Duke; "Pete Peaches & Duke"

O'Connell, Helen 158
O'Day, Darlene 177, 204
Off Beat Club, D.C. 33, 197
Oldest Nightclub in America 98, 100, 101
Oliver, Joseph "King" 78, 86–87, 87
Original Dixieland Jazz Band 175
O.V. Catto's Elks Lodge, PA 41, 44

Page, Oran Thaddeus "Hot Lips" 70, 198
Palace Theatre, IL 162
Palace Theatre, TN 201, 203
Palmer, Fats 88, 200
Panama Club, IL 78
Panama Trio 30, 210
Paradise Bowl 153
Paradise Club, NJ 19, 98
Paradise Theatre, MI 22, 57, 153
Paradise Valley 152, 153–156
Parker, Charlie "Bird" 8, 146, 155, 174
Parker, Delores 145, 200
Parker, Sonny 139, 159, 202, 206
Parks, Gordon 78
Parkway Ballroom, IL 149, 205
Paul, Tony 157
Paxton, George 73, 202
Pearl Theater, PA 68, 82, 93
Pearson, Ted 82
Pembrook, Dolly 54, 198
Pendennies, MI 153
Penn, Helen 112, 195, 198
Pennettes 112, 198
Penquin Walk (dance) 63
Perez, Emanuel "Manuel" 78
Perry, Jesse 87, 199

Perry, Lincoln; *see also* "Stepin Fetchit"
Pershing Hotel 87, 147, 150, 202
Peterson, Louise 52
Petrillo, James C. 81
Peyton, Dave 134
Philadelphia Independent (newspaper) 37, 38, 41, 44, 46
Pinier, "Fats" 33, 197
Pittsburg Courier (newspaper) 57, 96, 97, 134
The Plantation, MI 153
Plantation Café, IL 86–87, 167
Plantation Café, MO 19
Plantation Club, NY 216
Polly Goree Dancers 156, 203
Premier Hotel 104, 200
Previn, Andre 69
Prince, Ollie 52
Prince, Thelma 52
Princess Gomez 178
Prohibition 5, 9, 10, 25, 98, 133, 136, 158, 162, 175, 218
Pulling Trenches or Through the Trenches (dance) 44, 63, 215, 219, 220
Purple Gang 79

R&B 70, 75, 136, 151, 215, 222; *see also* rhythm and blues
race riots 7, 10, 25, 133
racism 1, 5, 7, 25, 38, 40, 106, 108, 121–124, 133–134, 151–154, 156, 162–163, 175–176, 182–185, 212; 214; *see also* Knights of the White Camellia; Ku Klux Klan
Raft, George 136, 218
ragtime 8, 40, 78, 151, 153, 165, 175, 181, 213
Rainey, Ma 40, 70, 118, 213, 214
rap 160
Ray, Charles 95, 201
Ray, Fay 168, 227
Rector, Eddie 93, 94, 95, 200, 213
Red and Curley 89, 200
Reed, Leonard 8, 143, 166
Regal Theatre, IL 19, 85, 89, 134–136, 141, 147, 149, 200
Remy, Dick 110, 201
Remy, Dot 110, 201
Rendezvouettes 54, 165, 196, 198
Republic Gardens, D.C. 33
revue format 22, 43, 44, 46, 57, 58, 70, 87, 99, 106, 135, 147, 161, 165, 166, 209, 210, 212, 215, 216; *see also* full show format
Rhumboogie Café, IL 19, 57, 87, 89, 141, 143–146, 199, 200
rhythm and blues 151, 181, 215; *see also* R&B
"Rhythm and Rhyme" (music) 61
Rhythm Tap (dance) 8, 10, 26, 54, 57, 62, 63, 72, 108, 165,

166, 184, 207, 209, 210, 212, 213, 215
Rhythmettes 37, 38
Rhythmites 149, 202, 205
Ricardo, Marie 33, 197
Richards, Daisy 168, 199
RKO Capitol Theatre 202
RKO Regent Theatre, NY 19
Roach, Max 146
Robeson, Paul 8, 136
Robinson, Ann 52, 198
Robinson, Bill "Bojangles" 8, 10, 17, 36, 44, 68, 80, 87, 182, 206, 207, 213–214
Robinson, Clarence 123, 166
Robinson, LaVaughn vii, 211
Robinson, Sugar Ray 167
Roche, Betty 87, 199
Rockadets 165, 177, 204
Rockhead's Paradise Café, QC 110, 174, 176–178, 180, 204
rock 'n' roll 71, 151, 160, 181, 182, 215
Rogers, Sinclair 156, 203
Rogers, Timmie 139–140, 210, 214; *see also* Gordon, Freddie
Roman Grill, PA 97
round the world circuit 19, 57, 82, 166
Roxyettes 165
Royal Blue Bar, MI 153
Royal Gardens, IN 78
Royal Palm Gardens, IN 160
Royal Theatre, MD 19, 22, 57, 82, 106, 115–120, 135, 196, 199, 201, 209
Running Wild (stage show) 8
Russell, Luis 44, 195

Saltis, "Polack Joe" 162
Sanchez, Baby 191
Santley Agency 57
Saunders, Gertrude 30, 70, 196, 197, 198
Saunders, Percy (Jackie P.) 161
Saunders, Red 170–171, 202, 203, 204, 205
Savoy Ballroom, Chicago 134, 135, 147
Savoy Ballroom, NY 13–14, 209
Scarne, John 157
Schiffman, Frank 17, 44, 64–66, 81
Schiffman, Jack 64, 67, 71, 213
Scott, Lord Essex 71, 87, 88, 89, 148, 149, 199, 200, 202, 205, 214
Scott, Kermit 71, 89, 200, 222
Sebree, Sonny 161
segregation 51, 97–99 103, 107, 109, 147, 175–176, 214; *see also* racism
sexism 1, 2, 19, 22, 34, 38, 94, 121, 158, 165, 182, 183, 184
sexuality 1, 2, 38, 46, 50, 118, 184, 188–189, 194
Shadowland Club, LA 128, 129, 201

Shaver, Charlie 22
Shaw, Buddy 162, 203
Shelton Sisters 149
Shim Sham Shimmy 60, 119, 137, 170, 191, 220
Shorty George (dance) 10, 63, 218, 220
show format 19; *see also* gillies & medicine; minstrels; revue format; vaudeville
Shubert Brothers 165
Shuffle Along (stage show) 7–8, 9, 30, 70, 93, 106, 165, 175
Silver Bells 1, 173, 191
Simm's Paradise Café, PA 41
Sinatra, Frank 97, 98, 158
Sing-Fionice 145, 200
Singing Weavers 46
Sissle, Noble 8, 30, 211, 123
Sister Sledge 191
Six (6) Marvelettes 115, 201
Six O Six (606) Horse Shoe Bar and Lounge, MI 153
Sky Club Theater and Supper Club, IN 161, 205
Sky Rockets 161; 205
Slatko's Theatrical Ventures 37
slumming 9, 175
Slyde, Jimmy 61, 212, 214, 216
Small, Clifton 89, 200
Smiley, Phyllis 144, 145, 199
Smith, Ada "Bricktop" 30, 210
Smith, Bessie 30, 93, 112, 118, 214–215, 216
Smith, Effie 69
Smith, Jimmy 52, 198
Smith, Mamie 93, 209, 215
Smith Sisters and Geri 33–34, 197
Smitty and Dotty 33
Snookie Marsh 144
Soft Shoe (dance) 10, 166, 169, 207, 209
Sonia 100, 171
soubrette 95, 166, 168, 201
Sparks, Jean 22, 115, 196
Spencer, Libby 191, 215
Spencer, Prince C. 72
Spic and Span 155, 209; *see also* Hunt, Edith "Baby Edwards"
Standard Theatre, PA 36, 92–93, 209
Stardust Inn, D.C. 19, 30, 106, 197, 198
Steel, Pecin' Joe 100–101
Steele, Larry 155, 166, 209
Stepherson, Stephany 89, 200
Stevens, George "Kingfish" 69; *see also* Moore, Tim
Strand Ballroom, PA 44
Strand Theatre, PA 68
Strawberry Russel & Julia 73–74, 202
"Streamline" Sue 33, 197
street corner tap (dance) 1, 8, 11, 14, 25, 36, 38, 39, 58, 160, 184
Struttin Time (stage show) 93

Stump and Stumpy 44, 46, 195, 212, 215
Styles, Lulu 38
Sublett, John "Bubbles" 8, 26, 210, 213, 215
Sullivan, Ed 131
Sunset Café, IL 78, 86, 167; *see also* Grand Terrace
Sunset Terrace Ballroom, IN 160, 161
Sussman, Morris 17
Suzy-Q (dance) 10, 218
swing 1, 8, 10, 13, 14, 19, 24, 28, 36, 52, 63, 106, 109, 151, 161, 179, 181, 207
swing era 3, 4–5, 24, 70, 92, 113, 136, 162, 164, 173, 180, 181–183, 191, 193, 213, 215
Swingland Café, IL 209

Tack Annie 220
Tallie's Minstrel 40–41
tap and vernacular dance; *see also* Black Bottom; B.S. Chorus; Bunny Hug; Cha-Cha; Challenge Dance; Charleston; Flash; Grizzly Bear; Jazz Tap; Jitterbug, Lindy Hop, Mambo; Penguin Walk; Pulling Trenches Or Through The Trenches; Rhythm Tap; Shim Sham Shimmy; Shorty George; Soft Shoe; Street Corner Tap; Susie-Q; Truckin'; Turkey Trot; Wings
Tatum, Art 8, 146
Taylor, Lovey 86
Taylor, Yack 95, 168, 201, 215
Tharpe, Sister Rosetta 22, 24, 69, 153
Theard, Sam "Spo-De-O-De" 28–29, 75, 161, 206
Theater Owners' Booking Association (TOBA) 116, 216
The Theatrical Grill, NY; *see also* Wells, Dickie
Thomas, Audrey 112, 198
Thomas, Eugene 88, 89, 200
Thomas, Harry 175
Thomas, Peggy 132, 203, 204
Thompson, Billy 89, 200
Thompson, Willard (Chops) 96, 201
Thorpe, Mildred "Candi" 3–5, 39–51, 192
Three Kaye Sisters 162, 203
Three (3) Maniacs of Rhythm 70, 153, 200, 210; *see also* Ford, Harris & Jones
Three Shades of Rhythm 22, 196
Tim and Vivian 69; *see also* Gravens Moore, Vivian; Moore, Tim
Tip Tap and Toe 24
Tonalayo and Lopez 46, 50, 196; *see also* Tondelayo and Calypso Boys

Tondelayo and Calypso Boys 97, 204; *see also* Tonalayo and Lopez
Travis, Dempsey 80
Trianon Ballroom, IL 147
Trianon Ballroom, IN 160
Trianon Ballroom, OH 157
Truckin' (dance) 10, 218
tuberculosis 24–25
Tucker, Sophie 102, 215
Turkey Trot (dance) 175
Turner, Big Joe 137
Two (2) Swing Maniacs 69, 198
Tynes, Gwen 148, 156, 202, 203

Underground Railroad 174
"ups" 170–171

Valdor Club, QC 77
Vanderhurst, Sammy 86
vaudeville format 19, 30, 32, 36, 40, 69, 70, 73, 92, 108, 109, 118, 162, 182, 208, 209, 210, 212, 213, 215, 216
Vaughan, Sarah 98, 110, 209, 216
Venable, Percy 22
vernacular dances; *see also* tap and vernacular dances
Victory Club, OH 517
Volstead Act 9

Walker, Arthur 71, 84, 87, 88, 89, 153, 199, 200, 214, 216
Walker, Madam C.J. 161, 222
Walker, Dianne 191, 216
Walker, James "Chuckles" 127; *see also* "Chuck and Chuckles"
Walker, Margaret 78
Walker, Red 72; *see also* The Four Step Brothers
Walker, T-Bone 144, 199
Walker Casino, IN 161
Wallace Brothers 97, 202
Waller, Thomas Wright "Fats" 1, 21–22, 46, 49, 50, 60, 64, 115, 196, 212
Walter Page's Blue Devils 70
Ware, Archie 108–109; *see also* Crackerjacks
Warner, Ruth 28, 197
Washington, Baby 159
Washington, Dinah 98, 110
Washington, Ford Lee "Buck"; *see also* "Buck and Bubbles"; Sublett, John "Bubbles"
Washington Bee (newspaper) 109
Waters, Ethel 8, 10, 79, 80, 87, 93, 98, 118, 210, 216
Waters, Muddy 78
Watkins, Margaret 46, 100, 101, 204
Watson, Margaret 177, 178, 204
Webb, Chick 8, 13, 37, 68
Webster Inn, OH 157
Wellman, Alan 177

Wells, Dickie 52; *see also* The Theatrical Grill
Wells, Ida B. 78
West, Mae 136
White, Charlie 75; *see also* The Checkers
White, Herbert "Whitey's" Lindy Hoppers 14
White, Slappy 98, 195, 216
White Caps 40
White City Amusement Park Ballroom, IL 147
Whitlow, Mildred 144–145, 199, 200
Whitman Sisters 40, 93, 112, 216
Whyte, Loretta 163, 204
Wilkey & Dare 73, 202

Williams, Al 72; *see also* The Four Step Brothers
Williams, Fess 134
Williams, Joe 137, 149, 202, 204, 205
Williams, Midge 44, 195
Wilson, Derby 39, 41, 68, 108, 198, 207, 209, 210, 211
Wilson, Iron Jaw 100, 101, 145, 178, 199, 204
Wilson, Lucille 167
Winburn, Anna Mae 115–116; 210
Wings (dance) 44, 219
Wintergarden, NJ 98
Women's Army Corp (WACs) 113

Woods, Bertye Lou 168, 169
Woods, Sonny 44, 195
World War I 7, 9, 92, 97, 162, 176
World War II 1, 5, 19, 25, 97, 113, 122, 134, 147, 154, 158, 168, 181, 182, 183, 211
Wright, Richard 78
Wright, Virginia 52

Young, Lester 76, 211
Young, Marl 144, 145, 199

Zanzibar, Club, NY 69
Ziegfeld, Florenz 165
Ziggyettes 155, 165

www.ingramcontent.com/pod-product-compliance
Lightning Source LLC
Chambersburg PA
CBHW081550300426
44116CB00015B/2824